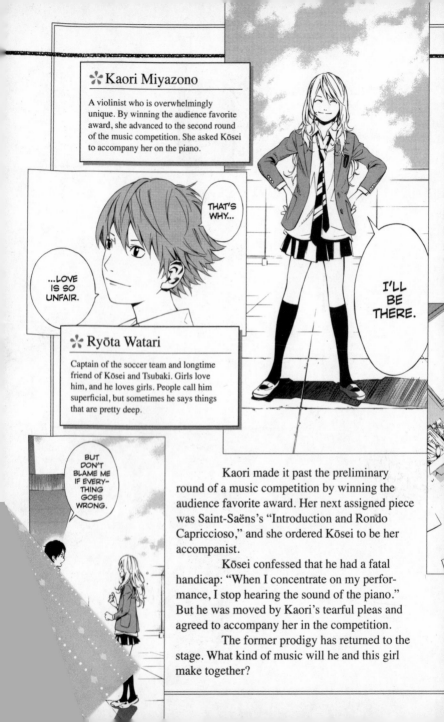

✻ Kaori Miyazono

A violinist who is overwhelmingly unique. By winning the audience favorite award, she advanced to the second round of the music competition. She asked Kōsei to accompany her on the piano.

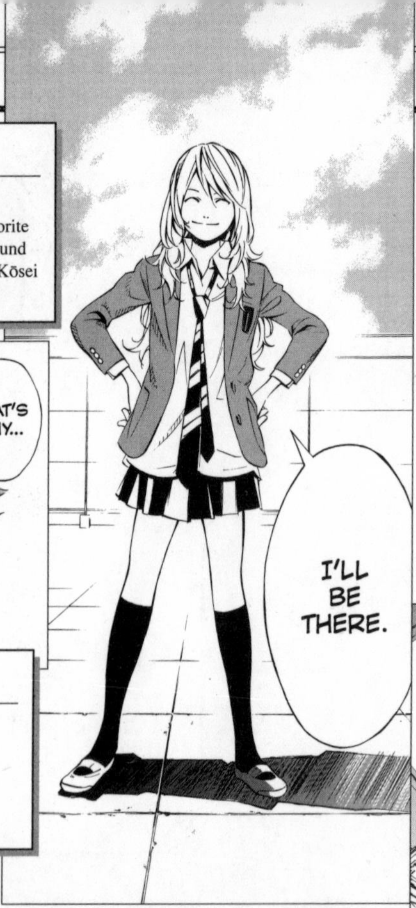
I'LL BE THERE.

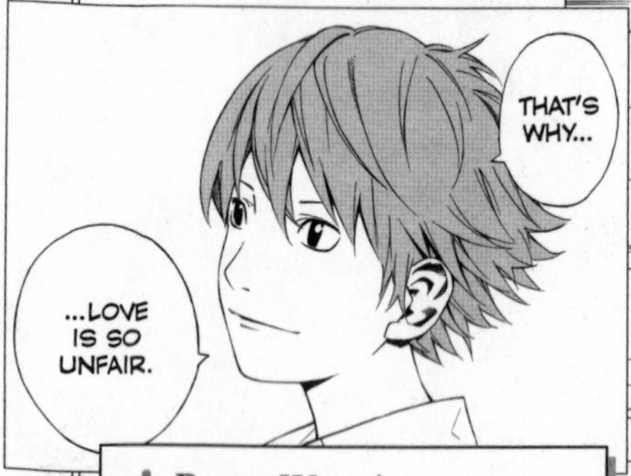
THAT'S WHY...
...LOVE IS SO UNFAIR.

✻ Ryōta Watari

Captain of the soccer team and longtime friend of Kōsei and Tsubaki. Girls love him, and he loves girls. People call him superficial, but sometimes he says things that are pretty deep.

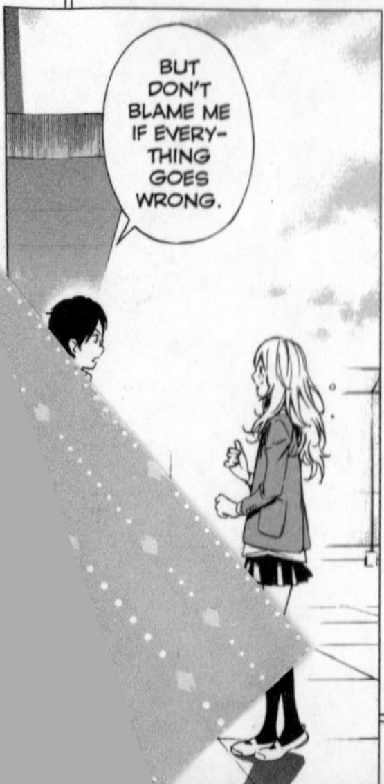
BUT DON'T BLAME ME IF EVERY-THING GOES WRONG.

Kaori made it past the preliminary round of a music competition by winning the audience favorite award. Her next assigned piece was Saint-Saëns's "Introduction and Rondo Capriccioso," and she ordered Kōsei to be her accompanist.

Kōsei confessed that he had a fatal handicap: "When I concentrate on my performance, I stop hearing the sound of the piano." But he was moved by Kaori's tearful pleas and agreed to accompany her in the competition.

The former prodigy has returned to the stage. What kind of music will he and this girl make together?

contents

Chapter 5: A Dark Ocean

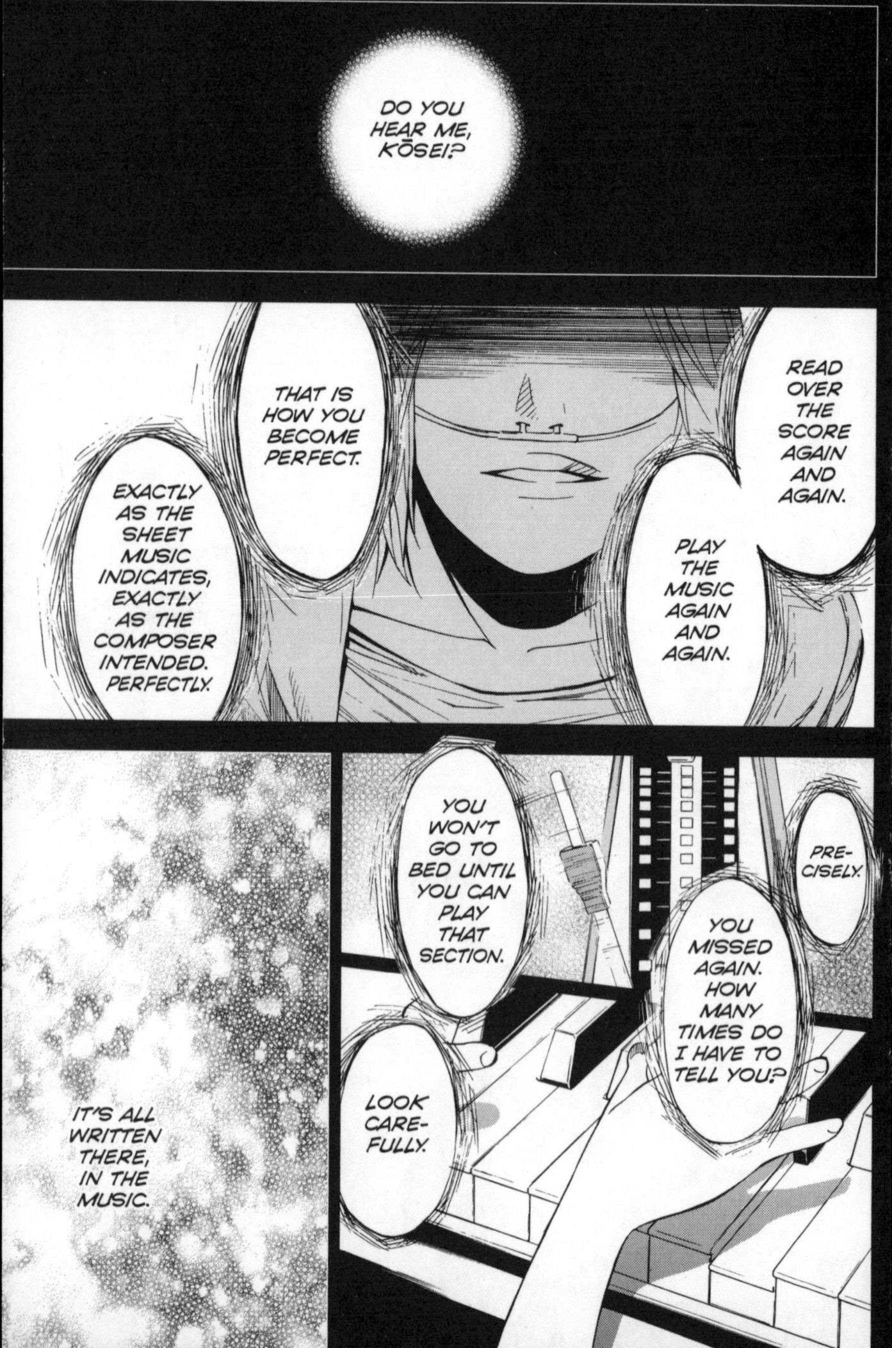
DO YOU HEAR ME, KŌSEI?
READ OVER THE SCORE AGAIN AND AGAIN.
PLAY THE MUSIC AGAIN AND AGAIN.
EXACTLY AS THE SHEET MUSIC INDICATES, EXACTLY AS THE COMPOSER INTENDED. PERFECTLY.
THAT IS HOW YOU BECOME PERFECT.
PRE-CISELY.
YOU WON'T GO TO BED UNTIL YOU CAN PLAY THAT SECTION.
YOU MISSED AGAIN. HOW MANY TIMES DO I HAVE TO TELL YOU?
LOOK CARE-FULLY.
IT'S ALL WRITTEN THERE, IN THE MUSIC.

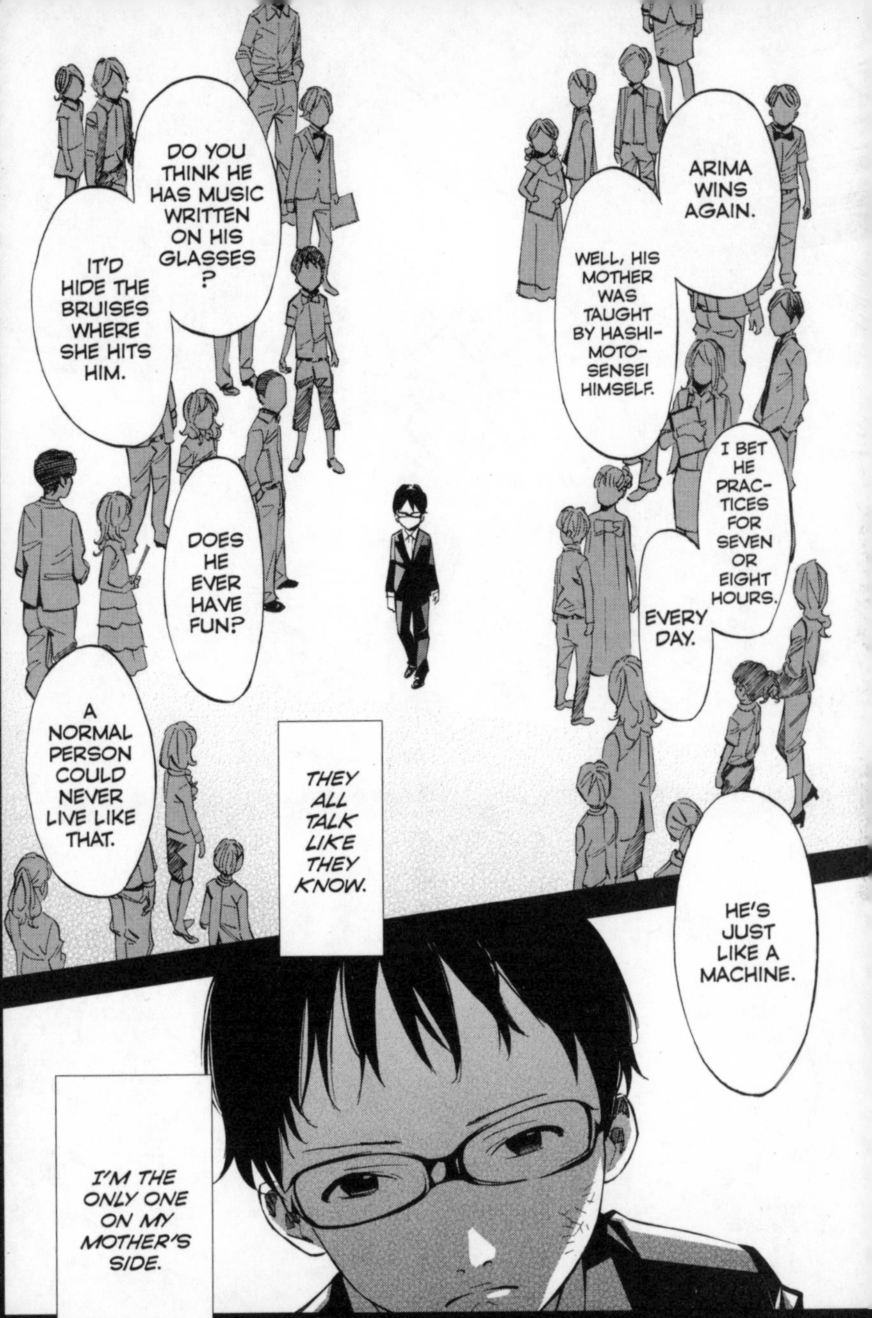
ARIMA WINS AGAIN.
WELL, HIS MOTHER WAS TAUGHT BY HASHIMOTO-SENSEI HIMSELF.
I BET HE PRACTICES FOR SEVEN OR EIGHT HOURS.
EVERY DAY.
DO YOU THINK HE HAS MUSIC WRITTEN ON HIS GLASSES?
IT'D HIDE THE BRUISES WHERE SHE HITS HIM.
DOES HE EVER HAVE FUN?
A NORMAL PERSON COULD NEVER LIVE LIKE THAT.
THEY ALL TALK LIKE THEY KNOW.
HE'S JUST LIKE A MACHINE.
I'M THE ONLY ONE ON MY MOTHER'S SIDE.

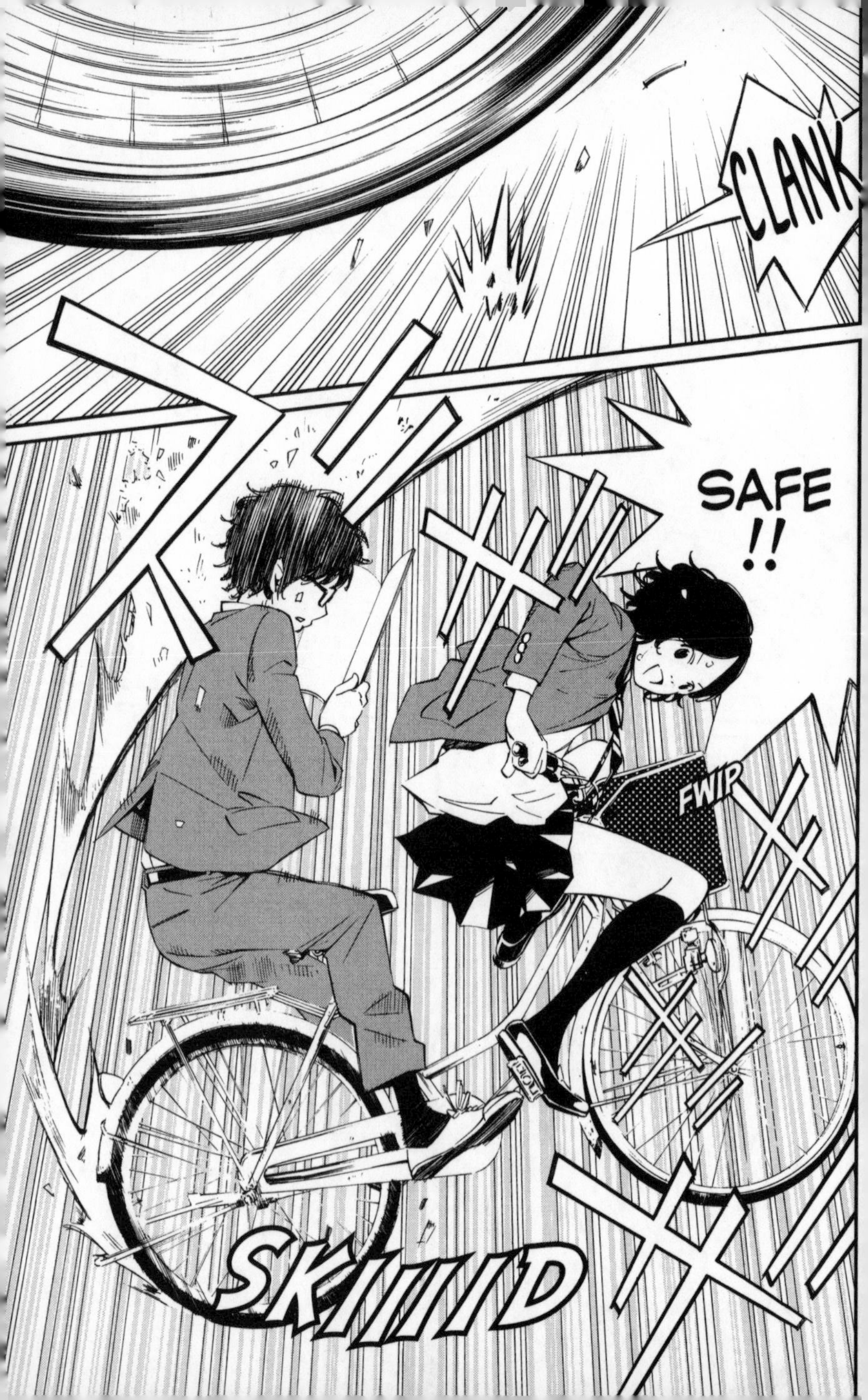
CLANK
SAFE !!
FWIP
SKIIIID

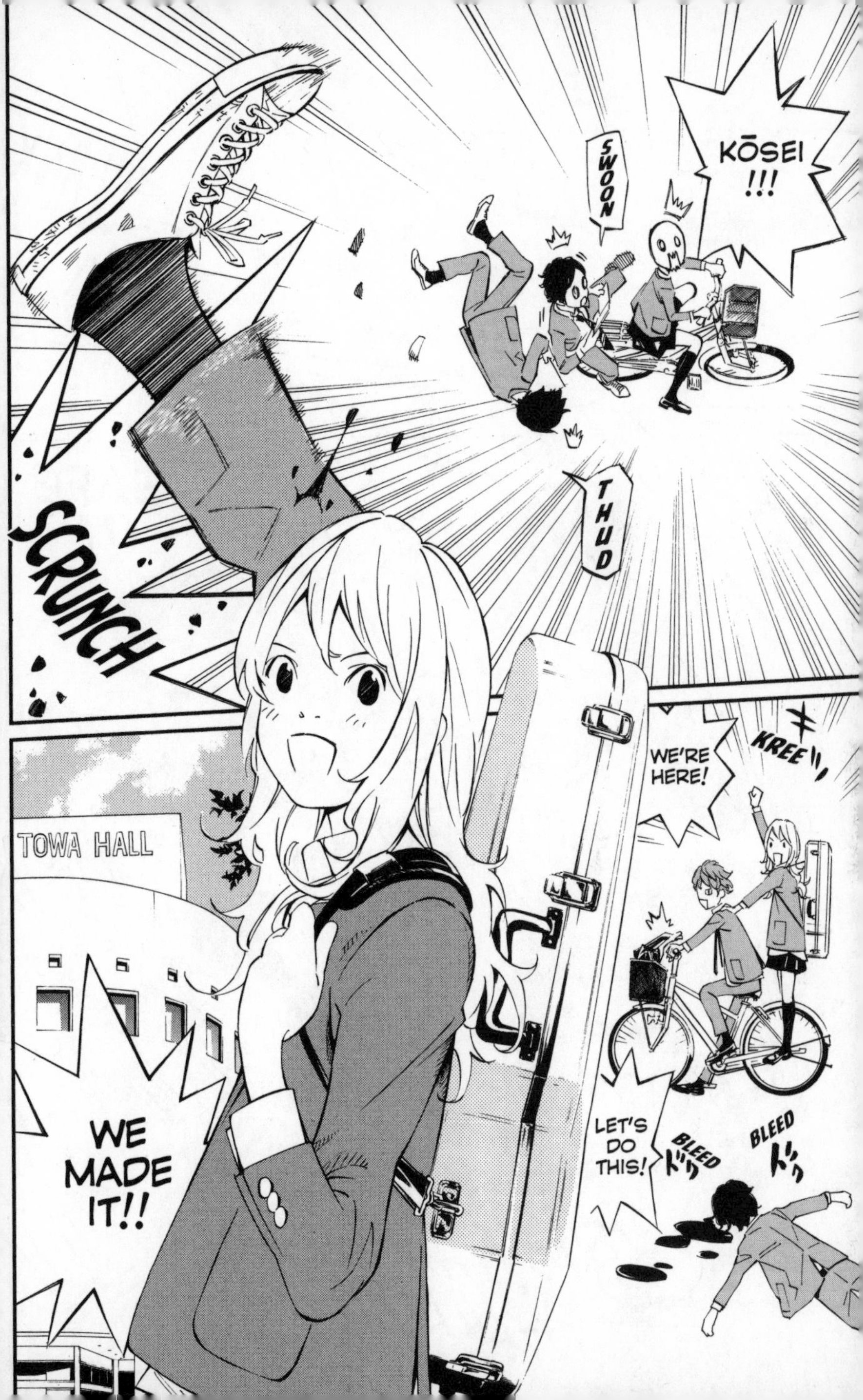
KŌSEI !!!
SWOON
THUD
SCRUNCH
KREE
WE'RE HERE!
LET'S DO THIS!
BLEED
BLEED
WE MADE IT!!
TOWA HALL

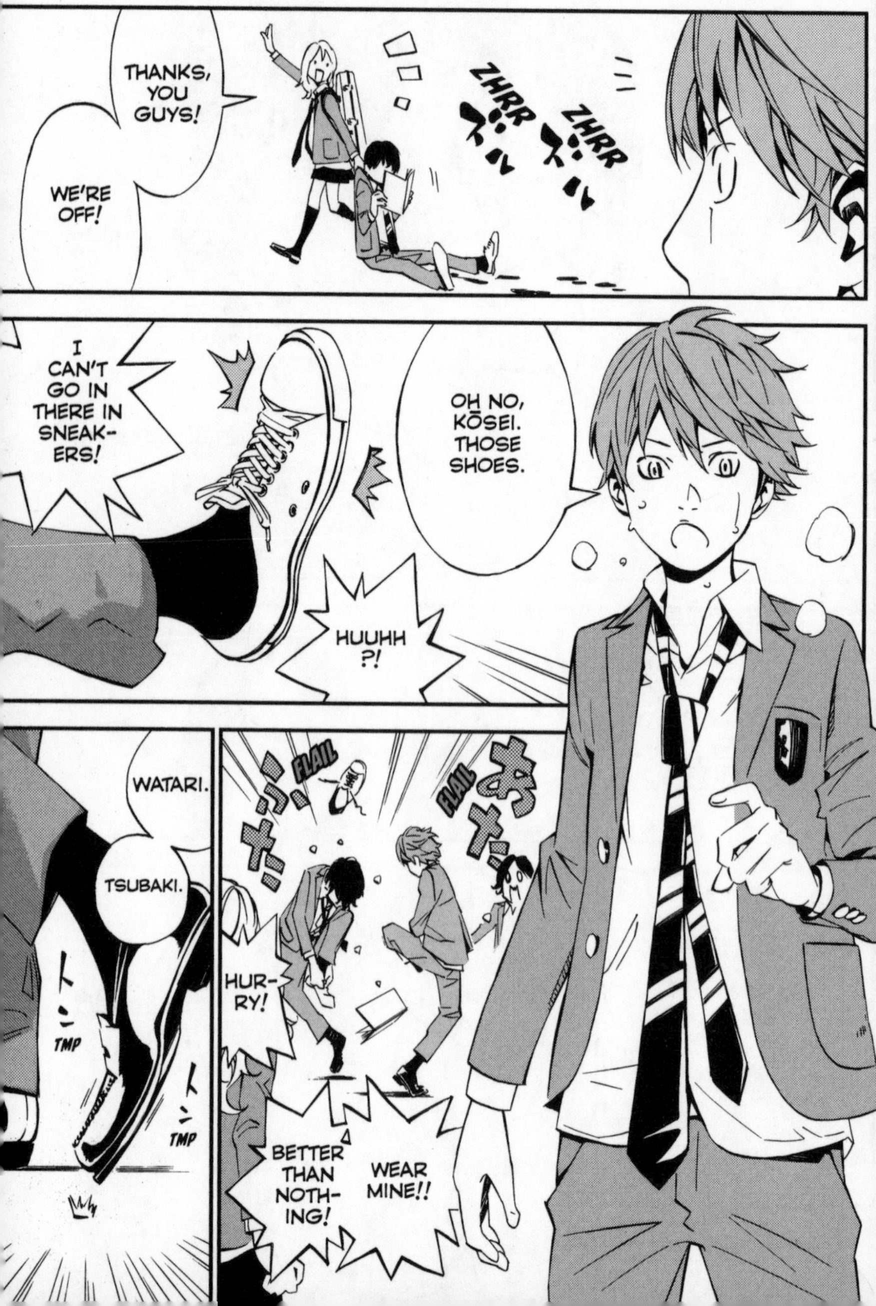
ZHRR
ZHRR
THANKS, YOU GUYS!
WE'RE OFF!
OH NO, KŌSEI. THOSE SHOES.
HUUHH?!
I CAN'T GO IN THERE IN SNEAKERS!
FLAIL
FLAIL
HURRY!
WEAR MINE!!
BETTER THAN NOTHING!
WATARI.
TSUBAKI.
TMP
TMP

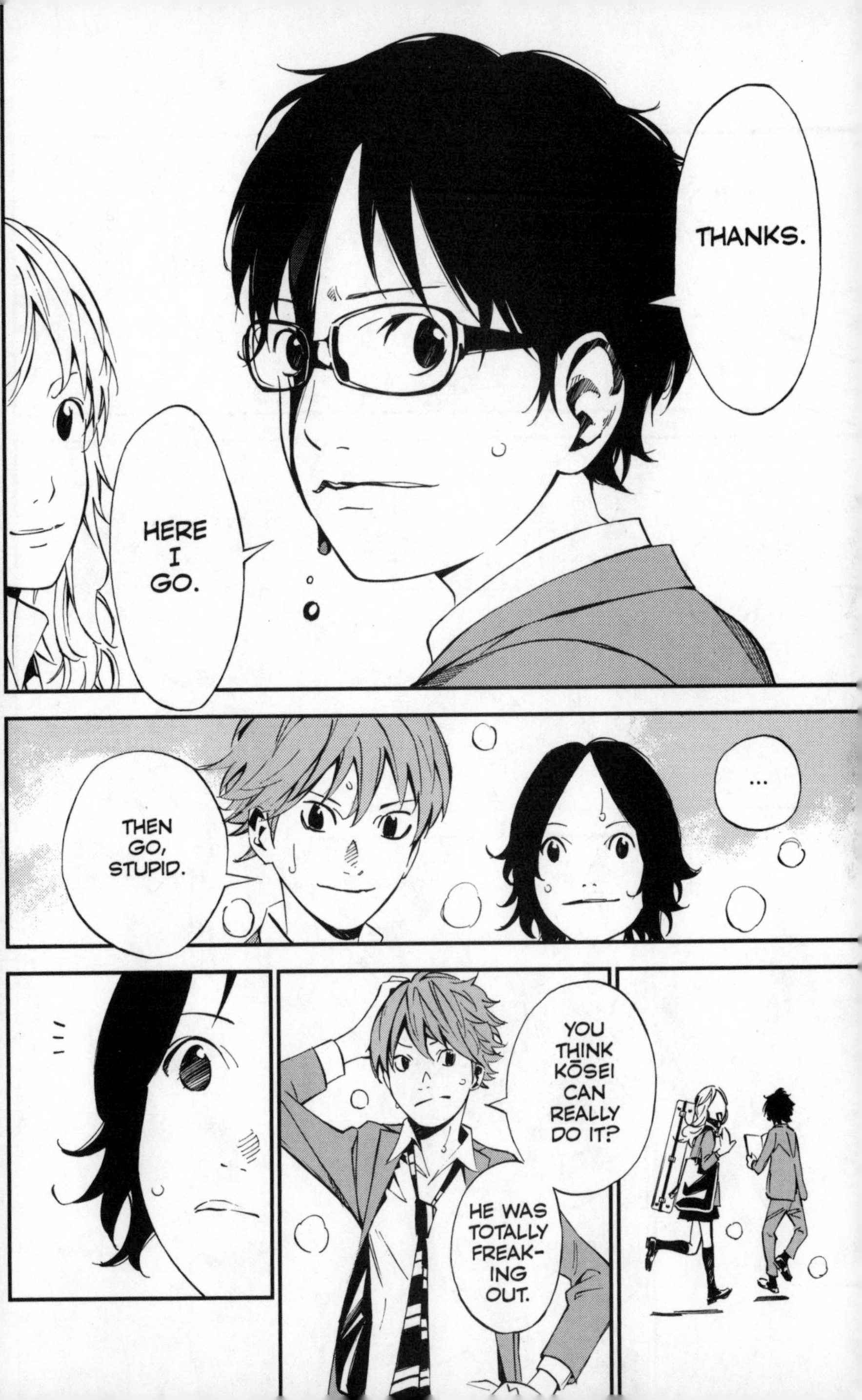
THANKS.
HERE I GO.
...
THEN GO, STUPID.
YOU THINK KŌSEI CAN REALLY DO IT?
HE WAS TOTALLY FREAKING OUT.

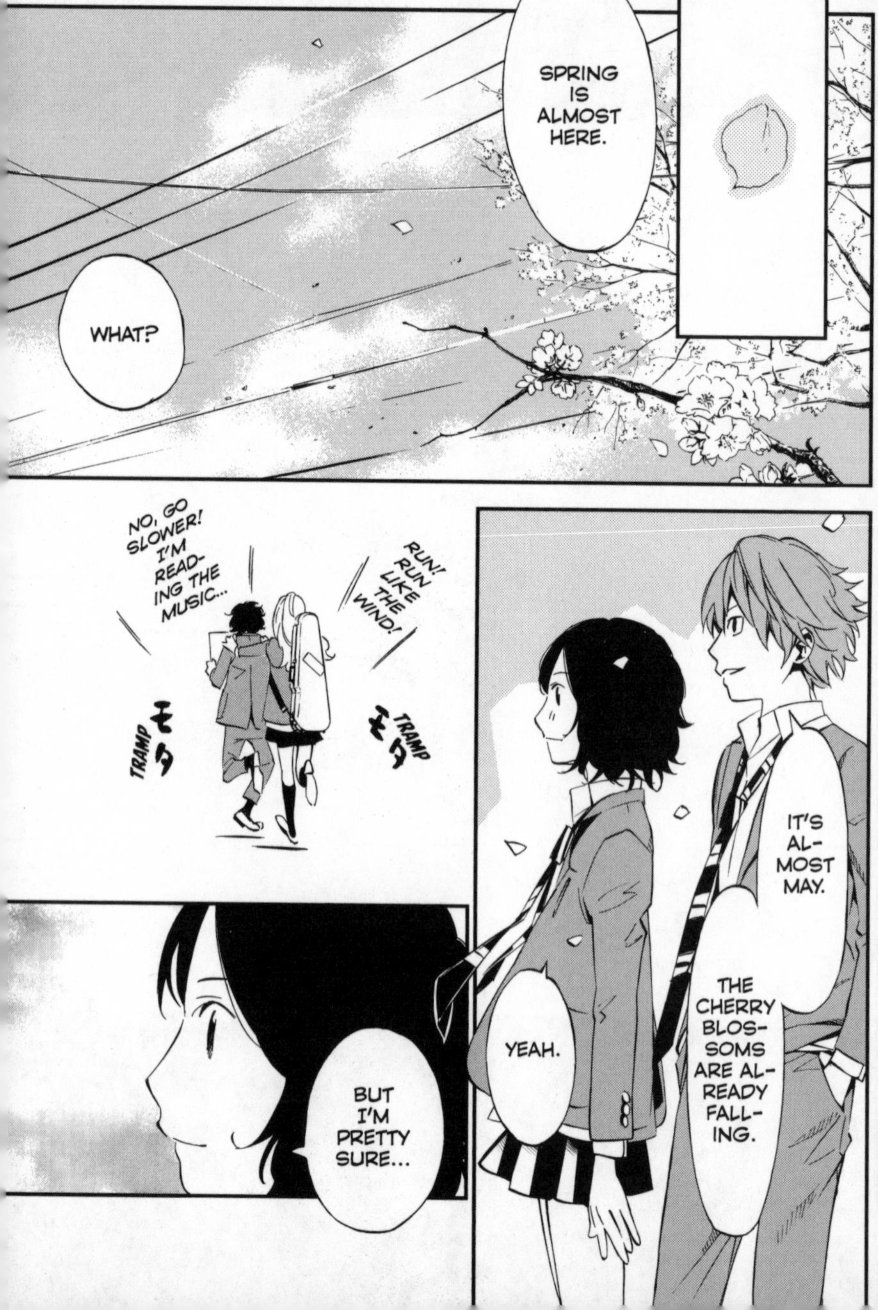
SPRING IS ALMOST HERE.
WHAT?
IT'S AL-MOST MAY.
THE CHERRY BLOS-SOMS ARE AL-READY FALL-ING.
YEAH.
RUN! RUN LIKE THE WIND!
NO, GO SLOWER! I'M READ-ING THE MUSIC...
モタ TRAMP
モタ TRAMP
BUT I'M PRETTY SURE...

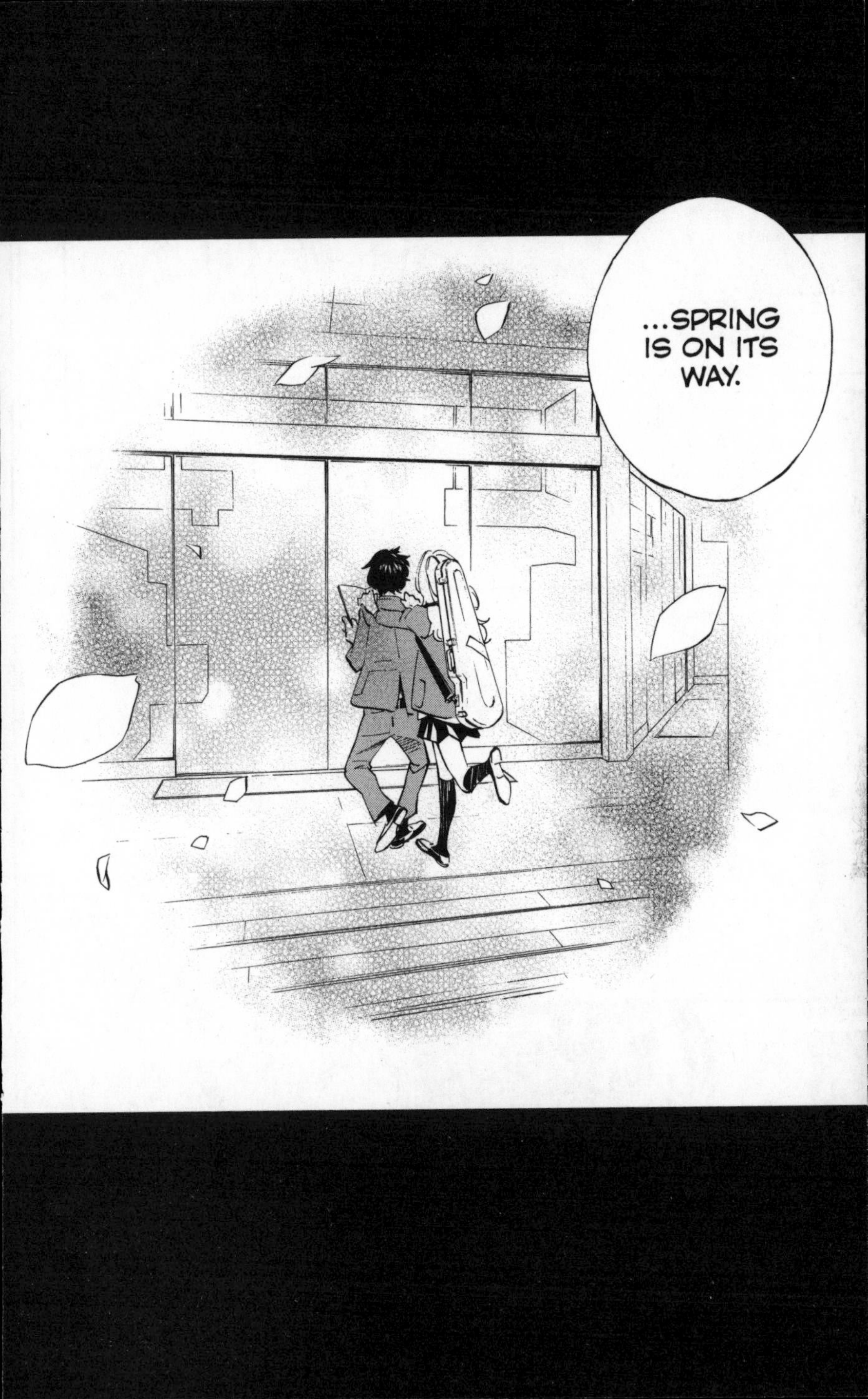
...SPRING IS ON ITS WAY.

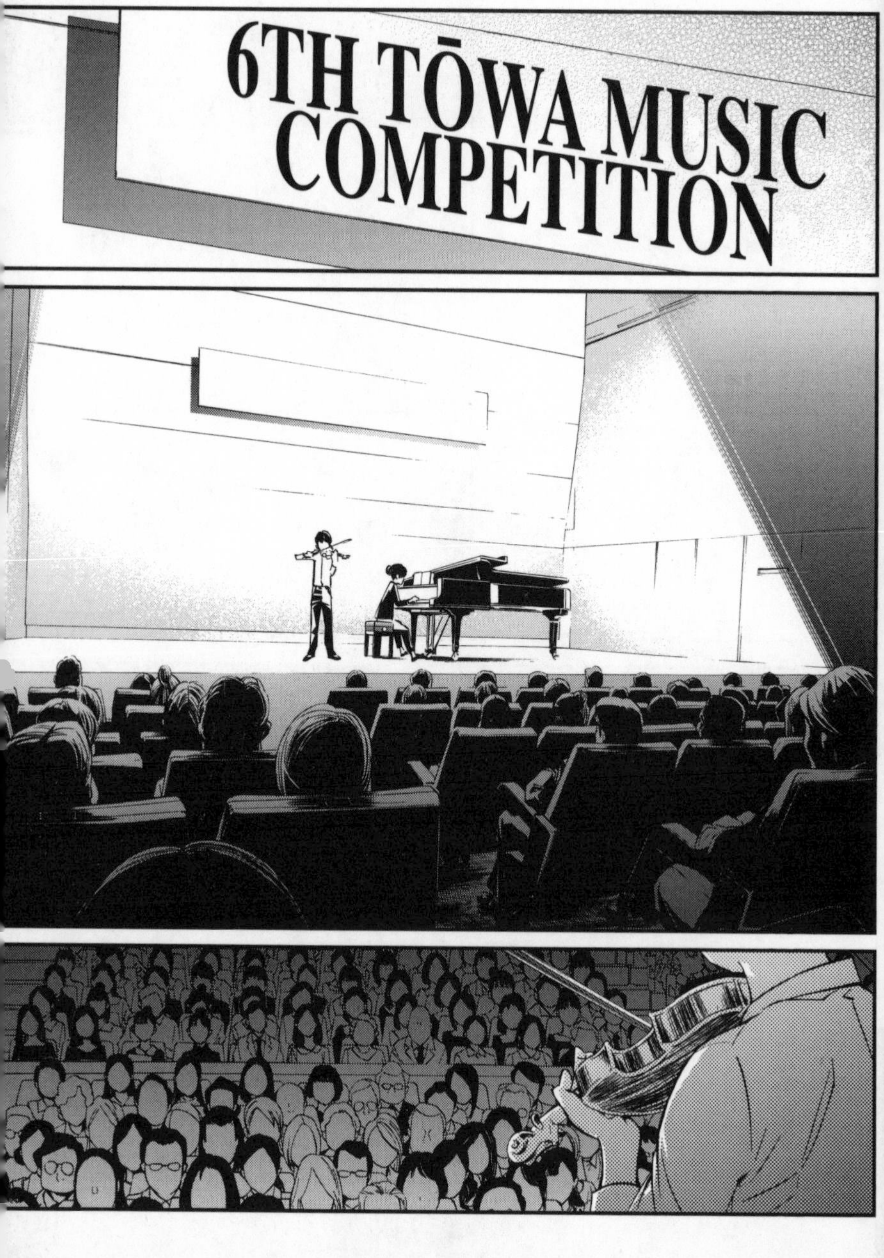
6TH TŌWA MUSIC COMPETITION

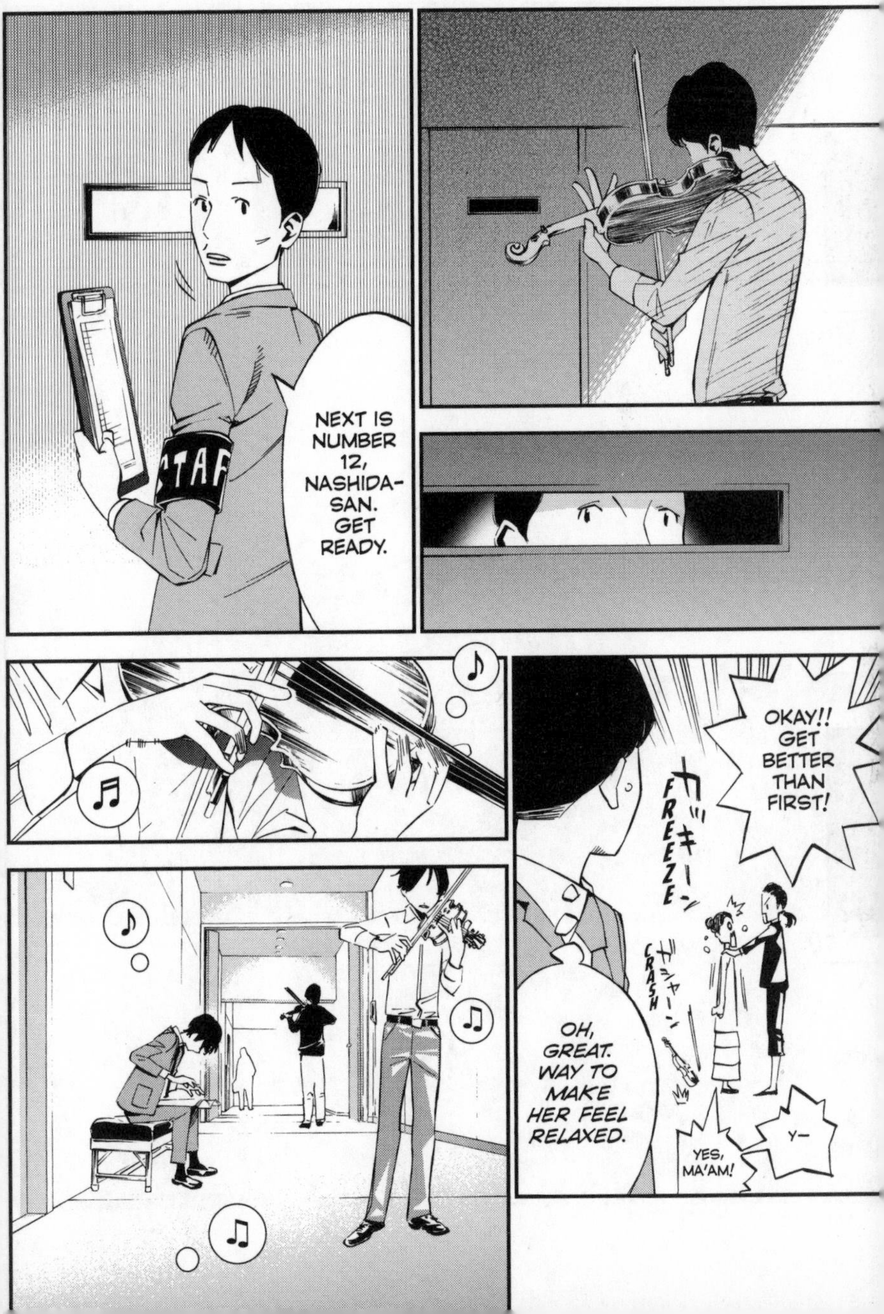
STAF
NEXT IS NUMBER 12, NASHIDA-SAN. GET READY.
OKAY!! GET BETTER THAN FIRST!
FREEZE
Y—
YES, MA'AM!
CRASH
OH, GREAT. WAY TO MAKE HER FEEL RELAXED.

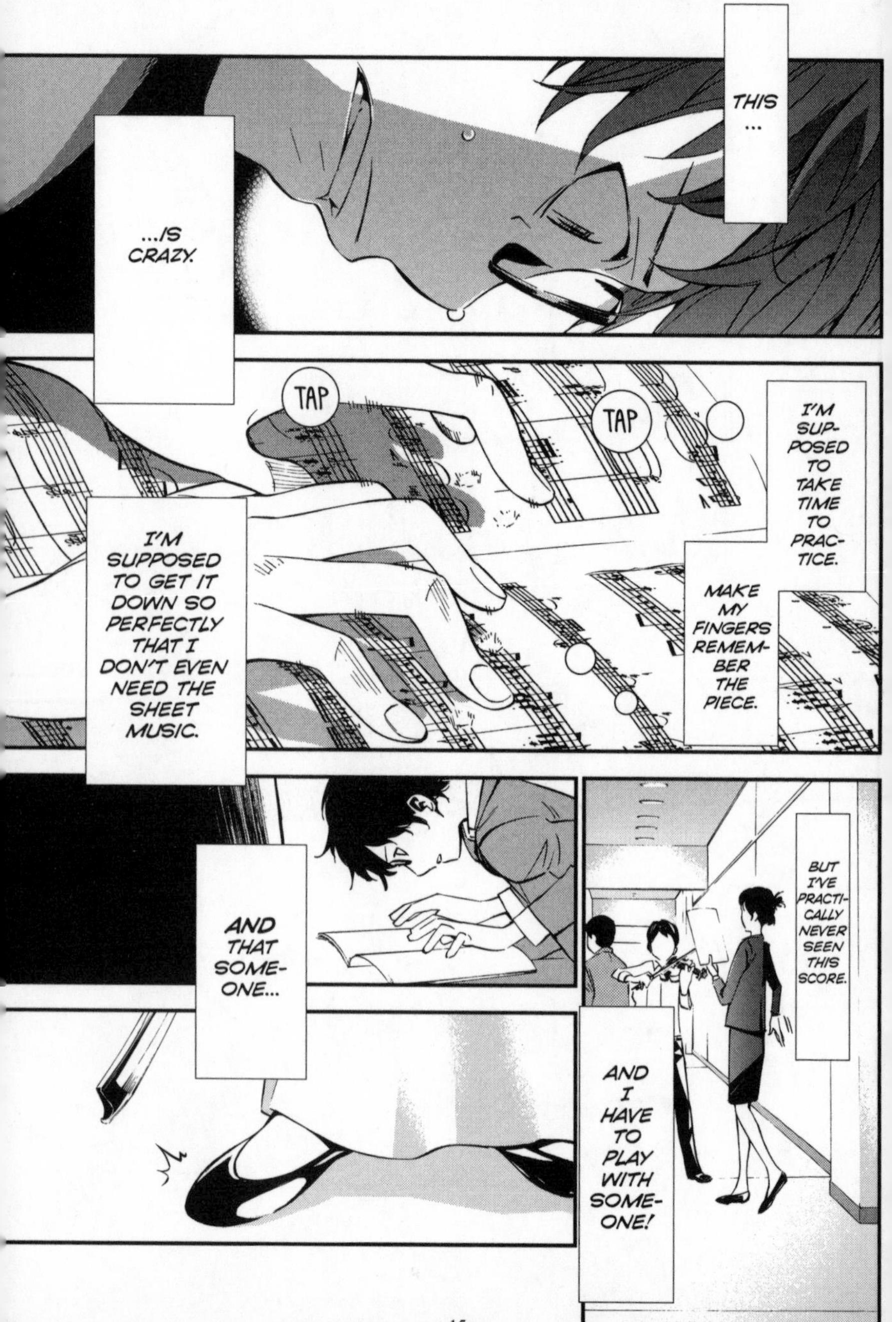
THIS ...
...IS CRAZY.
I'M SUPPOSED TO TAKE TIME TO PRACTICE.
TAP
TAP
MAKE MY FINGERS REMEMBER THE PIECE.
I'M SUPPOSED TO GET IT DOWN SO PERFECTLY THAT I DON'T EVEN NEED THE SHEET MUSIC.
BUT I'VE PRACTICALLY NEVER SEEN THIS SCORE.
AND I HAVE TO PLAY WITH SOMEONE!
AND THAT SOMEONE...

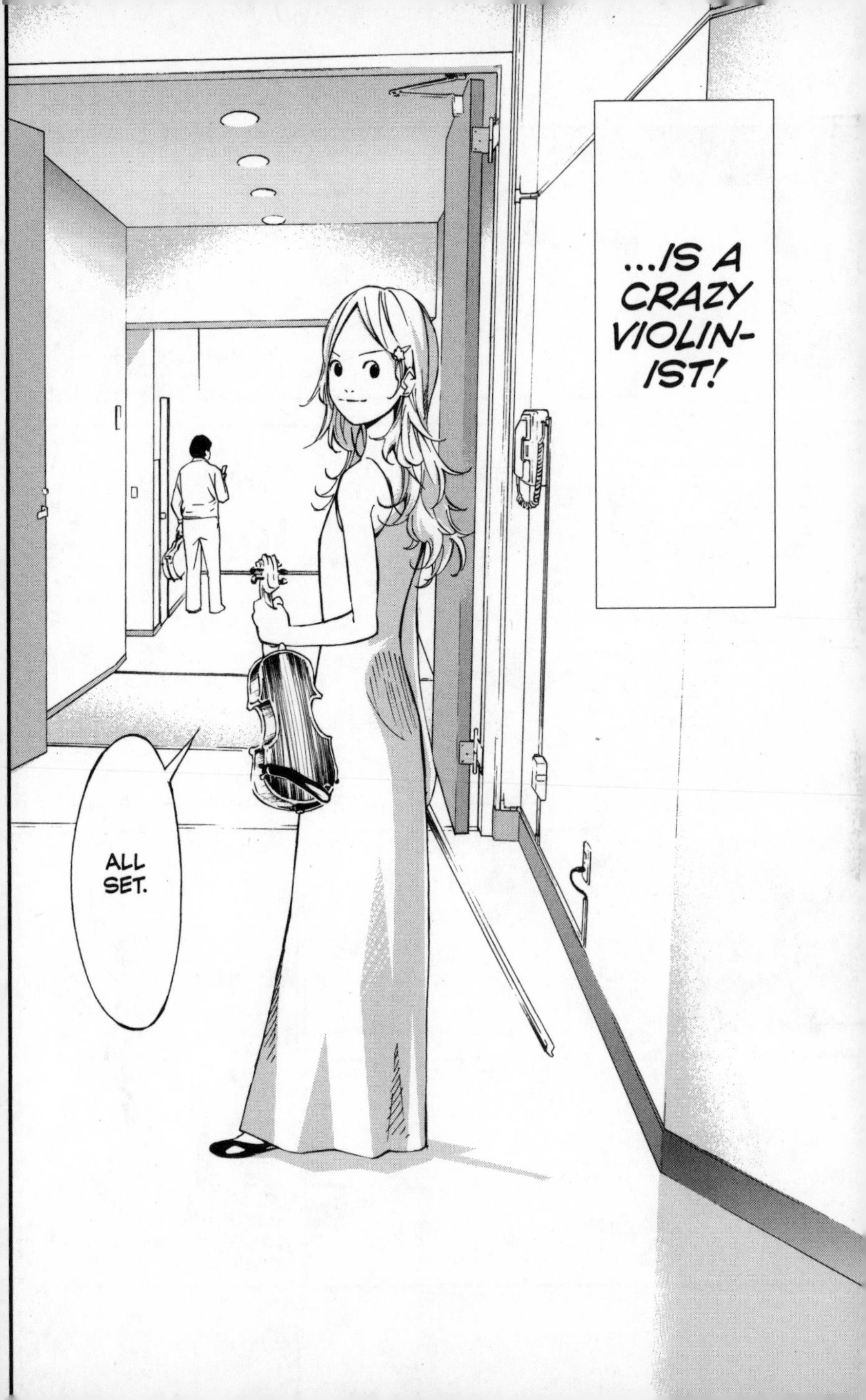
...IS A CRAZY VIOLIN-IST!
ALL SET.

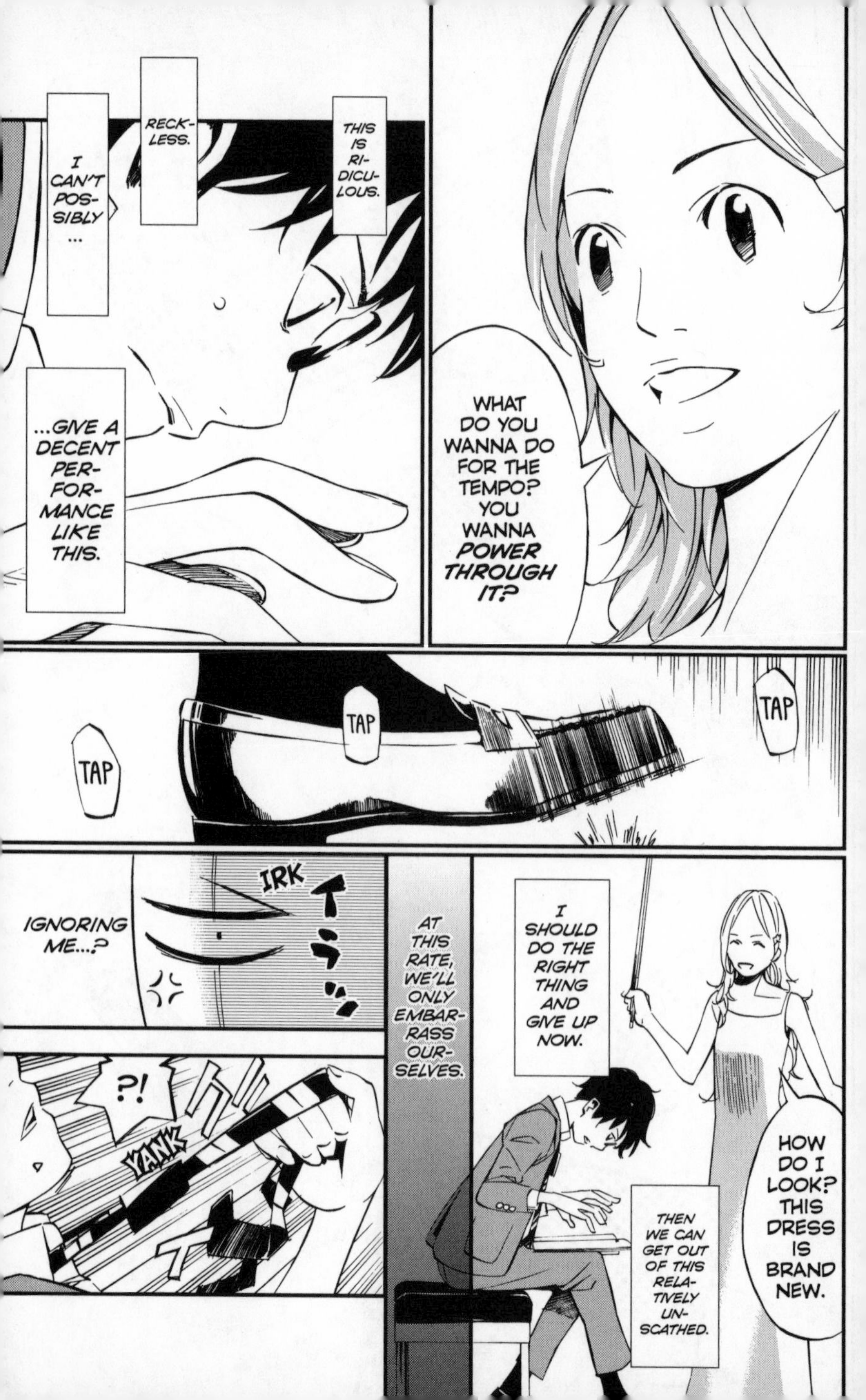
WHAT DO YOU WANNA DO FOR THE TEMPO? YOU WANNA POWER THROUGH IT?
THIS IS RIDICULOUS.
RECKLESS.
I CAN'T POSSIBLY...
...GIVE A DECENT PERFORMANCE LIKE THIS.
TAP
TAP
TAP
HOW DO I LOOK? THIS DRESS IS BRAND NEW.
I SHOULD DO THE RIGHT THING AND GIVE UP NOW.
THEN WE CAN GET OUT OF THIS RELATIVELY UNSCATHED.
AT THIS RATE, WE'LL ONLY EMBARRASS OURSELVES.
IRK
IGNORING ME...?
?!
YANK

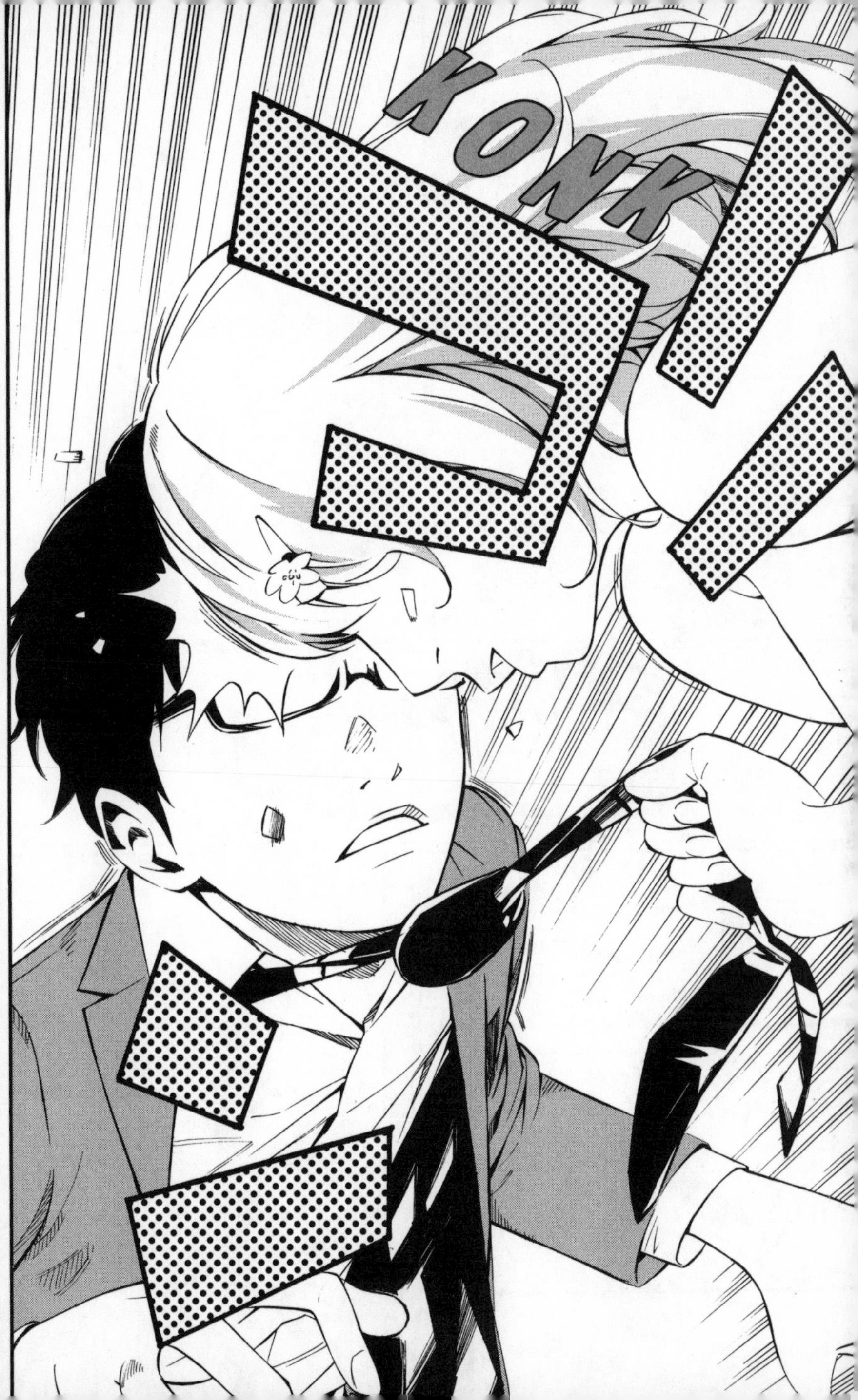
KONK

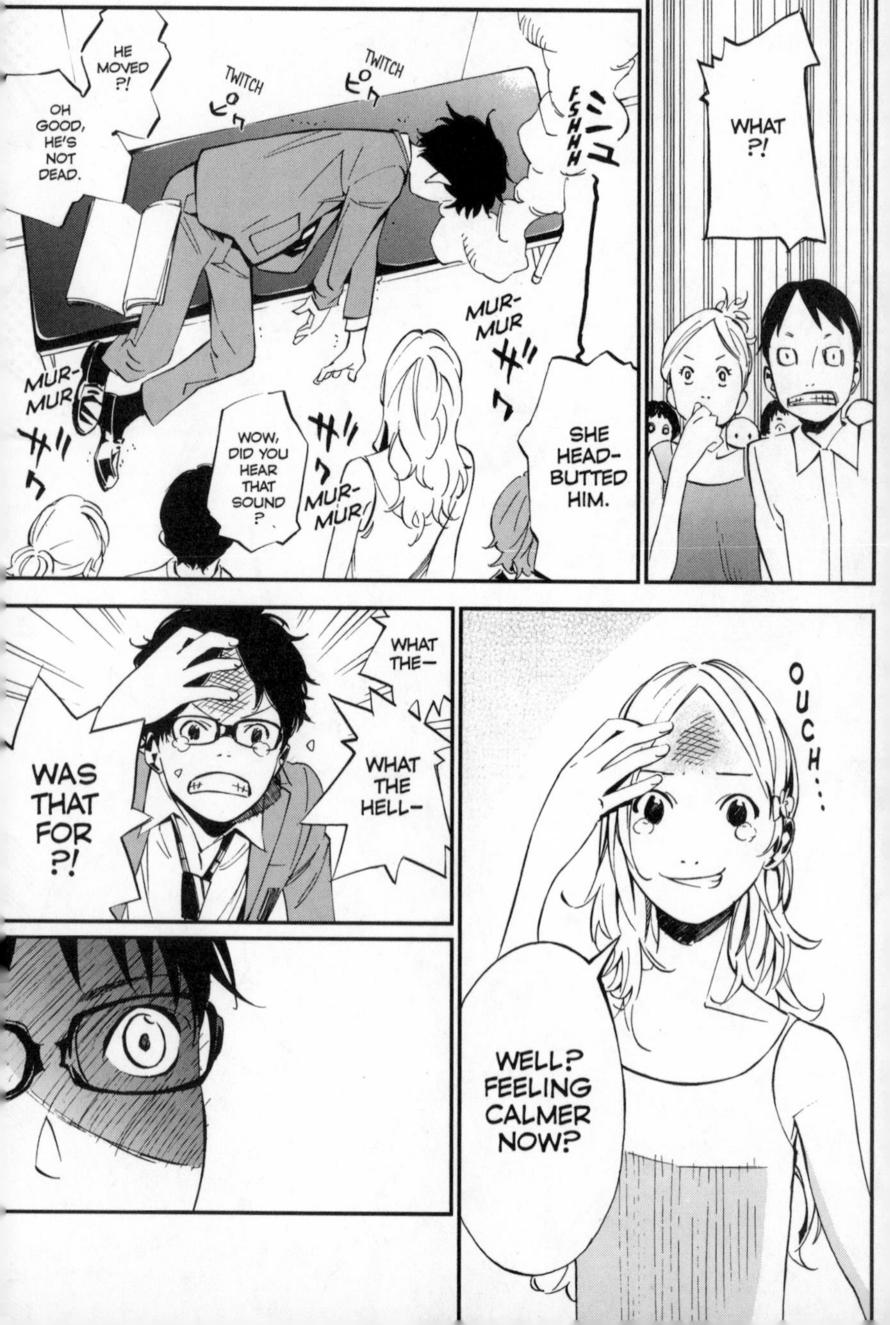
WHAT ?!
FSHHH
TWITCH
HE MOVED ?!
TWITCH
OH GOOD, HE'S NOT DEAD.
MUR-MUR
SHE HEAD-BUTTED HIM.
MUR-MUR
WOW, DID YOU HEAR THAT SOUND ?
MUR-MUR
WHAT THE—
WHAT THE HELL—
WAS THAT FOR ?!
OUCH...
WELL? FEELING CALMER NOW?

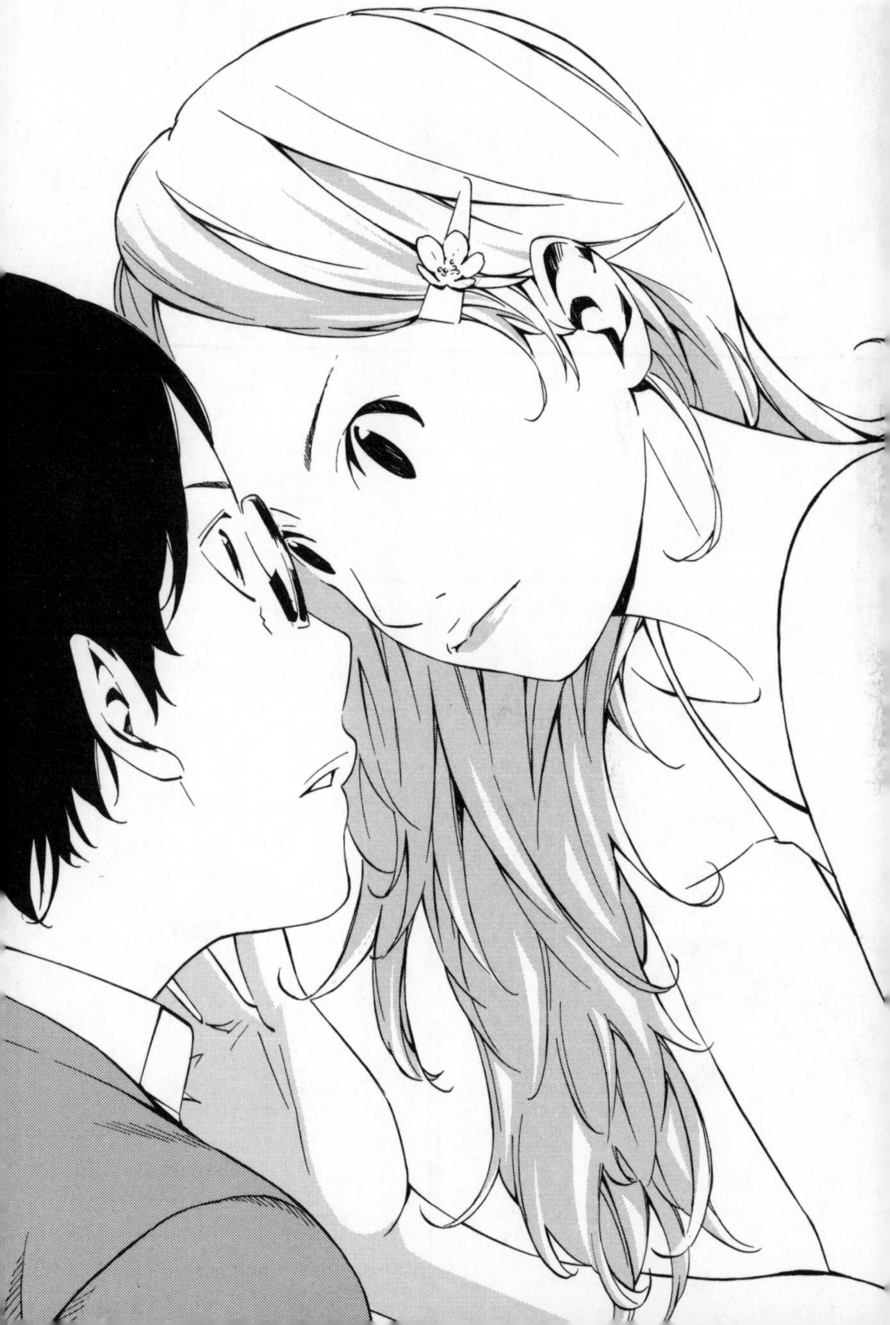

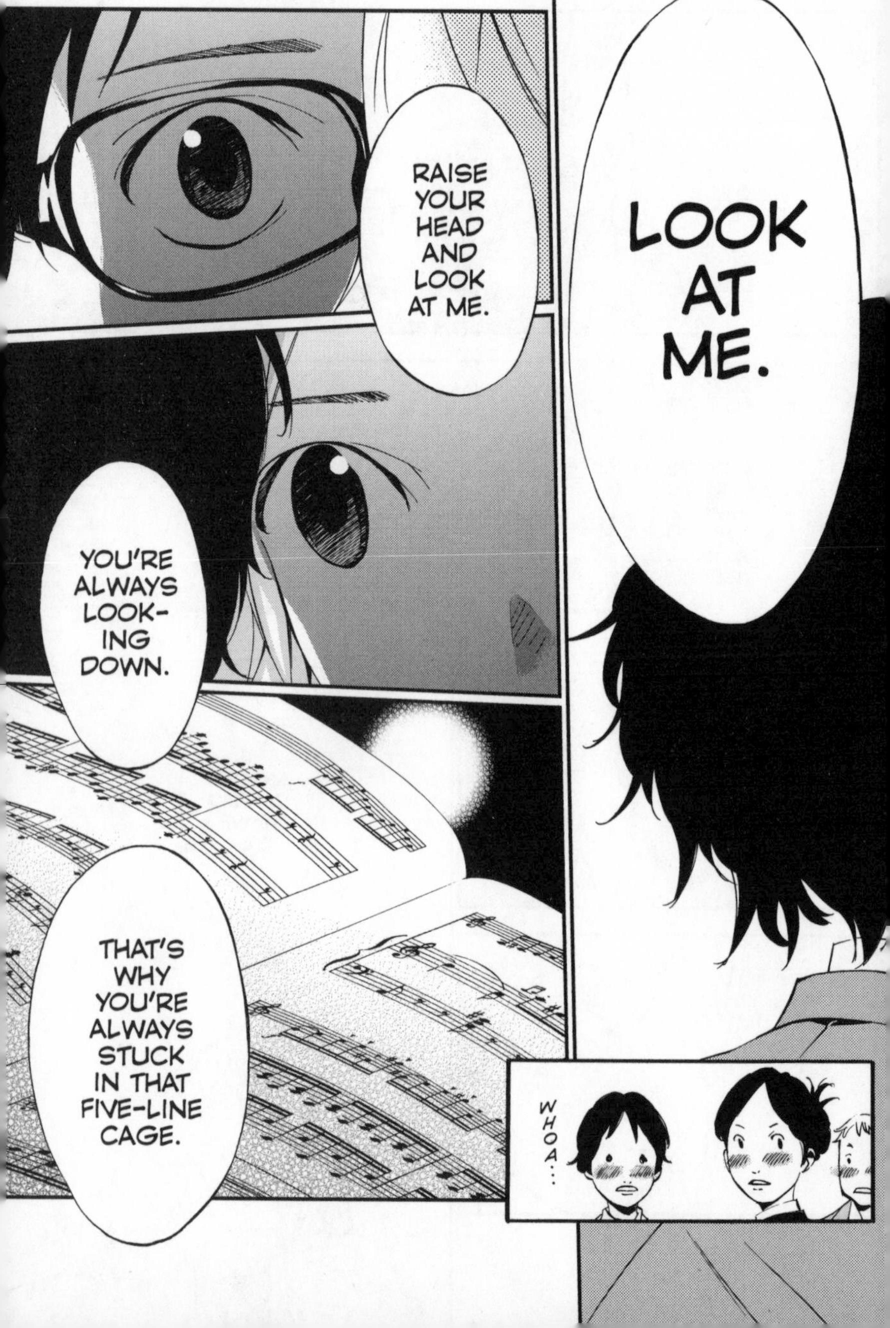
LOOK AT ME.
RAISE YOUR HEAD AND LOOK AT ME.
YOU'RE ALWAYS LOOKING DOWN.
THAT'S WHY YOU'RE ALWAYS STUCK IN THAT FIVE-LINE CAGE.
WHOA...

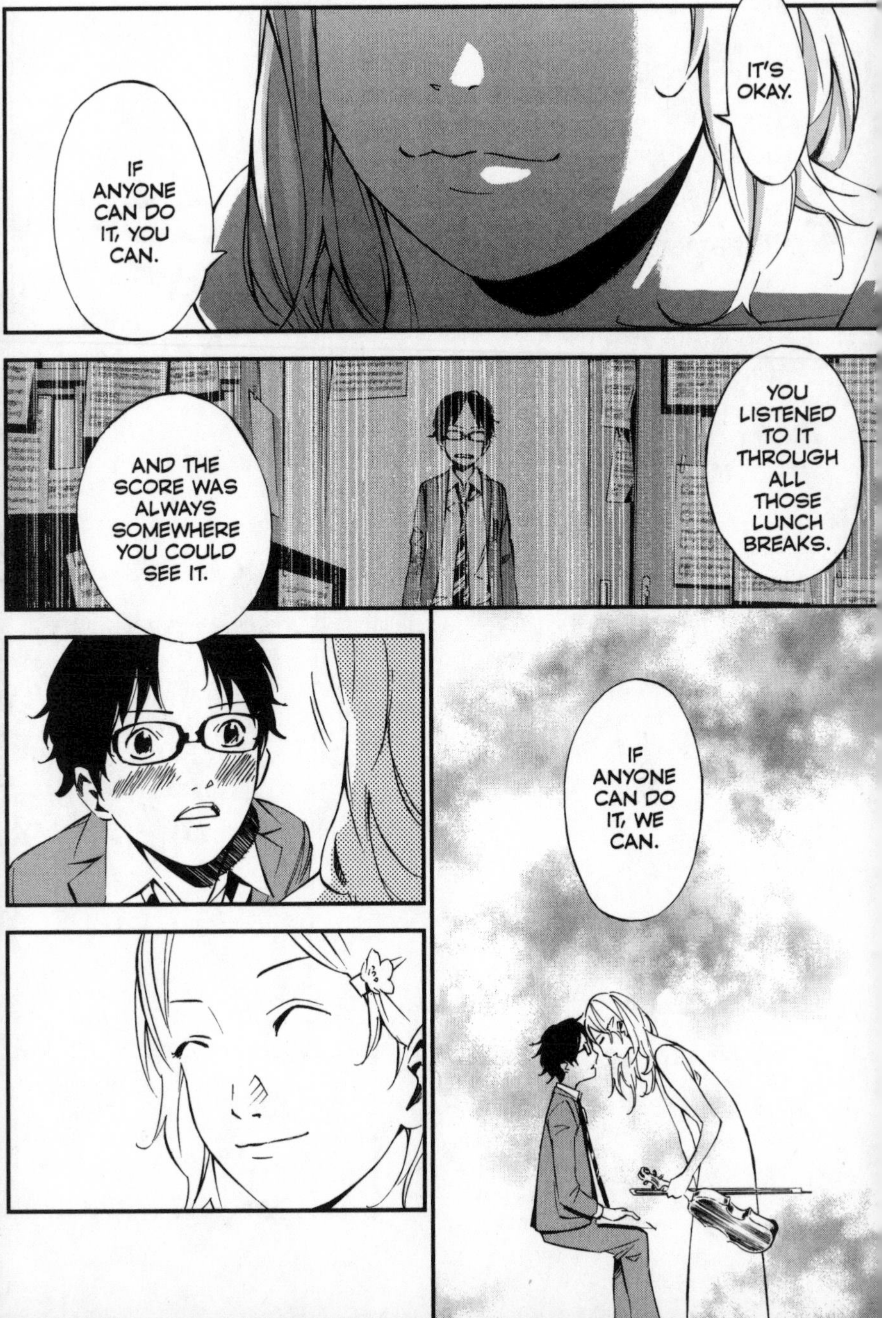
IT'S OKAY.
IF ANYONE CAN DO IT, YOU CAN.
YOU LISTENED TO IT THROUGH ALL THOSE LUNCH BREAKS.
AND THE SCORE WAS ALWAYS SOMEWHERE YOU COULD SEE IT.
IF ANYONE CAN DO IT, WE CAN.

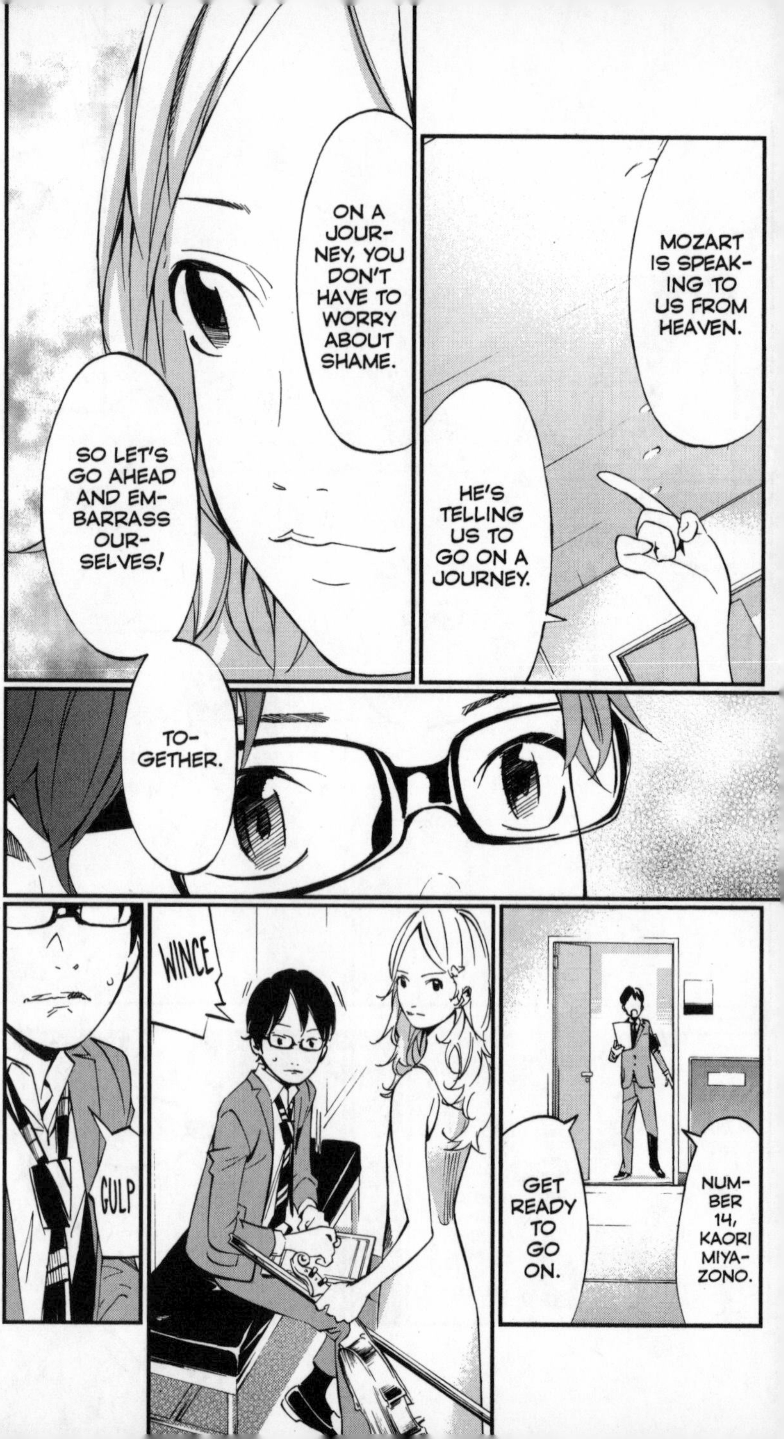
MOZART IS SPEAKING TO US FROM HEAVEN.
HE'S TELLING US TO GO ON A JOURNEY.
ON A JOURNEY, YOU DON'T HAVE TO WORRY ABOUT SHAME.
SO LET'S GO AHEAD AND EMBARRASS OURSELVES!
TOGETHER.
NUMBER 14, KAORI MIYAZONO.
GET READY TO GO ON.
WINCE
GULP

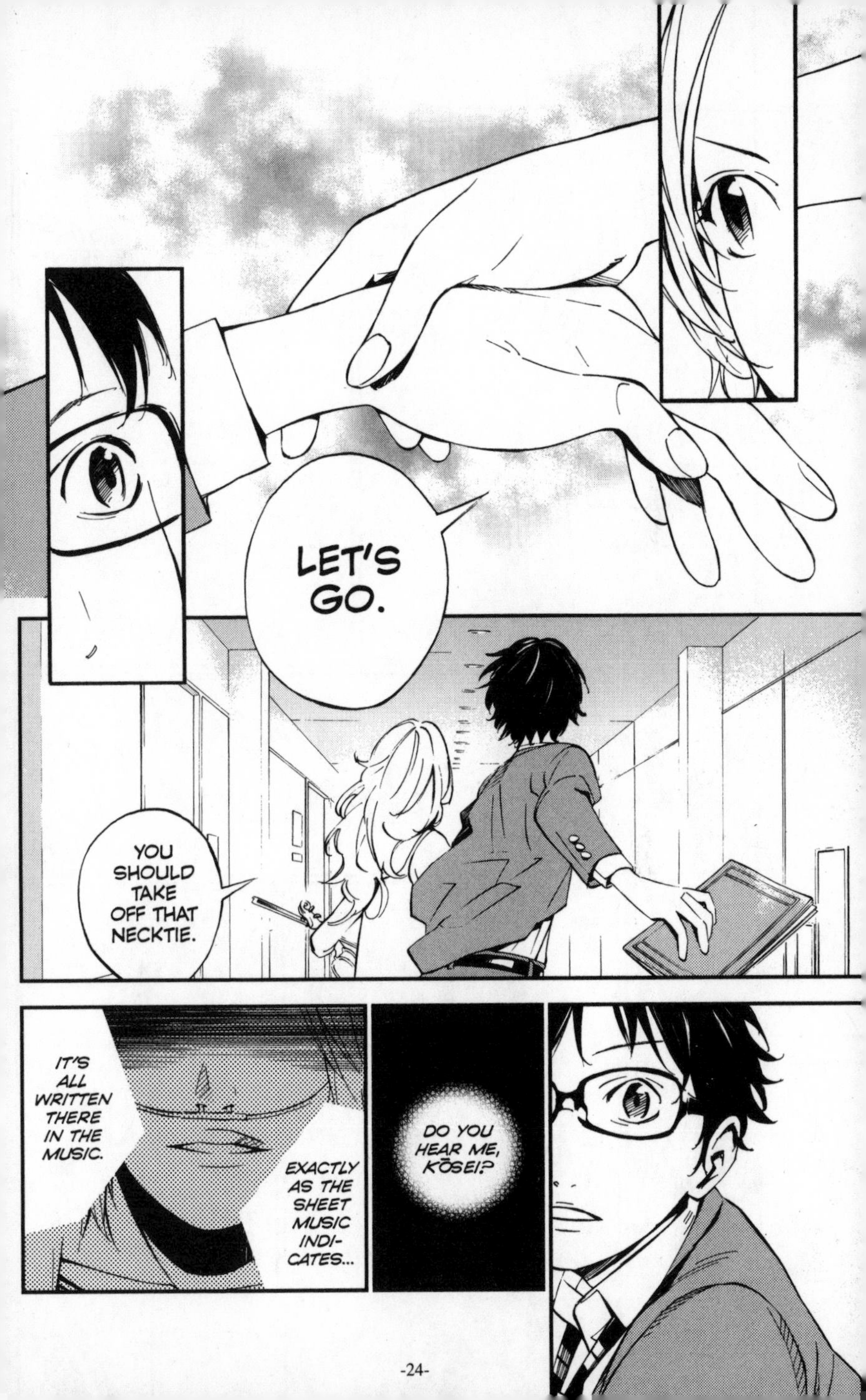
LET'S GO.
YOU SHOULD TAKE OFF THAT NECKTIE.
DO YOU HEAR ME, KŌSEI?
IT'S ALL WRITTEN THERE IN THE MUSIC.
EXACTLY AS THE SHEET MUSIC INDI-CATES...

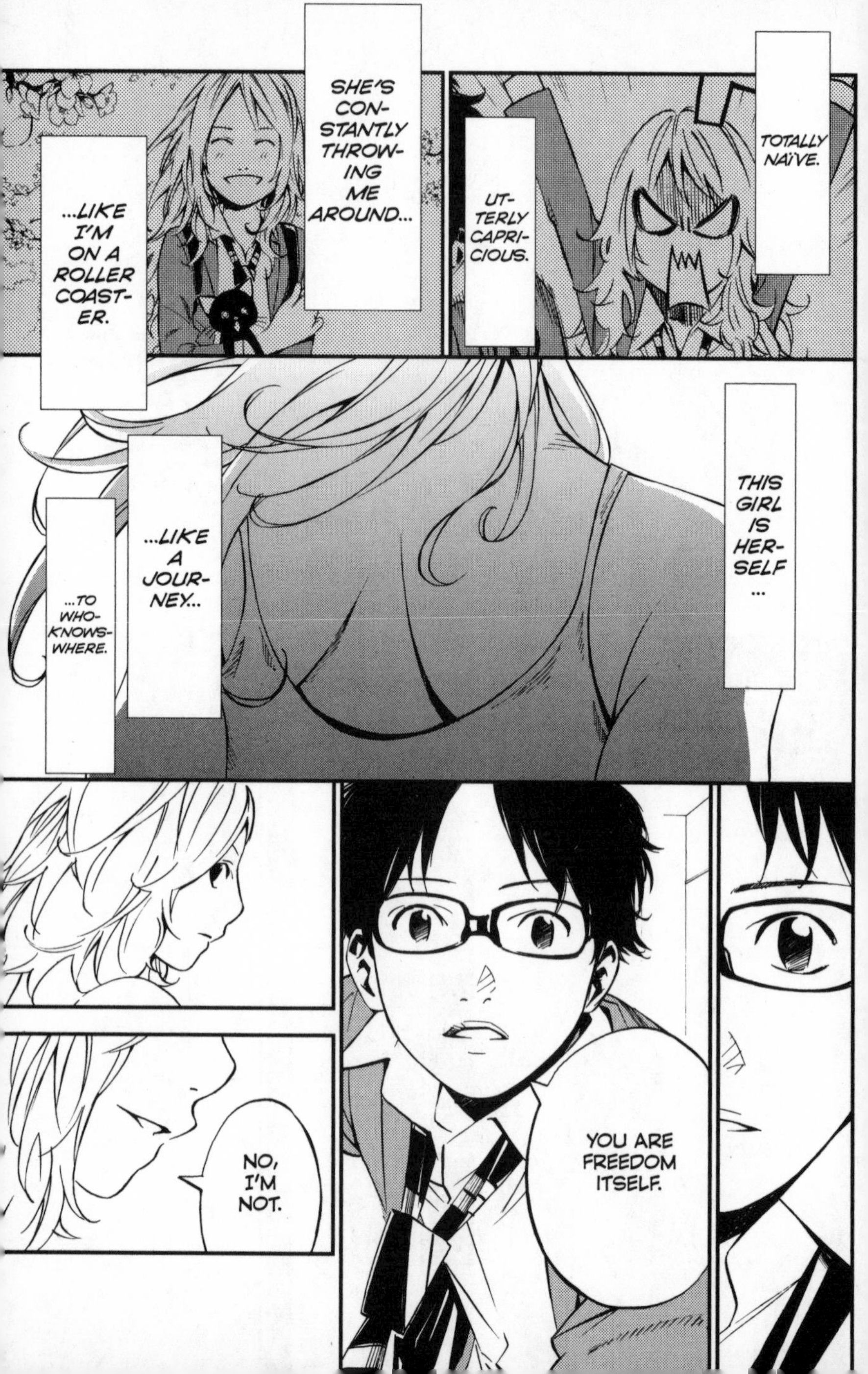
TOTALLY NAÏVE.
UTTERLY CAPRICIOUS.
SHE'S CONSTANTLY THROWING ME AROUND...
...LIKE I'M ON A ROLLER COASTER.
THIS GIRL IS HERSELF...
...LIKE A JOURNEY...
...TO WHO-KNOWS-WHERE.
YOU ARE FREEDOM ITSELF.
NO, I'M NOT.

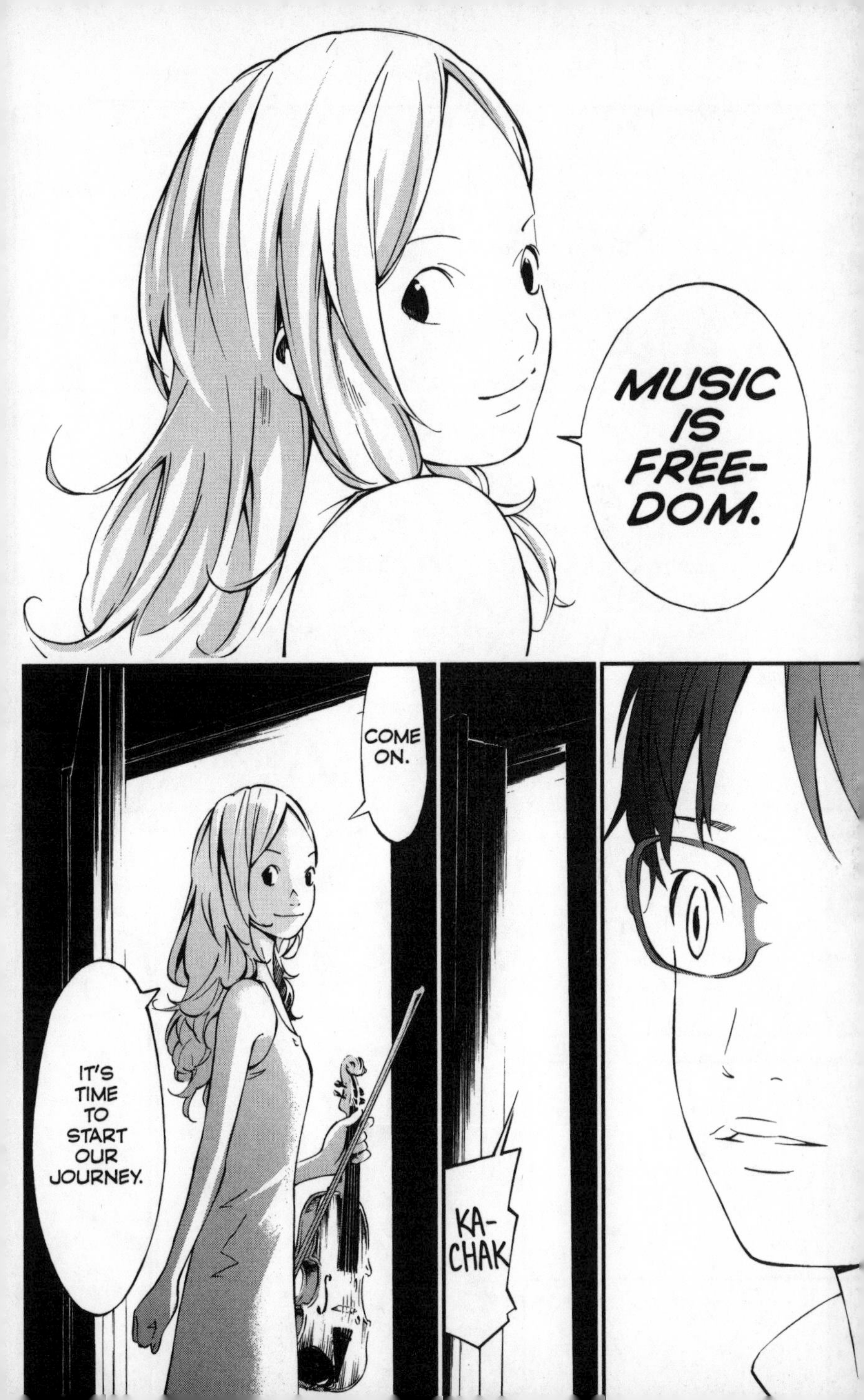
MUSIC IS FREE-DOM.
KA-CHAK
COME ON.
IT'S TIME TO START OUR JOURNEY.

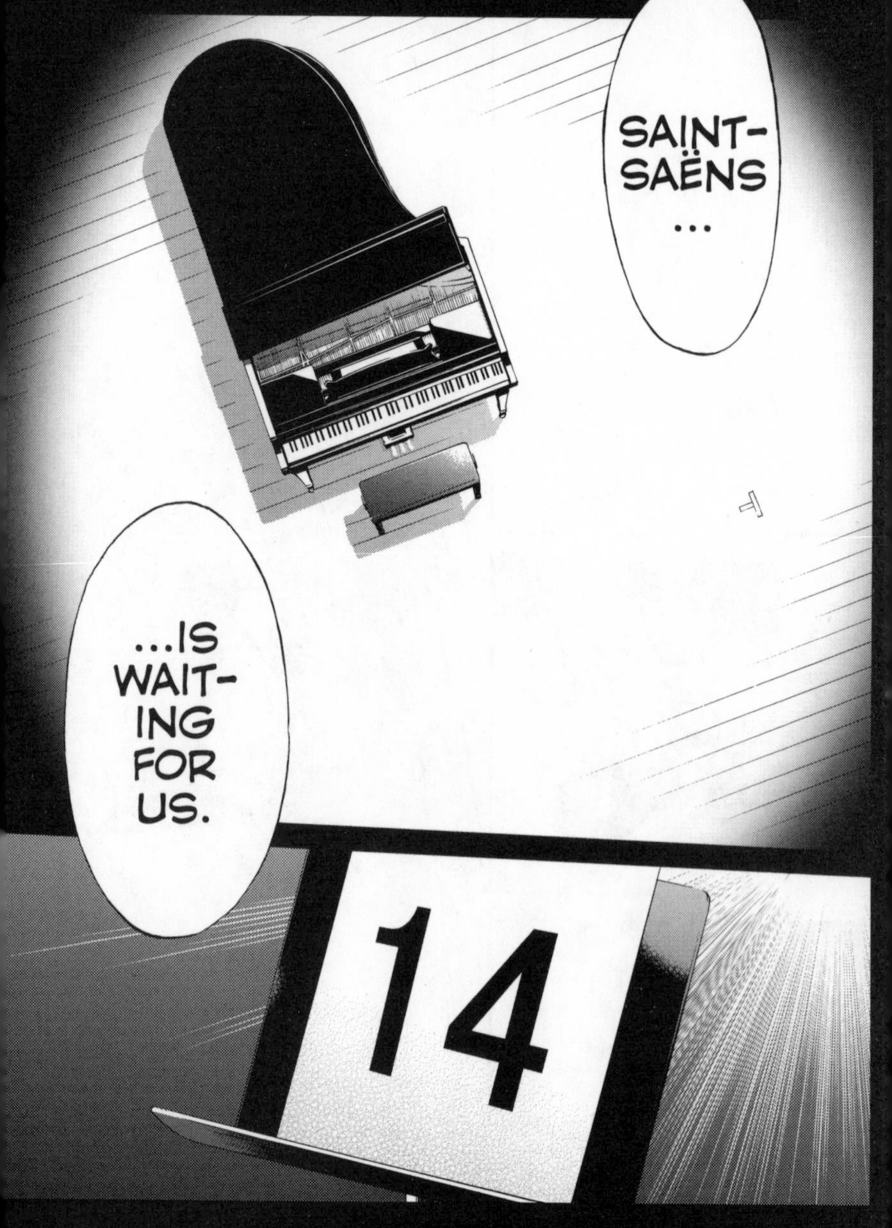
SAINT-SAËNS...
...IS WAITING FOR US.
14

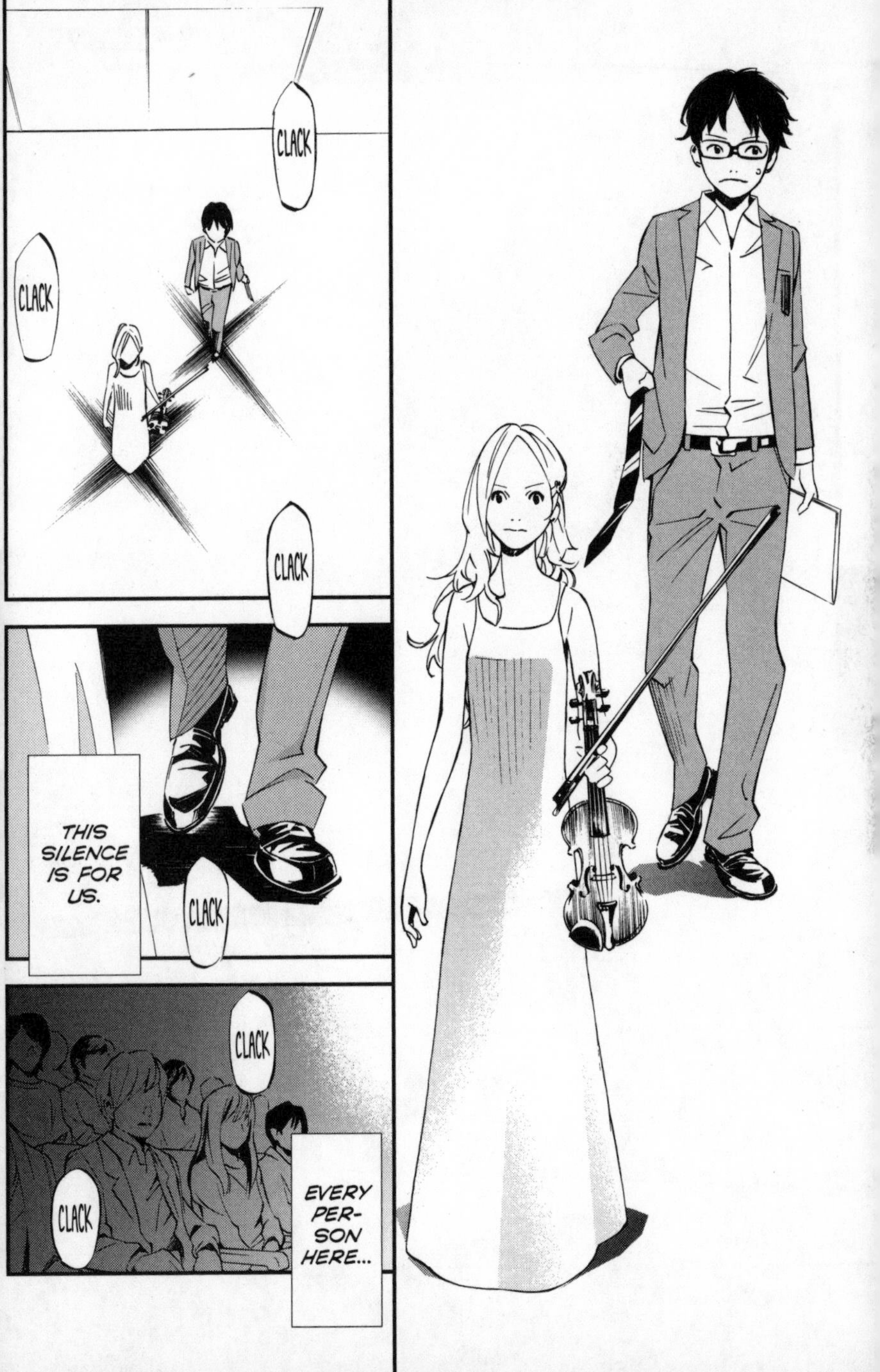
CLACK
CLACK
CLACK
THIS SILENCE IS FOR US.
CLACK
CLACK
EVERY PER-SON HERE...
CLACK

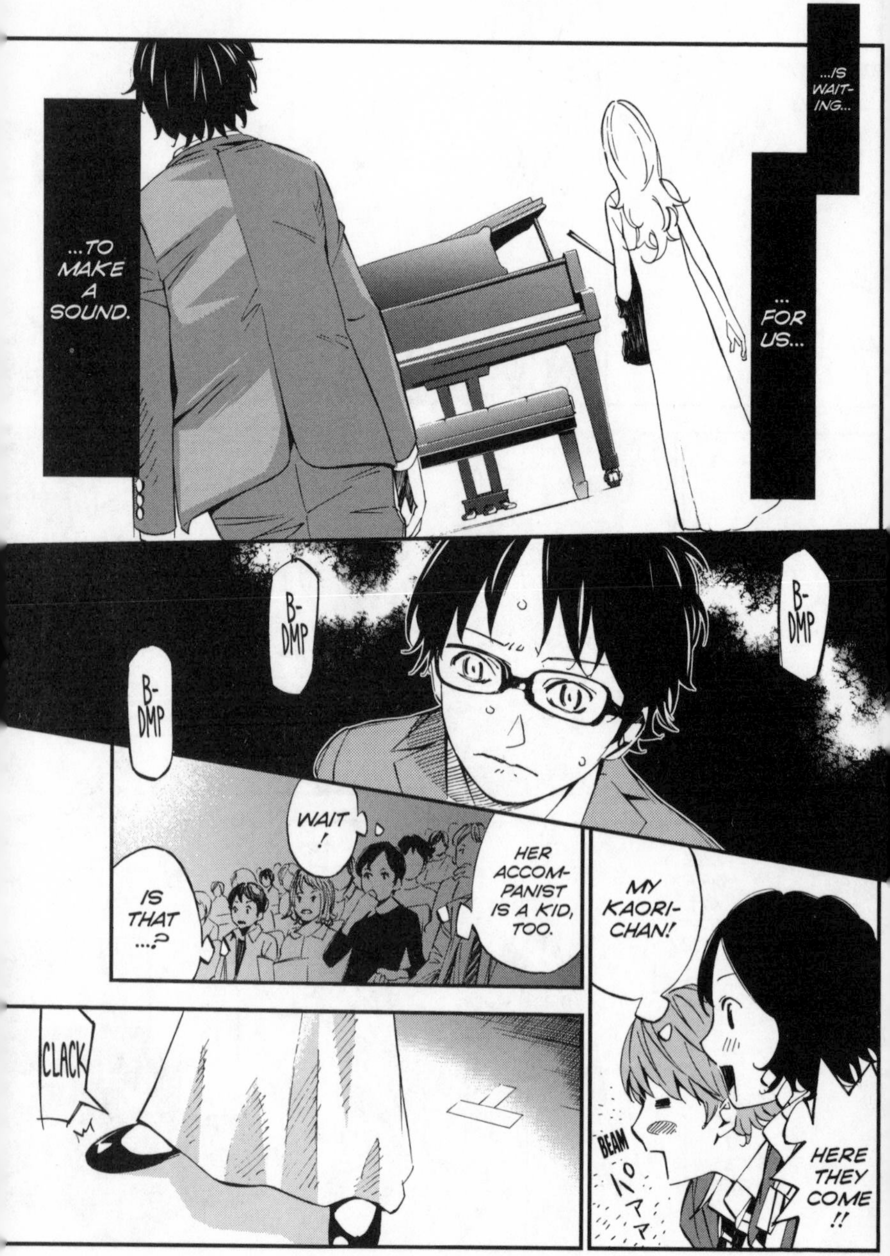
...IS WAIT-ING...
... FOR US...
...TO MAKE A SOUND.
B-DMP
B-DMP
B-DMP
MY KAORI-CHAN!
HERE THEY COME!!
BEAM
HER ACCOMPANIST IS A KID, TOO.
WAIT!
IS THAT ...?
CLACK

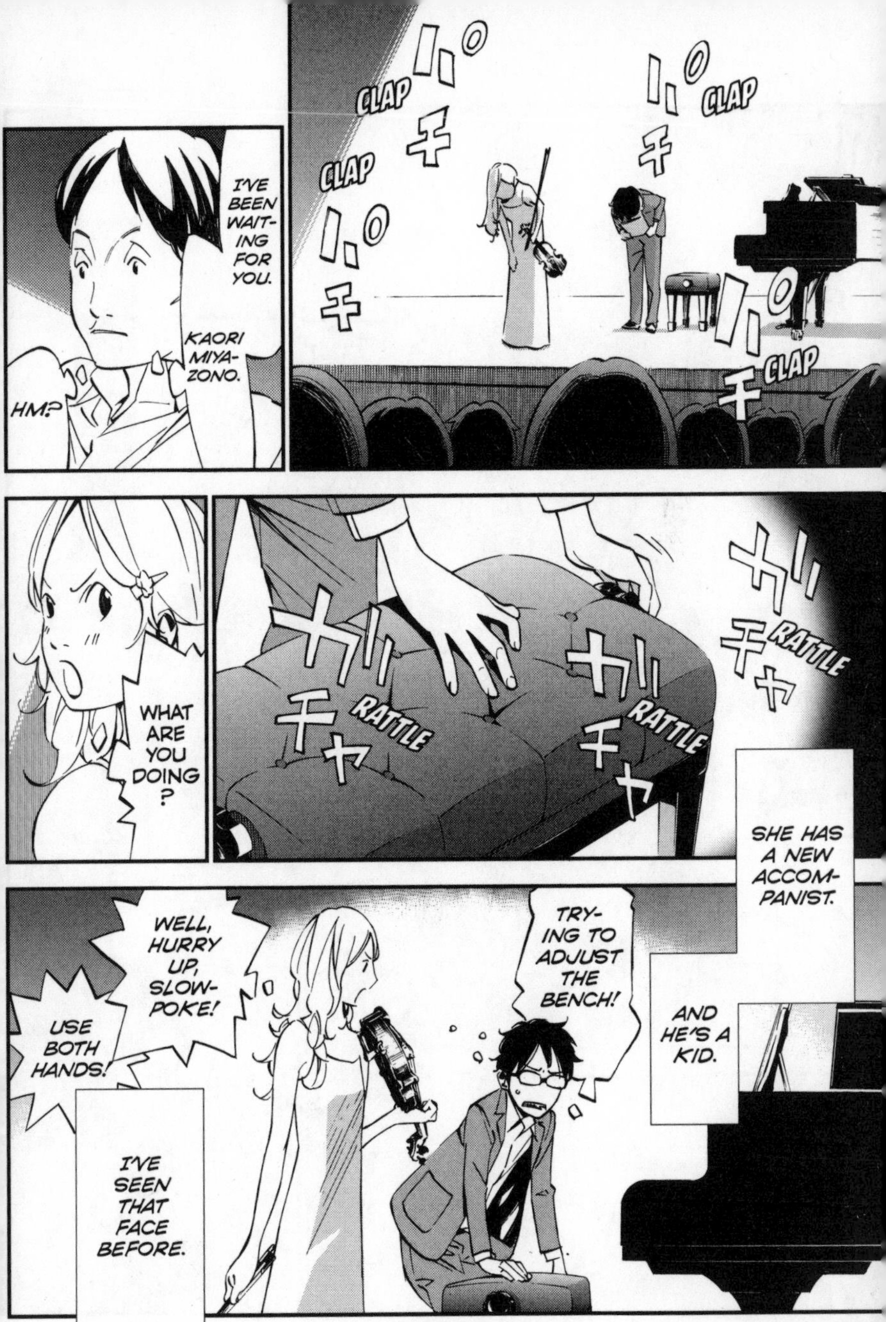
パチ CLAP
パチ CLAP
パチ CLAP
パチ CLAP
I'VE BEEN WAITING FOR YOU.
KAORI MIYAZONO.
HM?
カチャ RATTLE
カチャ RATTLE
カチャ RATTLE
WHAT ARE YOU DOING?
SHE HAS A NEW ACCOMPANIST.
AND HE'S A KID.
TRYING TO ADJUST THE BENCH!
WELL, HURRY UP, SLOWPOKE!
USE BOTH HANDS!
I'VE SEEN THAT FACE BEFORE.

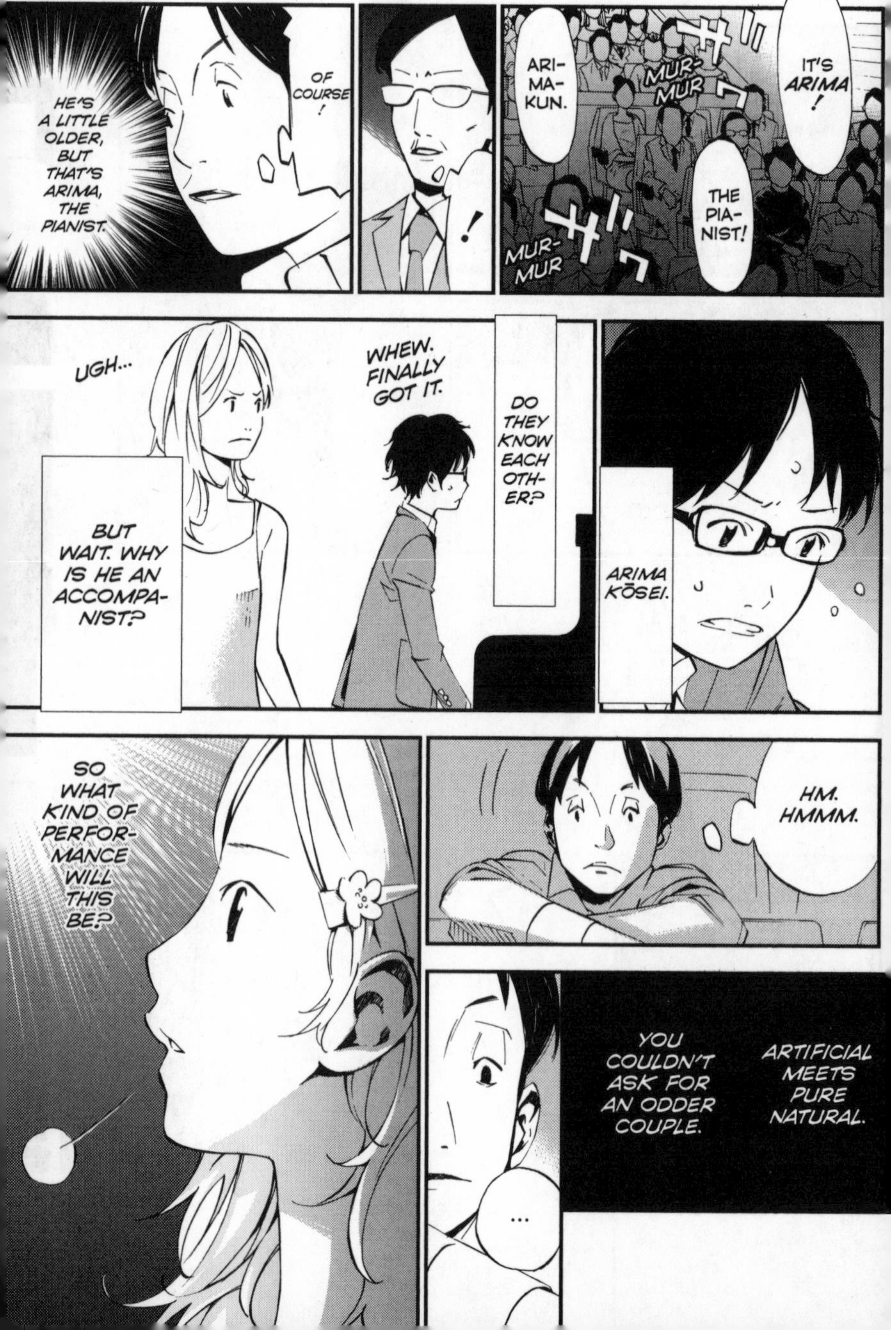
IT'S ARIMA!
MUR-MUR
ARI-MA-KUN.
THE PIA-NIST!
MUR-MUR
!
OF COURSE!
HE'S A LITTLE OLDER, BUT THAT'S ARIMA, THE PIANIST.
ARIMA KŌSEI.
DO THEY KNOW EACH OTH-ER?
WHEW. FINALLY GOT IT.
UGH...
BUT WAIT. WHY IS HE AN ACCOMPA-NIST?
HM. HMMM.
ARTIFICIAL MEETS PURE NATURAL.
YOU COULDN'T ASK FOR AN ODDER COUPLE.
...
SO WHAT KIND OF PERFOR-MANCE WILL THIS BE?

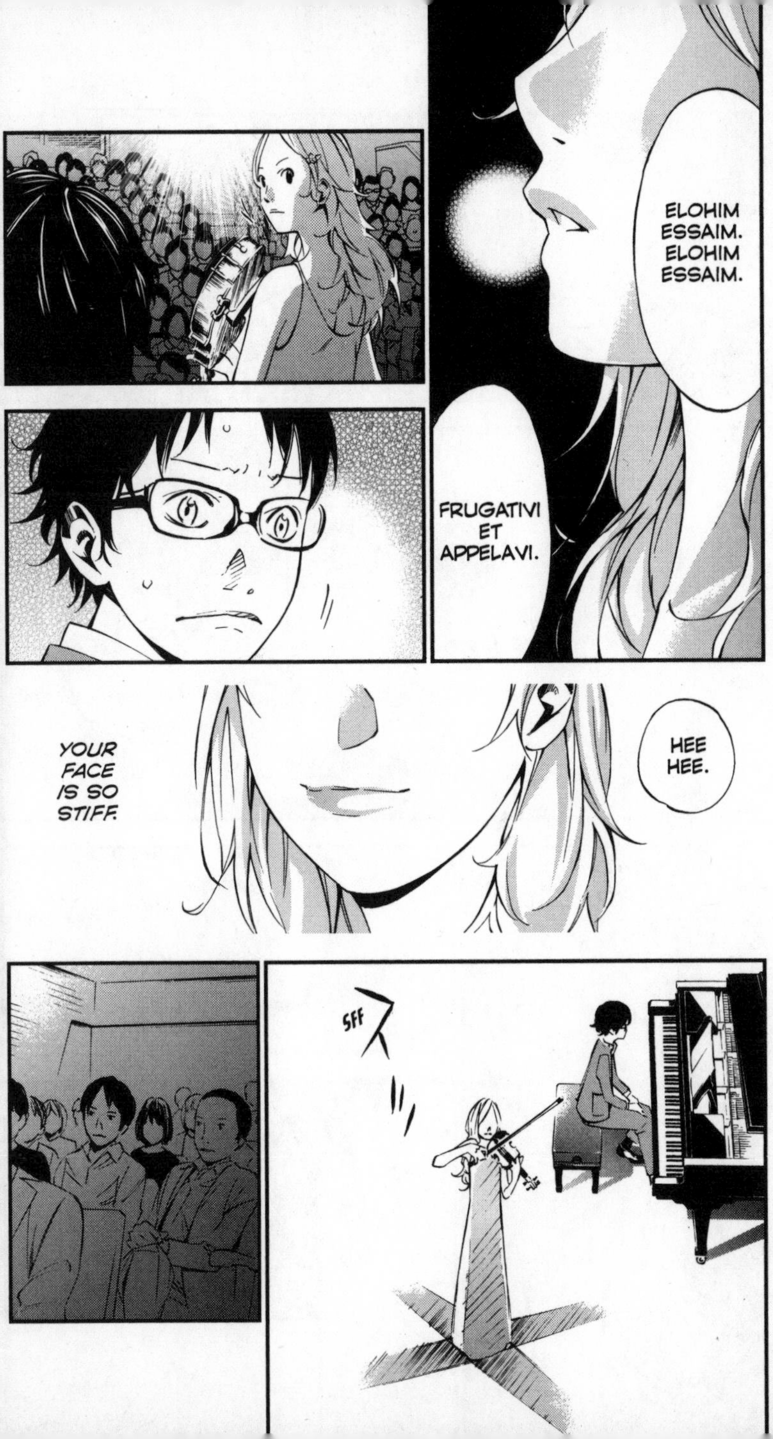
ELOHIM ESSAIM. ELOHIM ESSAIM.
FRUGATIVI ET APPELAVI.
HEE HEE.
YOUR FACE IS SO STIFF.
SFF

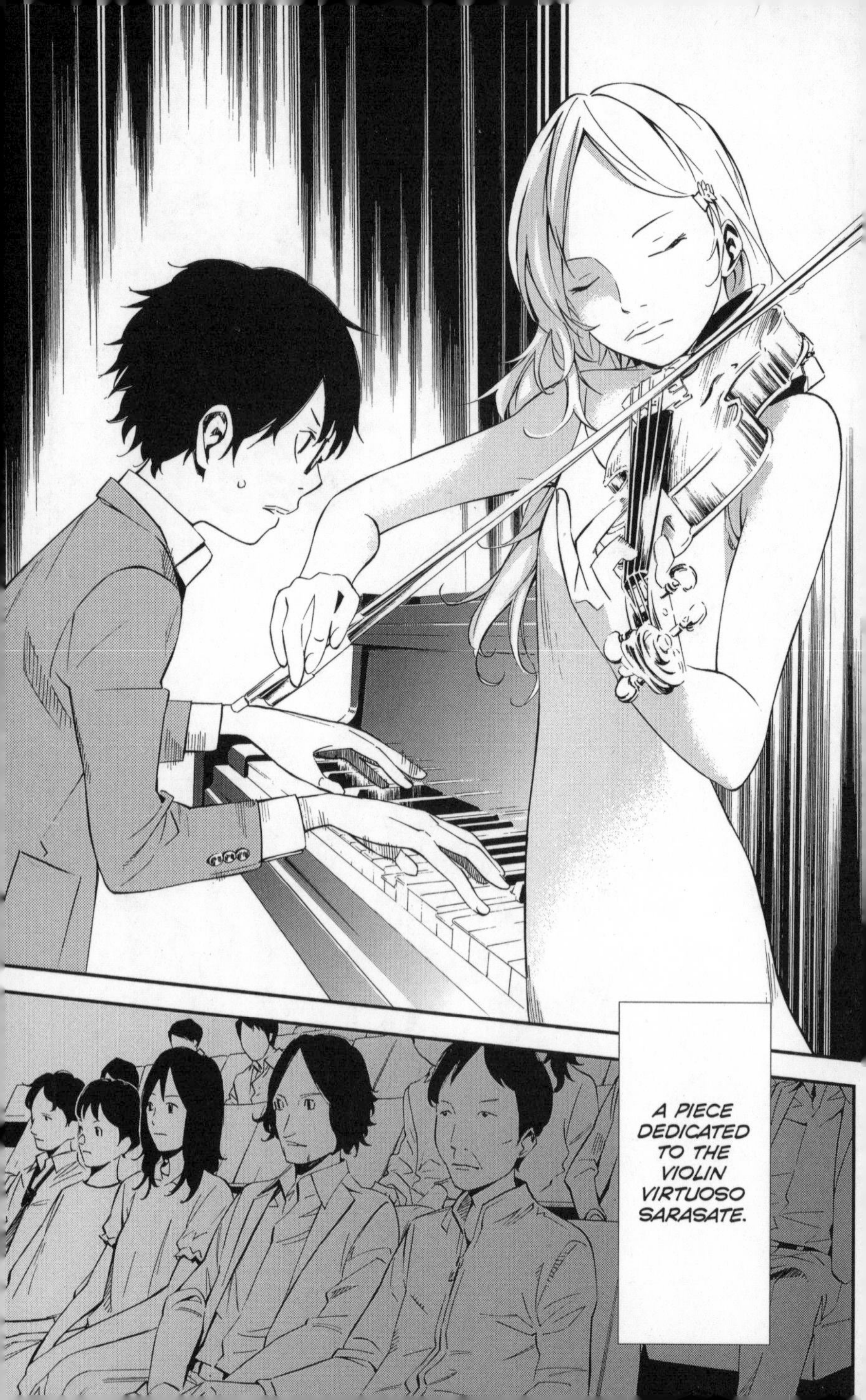
A PIECE DEDICATED TO THE VIOLIN VIRTUOSO SARASATE.

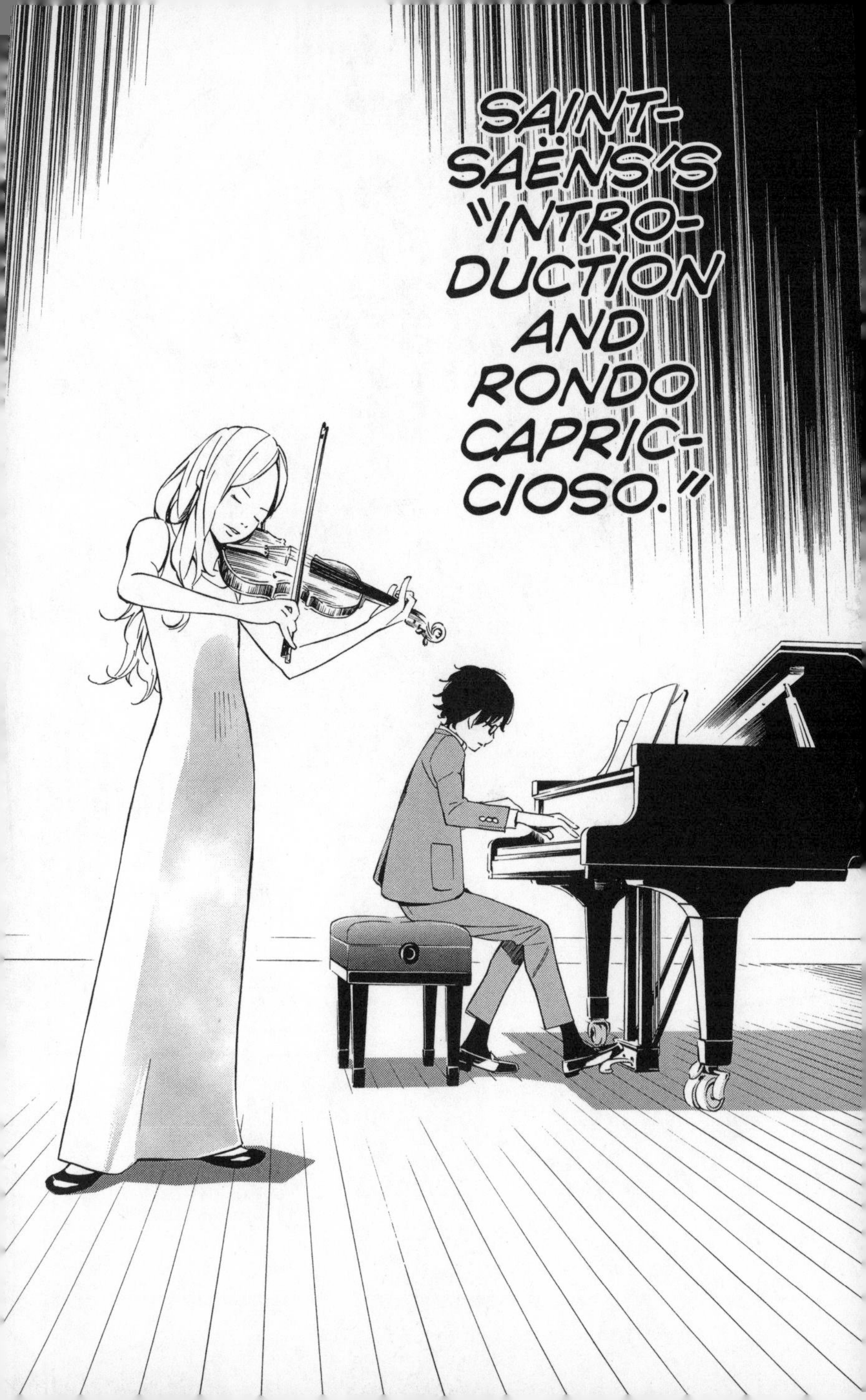
SAINT-SAËNS'S "INTRODUCTION AND RONDO CAPRICCIOSO."

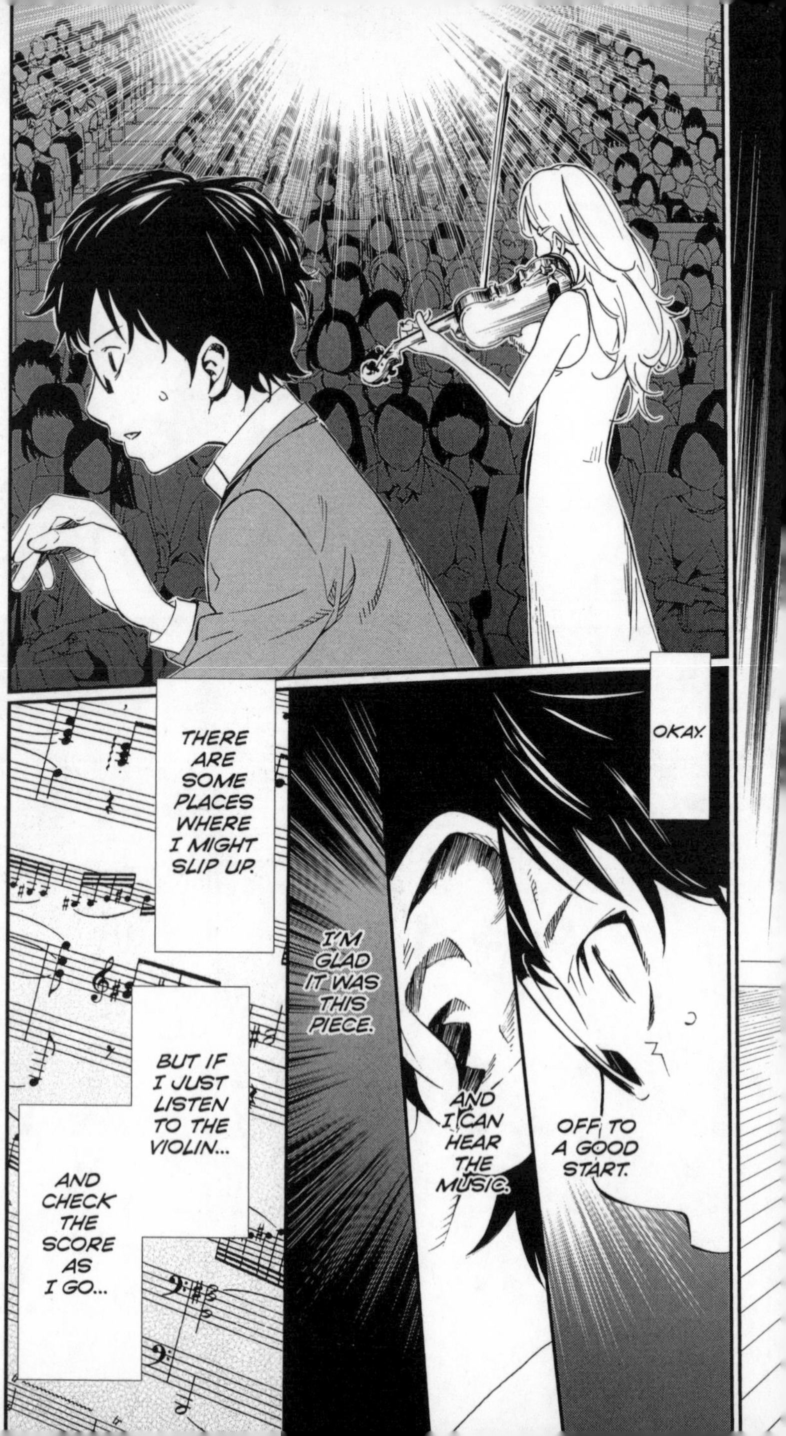
OKAY.
OFF TO A GOOD START.
AND I CAN HEAR THE MUSIC.
I'M GLAD IT WAS THIS PIECE.
THERE ARE SOME PLACES WHERE I MIGHT SLIP UP.
BUT IF I JUST LISTEN TO THE VIOLIN...
AND CHECK THE SCORE AS I GO...

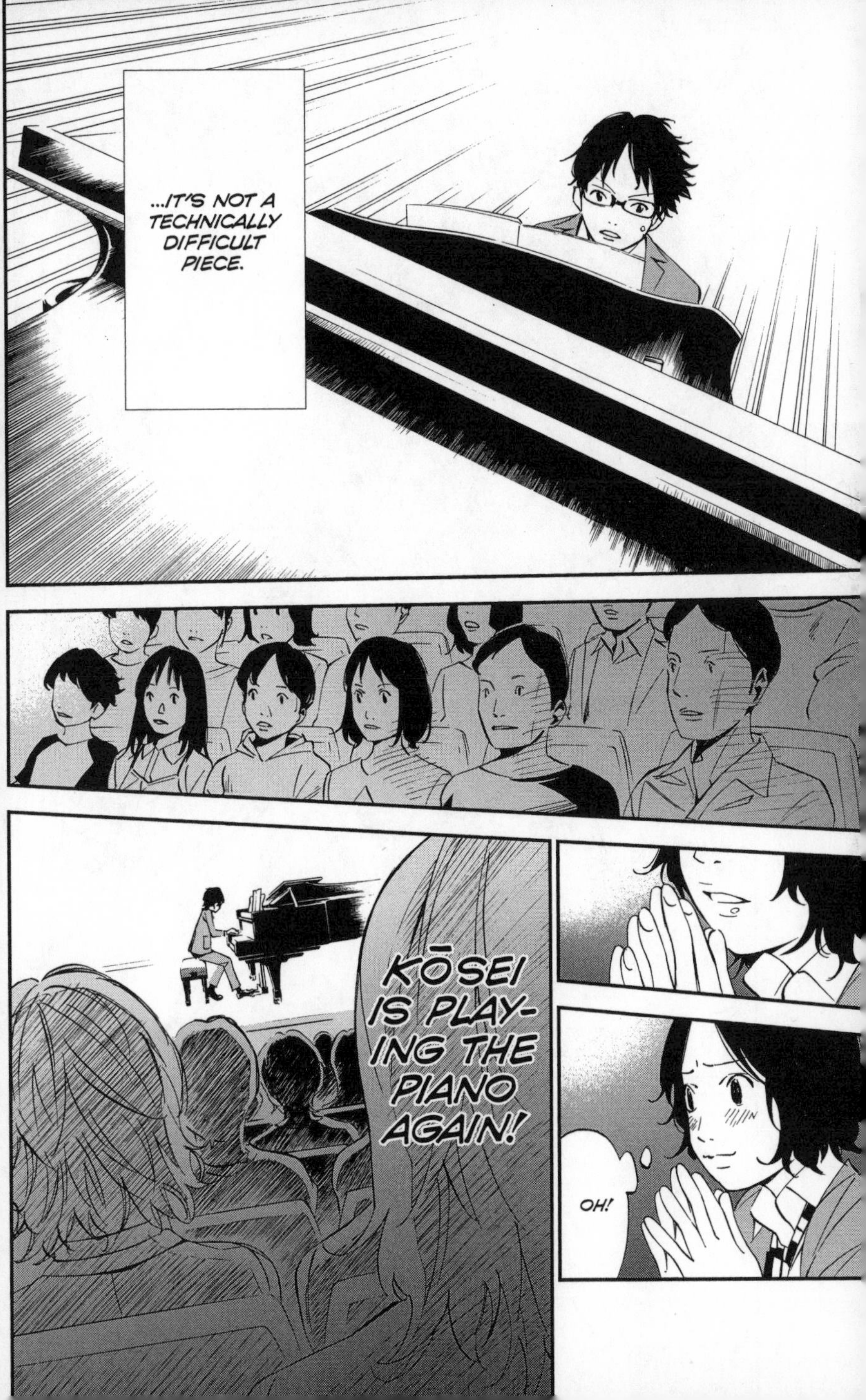
...IT'S NOT A TECHNICALLY DIFFICULT PIECE.
KŌSEI IS PLAYING THE PIANO AGAIN!
OH!

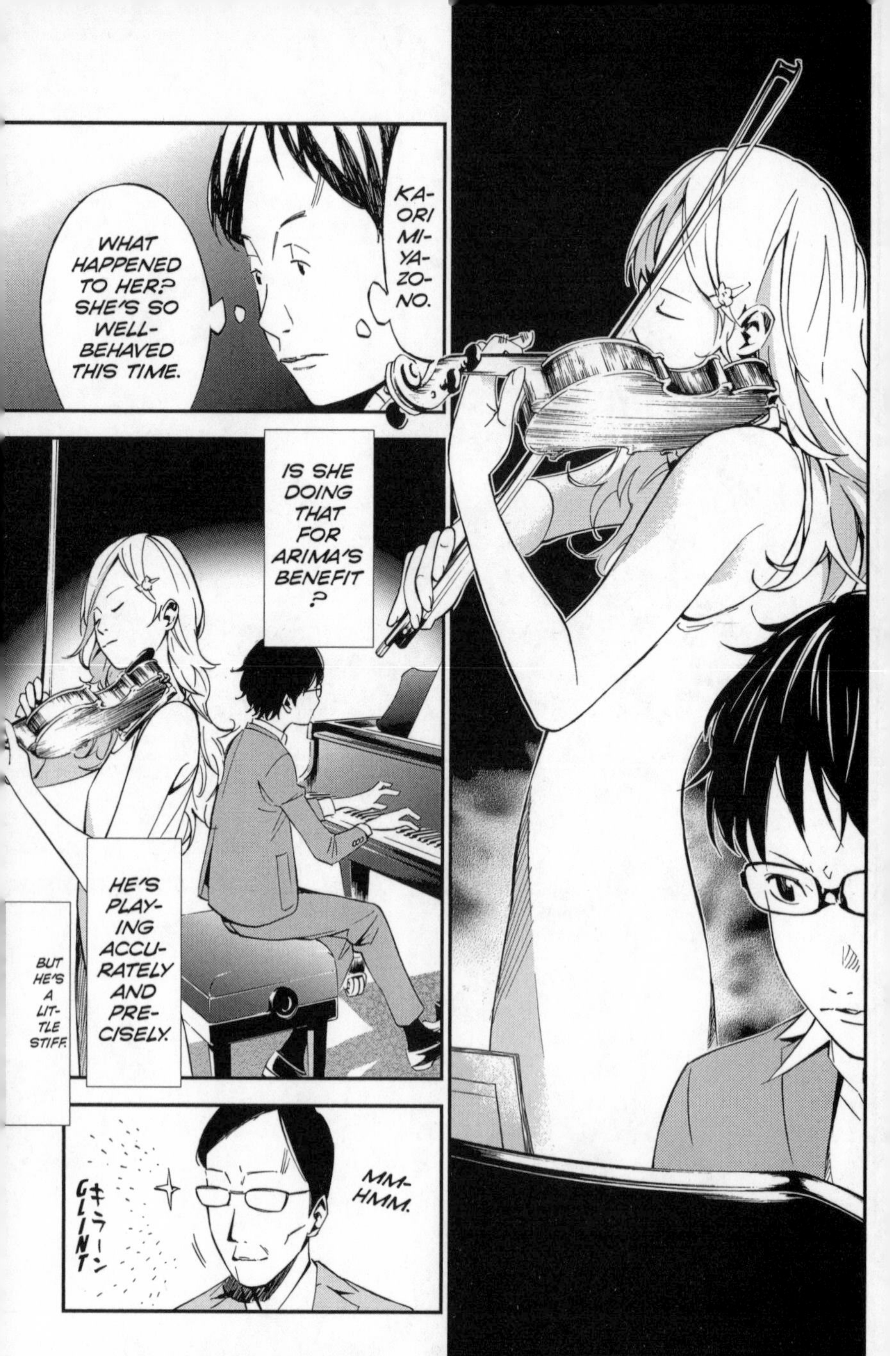
KA-ORI MI-YA-ZO-NO.
WHAT HAPPENED TO HER? SHE'S SO WELL-BEHAVED THIS TIME.
IS SHE DOING THAT FOR ARIMA'S BENEFIT?
HE'S PLAY-ING ACCU-RATELY AND PRE-CISELY.
BUT HE'S A LIT-TLE STIFF.
MM-HMM.
キラーン
GLINT

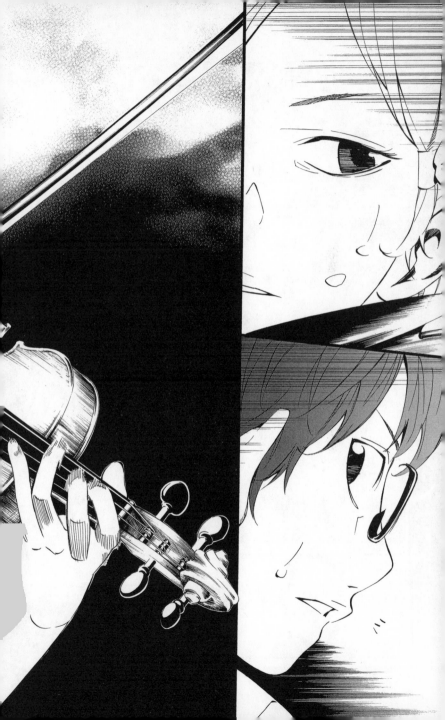

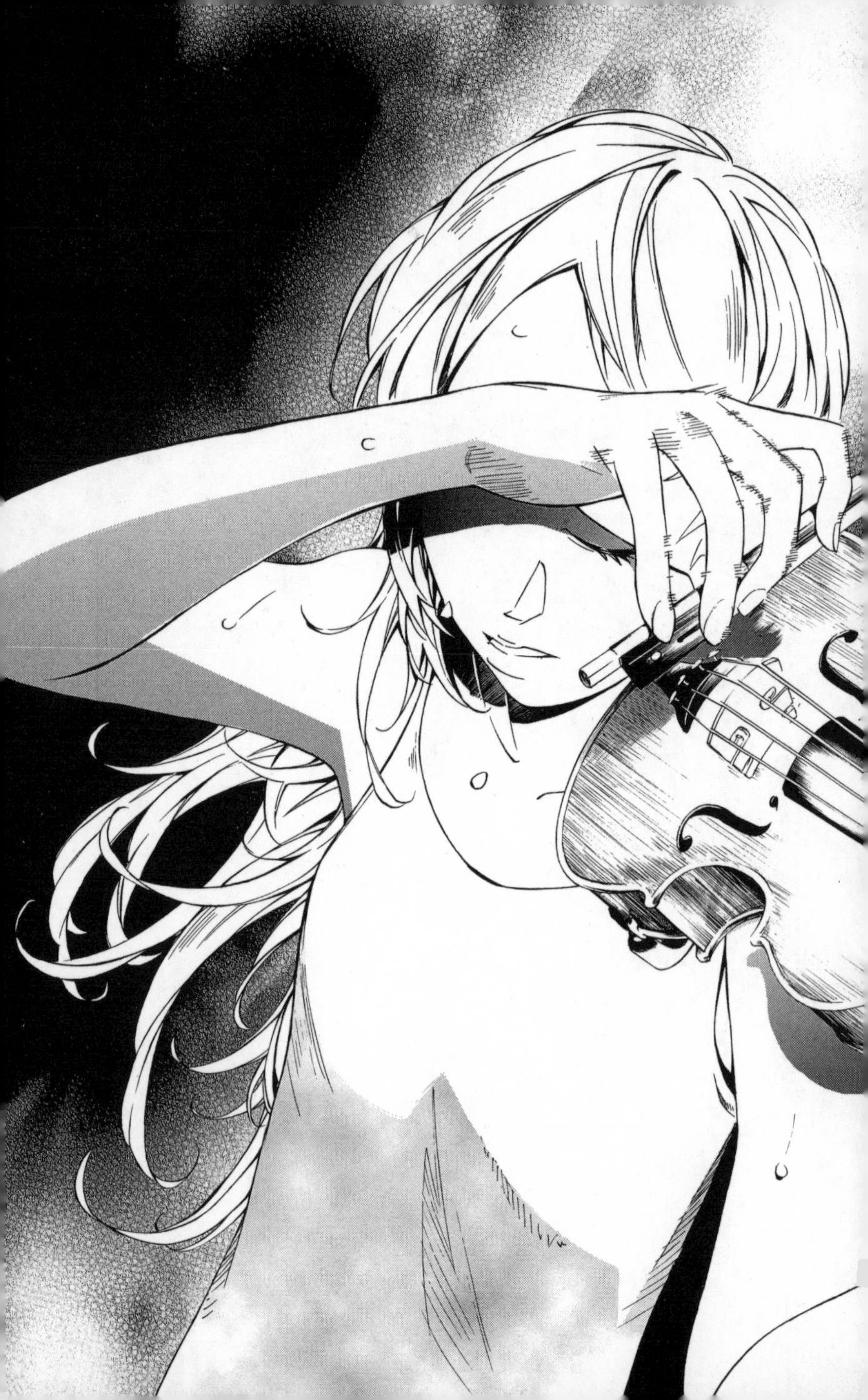

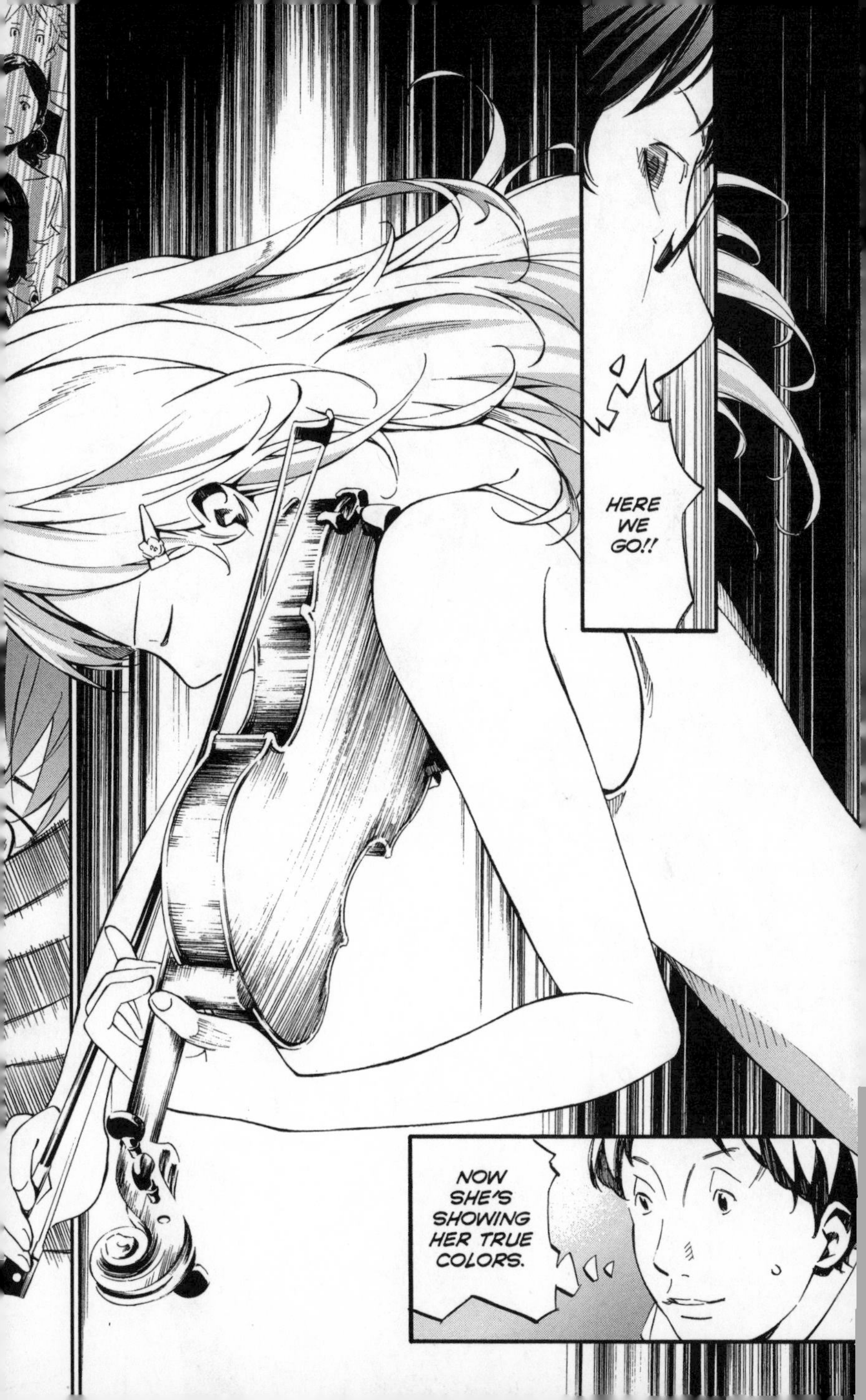
HERE WE GO!!
NOW SHE'S SHOWING HER TRUE COLORS.

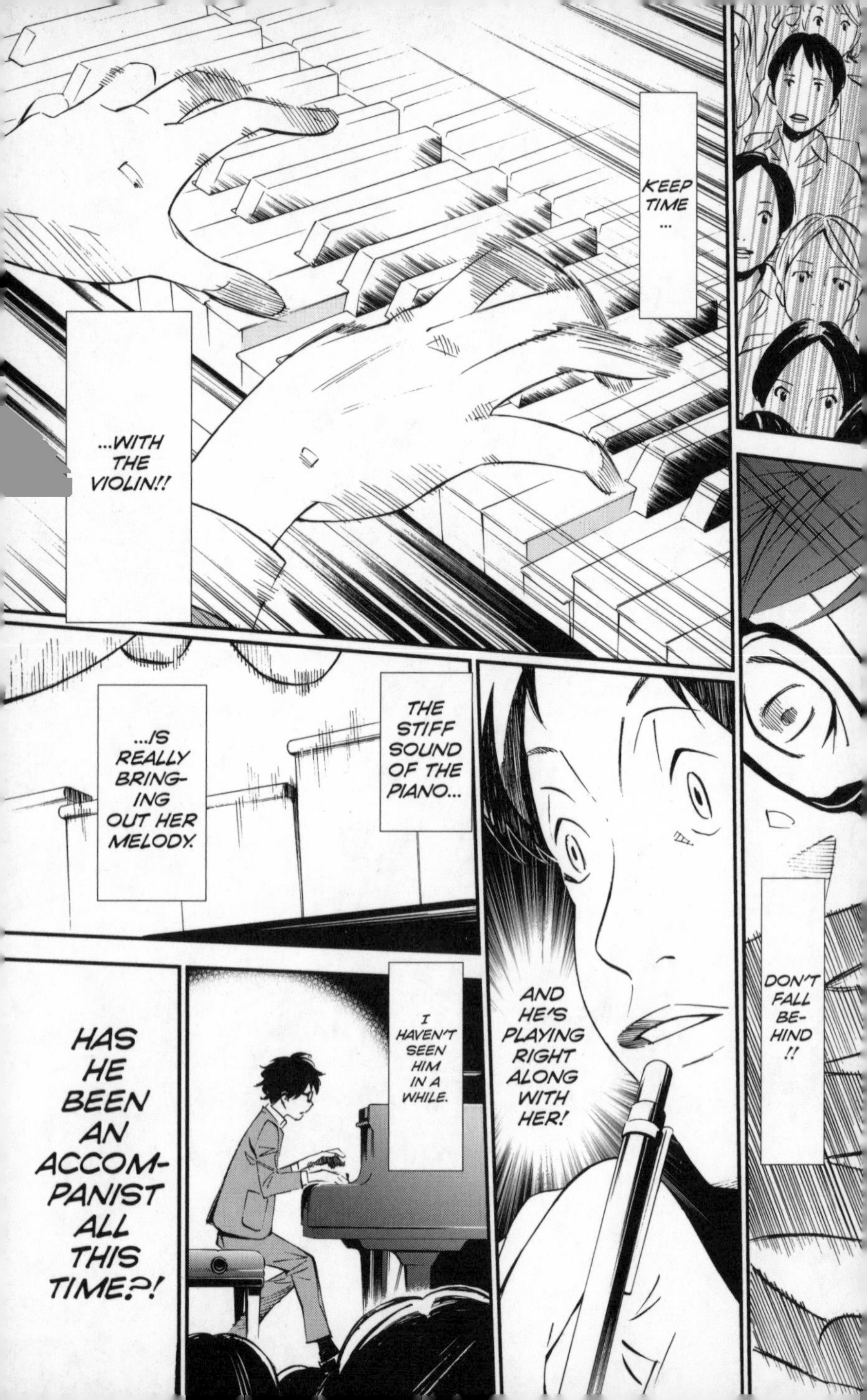
KEEP TIME...
...WITH THE VIOLIN!!
DON'T FALL BEHIND!!
AND HE'S PLAYING RIGHT ALONG WITH HER!
THE STIFF SOUND OF THE PIANO...
...IS REALLY BRINGING OUT HER MELODY.
I HAVEN'T SEEN HIM IN A WHILE.
HAS HE BEEN AN ACCOMPANIST ALL THIS TIME?!

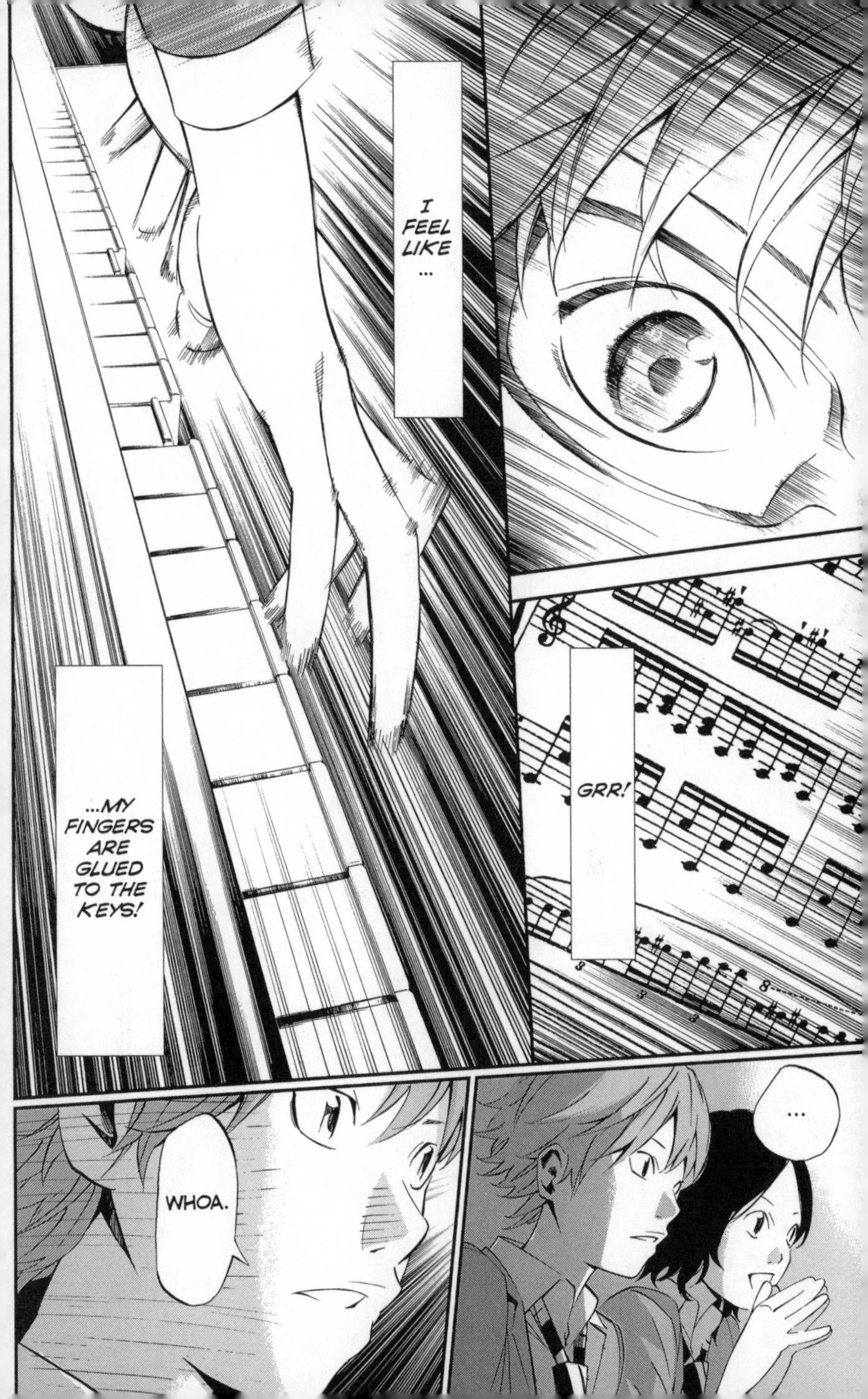
GRR!
I FEEL LIKE...
...MY FINGERS ARE GLUED TO THE KEYS!
...
WHOA.

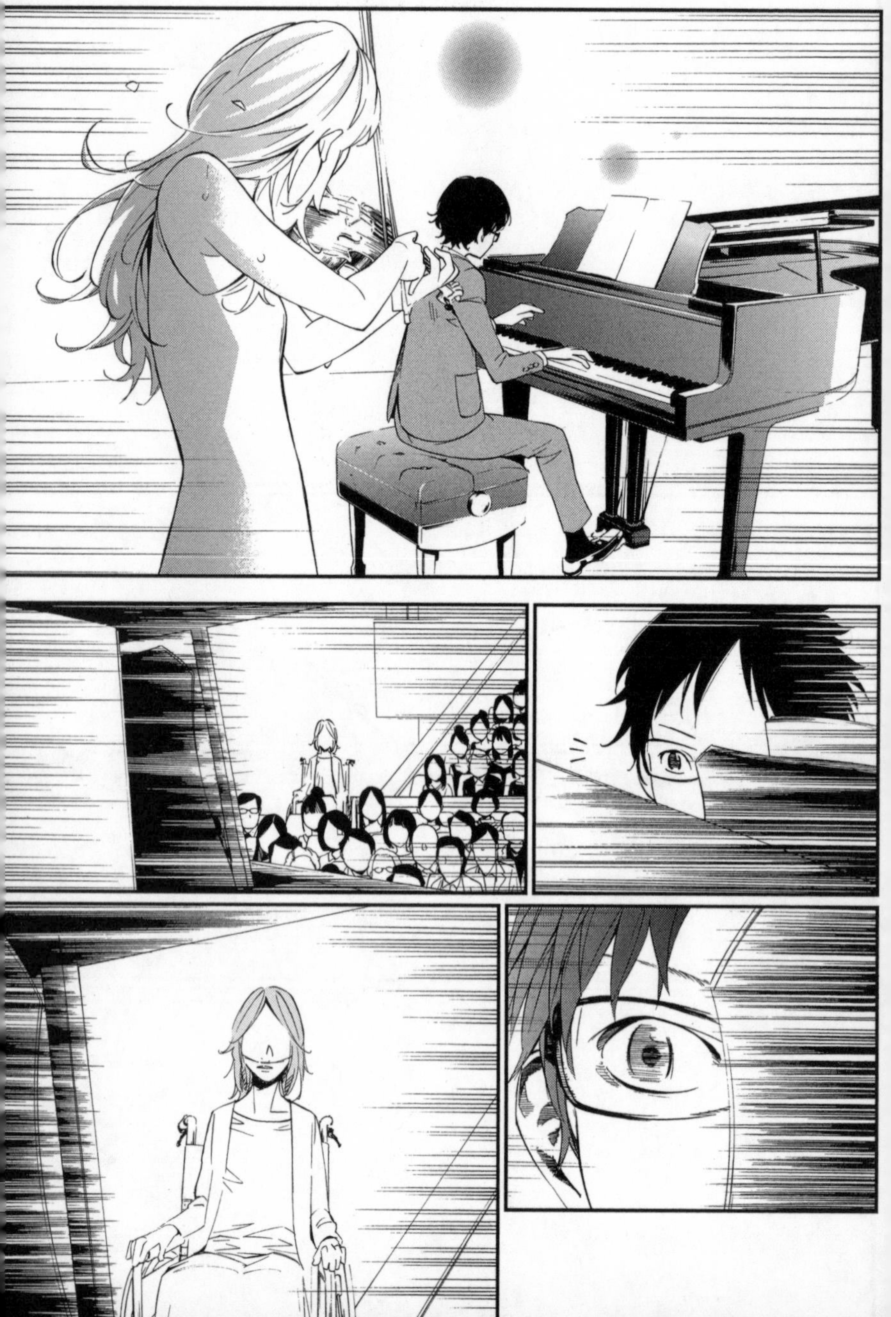

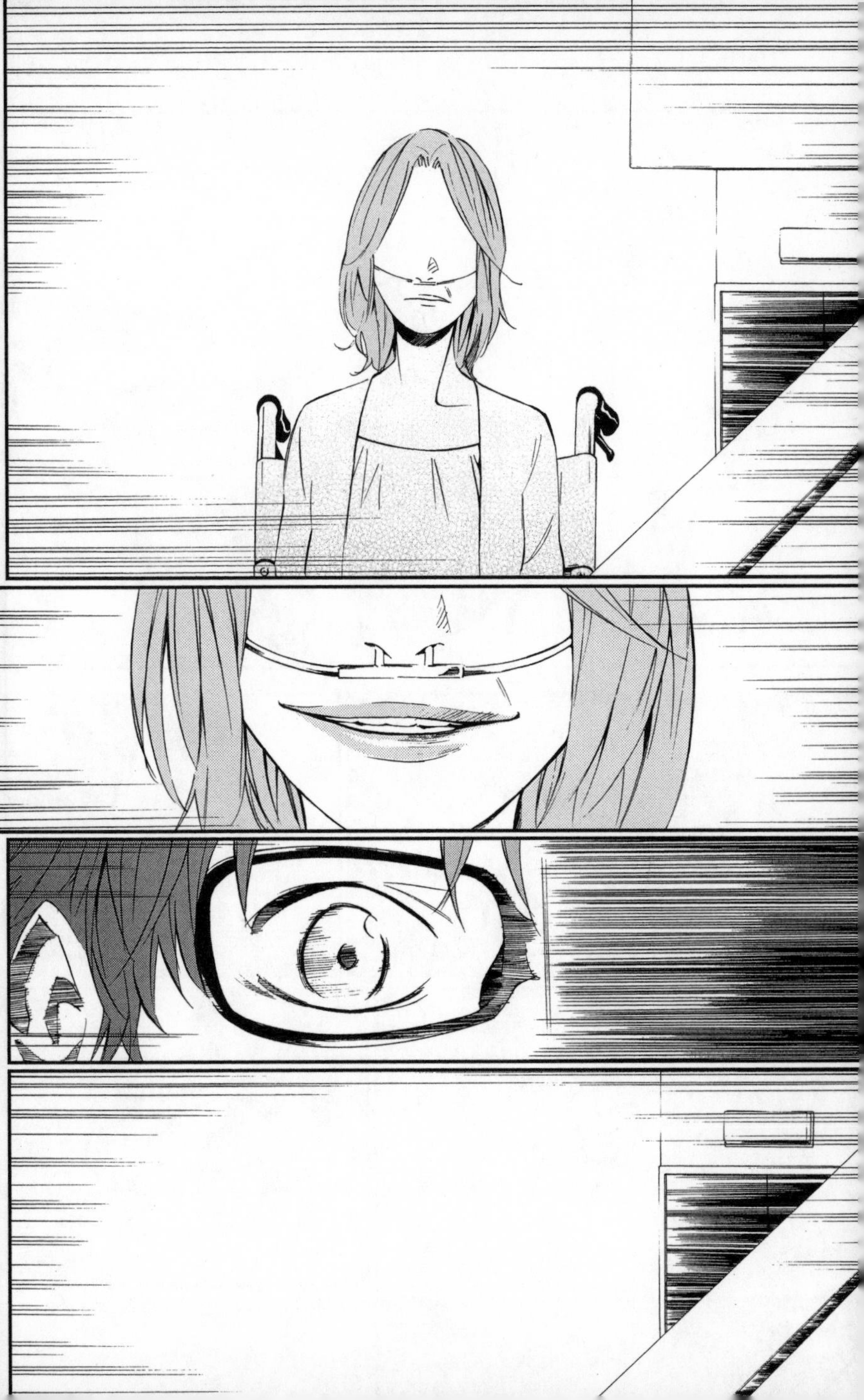

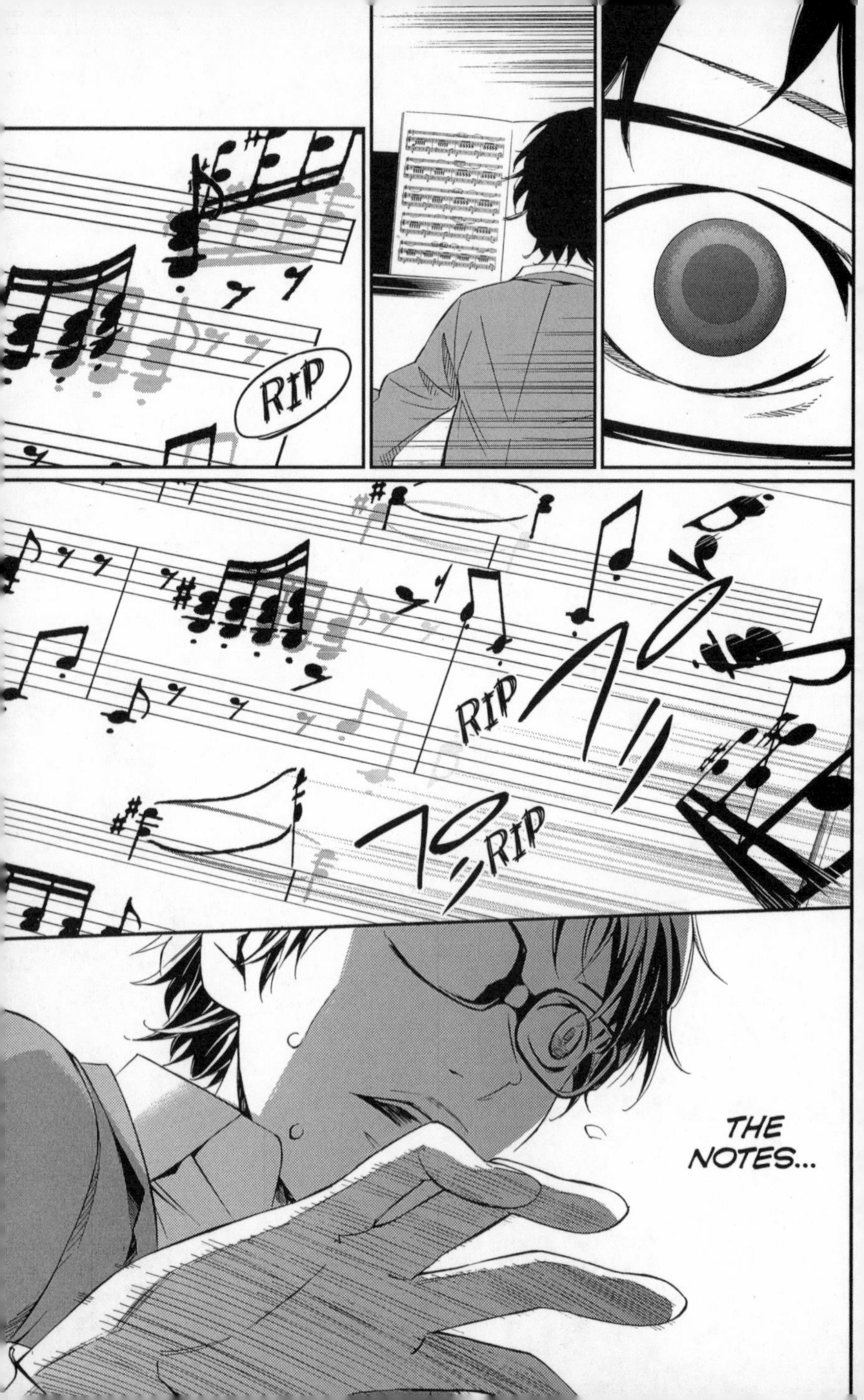
RIP
RIP
RIP
THE NOTES...

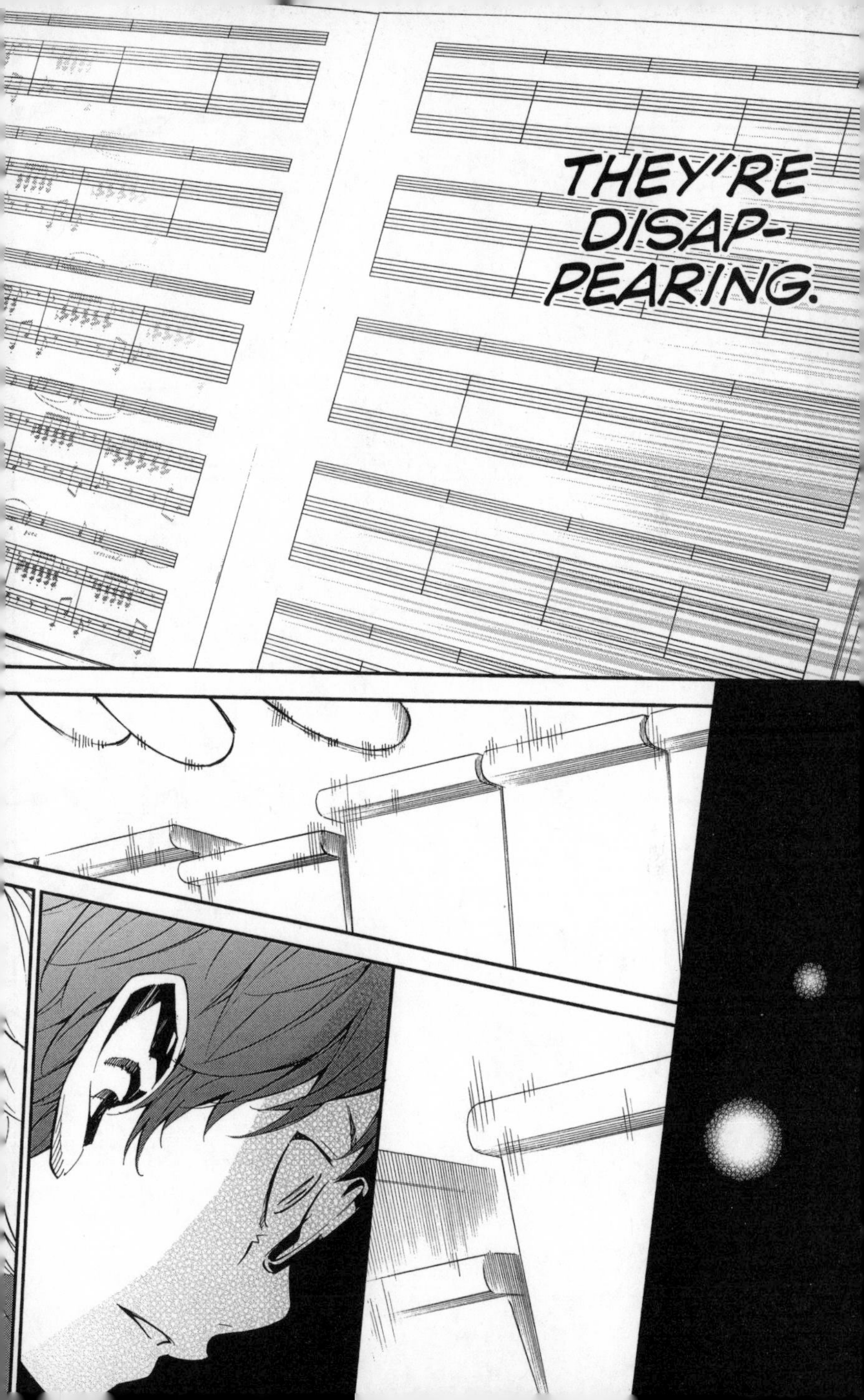
THEY'RE DISAP- PEARING.

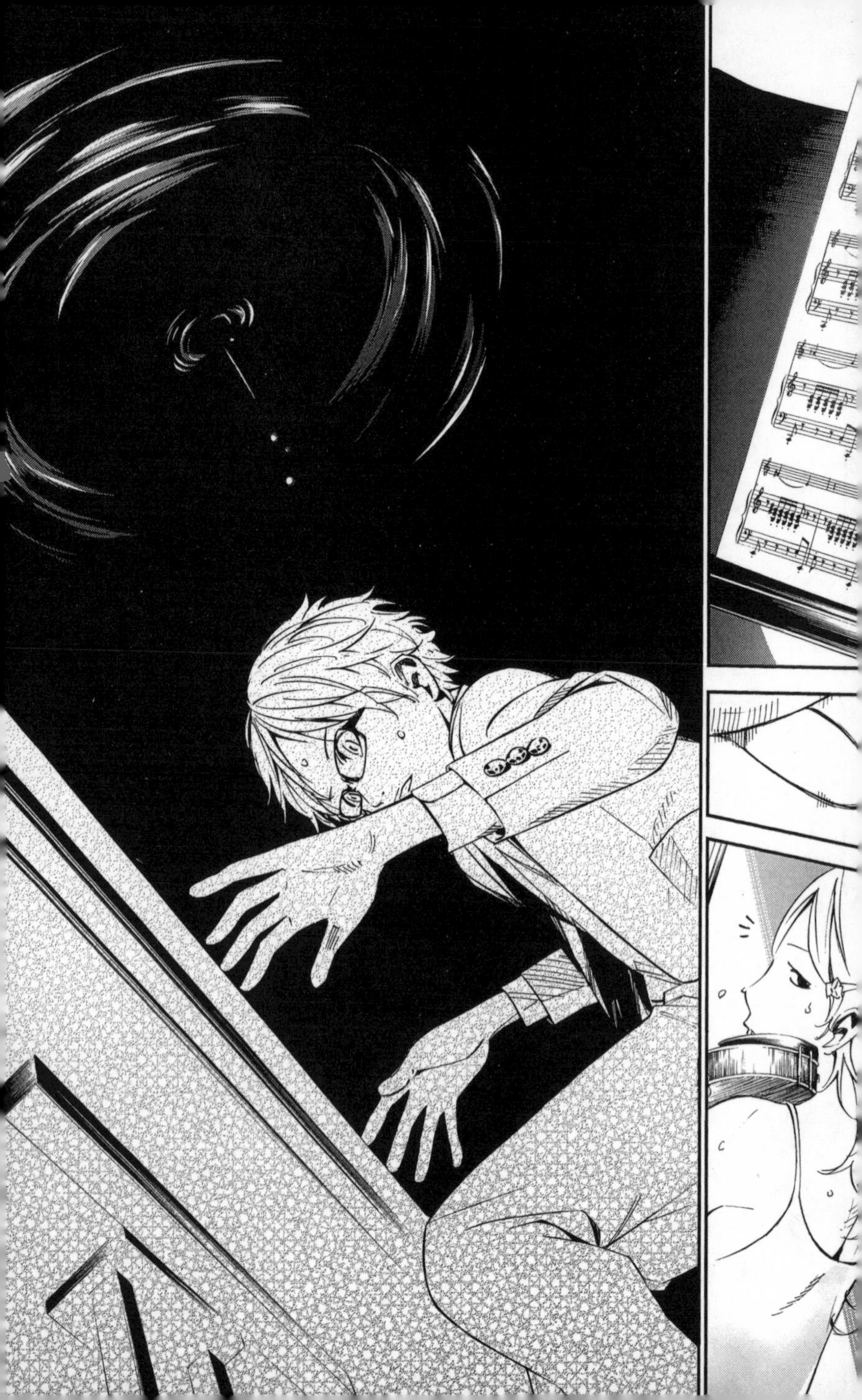

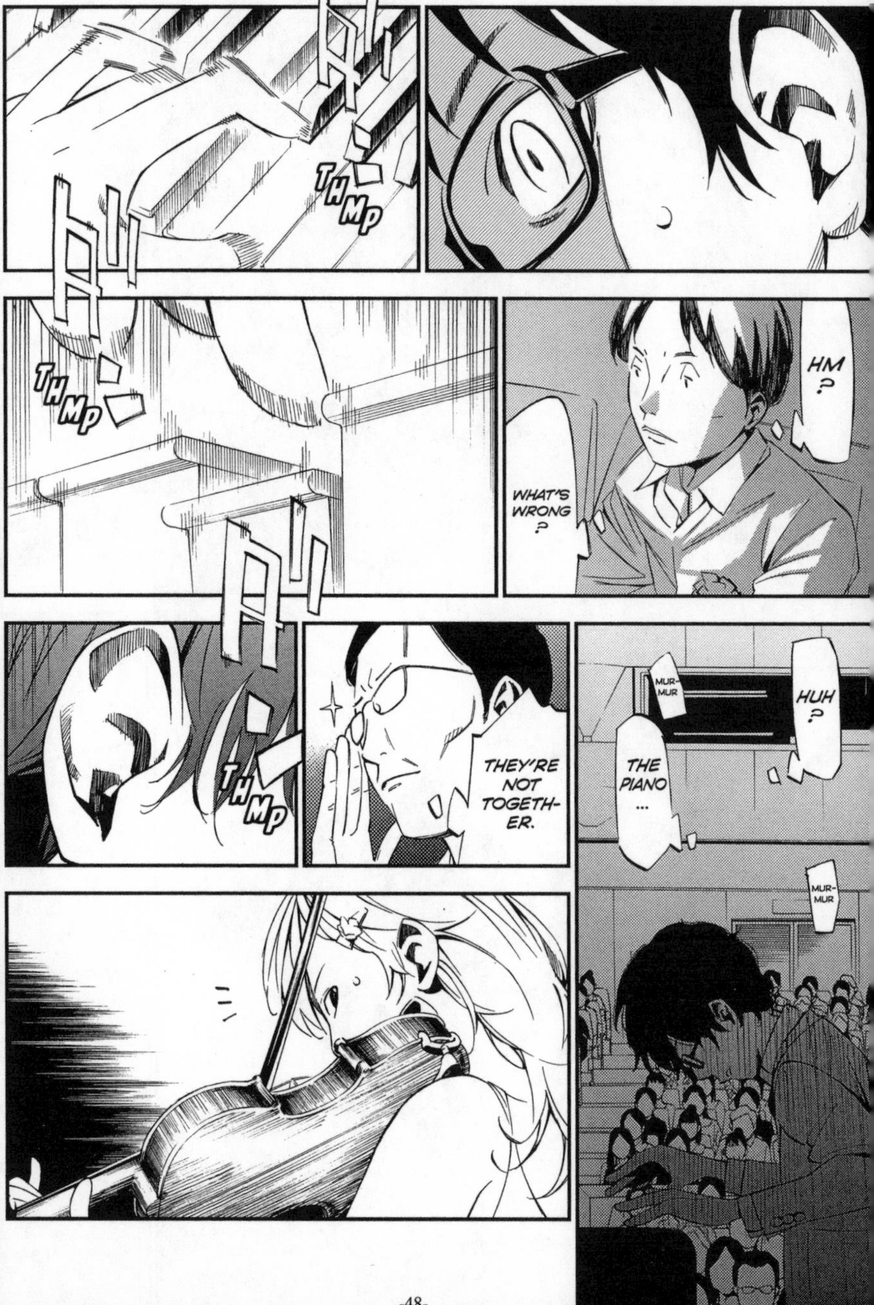
THMP
HM?
WHAT'S WRONG?
THMP
HUH?
MUR-MUR
THE PIANO ...
MUR-MUR
THEY'RE NOT TOGETHER.
THMP

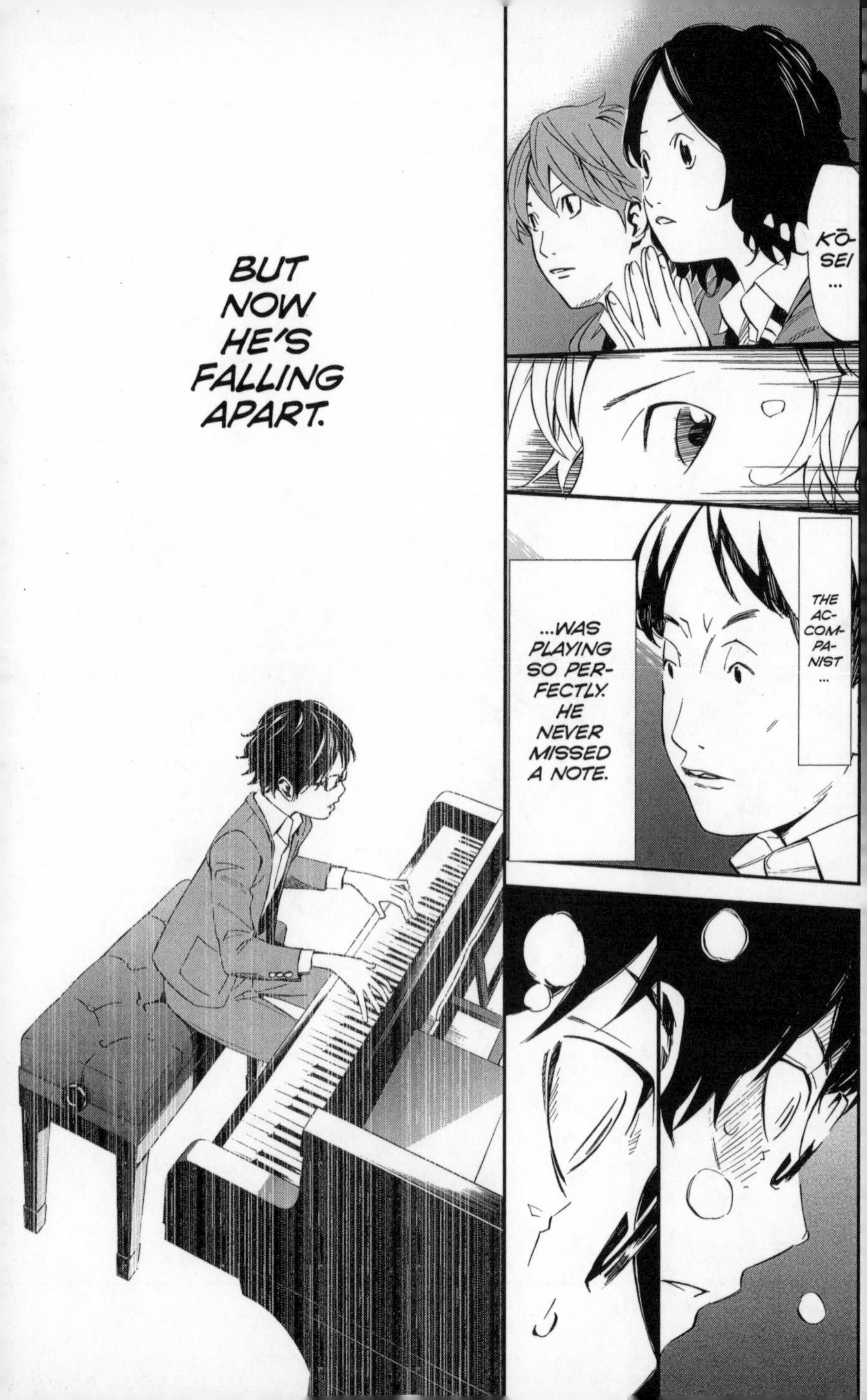
KŌSEI ...
THE AC-COMPA-NIST ...
...WAS PLAYING SO PER-FECTLY. HE NEVER MISSED A NOTE.
BUT NOW HE'S FALLING APART.

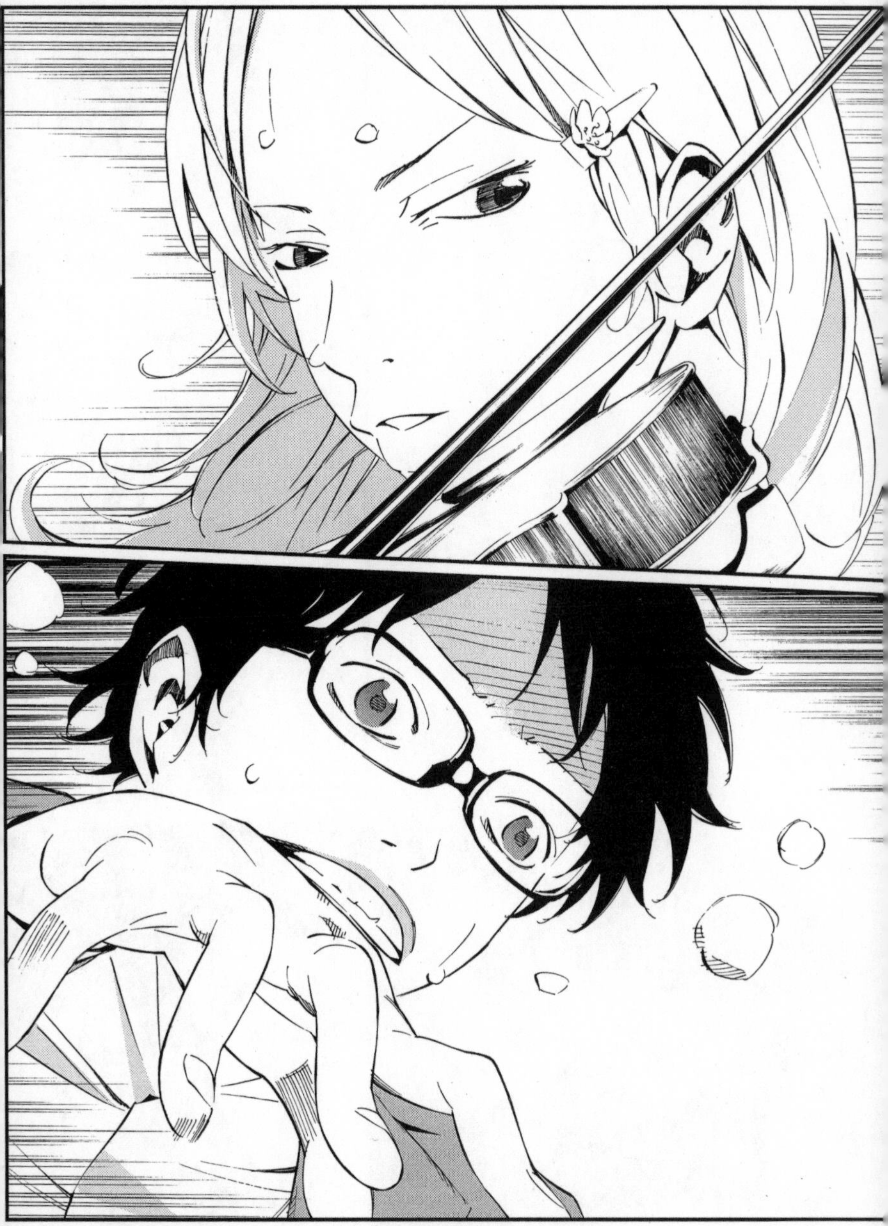

A DARK OCEAN / END

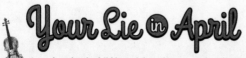

I met the girl under full-bloomed cherry blossoms, and my fate has begun to change.

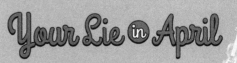

I met the girl under full-bloomed cherry blossoms, and my fate has begun to change.

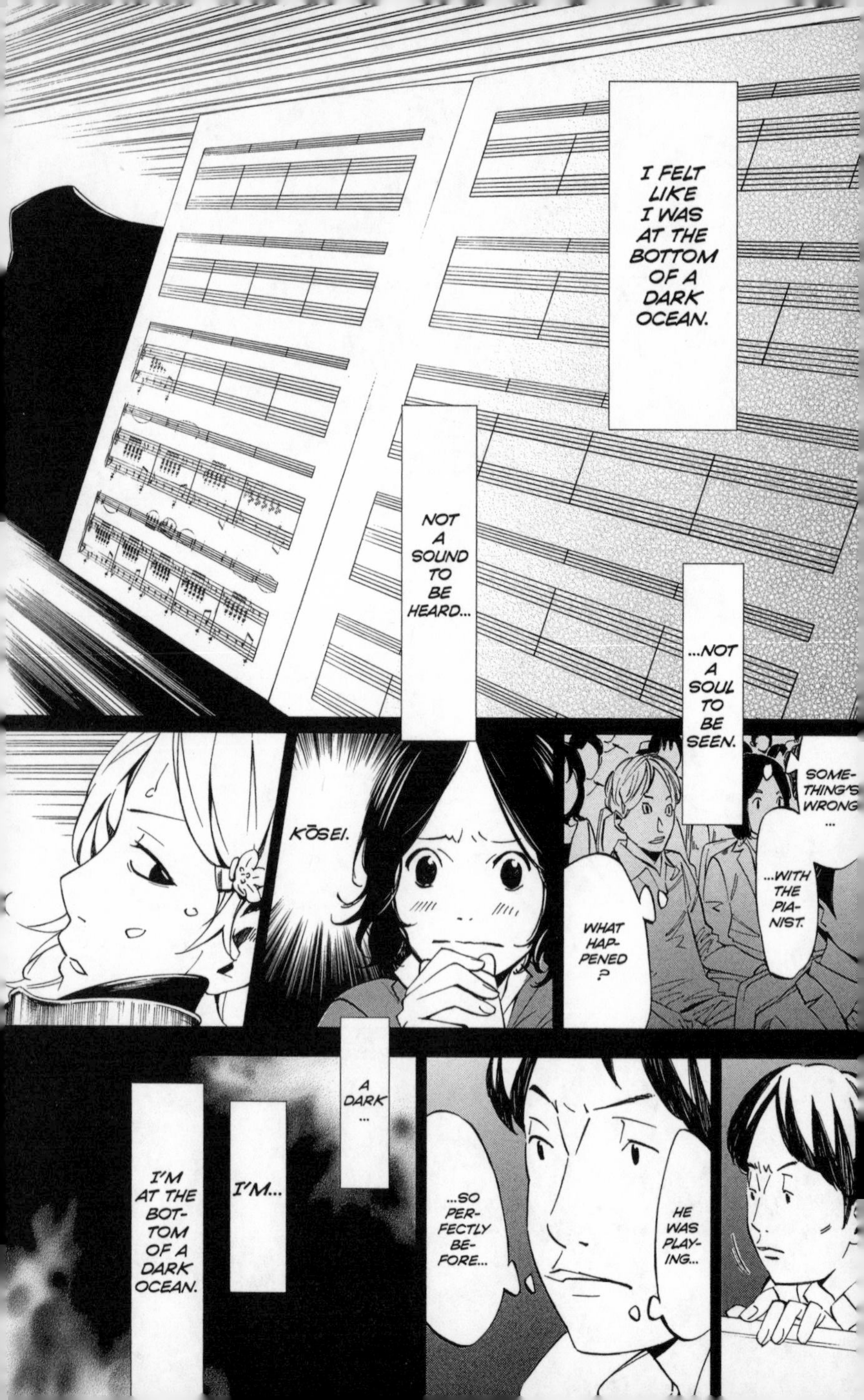
I FELT LIKE I WAS AT THE BOTTOM OF A DARK OCEAN.
NOT A SOUND TO BE HEARD...
...NOT A SOUL TO BE SEEN.
SOME-THING'S WRONG...
...WITH THE PIA-NIST.
WHAT HAP-PENED?
KŌSEI.
HE WAS PLAY-ING...
...SO PER-FECTLY BE-FORE...
A DARK...
I'M...
I'M AT THE BOT-TOM OF A DARK OCEAN.

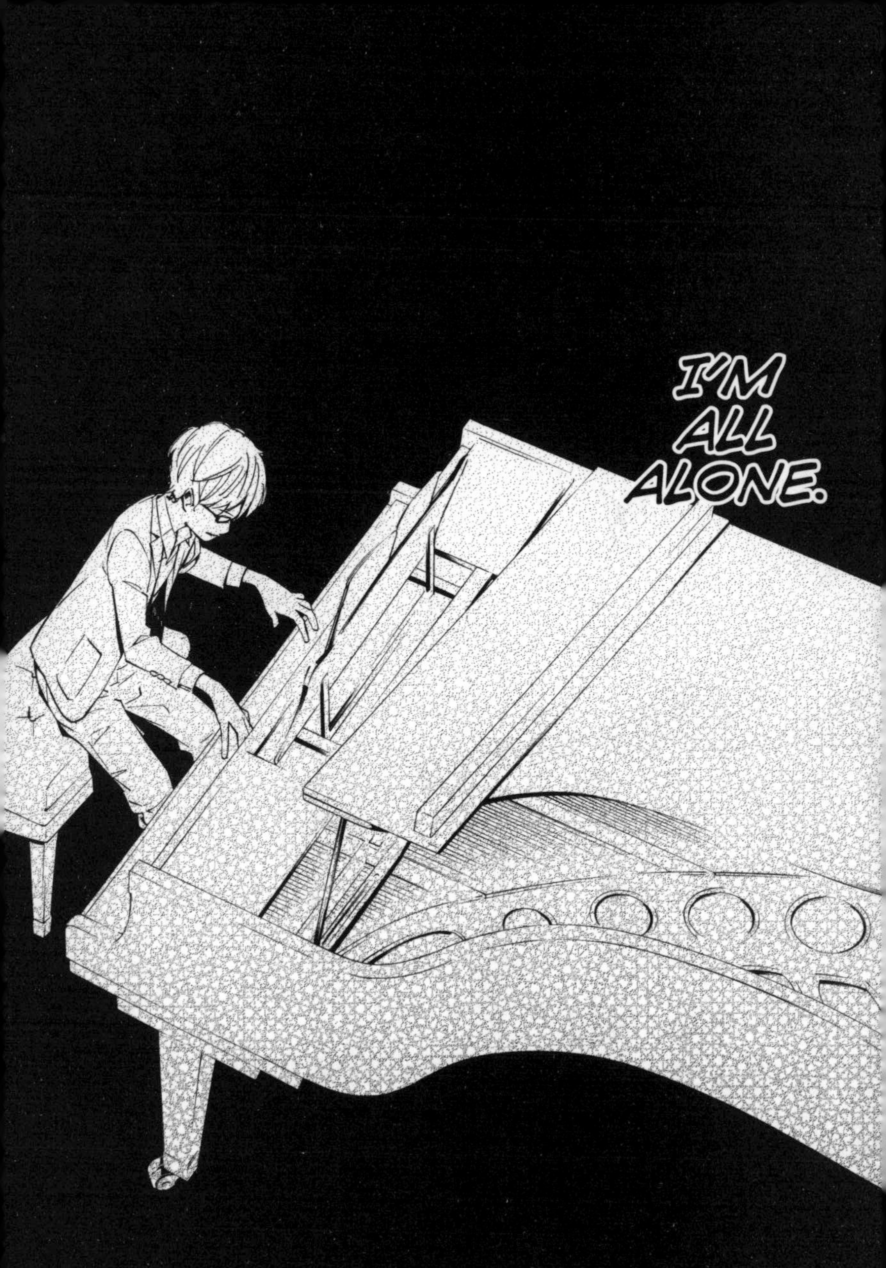
I'M ALL ALONE.

Chapter 6: From Behind

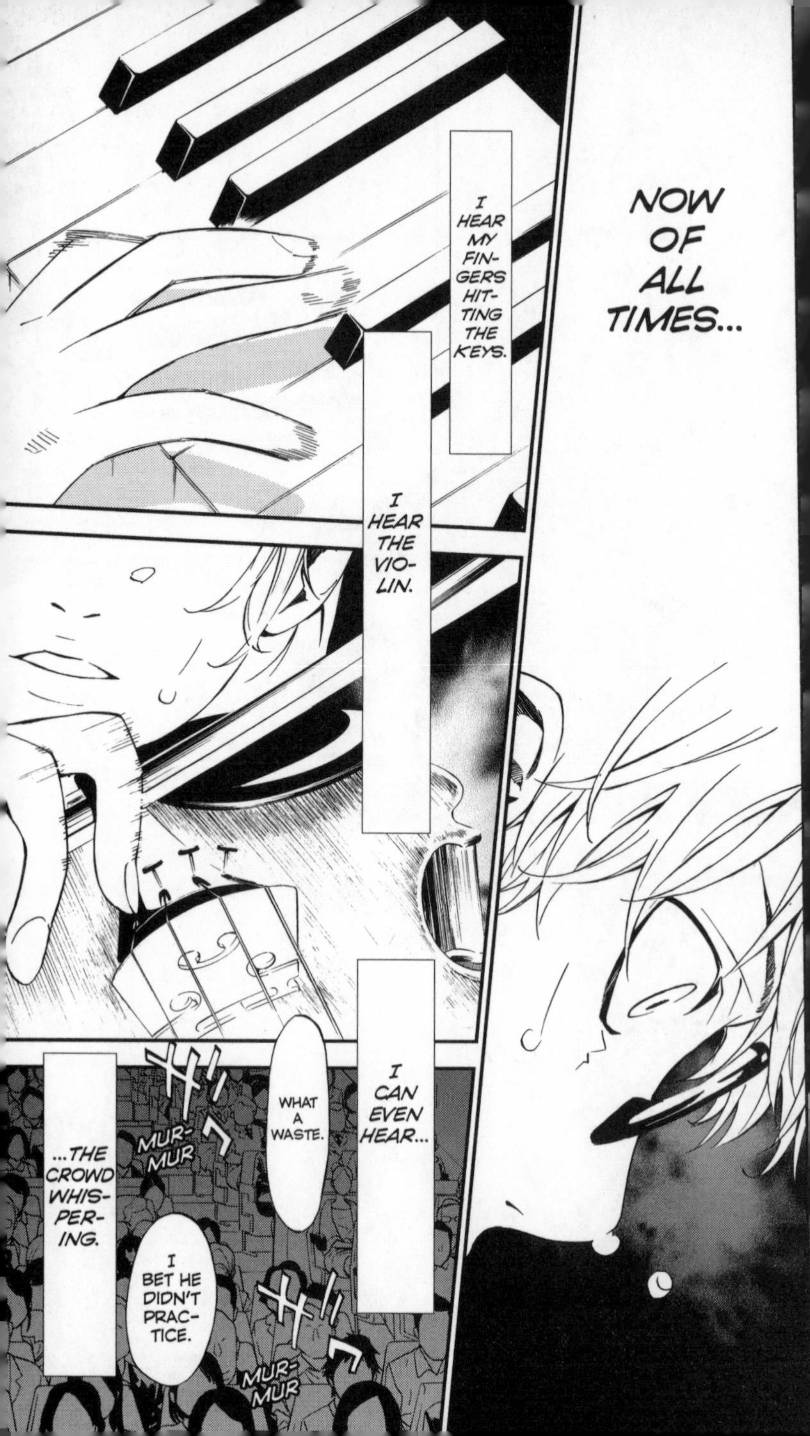
NOW OF ALL TIMES...
I HEAR MY FIN-GERS HIT-TING THE KEYS.
I HEAR THE VIO-LIN.
I CAN EVEN HEAR...
WHAT A WASTE.
MUR-MUR
...THE CROWD WHIS-PER-ING.
I BET HE DIDN'T PRAC-TICE.
MUR-MUR

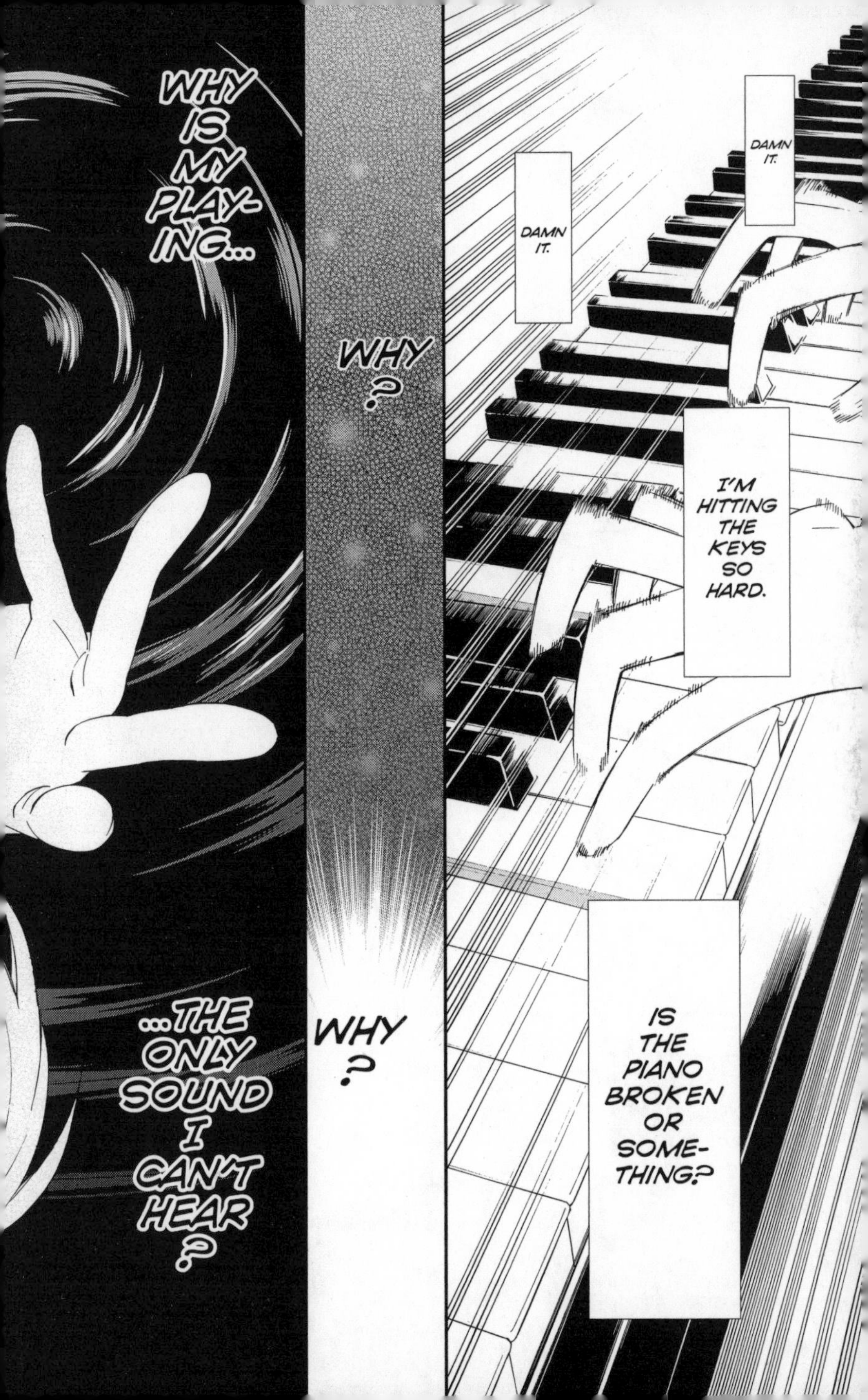
DAMN IT.
DAMN IT.
I'M HITTING THE KEYS SO HARD.
IS THE PIANO BROKEN OR SOME-THING?
WHY?
WHY?
WHY IS MY PLAY-ING...
...THE ONLY SOUND I CAN'T HEAR?

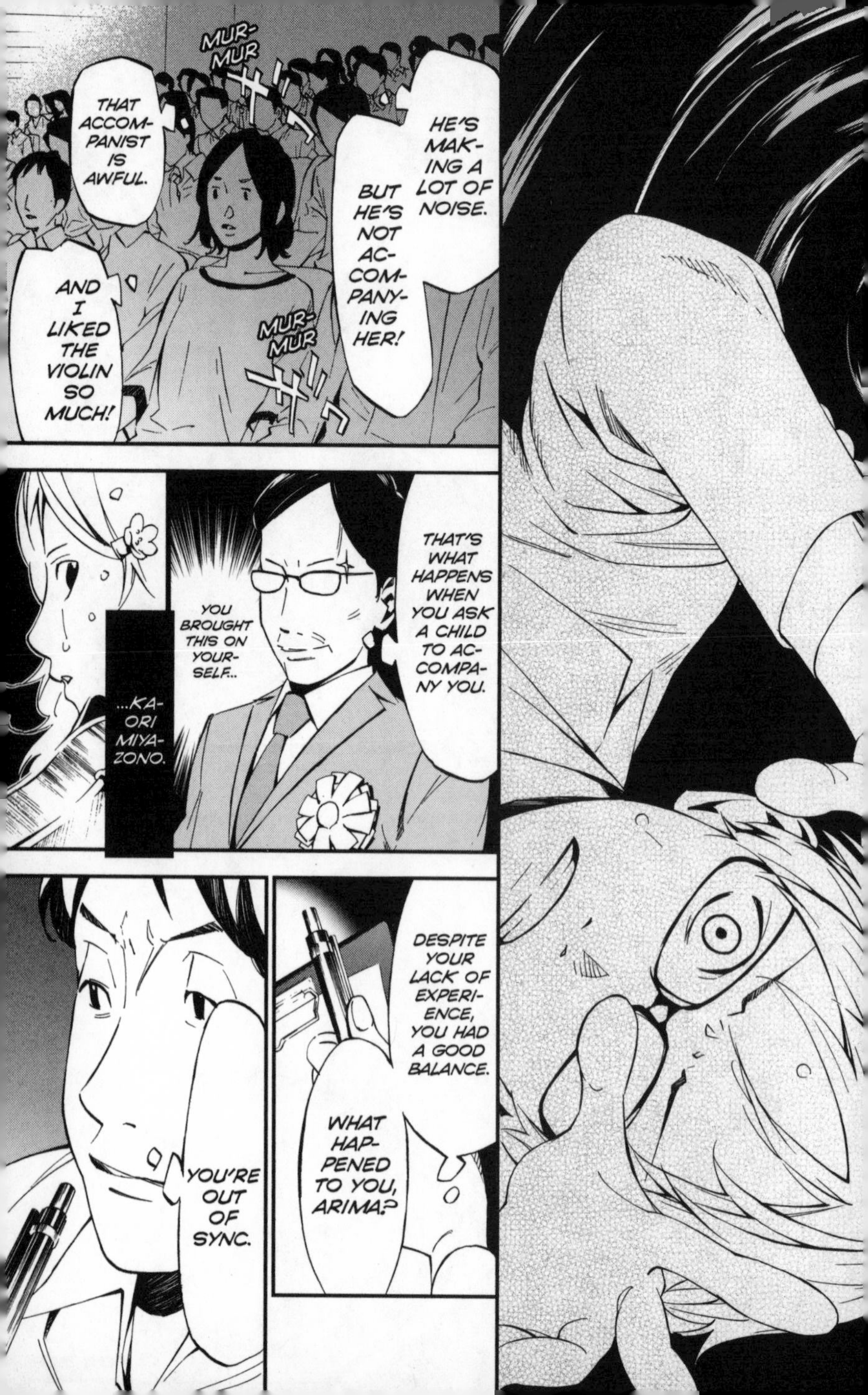
HE'S MAKING A LOT OF NOISE.
BUT HE'S NOT ACCOMPANYING HER!
MUR-MUR
THAT ACCOMPANIST IS AWFUL.
MUR-MUR
AND I LIKED THE VIOLIN SO MUCH!
THAT'S WHAT HAPPENS WHEN YOU ASK A CHILD TO ACCOMPANY YOU.
YOU BROUGHT THIS ON YOURSELF...
...KAORI MIYAZONO.
DESPITE YOUR LACK OF EXPERIENCE, YOU HAD A GOOD BALANCE.
WHAT HAPPENED TO YOU, ARIMA?
YOU'RE OUT OF SYNC.

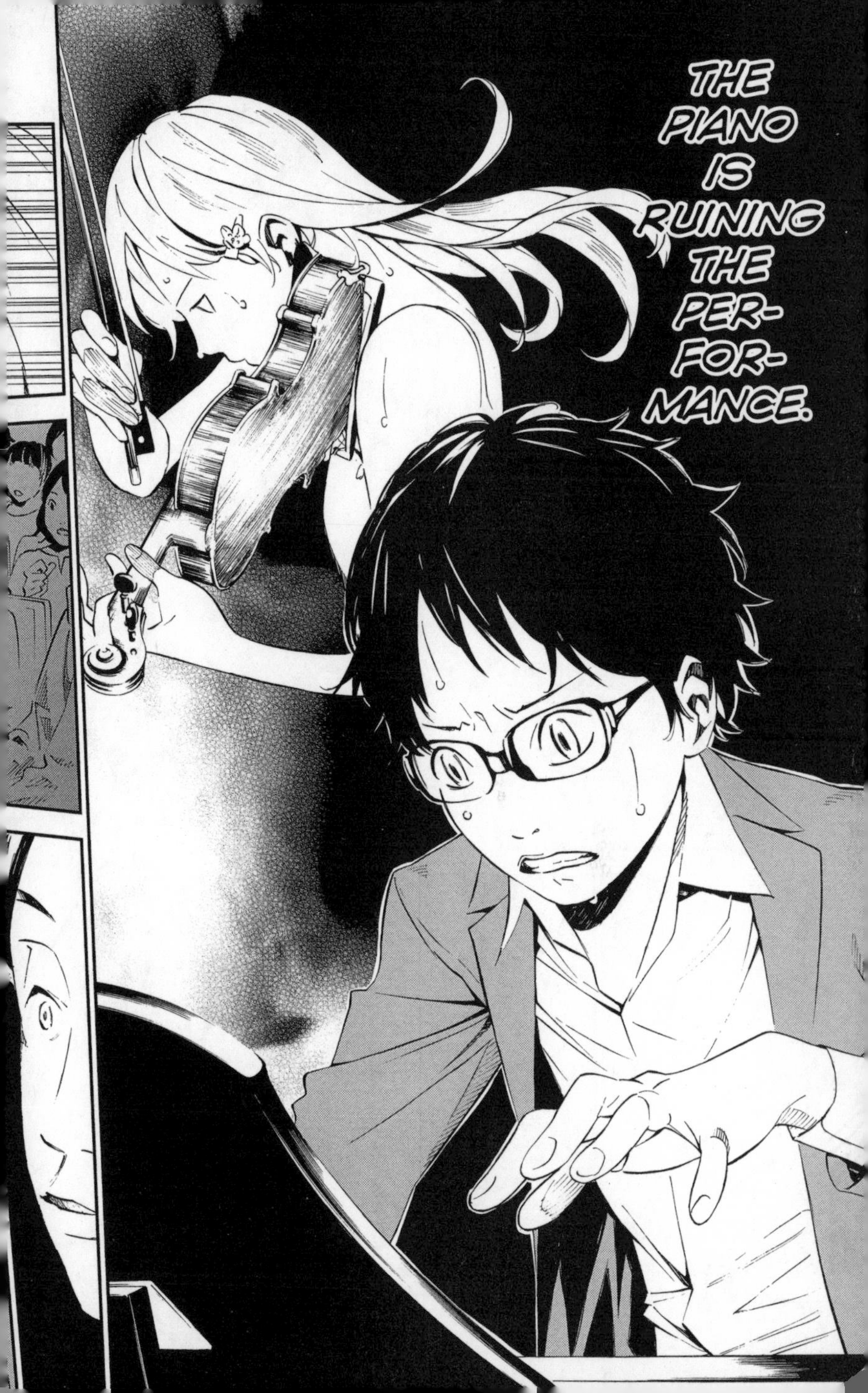
THE PIANO IS RUINING THE PER-FOR-MANCE.

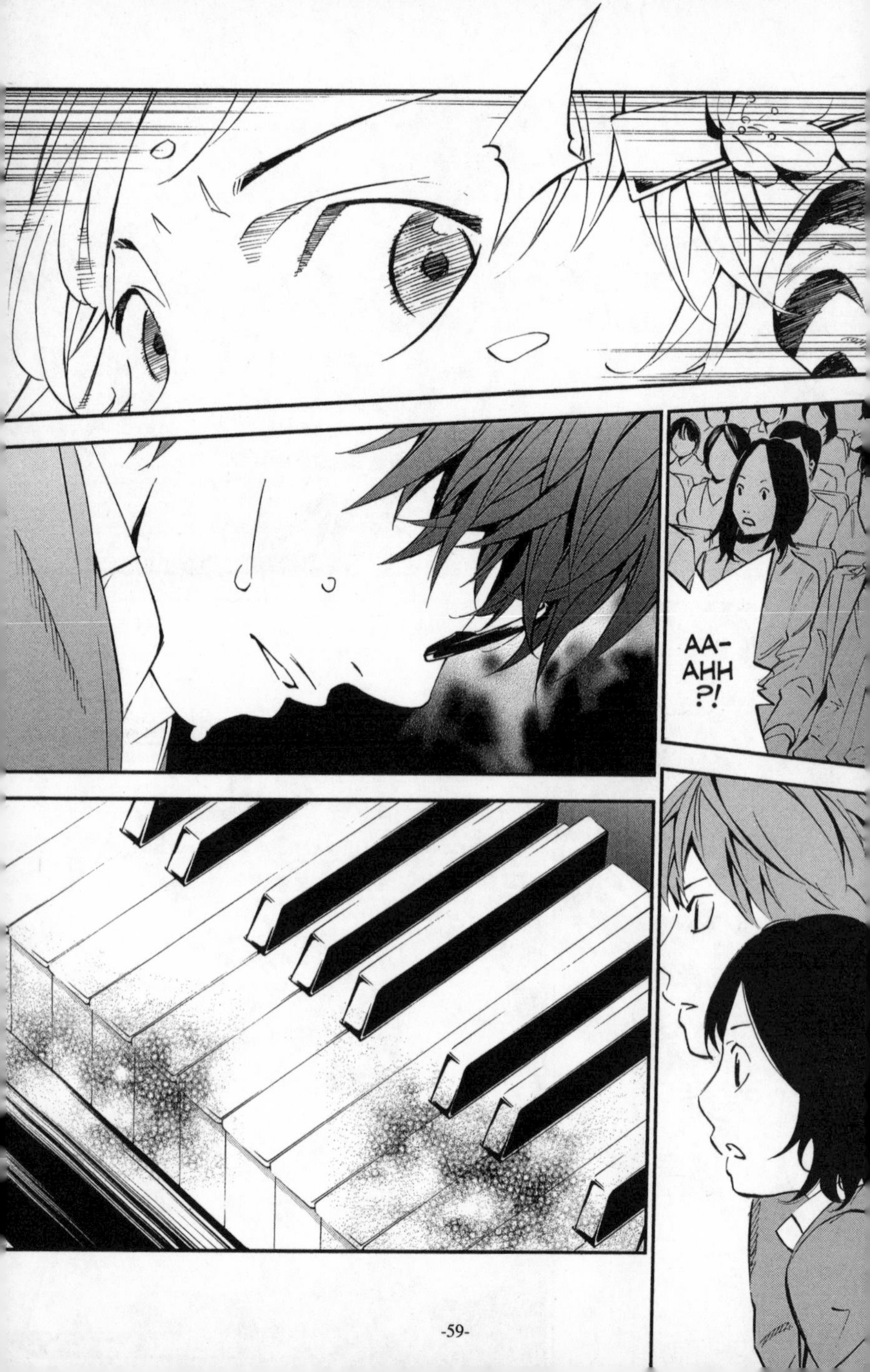
AA-
AHH
?!

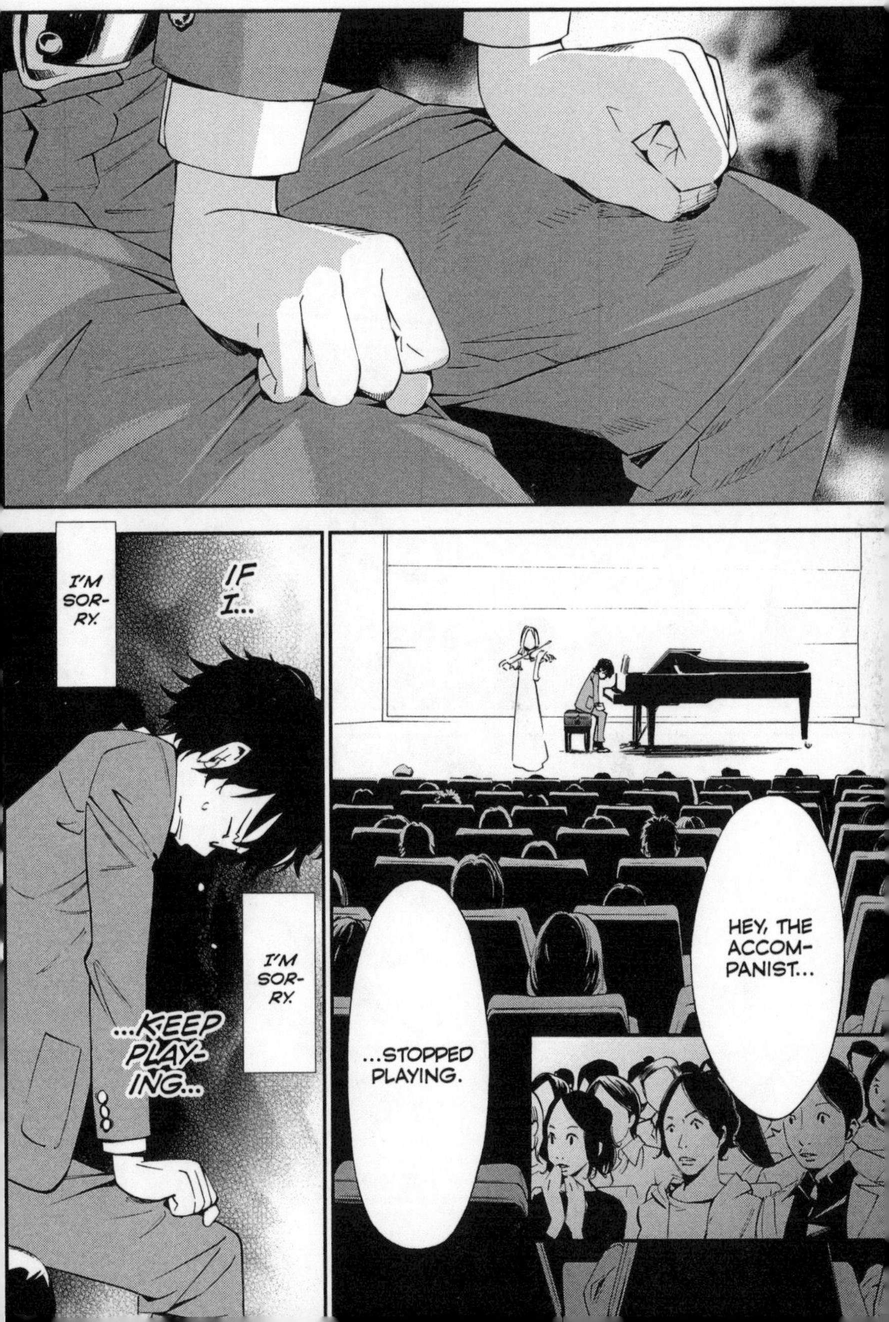
HEY, THE ACCOMPANIST...
...STOPPED PLAYING.
IF I...
I'M SORRY.
I'M SORRY.
...KEEP PLAYING...

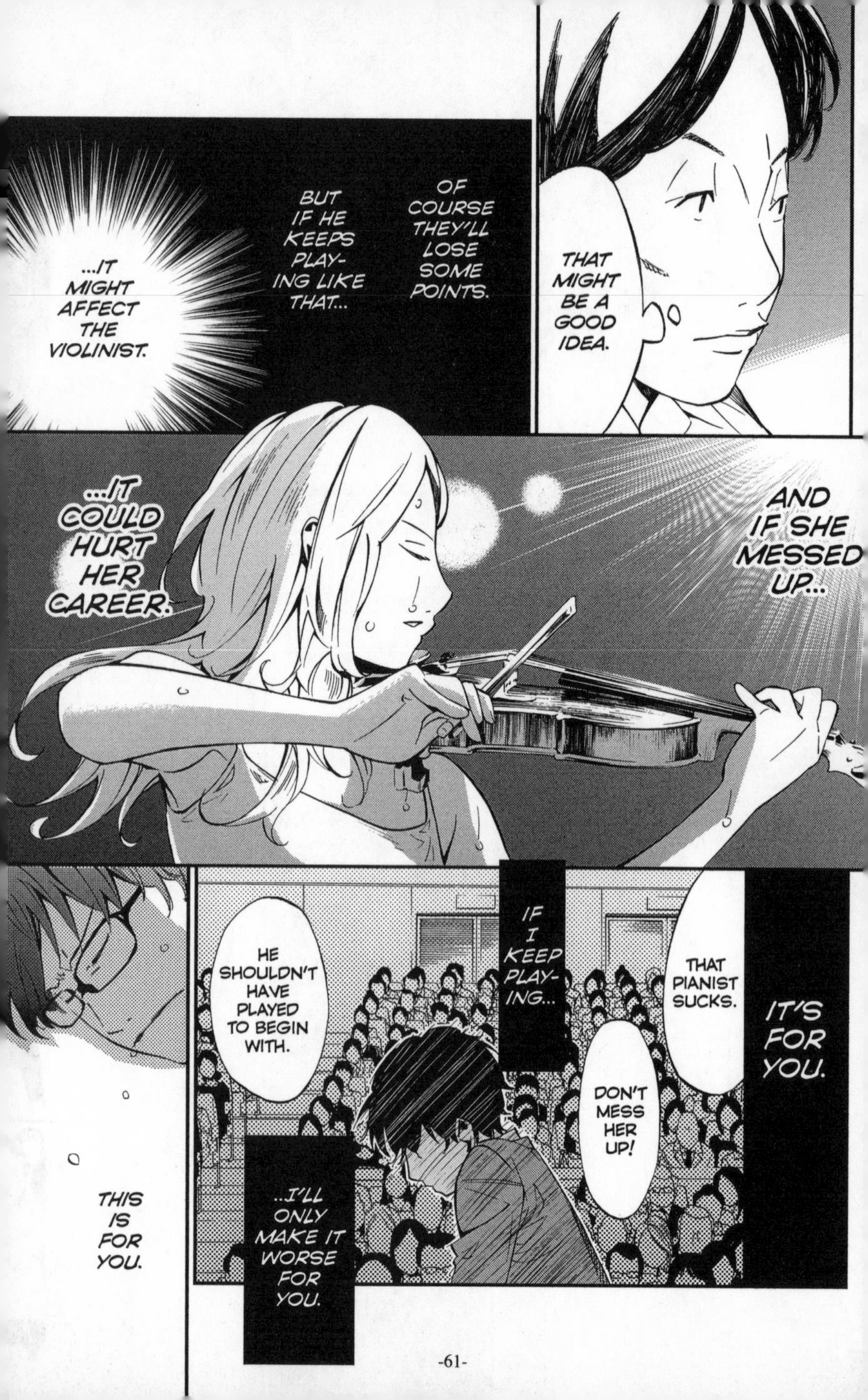
THAT MIGHT BE A GOOD IDEA.
OF COURSE THEY'LL LOSE SOME POINTS.
BUT IF HE KEEPS PLAY-ING LIKE THAT...
...IT MIGHT AFFECT THE VIOLINIST.
AND IF SHE MESSED UP...
...IT COULD HURT HER CAREER.
IT'S FOR YOU.
THAT PIANIST SUCKS.
IF I KEEP PLAY-ING...
DON'T MESS HER UP!
HE SHOULDN'T HAVE PLAYED TO BEGIN WITH.
...I'LL ONLY MAKE IT WORSE FOR YOU.
THIS IS FOR YOU.

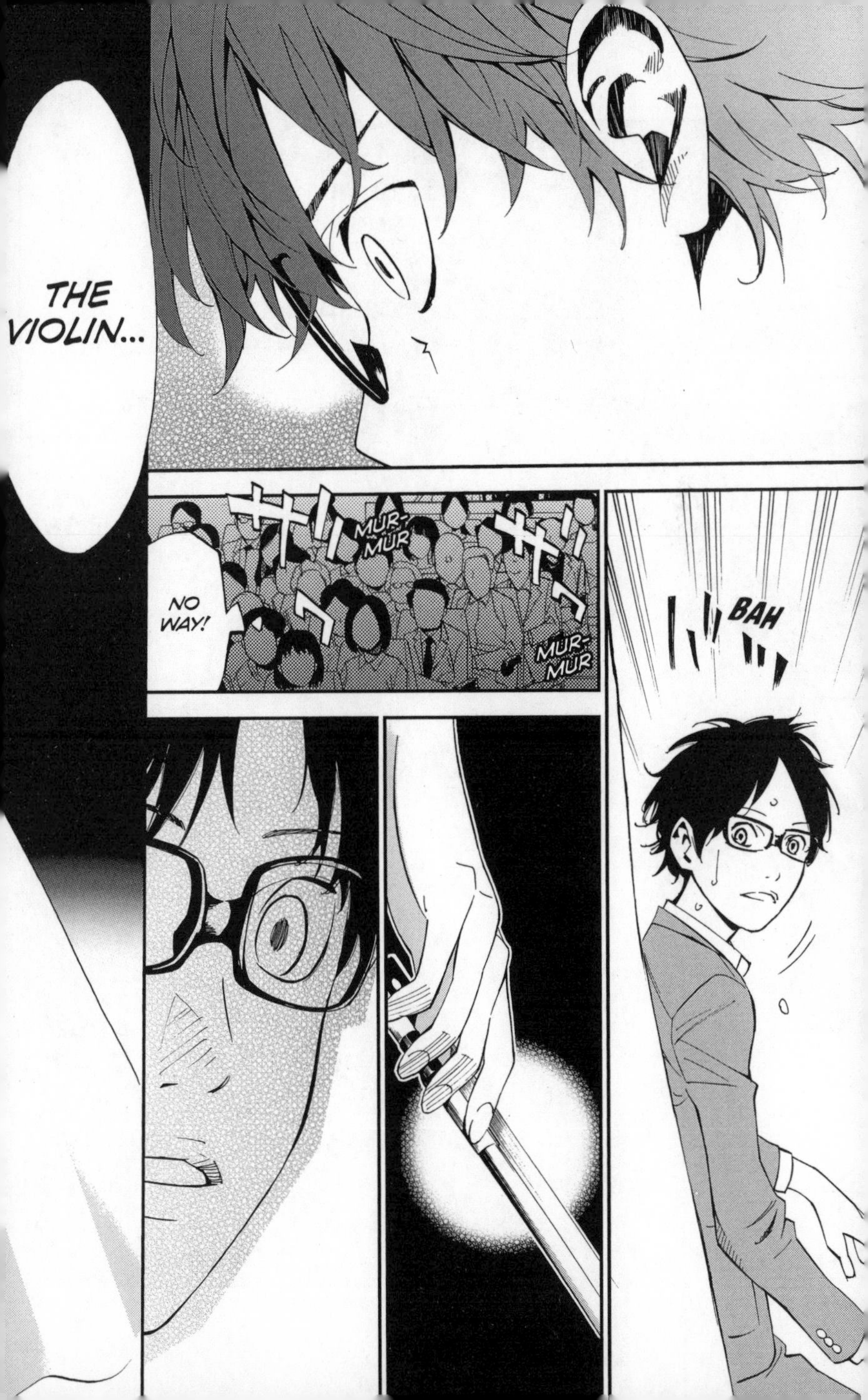
THE VIOLIN...
BAH
MUR-MUR
MUR-MUR
NO WAY!

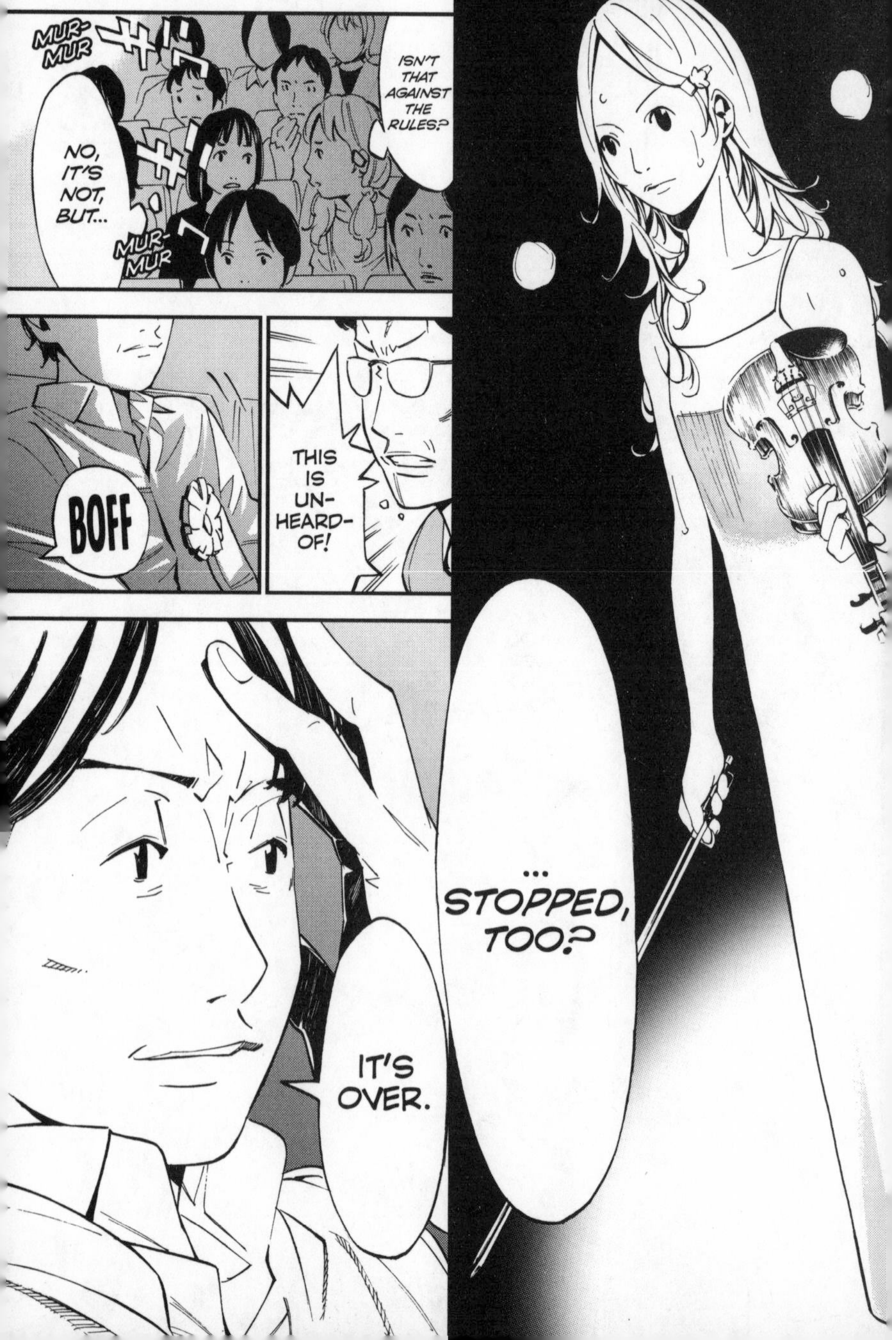
...STOPPED, TOO?
ISN'T THAT AGAINST THE RULES?
MUR-MUR
NO, IT'S NOT, BUT...
MUR-MUR
THIS IS UN-HEARD-OF!
BOFF
IT'S OVER.

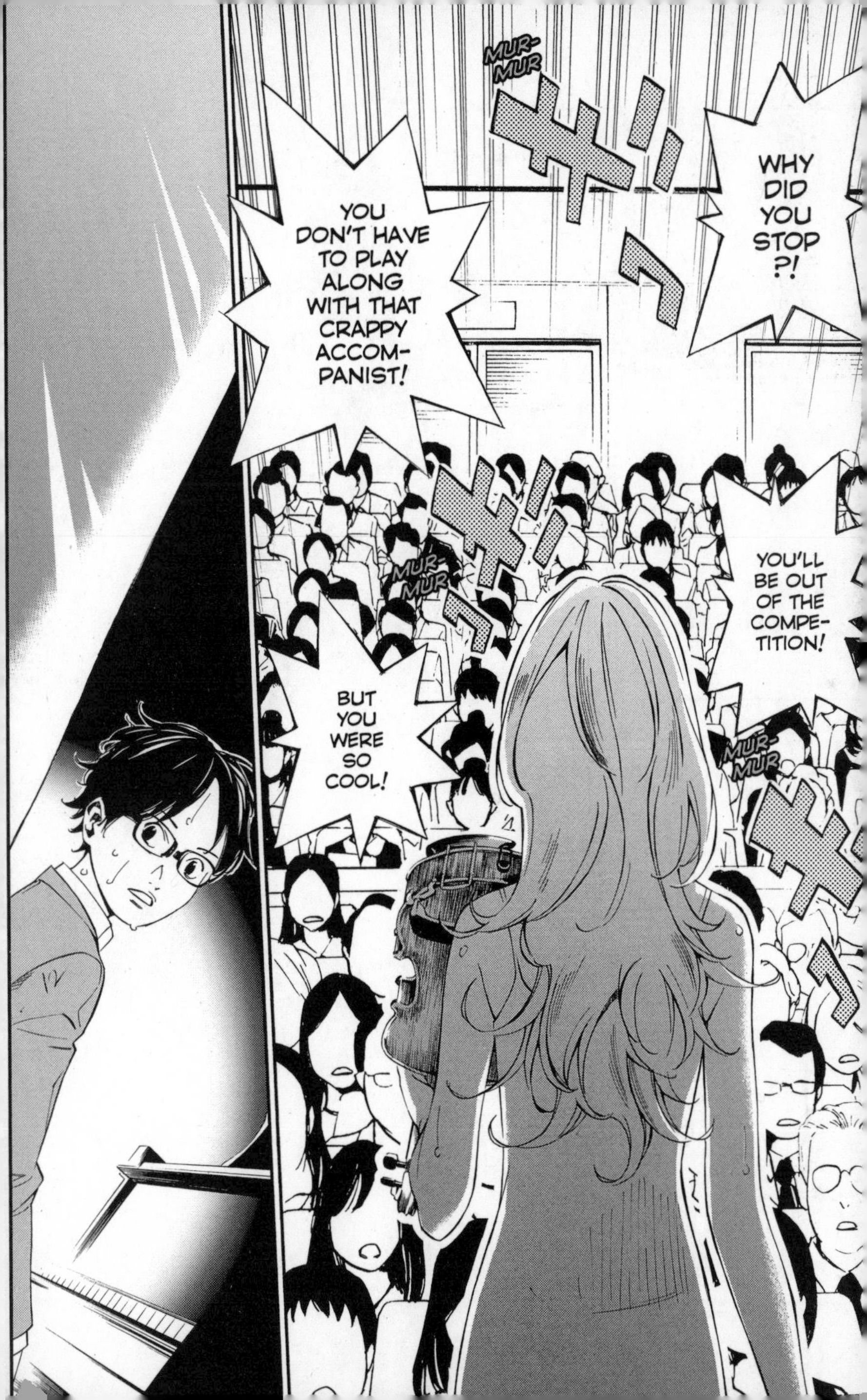
MUR-MUR
WHY DID YOU STOP?!
YOU DON'T HAVE TO PLAY ALONG WITH THAT CRAPPY ACCOMPANIST!
YOU'LL BE OUT OF THE COMPETITION!
MUR-MUR
MUR-MUR
BUT YOU WERE SO COOL!

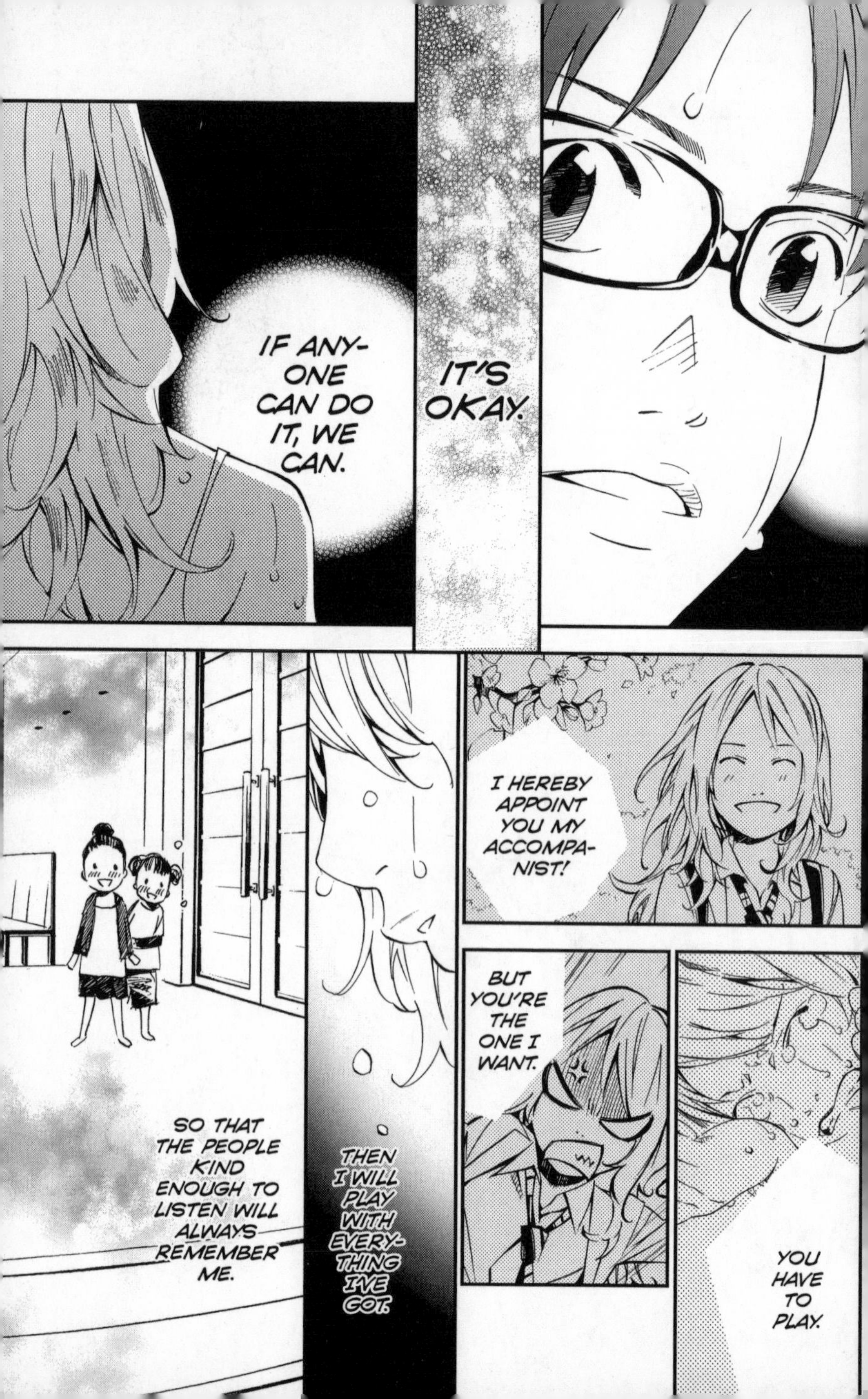
IT'S OKAY.
IF ANY-ONE CAN DO IT, WE CAN.
I HEREBY APPOINT YOU MY ACCOMPA-NIST!
YOU HAVE TO PLAY.
BUT YOU'RE THE ONE I WANT.
THEN I WILL PLAY WITH EVERY-THING I'VE GOT.
SO THAT THE PEOPLE KIND ENOUGH TO LISTEN WILL ALWAYS REMEMBER ME.

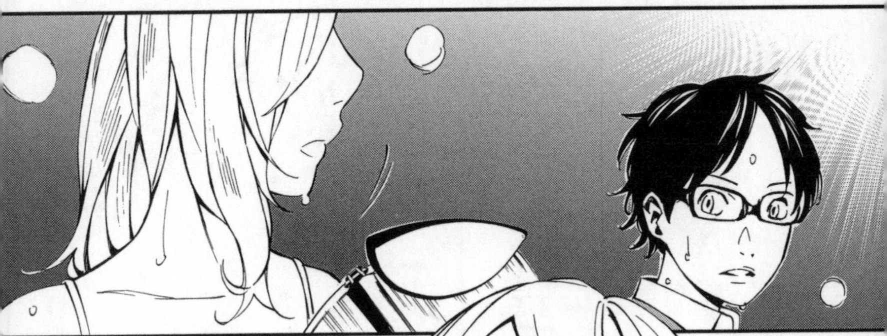
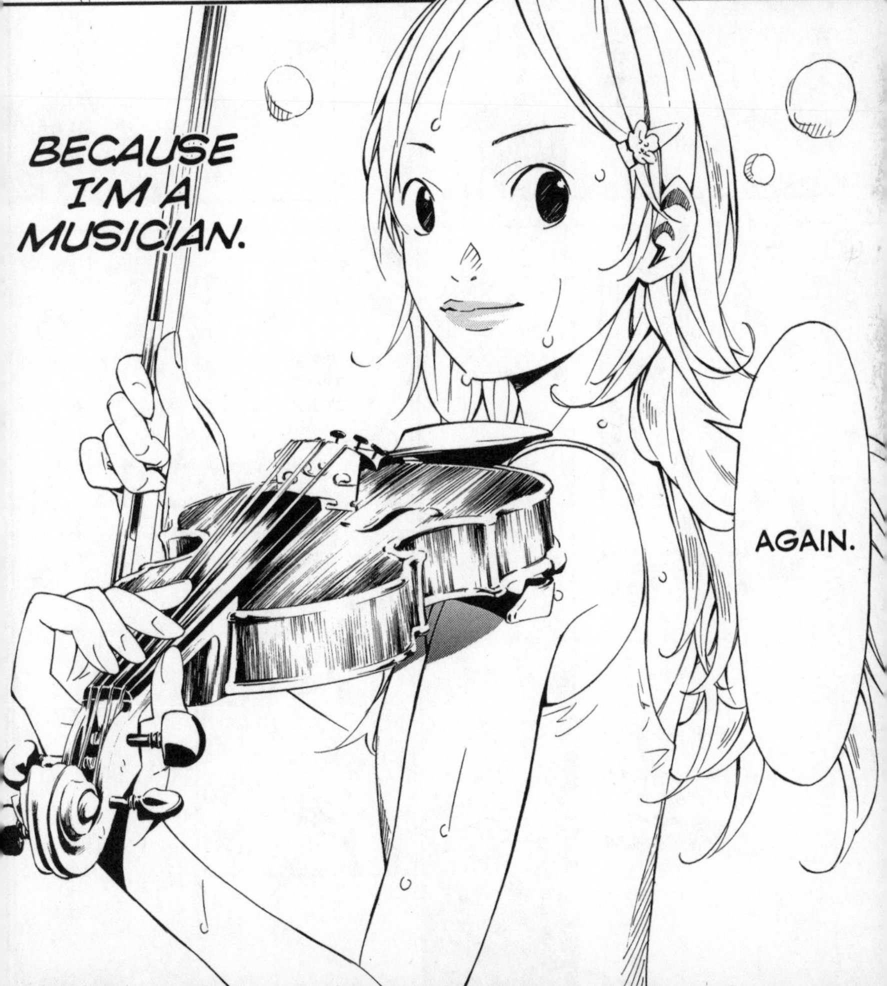
AGAIN.
BECAUSE I'M A MUSICIAN.

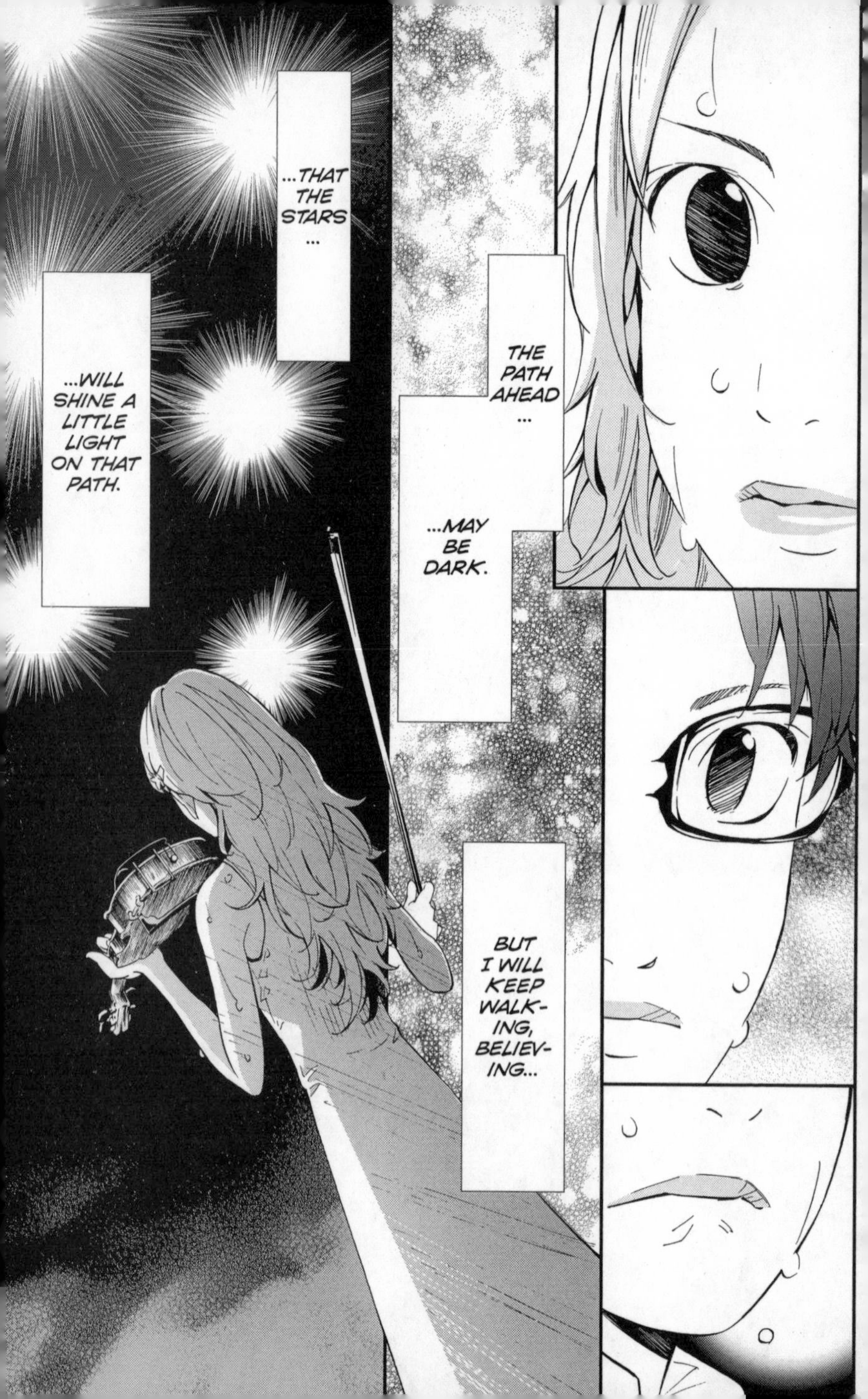
THE PATH AHEAD...
...MAY BE DARK.
BUT I WILL KEEP WALKING, BELIEVING...
...THAT THE STARS...
...WILL SHINE A LITTLE LIGHT ON THAT PATH.

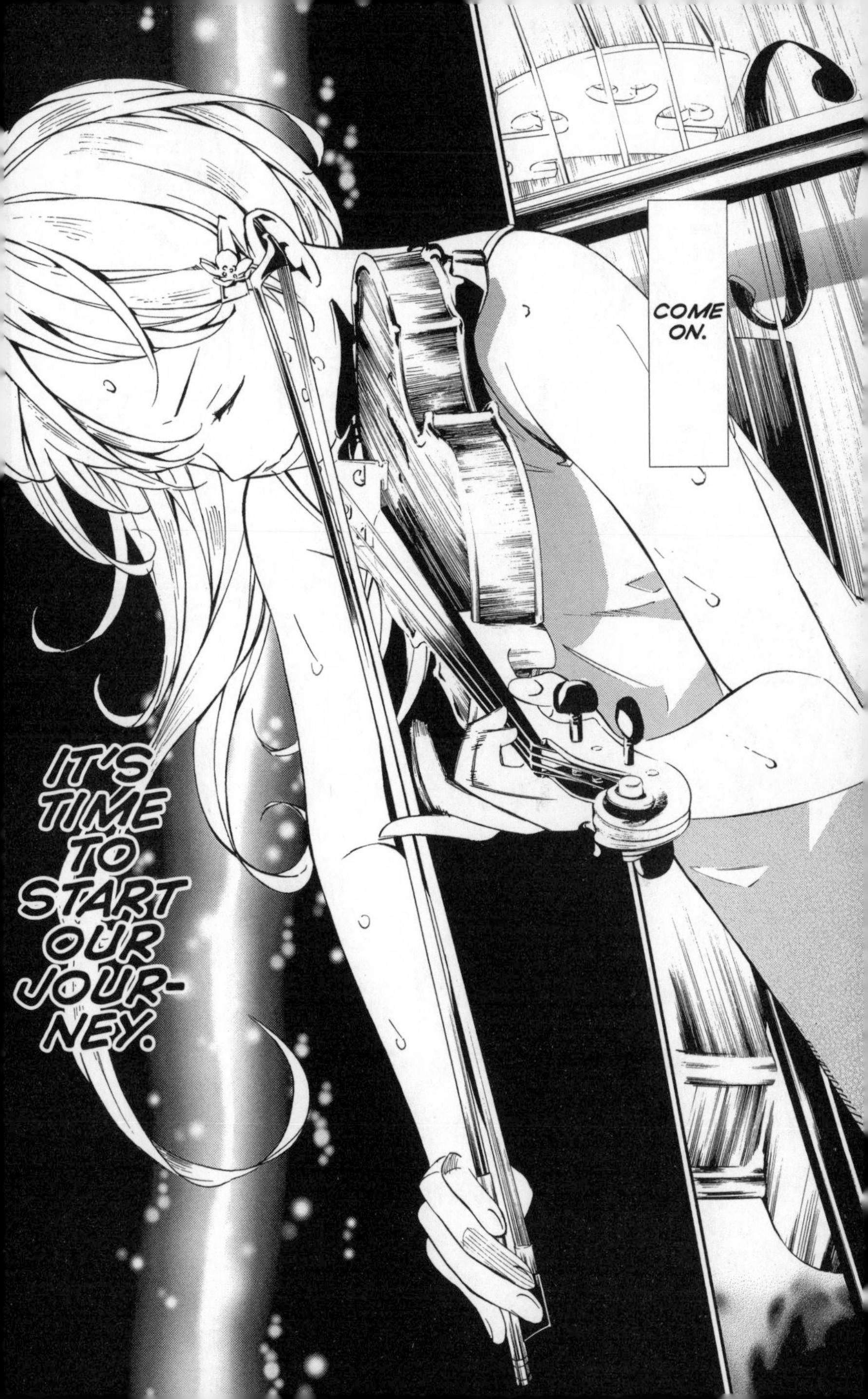
COME ON.
IT'S TIME TO START OUR JOUR-NEY.

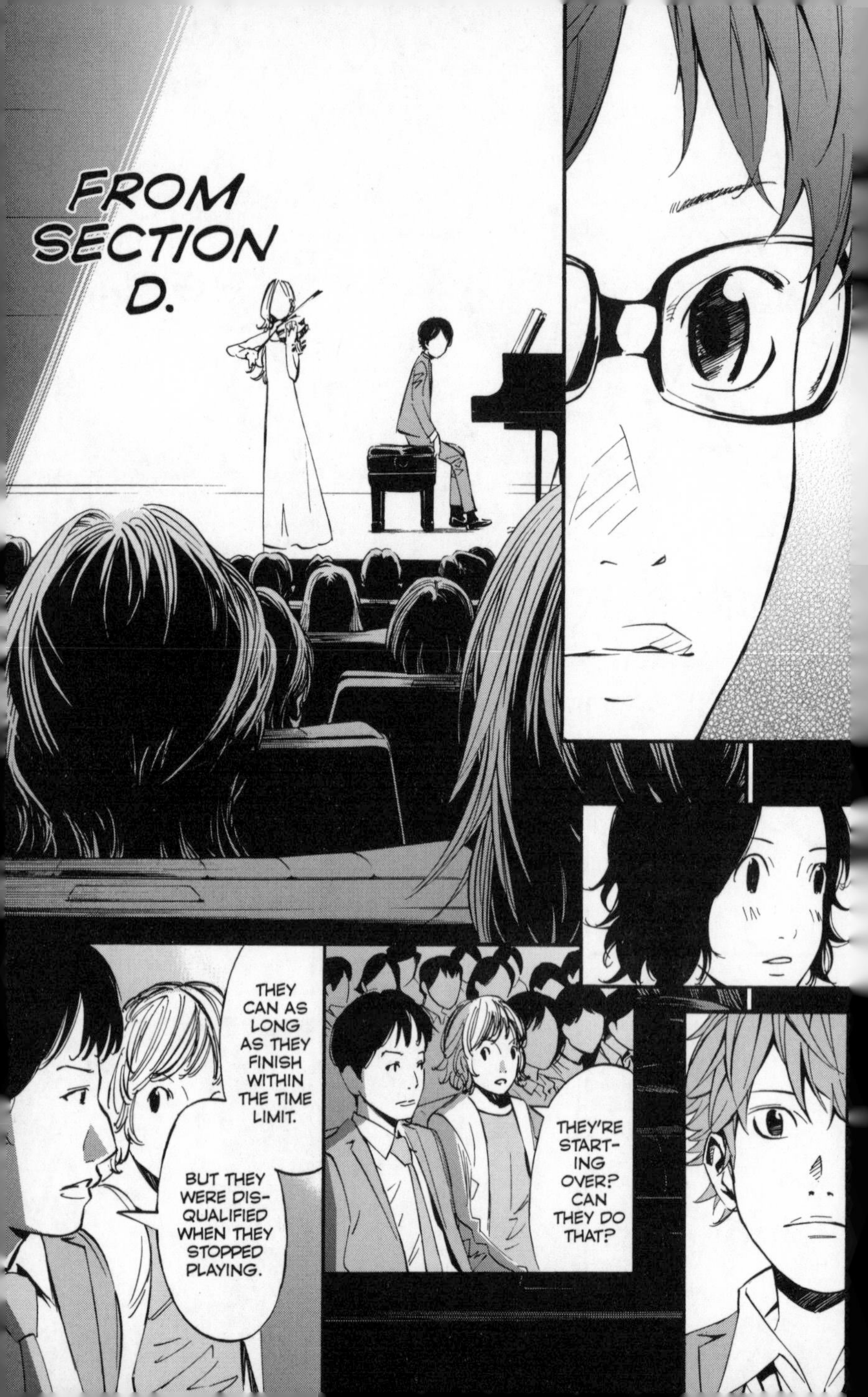
FROM SECTION D.
THEY'RE STARTING OVER? CAN THEY DO THAT?
THEY CAN AS LONG AS THEY FINISH WITHIN THE TIME LIMIT.
BUT THEY WERE DISQUALIFIED WHEN THEY STOPPED PLAYING.

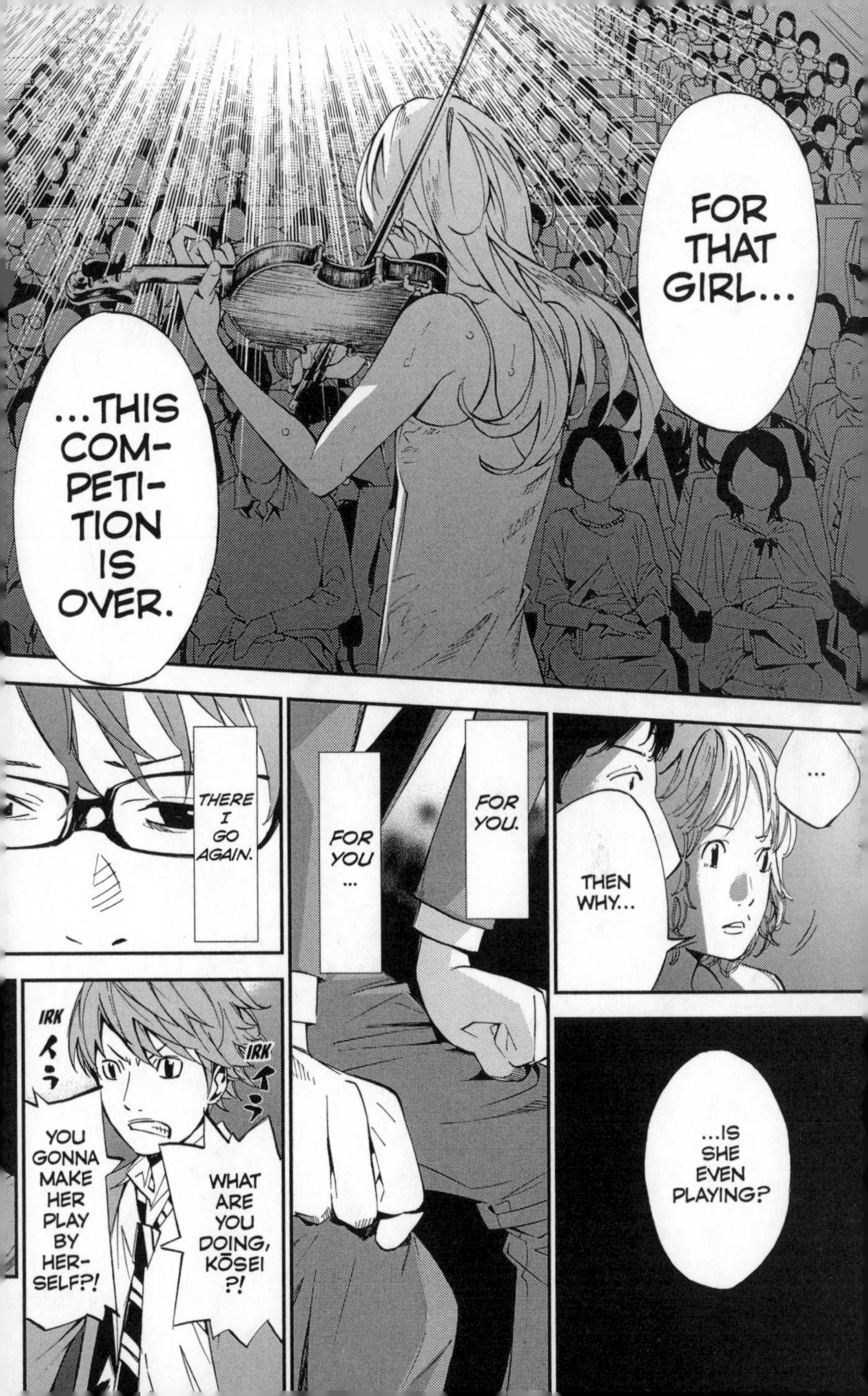
FOR THAT GIRL...
...THIS COMPETITION IS OVER.
...
THEN WHY...
FOR YOU.
FOR YOU ...
THERE I GO AGAIN.
...IS SHE EVEN PLAYING?
IRK
IRK
WHAT ARE YOU DOING, KŌSEI?!
YOU GONNA MAKE HER PLAY BY HERSELF?!

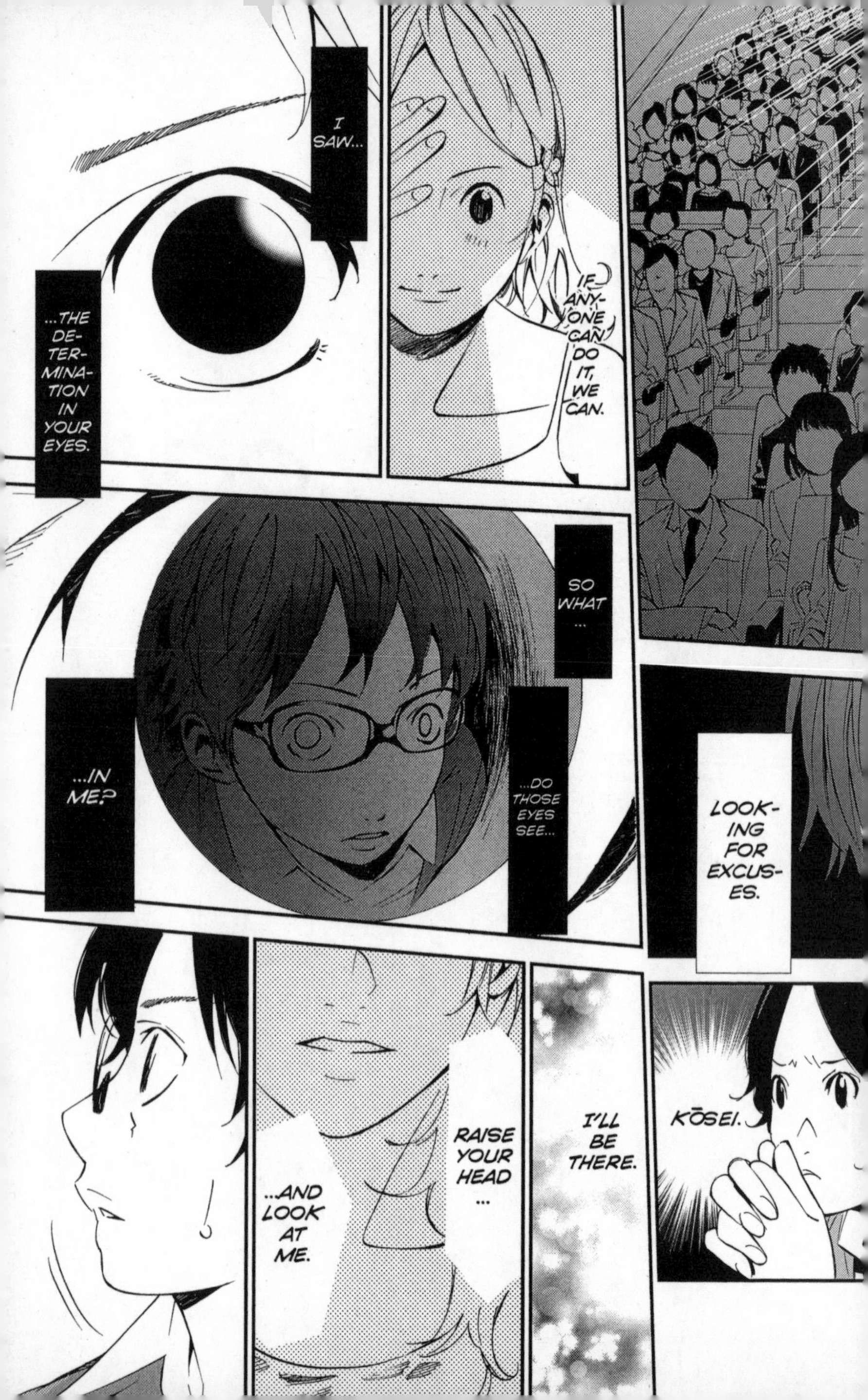
IF ANYONE CAN DO IT, WE CAN.
I SAW...
...THE DETERMINATION IN YOUR EYES.
LOOKING FOR EXCUSES.
SO WHAT ...
...DO THOSE EYES SEE...
...IN ME?
KŌSEI.
I'LL BE THERE.
RAISE YOUR HEAD ...
...AND LOOK AT ME.

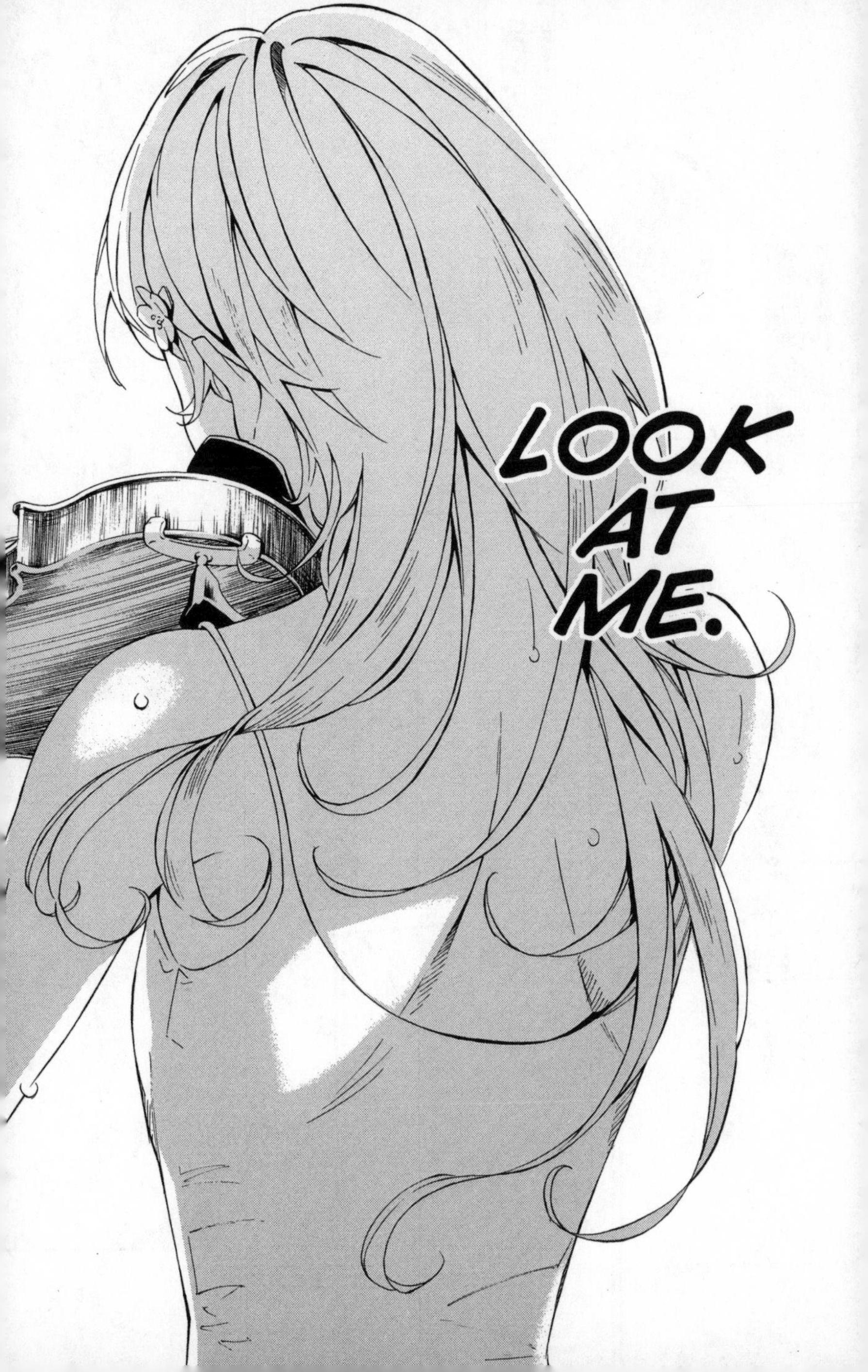
LOOK AT ME.

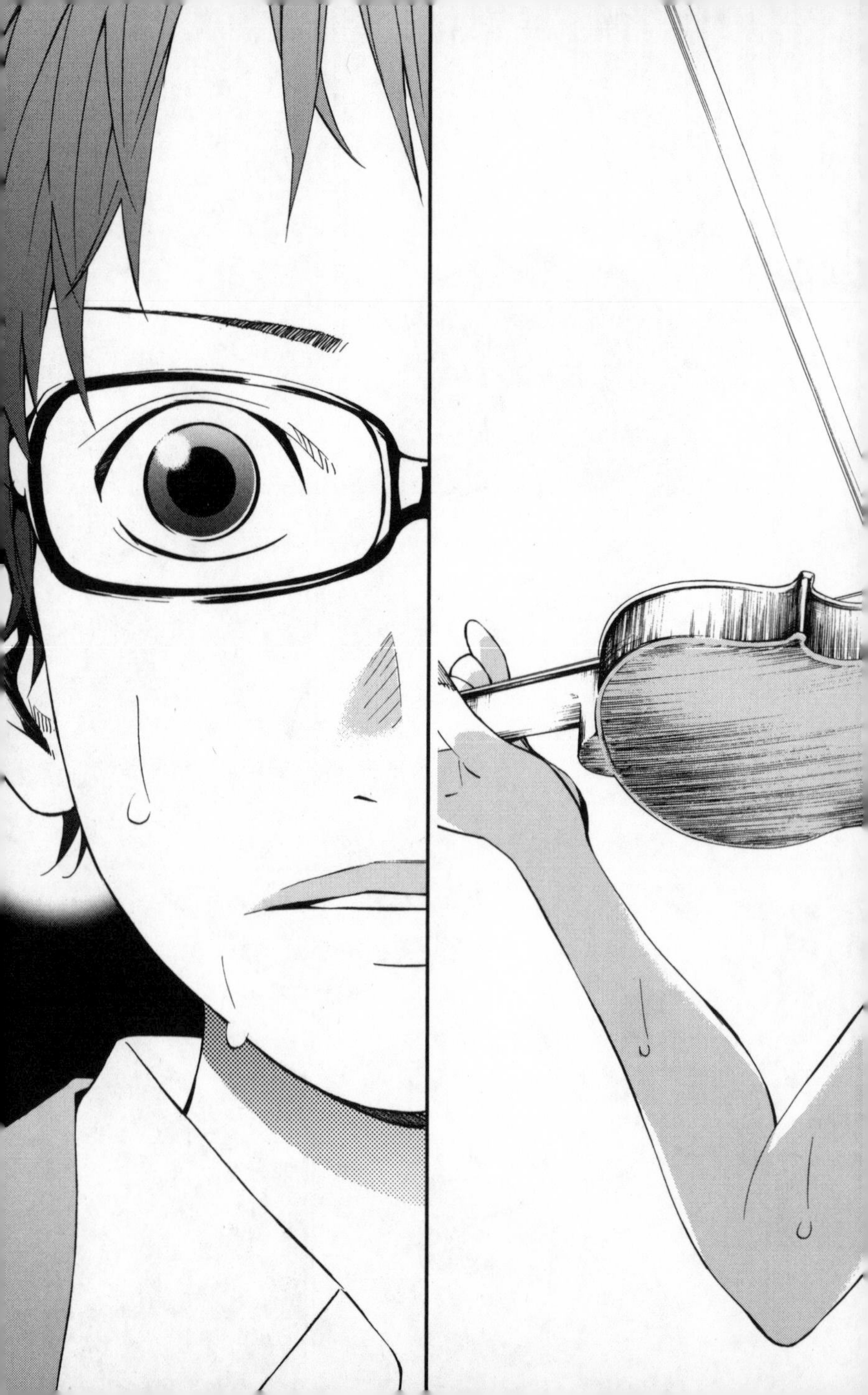

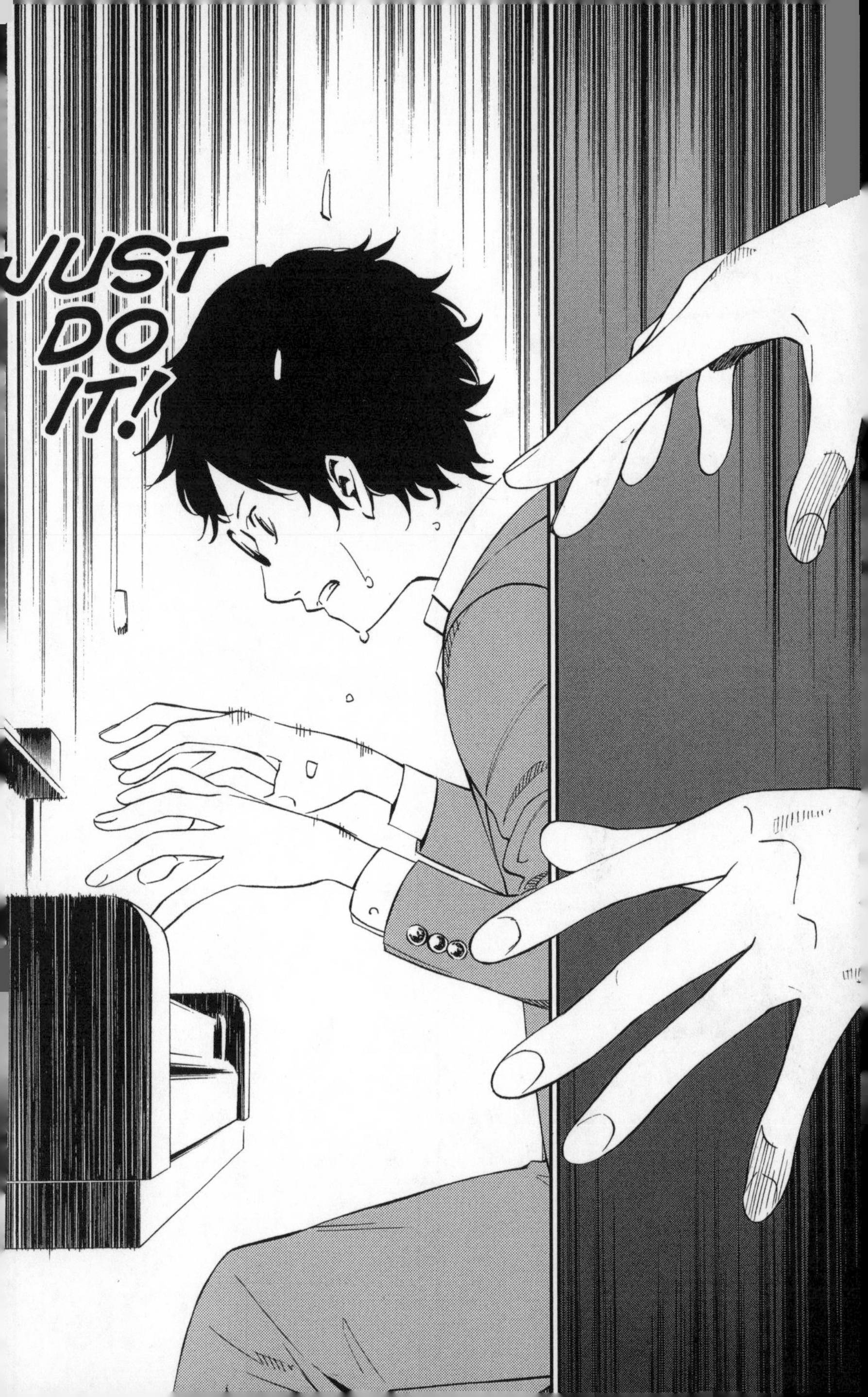
JUST
DO
IT!

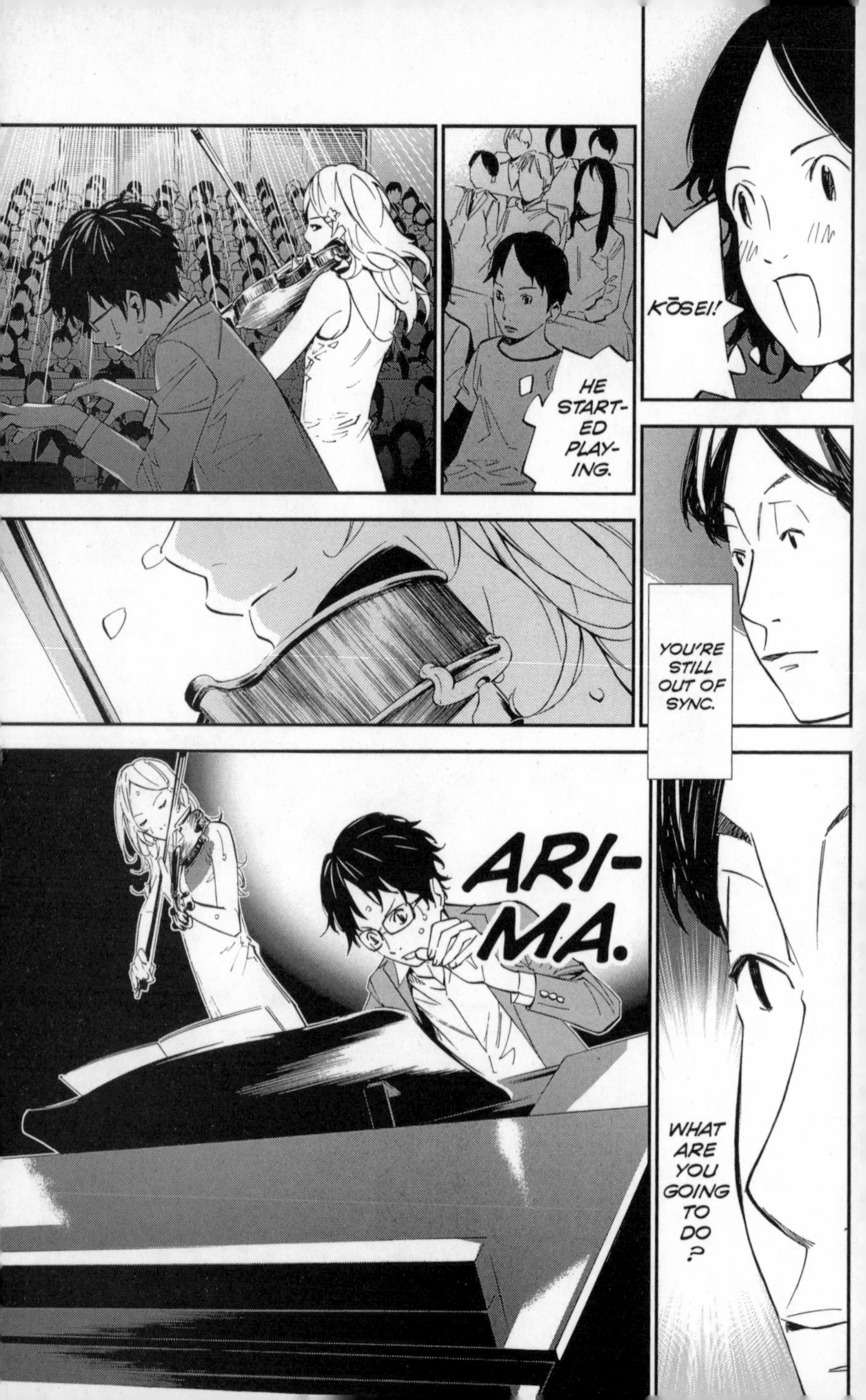
KŌSEI!
HE STARTED PLAYING.
YOU'RE STILL OUT OF SYNC.
ARIMA.
WHAT ARE YOU GOING TO DO?

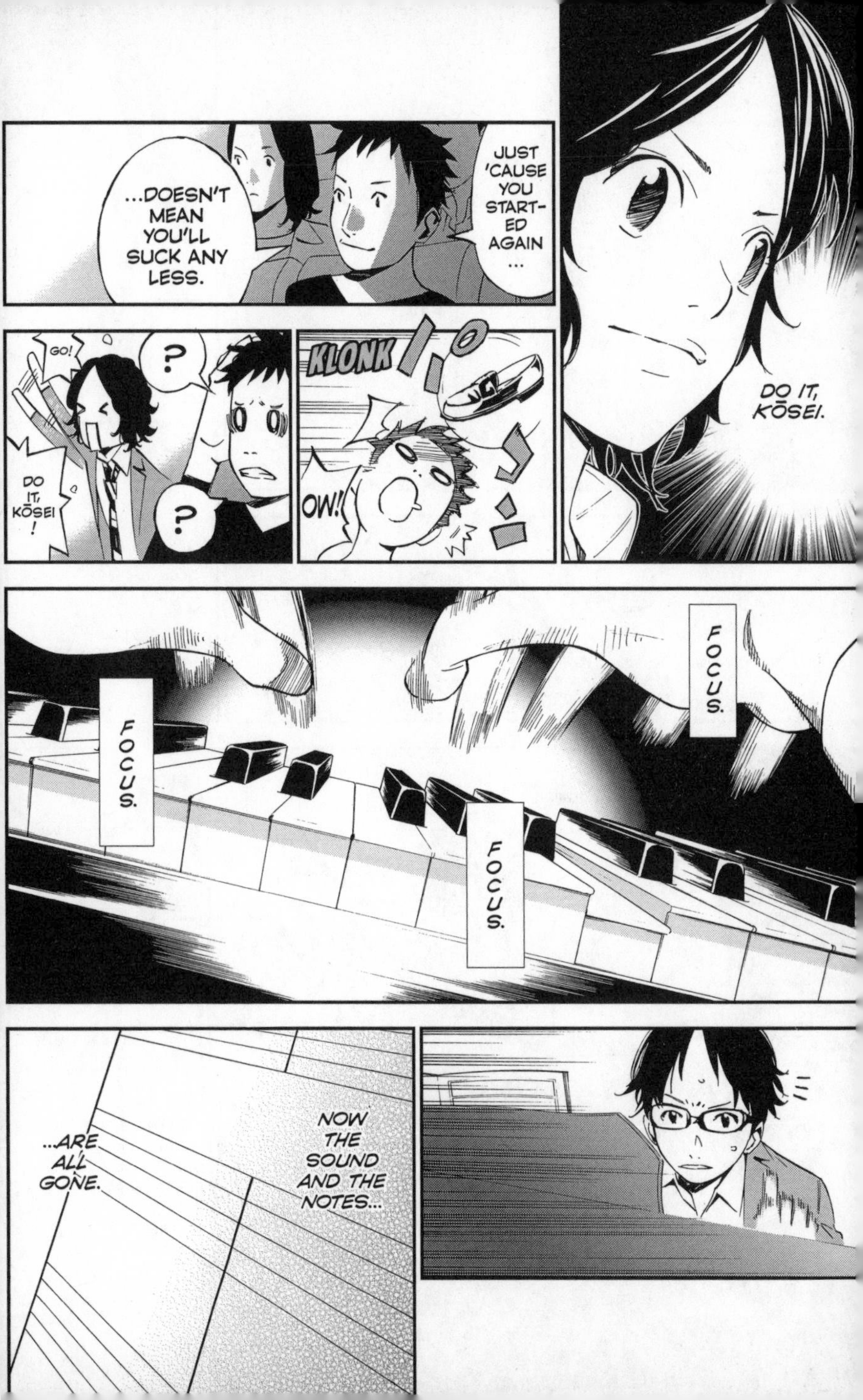
JUST 'CAUSE YOU START-ED AGAIN ...
...DOESN'T MEAN YOU'LL SUCK ANY LESS.
DO IT, KŌSEI.
KLONK
OW!
GO!
?
?
DO IT, KŌSEI !
FOCUS.
FOCUS.
FOCUS.
NOW THE SOUND AND THE NOTES...
...ARE ALL GONE.

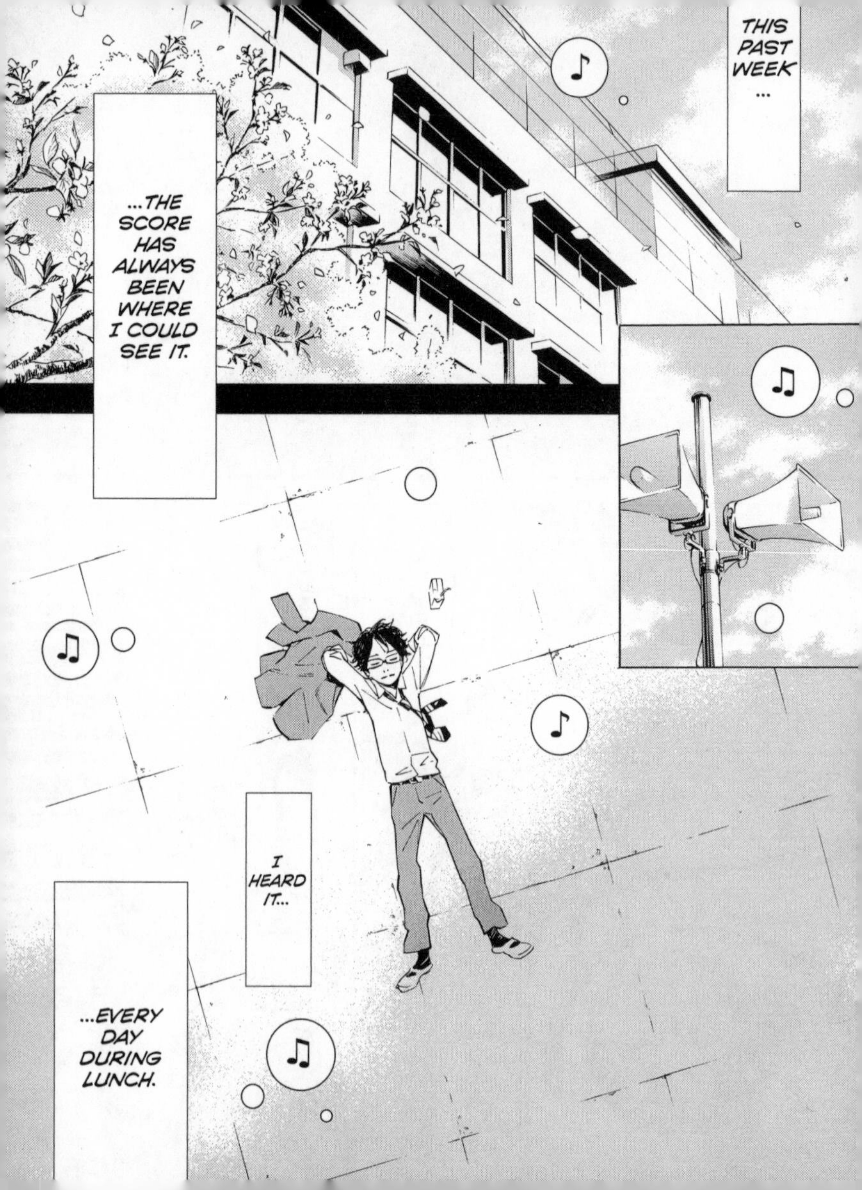
THIS PAST WEEK...
...THE SCORE HAS ALWAYS BEEN WHERE I COULD SEE IT.
I HEARD IT...
...EVERY DAY DURING LUNCH.

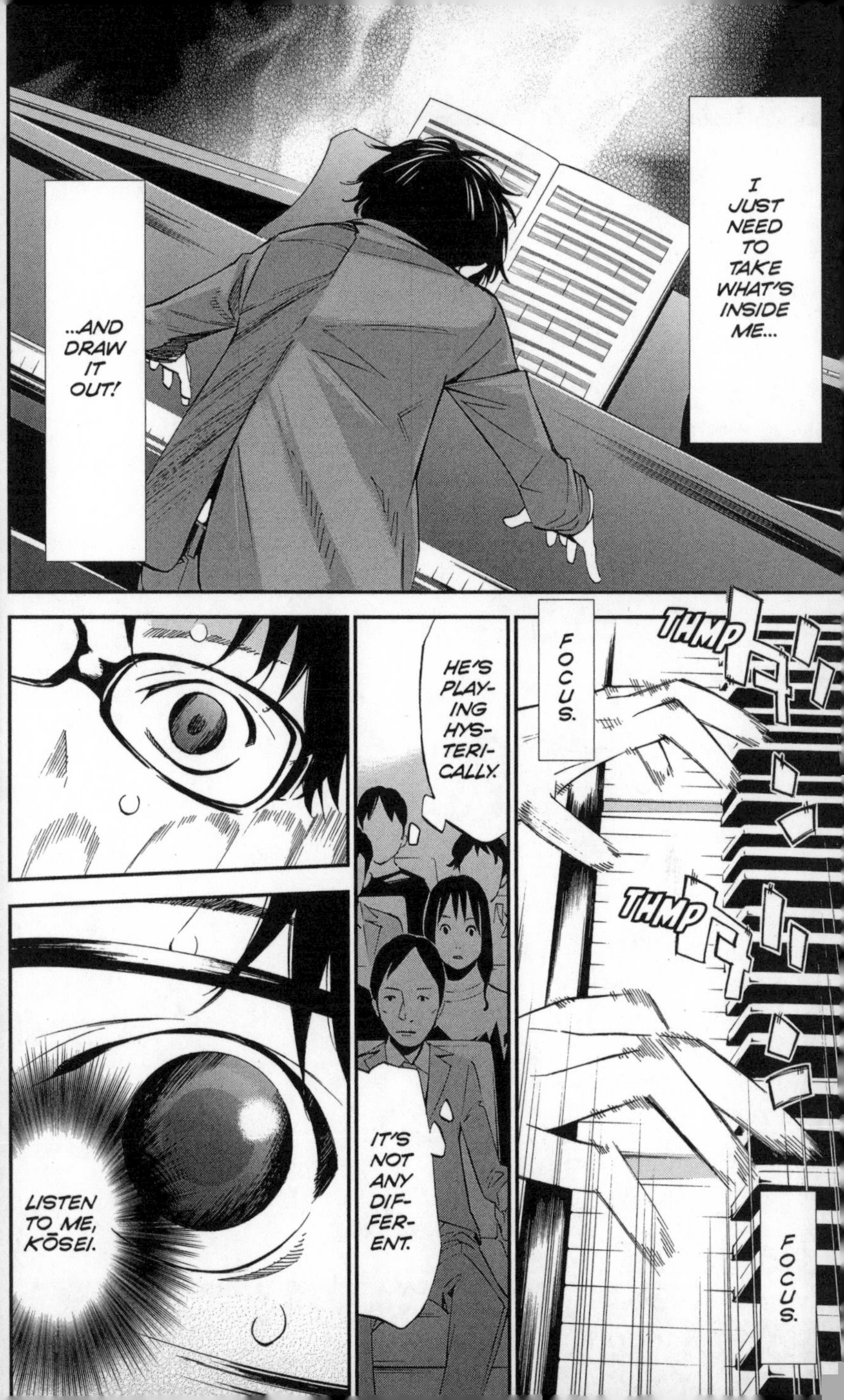

I JUST NEED TO TAKE WHAT'S INSIDE ME...
...AND DRAW IT OUT!
THMP
FOCUS.
THMP
FOCUS.
HE'S PLAYING HYS-TERI-CALLY.
IT'S NOT ANY DIF-FER-ENT.
LISTEN TO ME, KŌSEI.

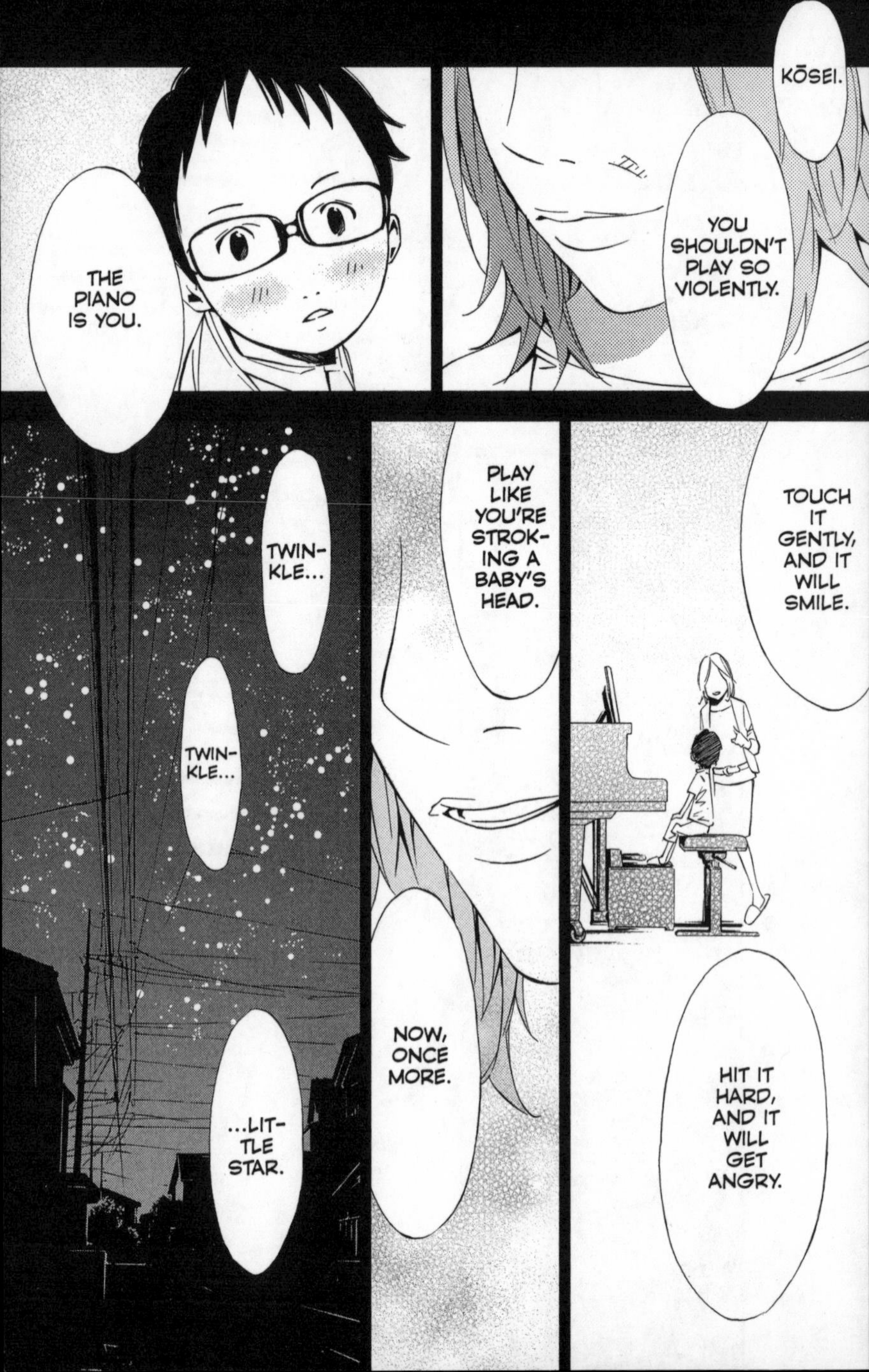
KŌSEI.
YOU SHOULDN'T PLAY SO VIOLENTLY.
THE PIANO IS YOU.
TOUCH IT GENTLY, AND IT WILL SMILE.
HIT IT HARD, AND IT WILL GET ANGRY.
PLAY LIKE YOU'RE STROKING A BABY'S HEAD.
NOW, ONCE MORE.
TWINKLE...
TWINKLE...
...LITTLE STAR.

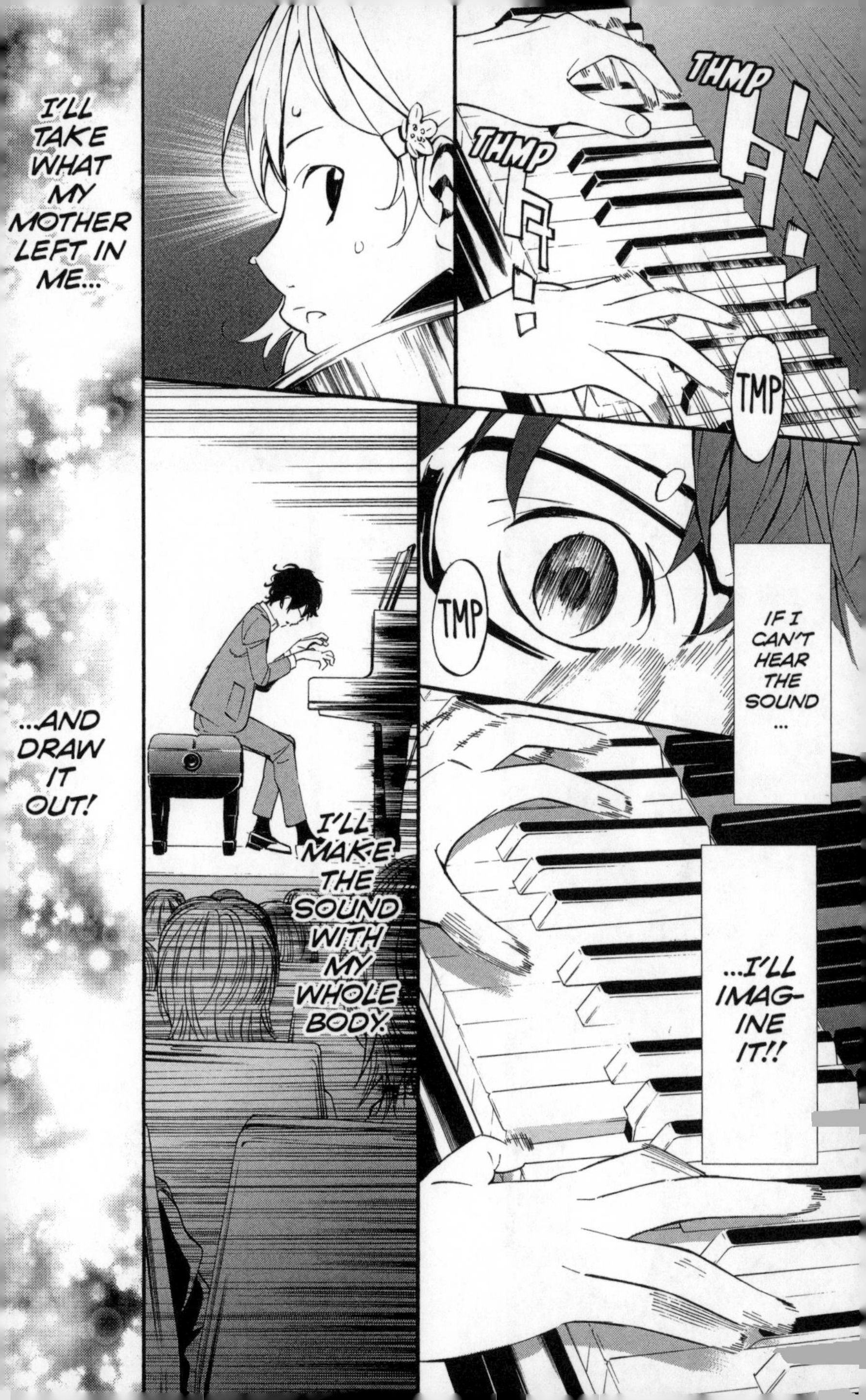
THMP
THMP
TMP
TMP
IF I CAN'T HEAR THE SOUND...
...I'LL IMAGINE IT!!
I'LL MAKE THE SOUND WITH MY WHOLE BODY.
I'LL TAKE WHAT MY MOTHER LEFT IN ME...
...AND DRAW IT OUT!

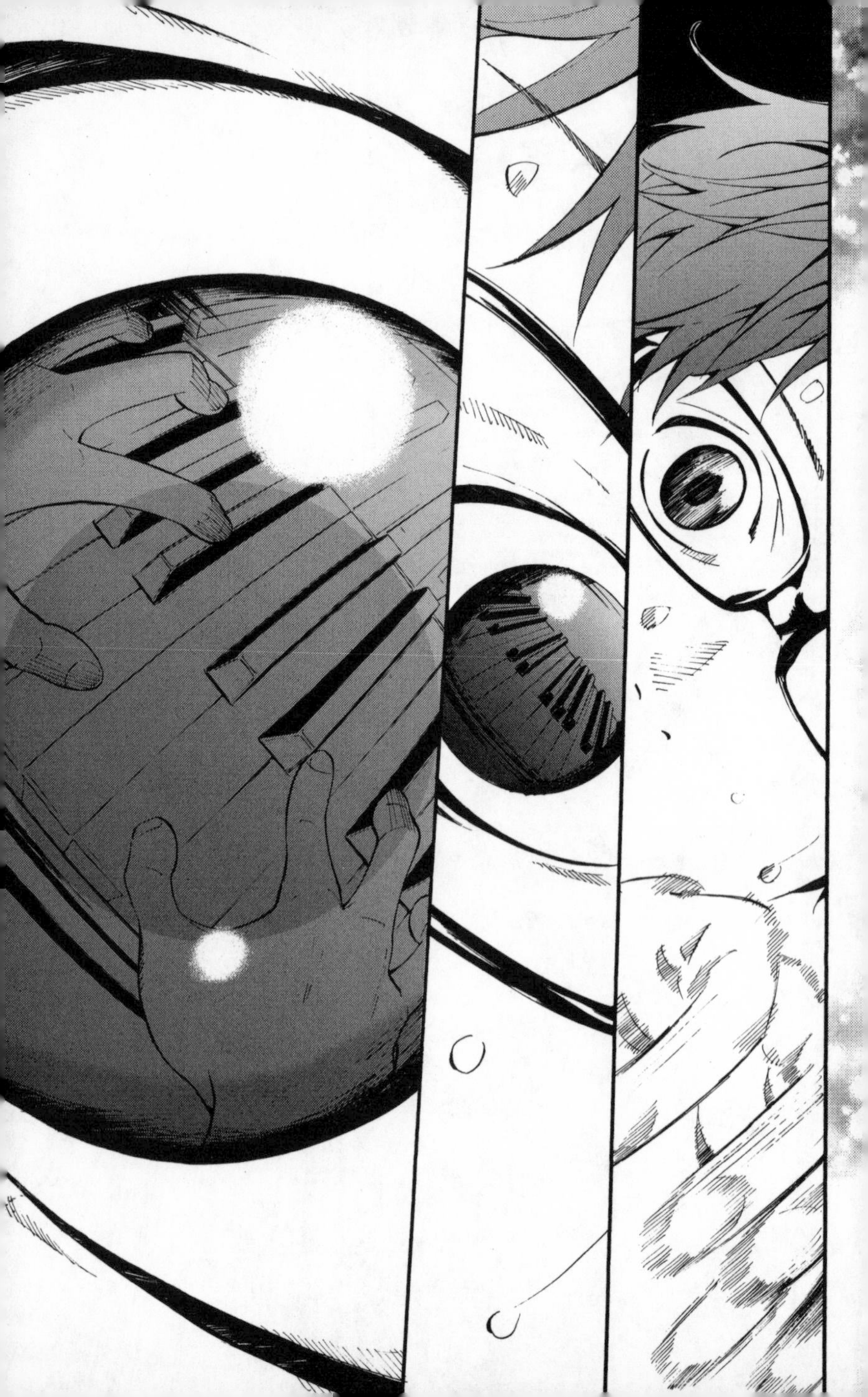

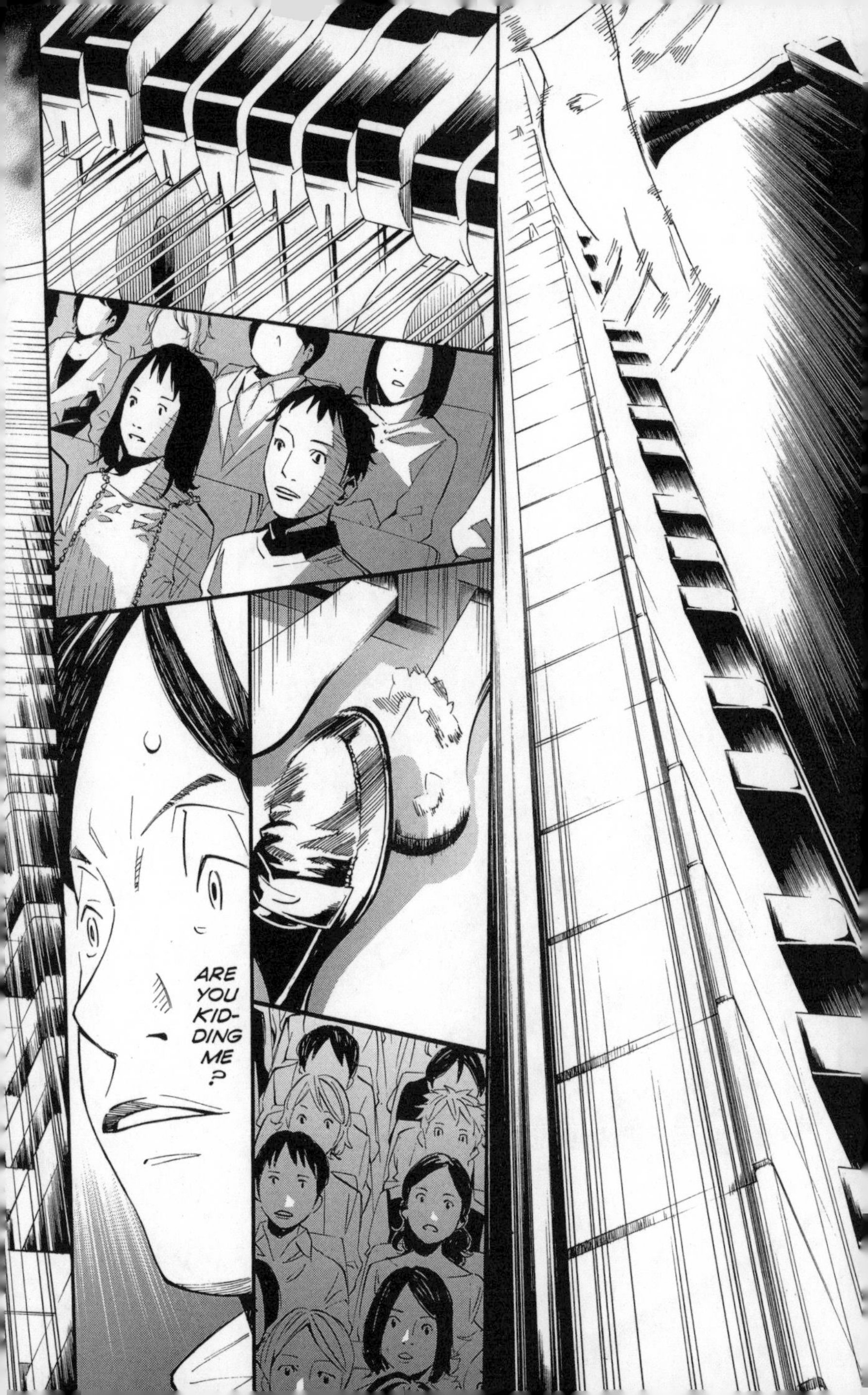
ARE YOU KID-DING ME?

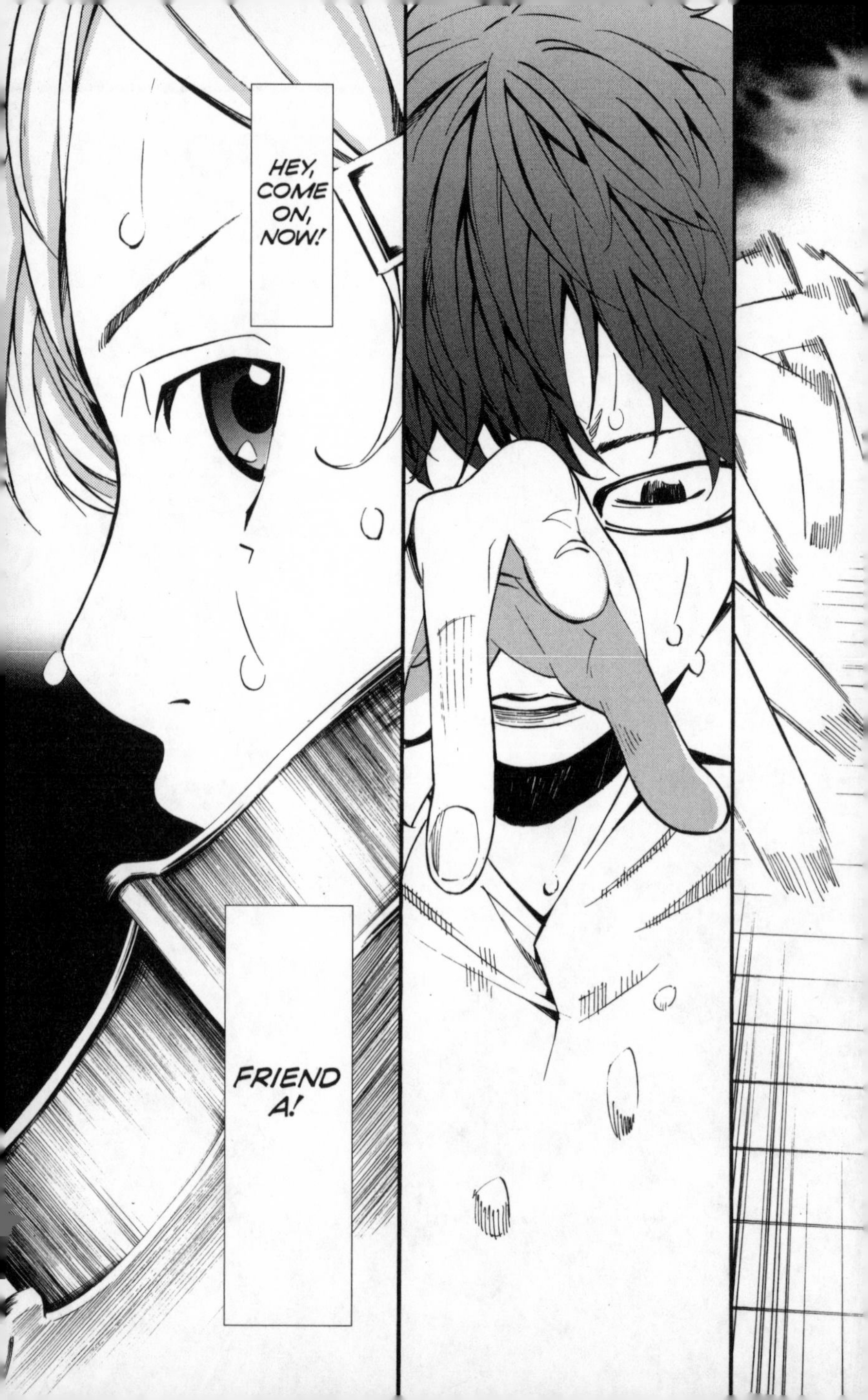
HEY, COME ON, NOW!
FRIEND A!

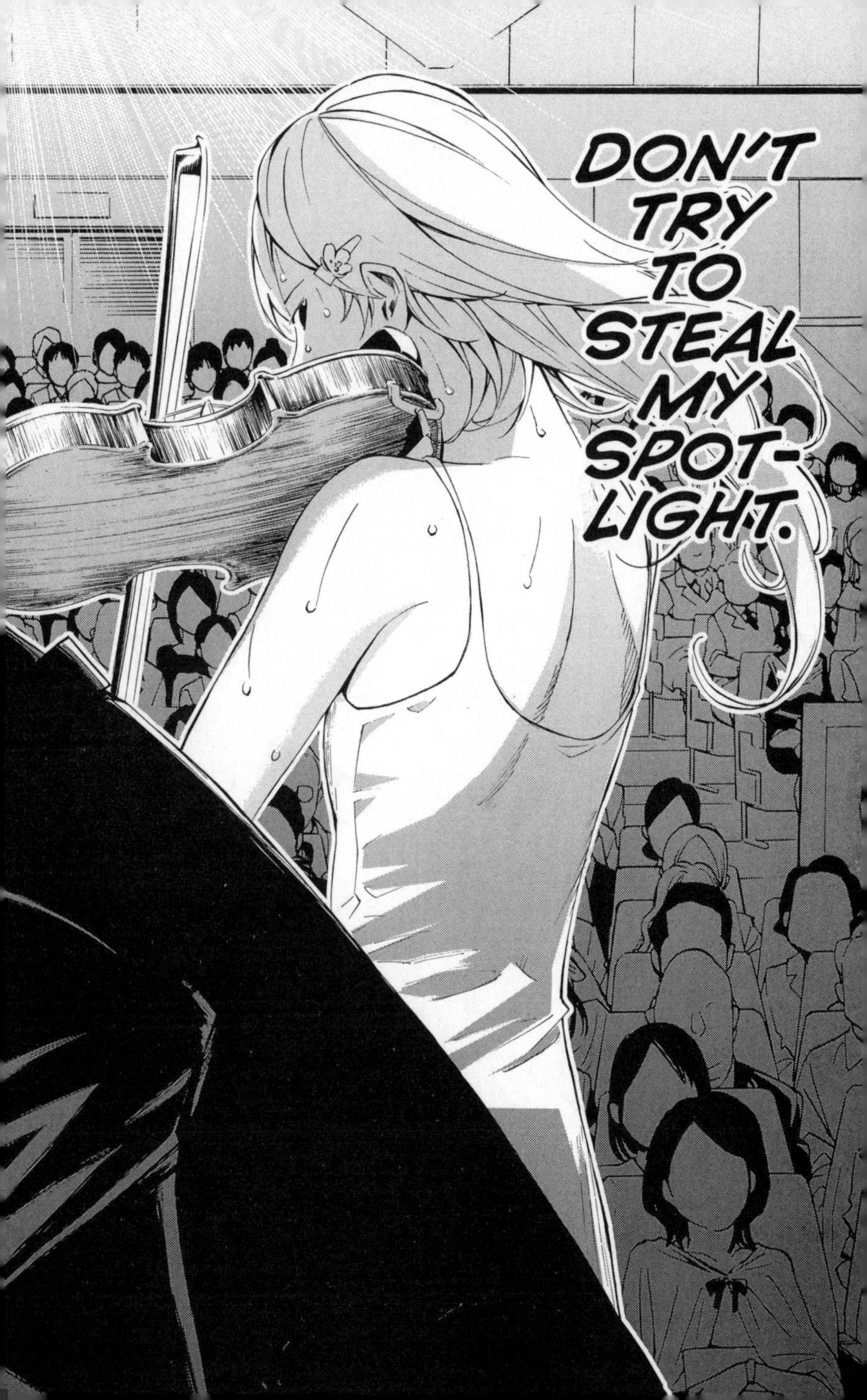
DON'T TRY TO STEAL MY SPOT-LIGHT.

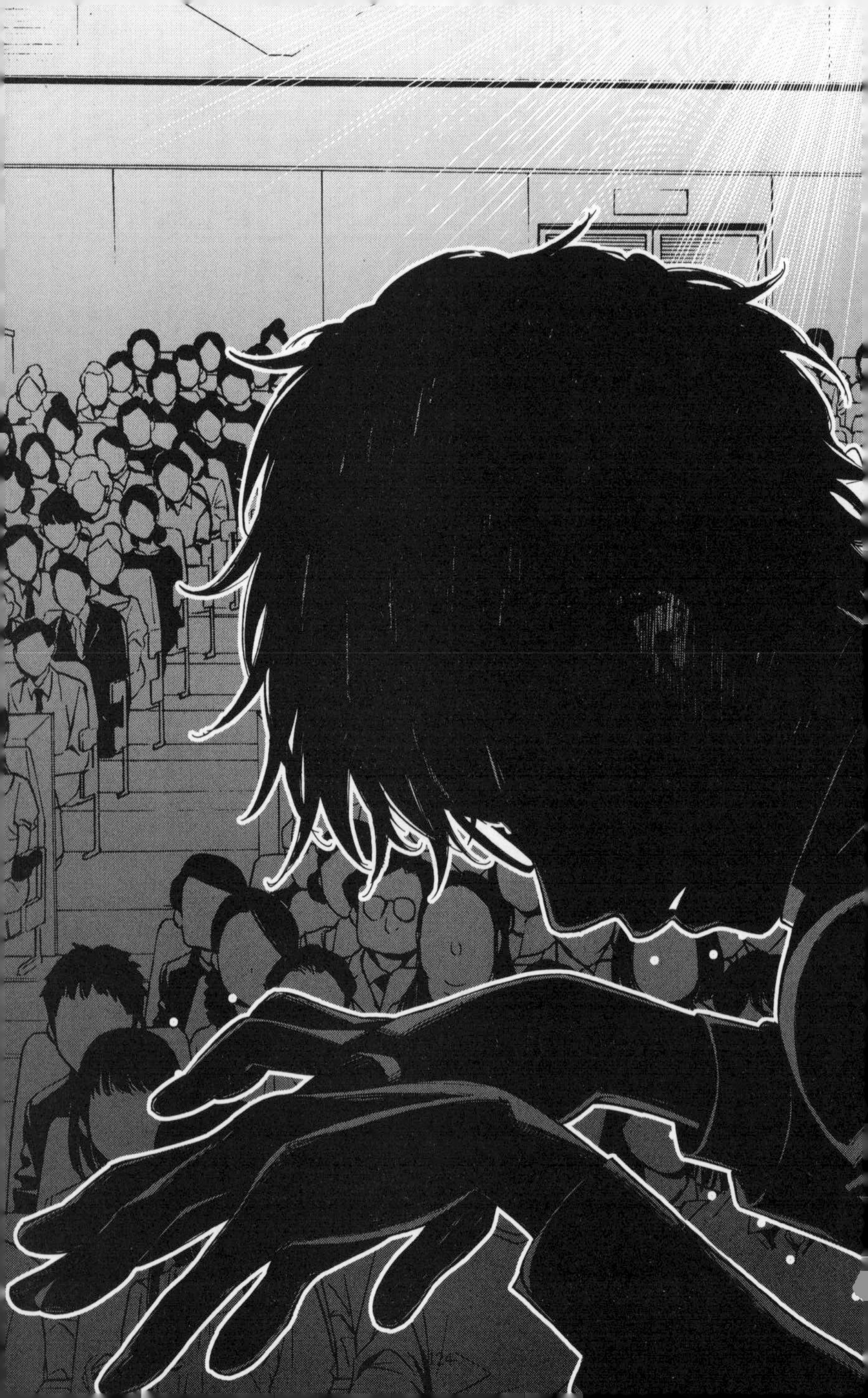

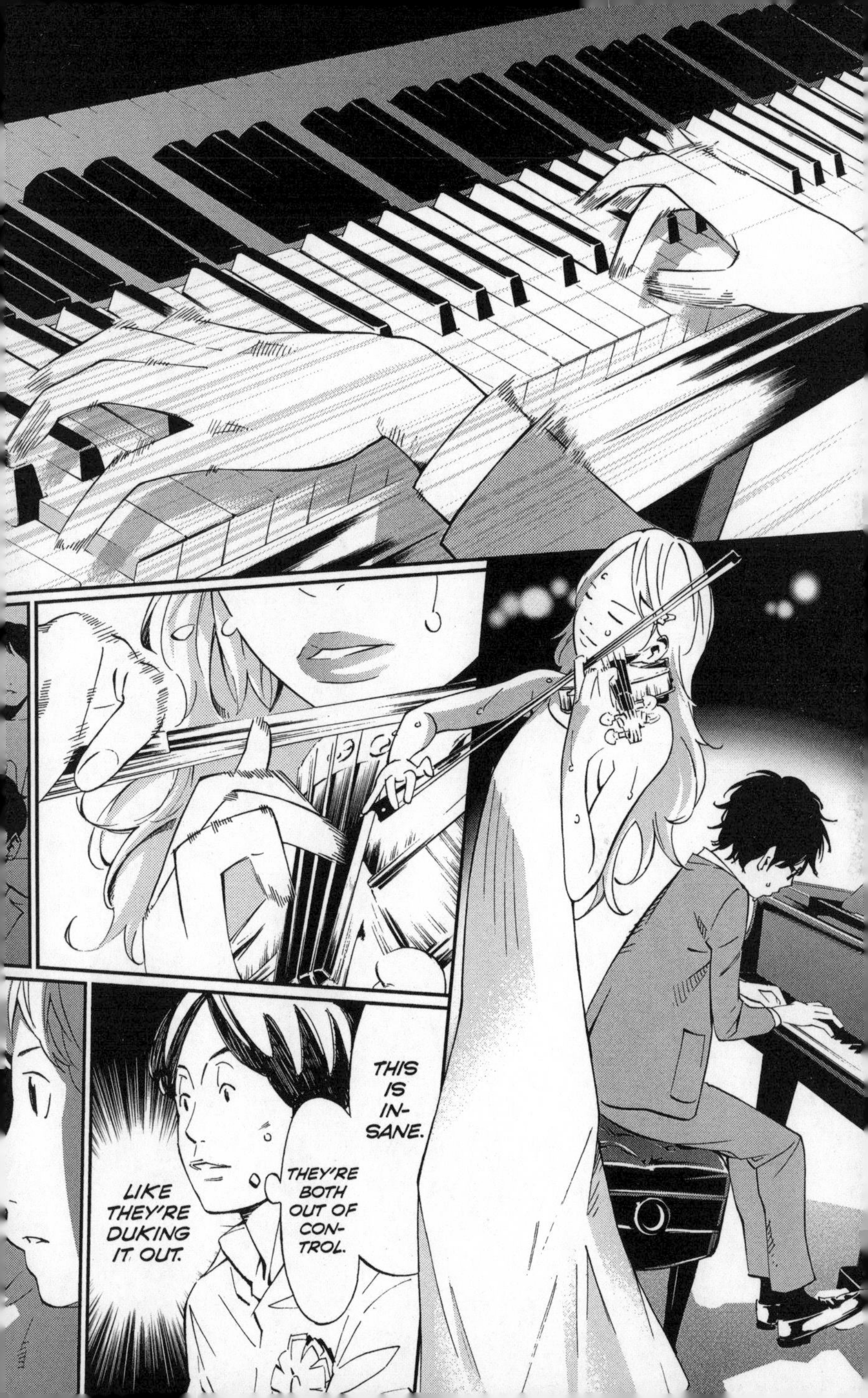
THIS IS IN-SANE.
THEY'RE BOTH OUT OF CON-TROL.
LIKE THEY'RE DUKING IT OUT.

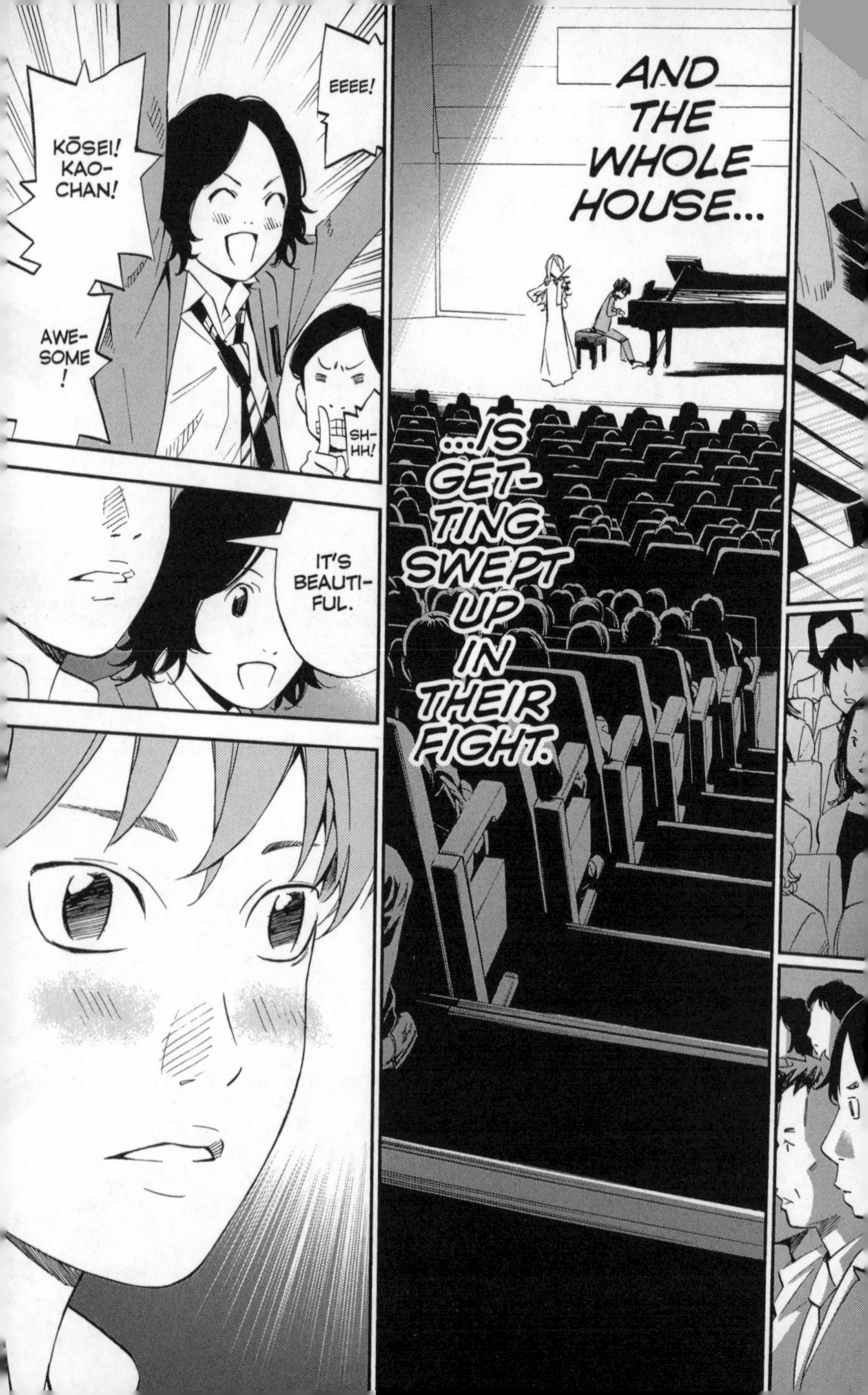
AND THE WHOLE HOUSE...
...IS GETTING SWEPT UP IN THEIR FIGHT.
EEEE!
KŌSEI! KAO-CHAN!
AWESOME!
SHHH!
IT'S BEAUTIFUL.

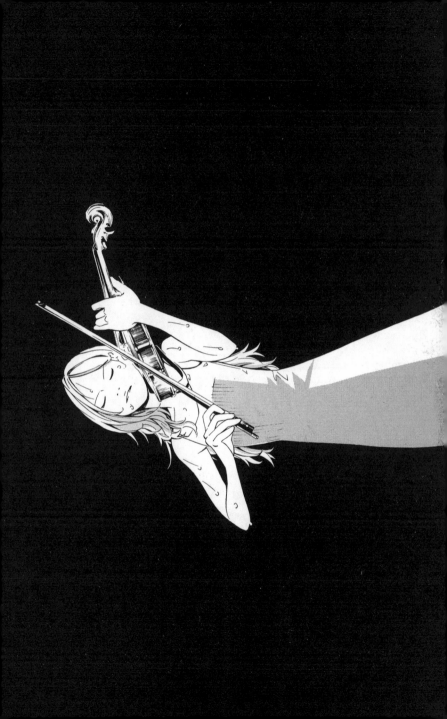

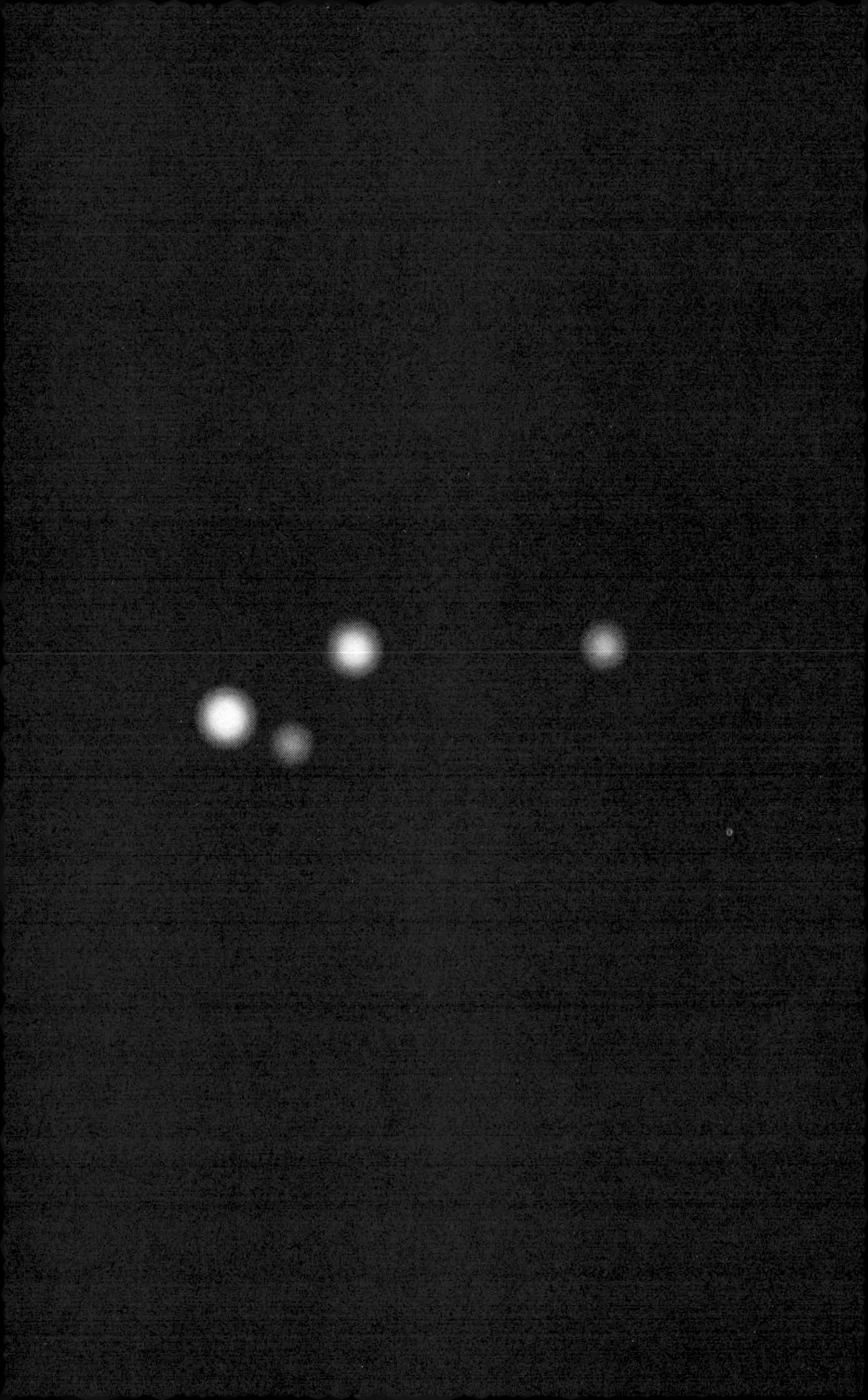

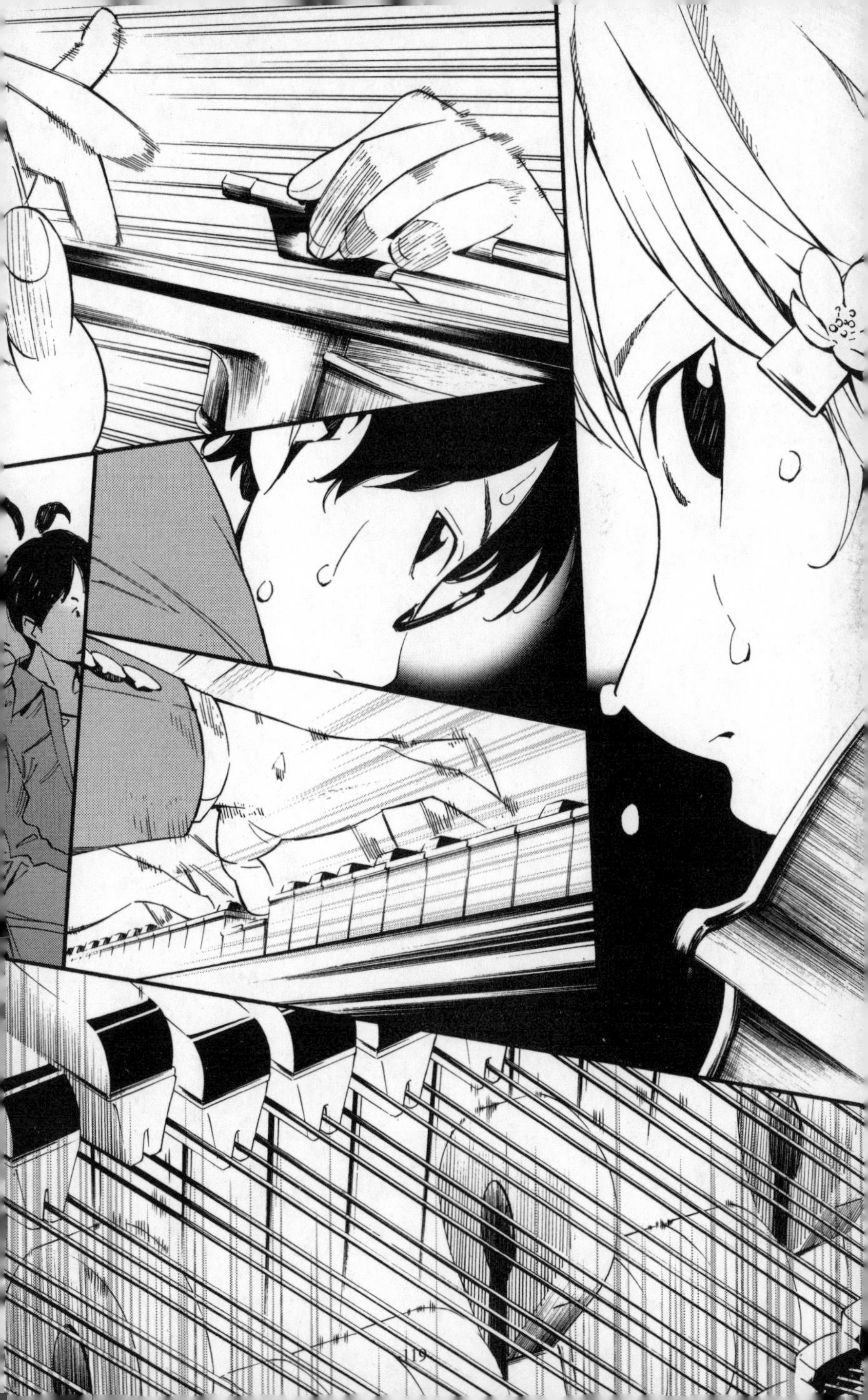

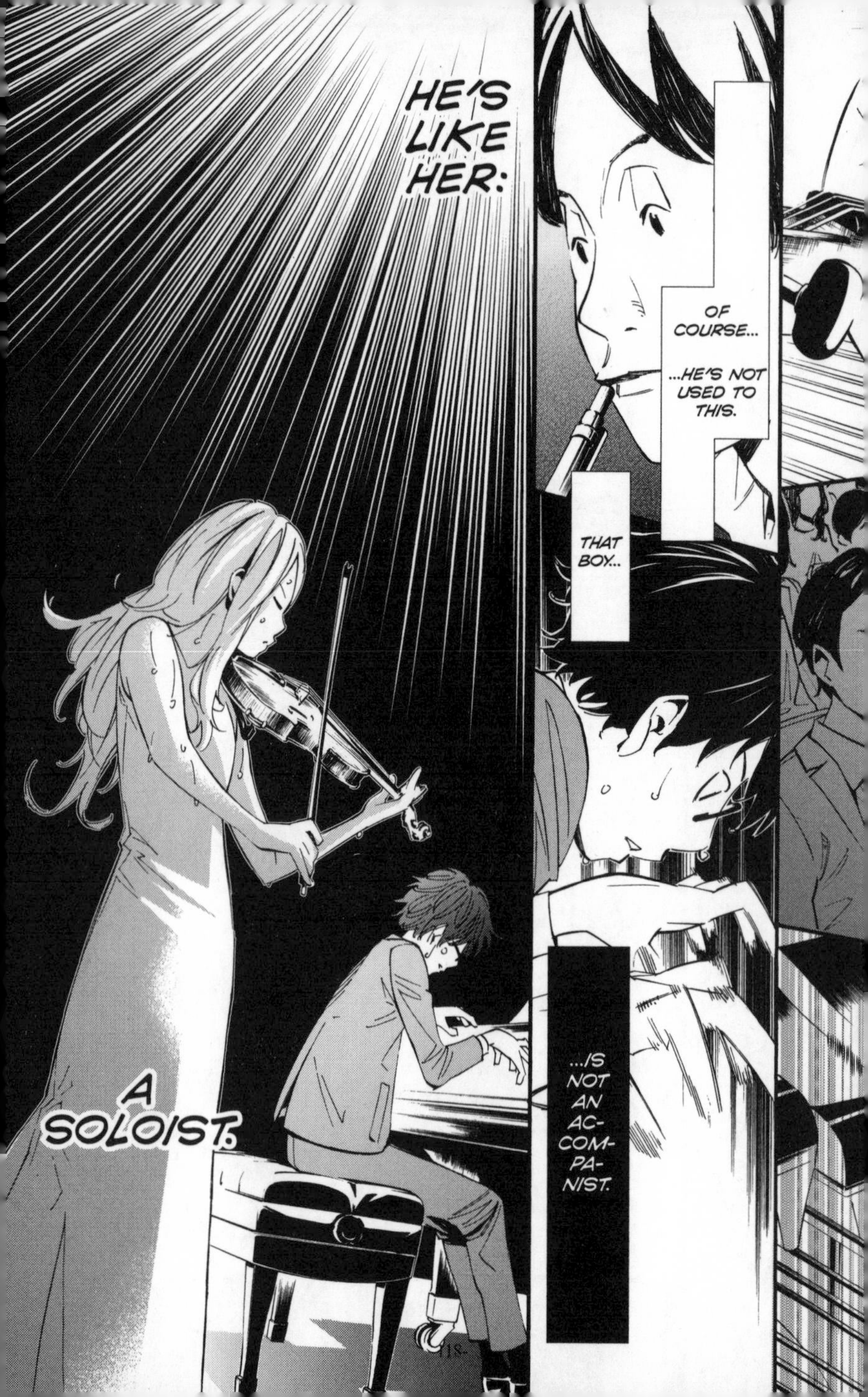
OF COURSE...
...HE'S NOT USED TO THIS.
THAT BOY...
...IS NOT AN AC-COM-PA-NIST.
HE'S LIKE HER:
A SOLOIST.

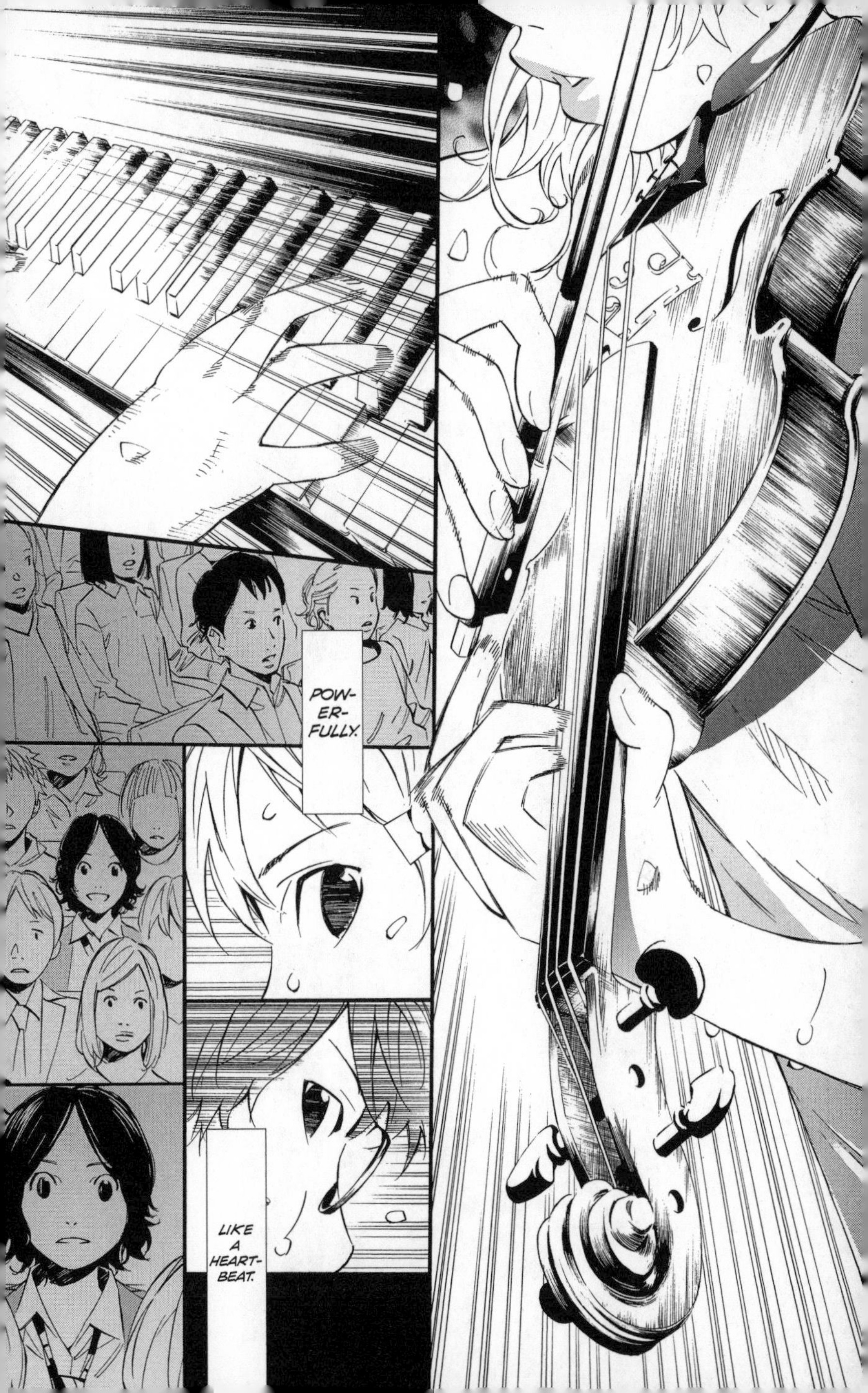
POW-
ER-
FULLY.
LIKE
A
HEART-
BEAT.

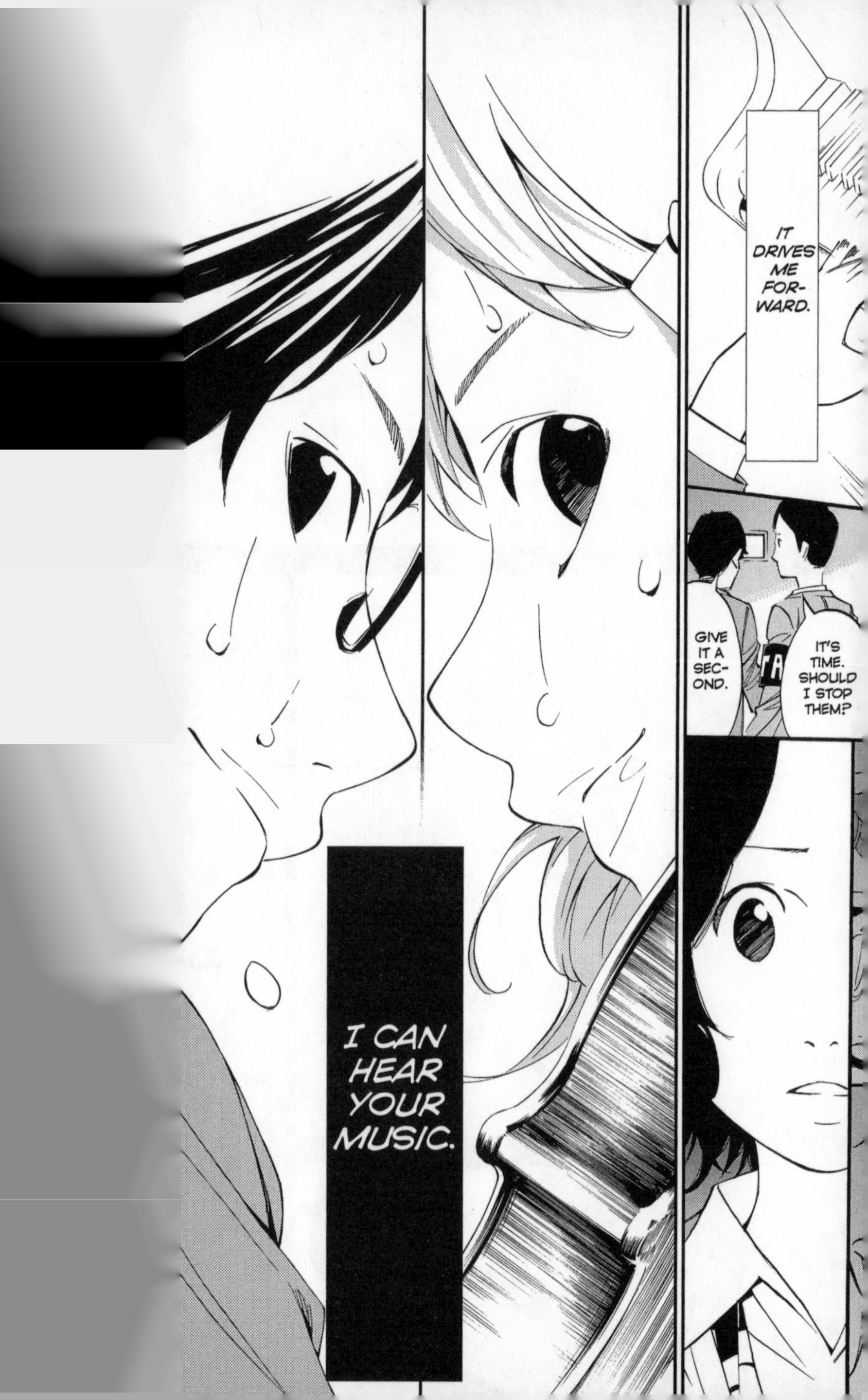
IT DRIVES ME FOR-WARD.
IT'S TIME. SHOULD I STOP THEM?
GIVE IT A SEC-OND.
I CAN HEAR YOUR MUSIC.

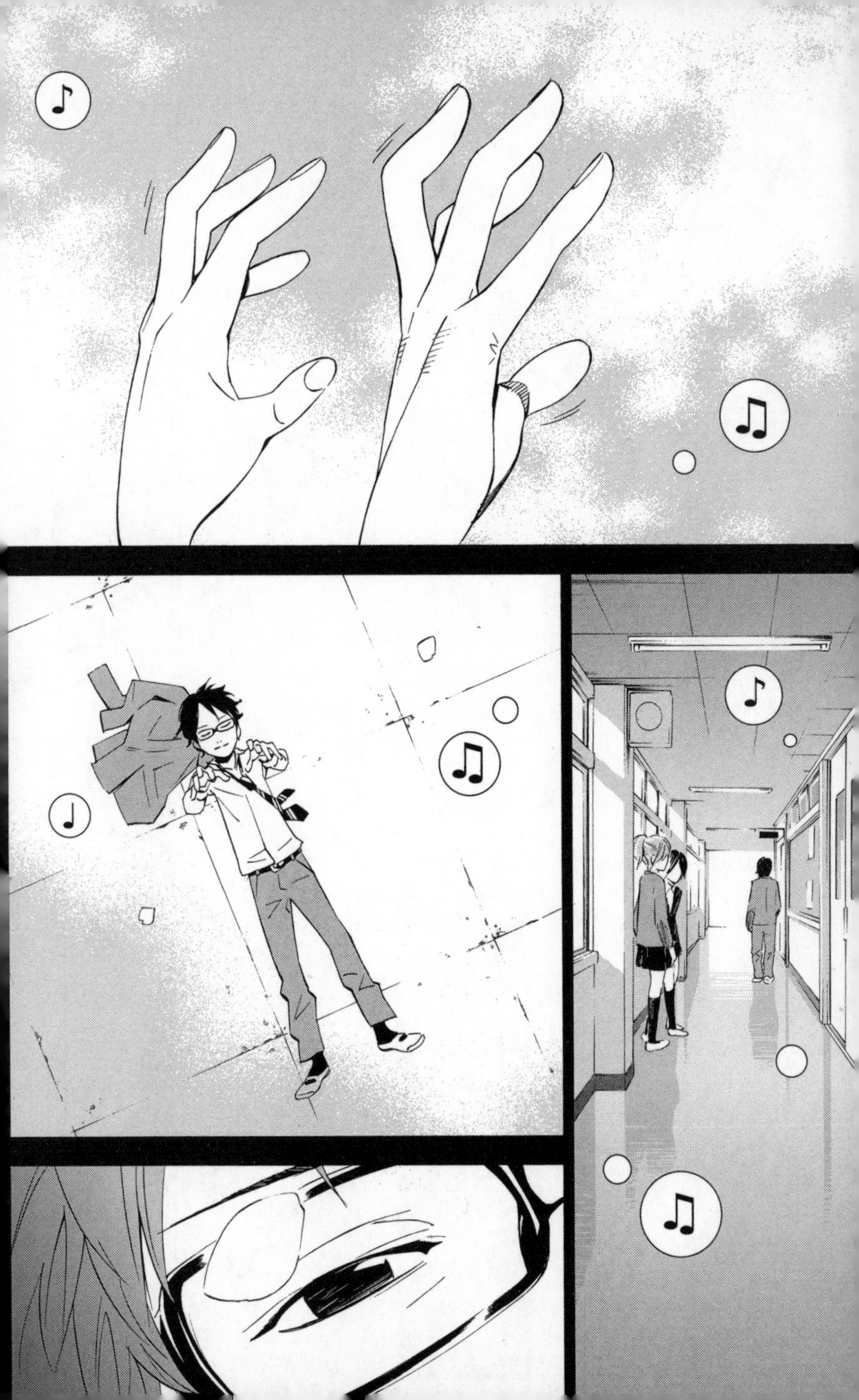

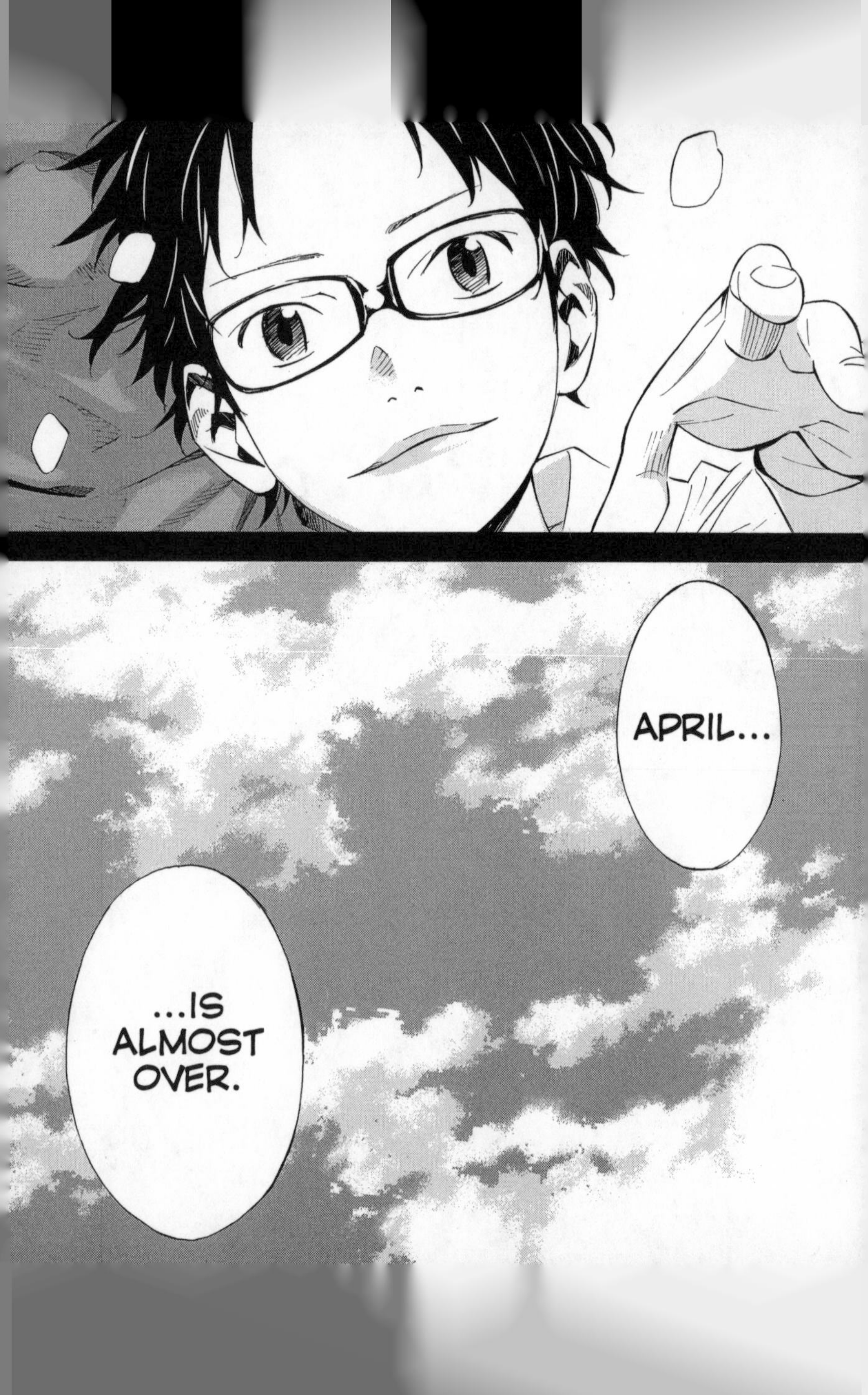
APRIL...
...IS ALMOST OVER.

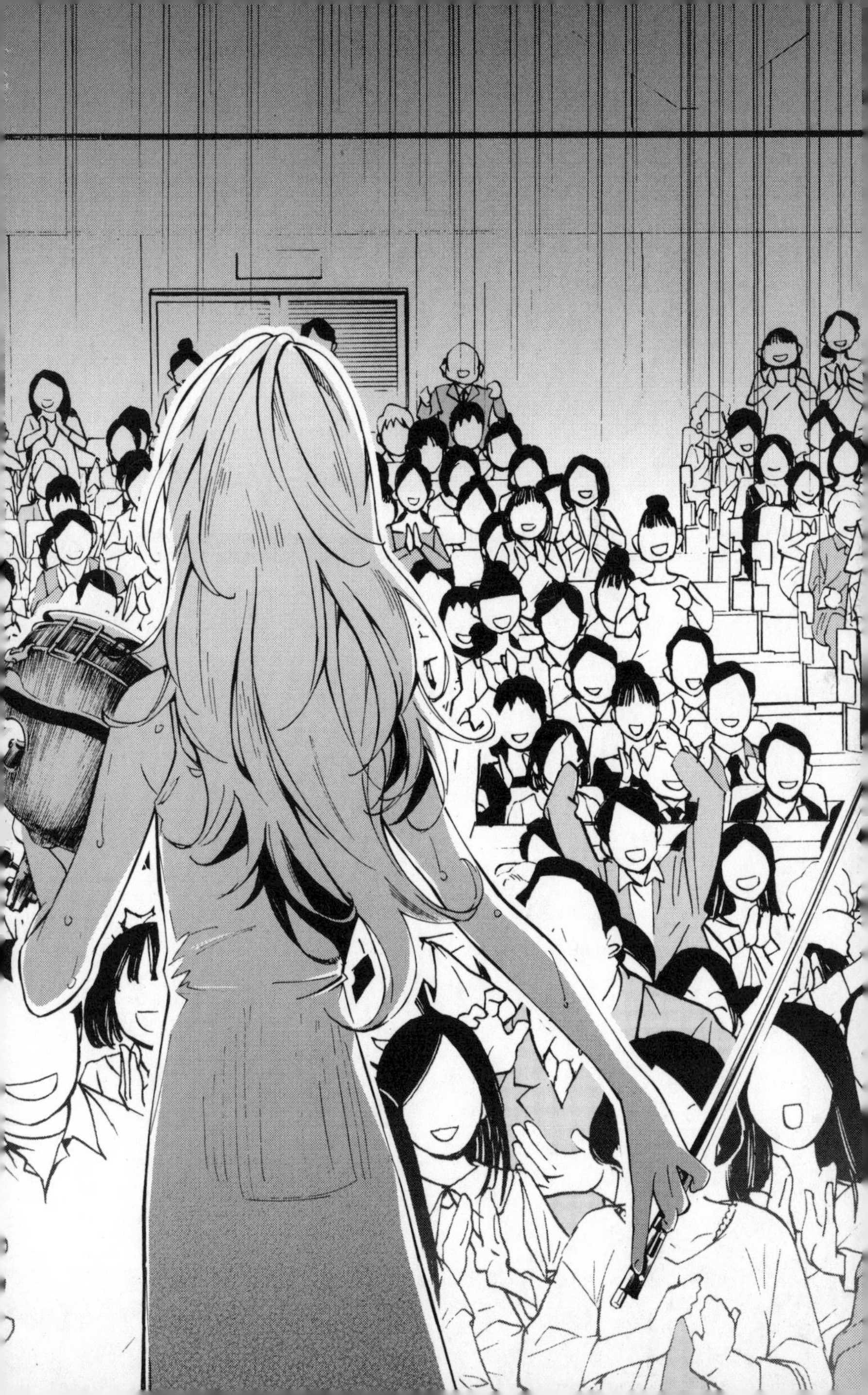

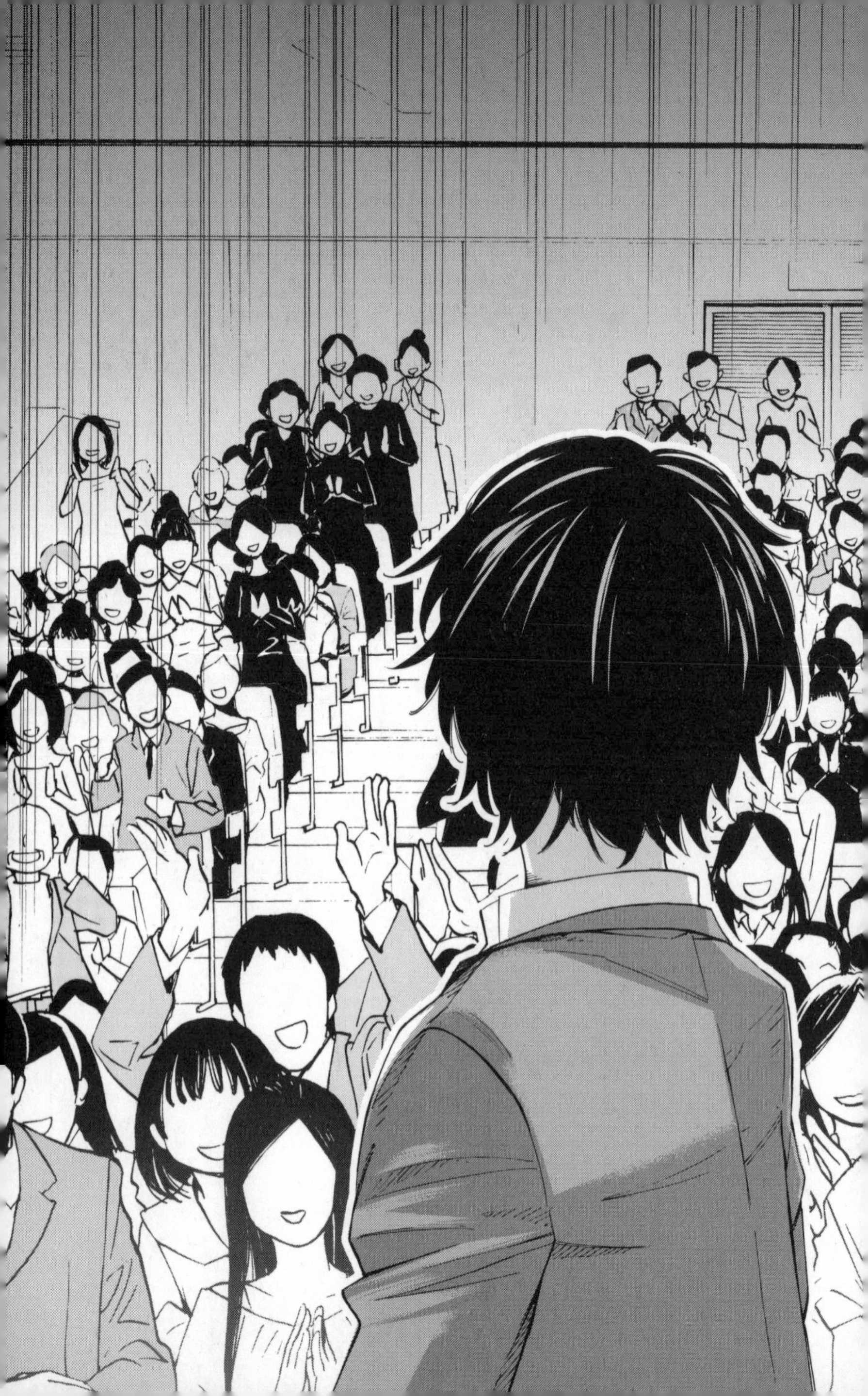

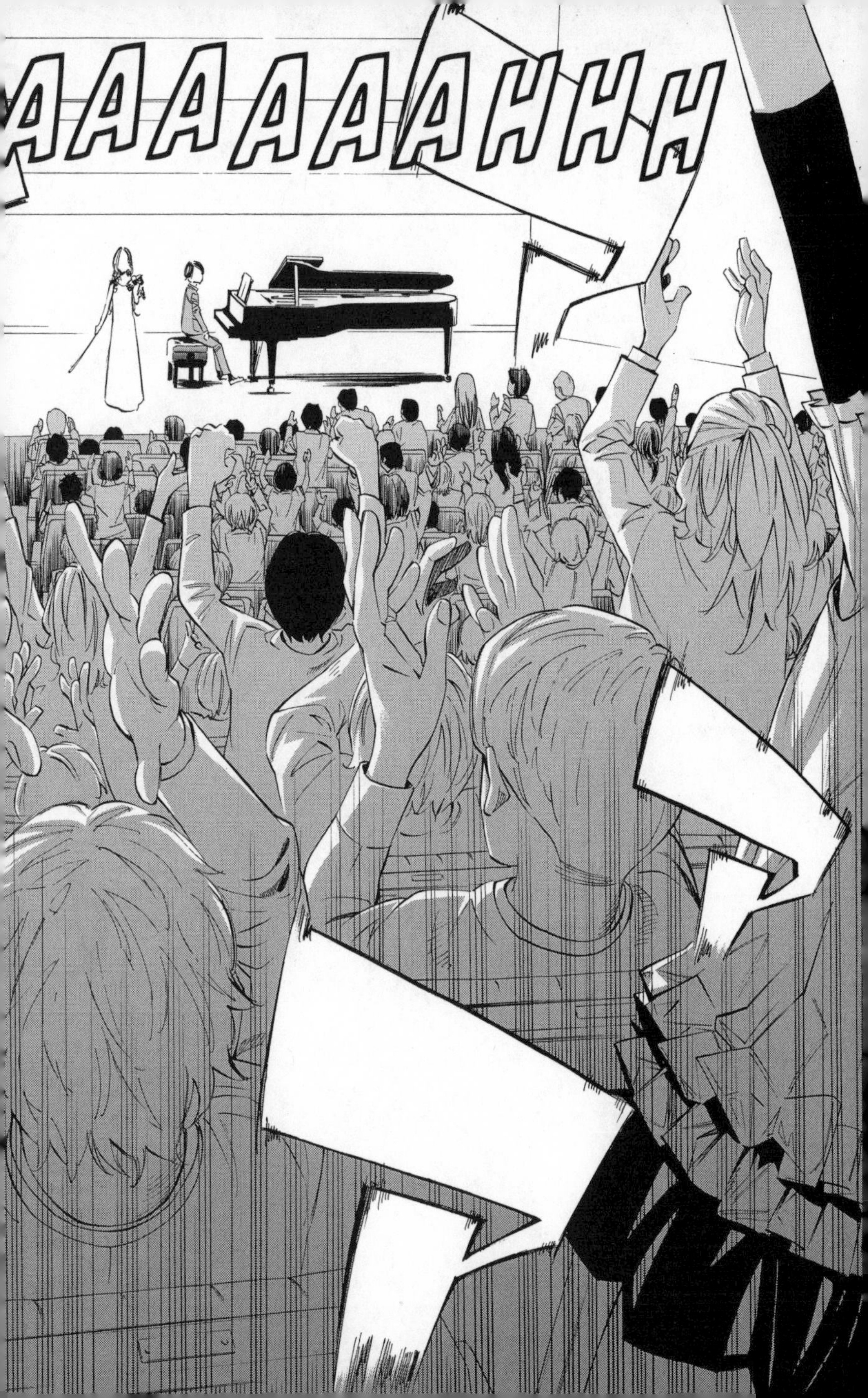
AAAAAAAHHH

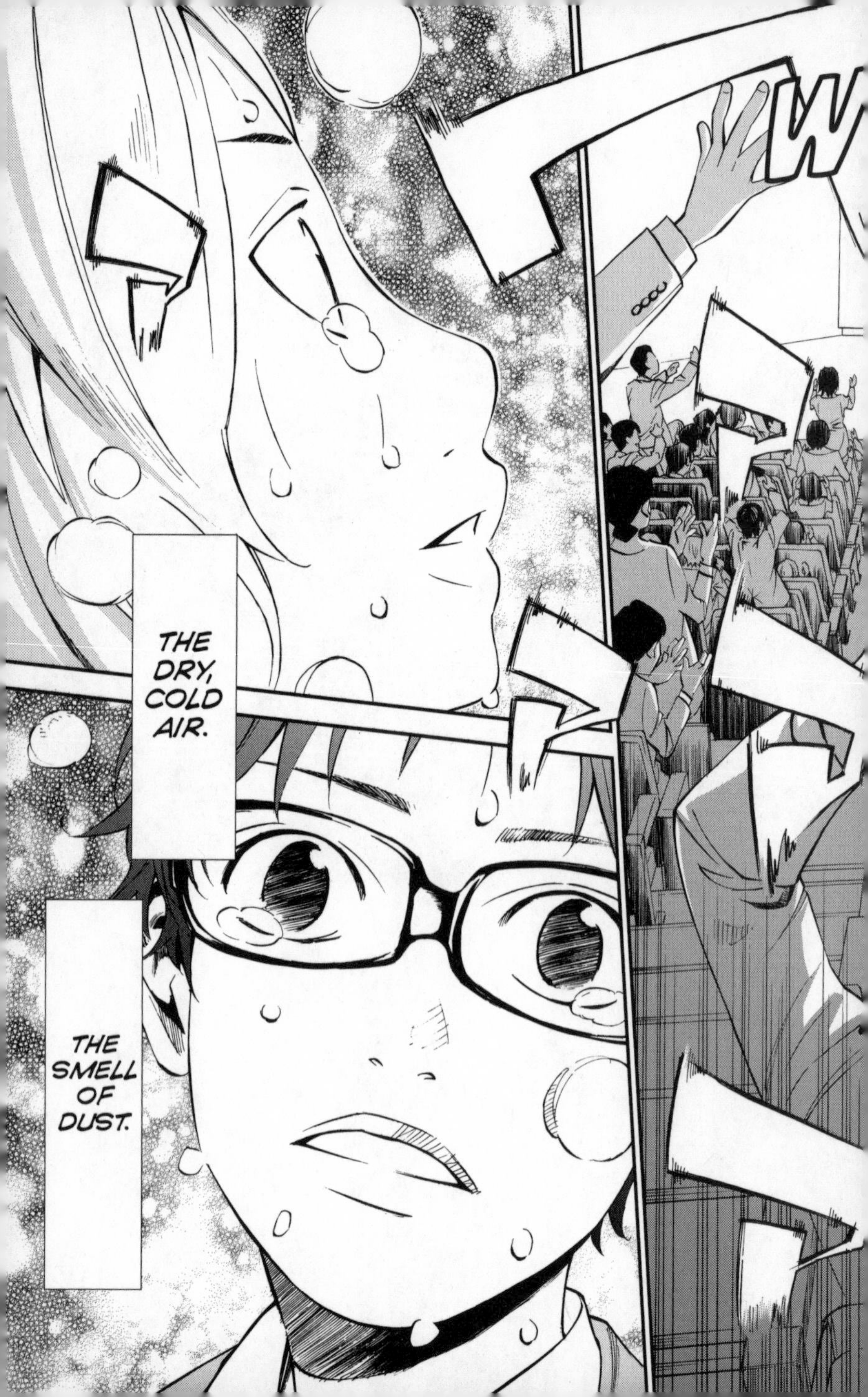
THE DRY, COLD AIR.
THE SMELL OF DUST.

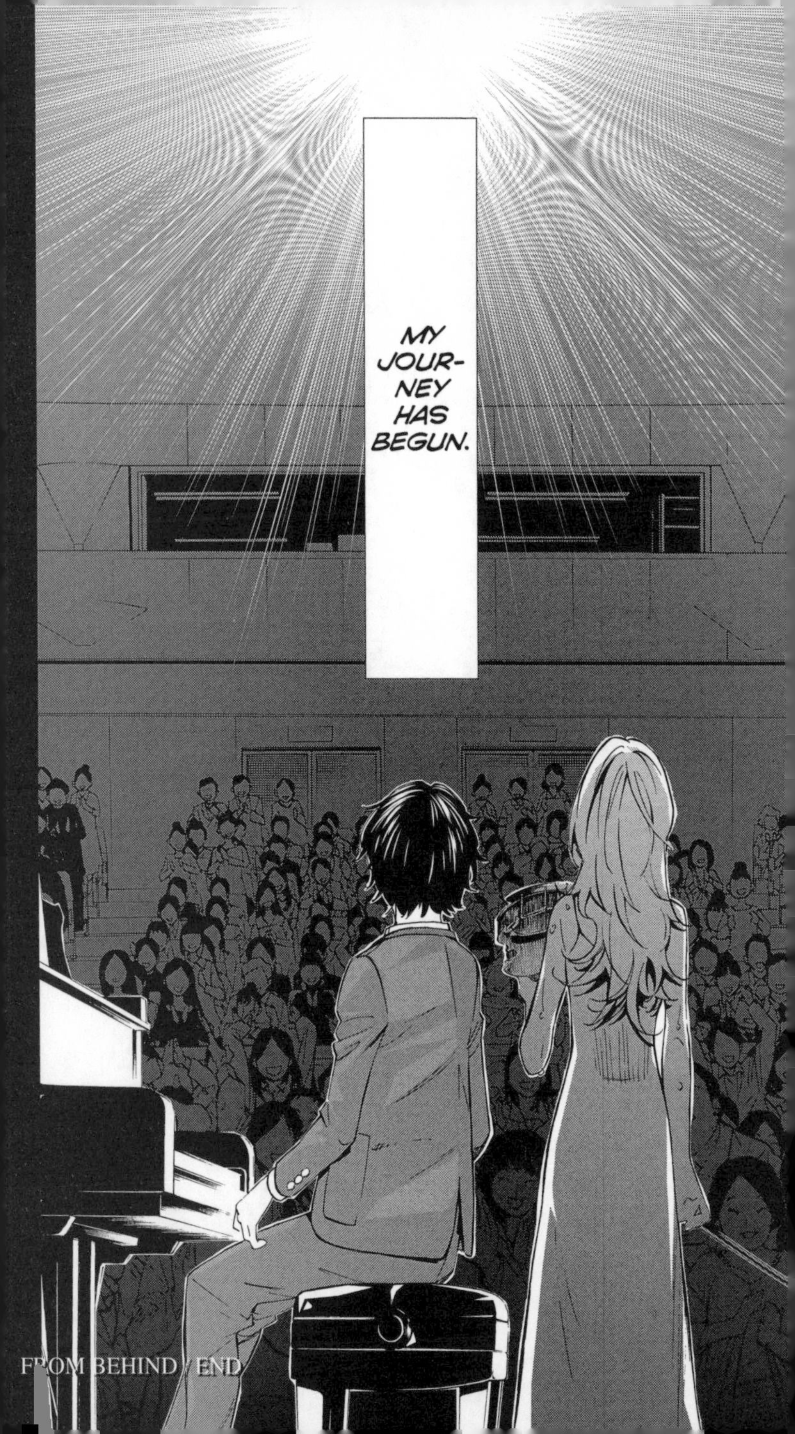
MY JOURNEY HAS BEGUN.
FROM BEHIND / END

YOUR LIE IN APRIL FEATURED MUSIC

SAINT-SAËNS'S INTRODUCTION AND RONDO CAPRICCIOSO

Originally written for violin and orchestra, making it a violin concerto, this piece is eight to nine minutes long. It was dedicated to the great violinist and composer, Pablo de Sarasate (known for his "Zigeunerweisen").

A violinist can show off a wide range of techniques with this piece and express his or her feelings romantically to impress everyone in the audience with its glowing beauty.

Even today, it is still one of Saint-Saëns's most popular pieces.

Watch it on Youtube
(Search for "Kodansha Your Lie in April featured music")

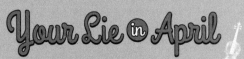

I met the girl under full-bloomed cherry blossoms, and my fate has begun to change.

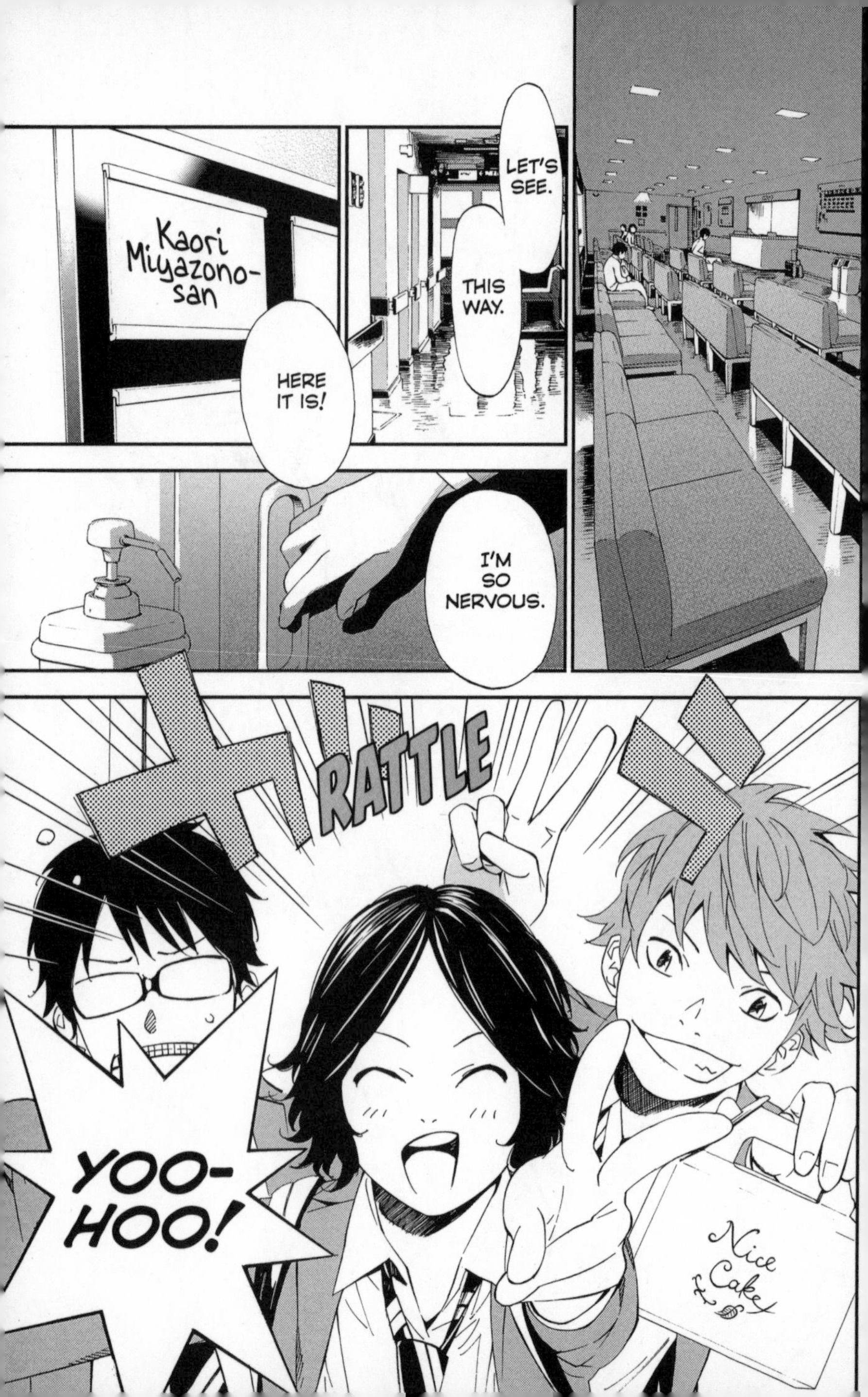
LET'S SEE.
THIS WAY.
Kaori Miyazono-san
HERE IT IS!
I'M SO NERVOUS.
RATTLE
YOO-HOO!
Nice Cake

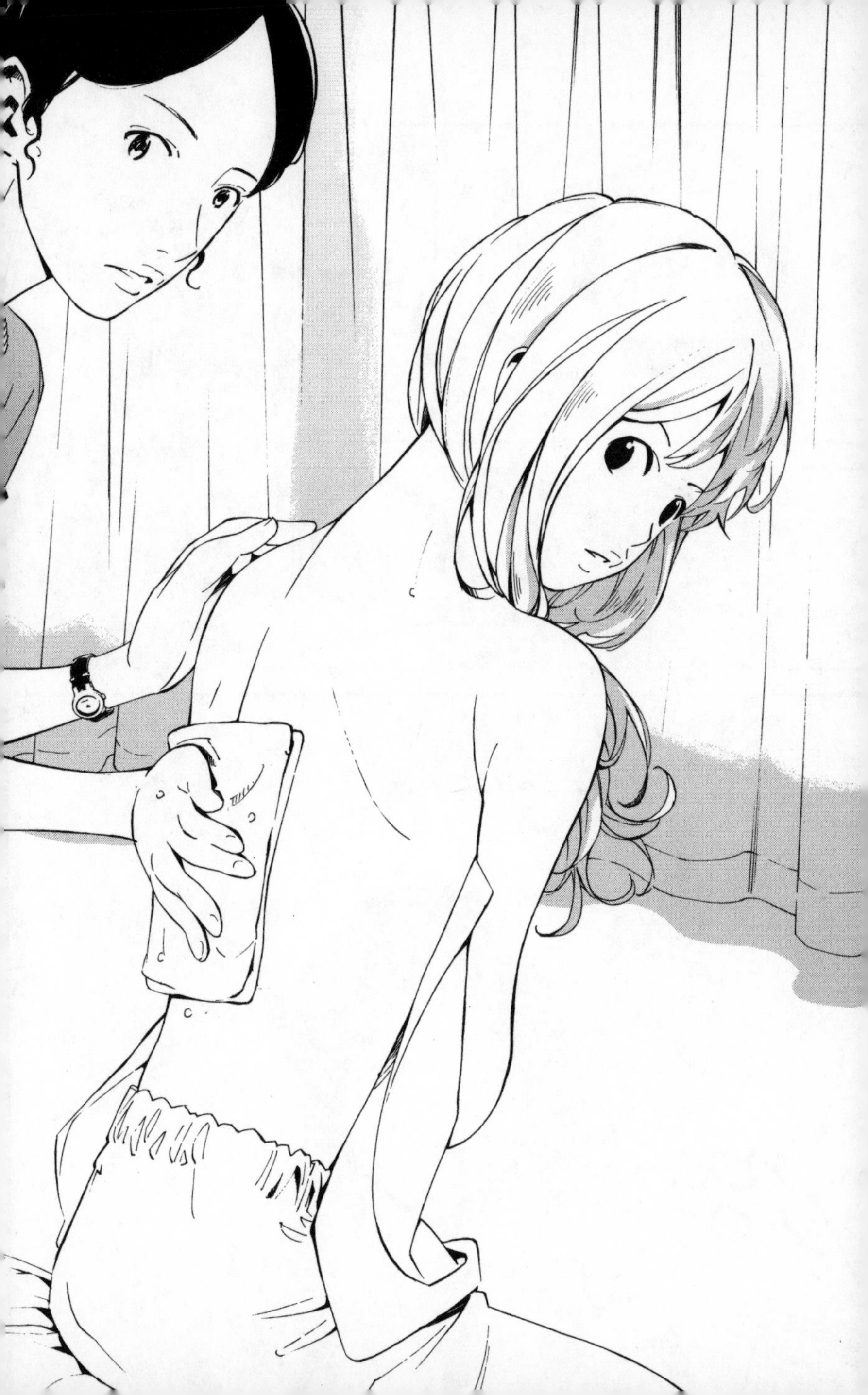

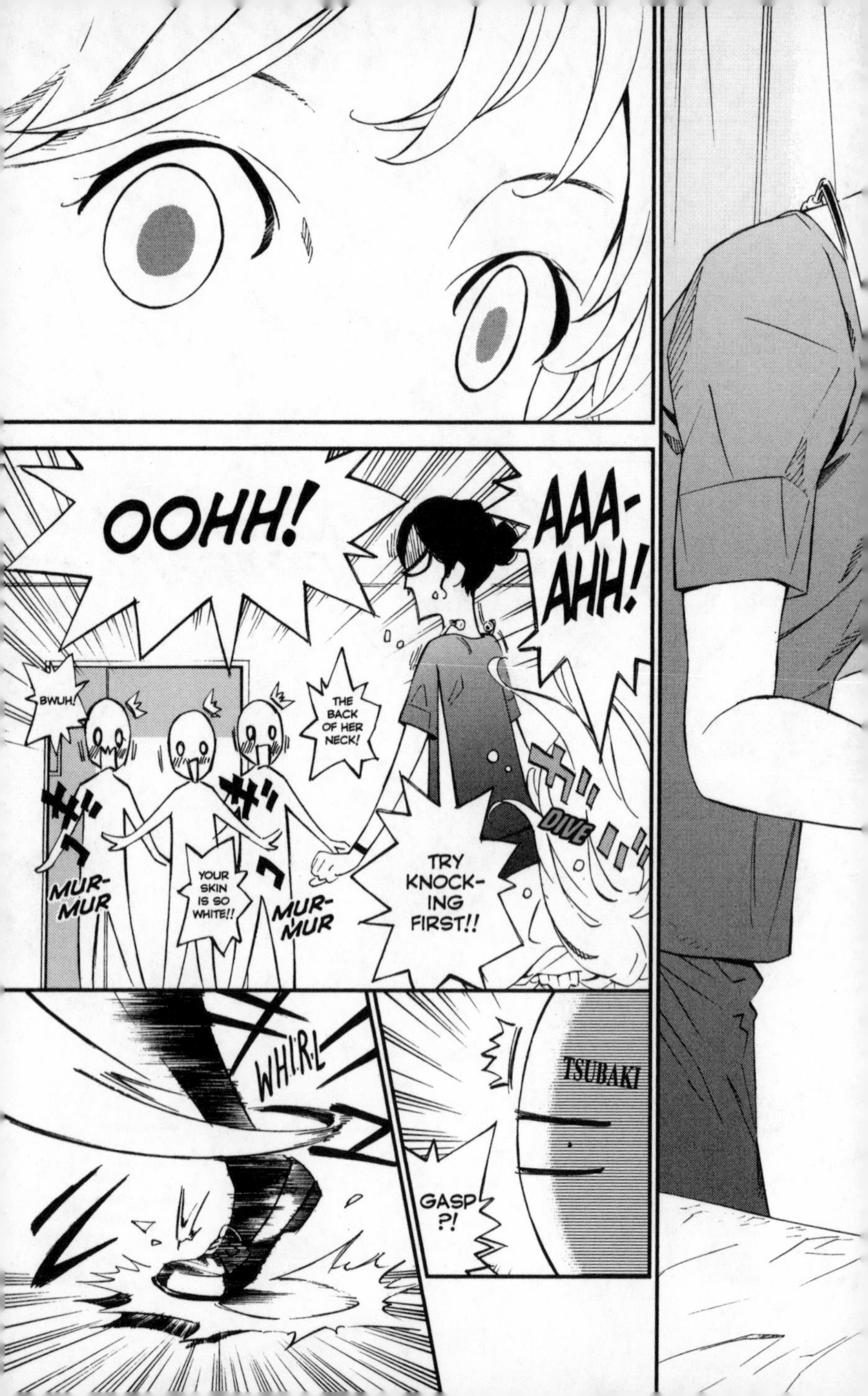
AAA-AHH!
OOHH!
THE BACK OF HER NECK!
BWUH!
DIVE
TRY KNOCKING FIRST!!
YOUR SKIN IS SO WHITE!!
MUR-MUR
MUR-MUR
TSUBAKI
GASP ?!
WHIRL

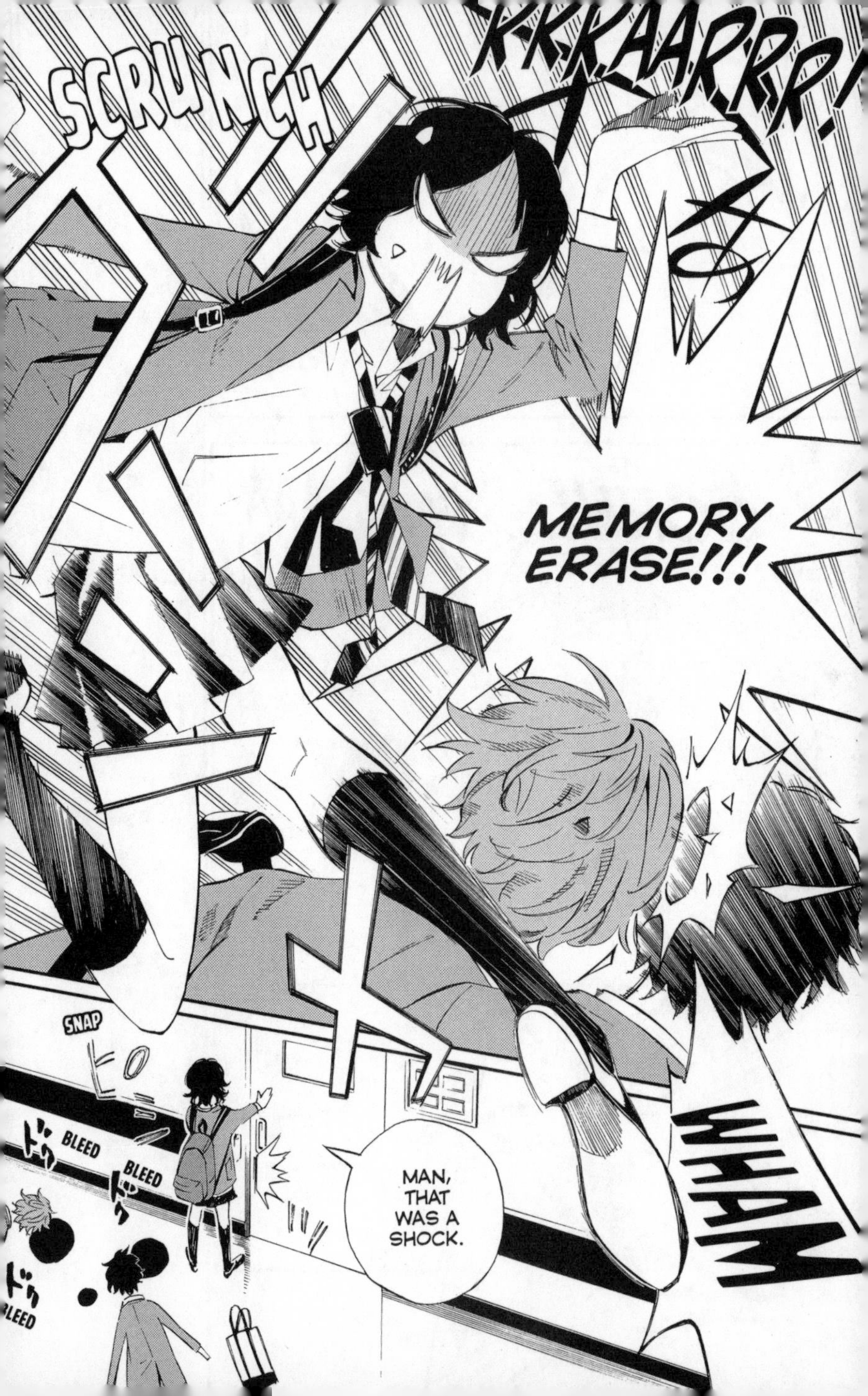

KKKAARRR!
SCRUNCH
MEMORY ERASE!!!
WHAM
MAN, THAT WAS A SHOCK.
SNAP
BLEED
BLEED
BLEED

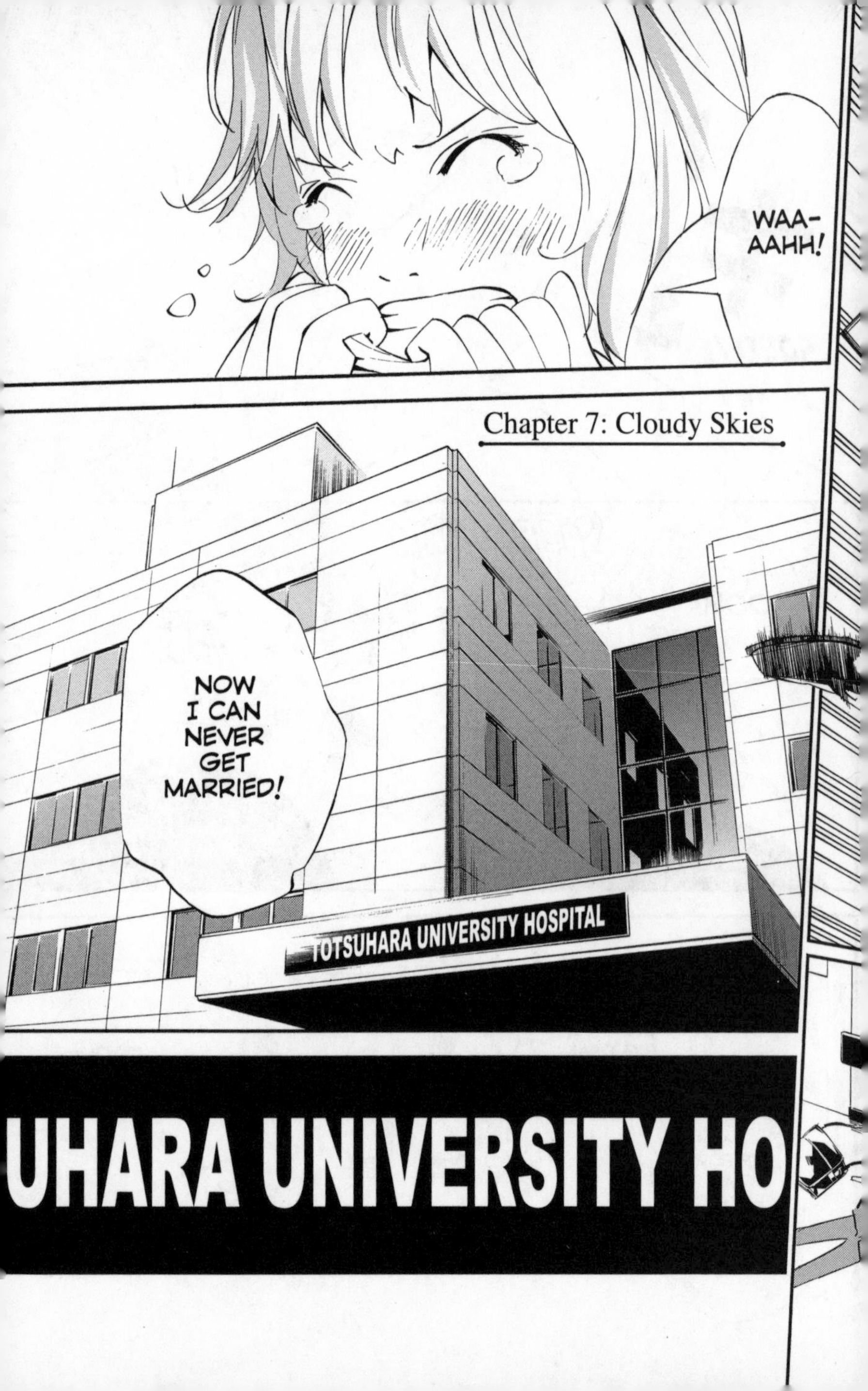
WAA-AAHH!
Chapter 7: Cloudy Skies
NOW I CAN NEVER GET MARRIED!
TOTSUHARA UNIVERSITY HOSPITAL
UHARA UNIVERSITY HO

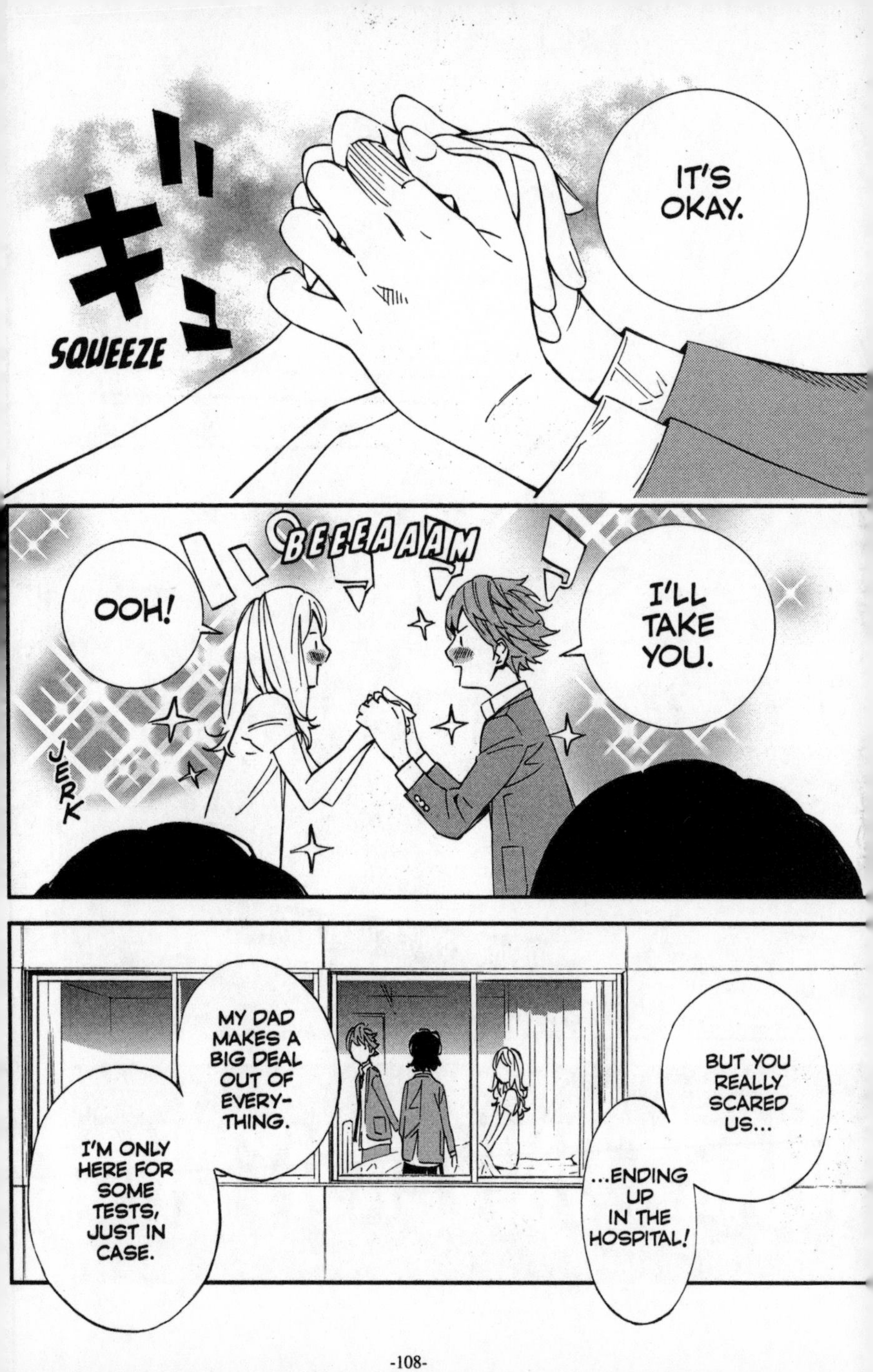
IT'S OKAY.
ギュ
SQUEEZE
I'LL TAKE YOU.
BEEEAAAAM
OOH!
JERK
BUT YOU REALLY SCARED US...
...ENDING UP IN THE HOSPITAL!
MY DAD MAKES A BIG DEAL OUT OF EVERY-THING.
I'M ONLY HERE FOR SOME TESTS, JUST IN CASE.

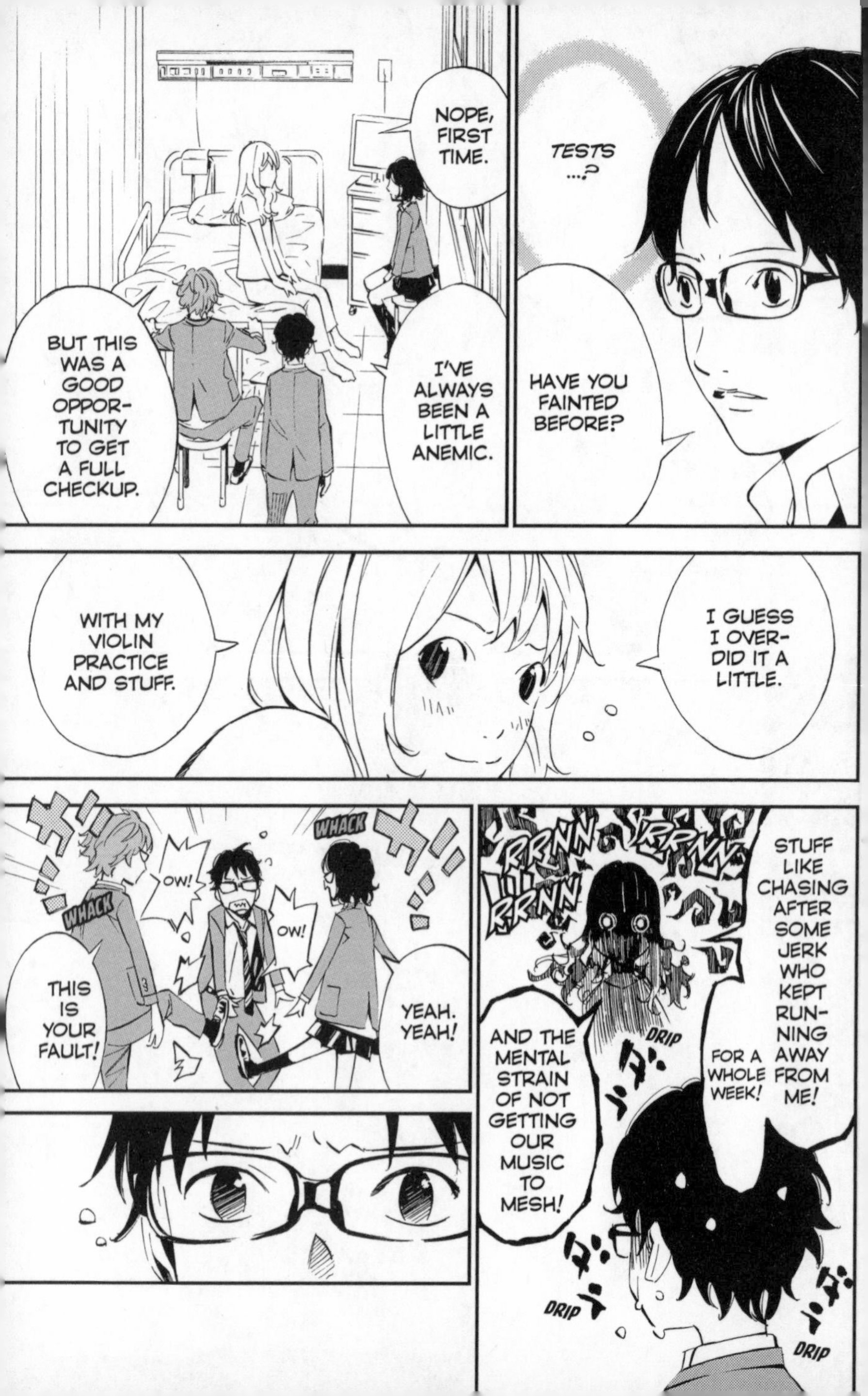
TESTS ...?
HAVE YOU FAINTED BEFORE?
NOPE, FIRST TIME.
I'VE ALWAYS BEEN A LITTLE ANEMIC.
BUT THIS WAS A GOOD OPPORTUNITY TO GET A FULL CHECKUP.
I GUESS I OVERDID IT A LITTLE.
WITH MY VIOLIN PRACTICE AND STUFF.
RRNN RRNN RRNN
STUFF LIKE CHASING AFTER SOME JERK WHO KEPT RUNNING AWAY FROM ME!
FOR A WHOLE WEEK!
AND THE MENTAL STRAIN OF NOT GETTING OUR MUSIC TO MESH!
DRIP
DRIP
DRIP
WHACK
WHACK
OW!
OW!
THIS IS YOUR FAULT!
YEAH. YEAH!

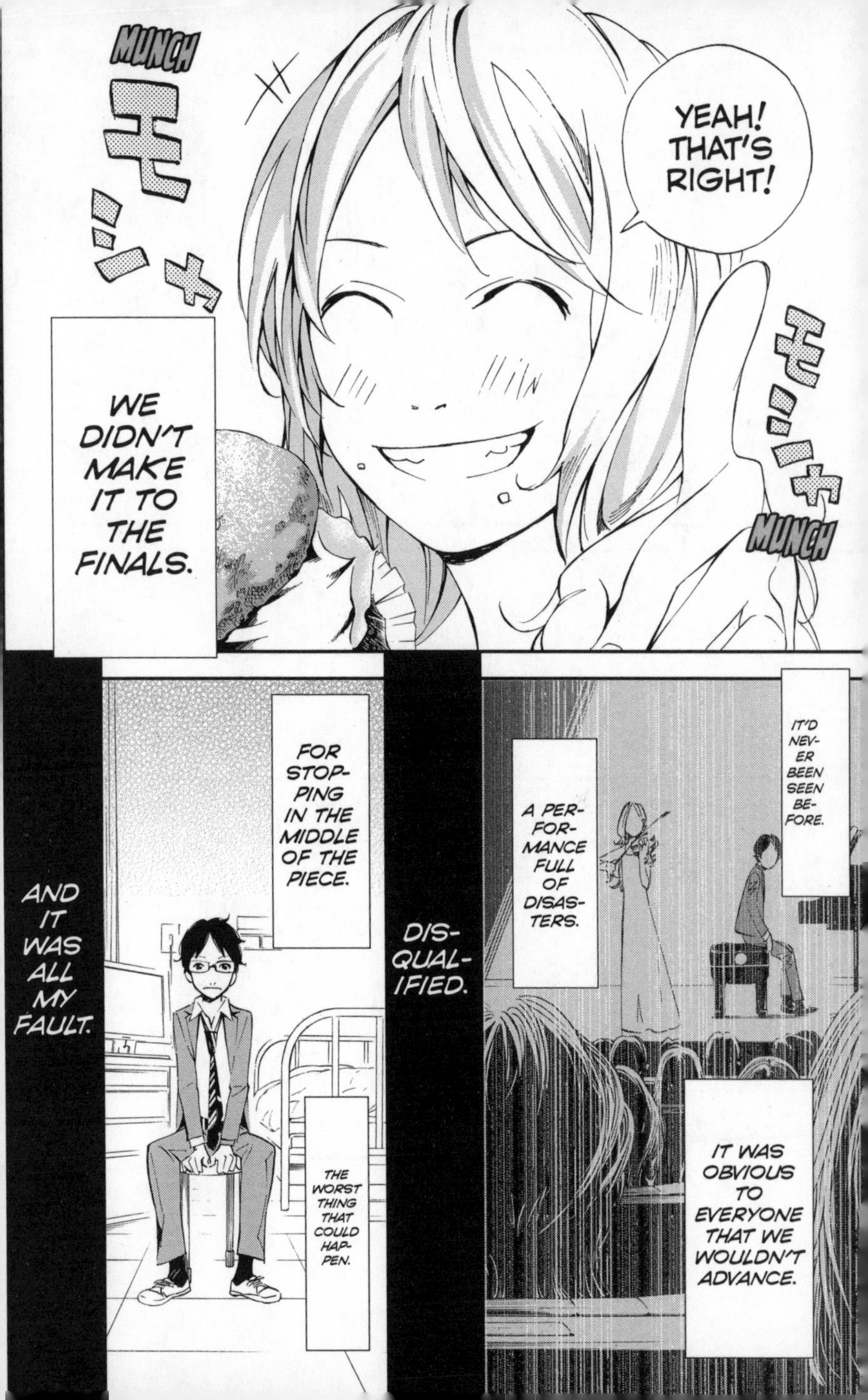
YEAH! THAT'S RIGHT!
MUNCH
MUNCH
WE DIDN'T MAKE IT TO THE FINALS.
IT'D NEVER BEEN SEEN BEFORE.
A PERFORMANCE FULL OF DISASTERS.
IT WAS OBVIOUS TO EVERYONE THAT WE WOULDN'T ADVANCE.
DISQUALIFIED.
FOR STOPPING IN THE MIDDLE OF THE PIECE.
THE WORST THING THAT COULD HAPPEN.
AND IT WAS ALL MY FAULT.

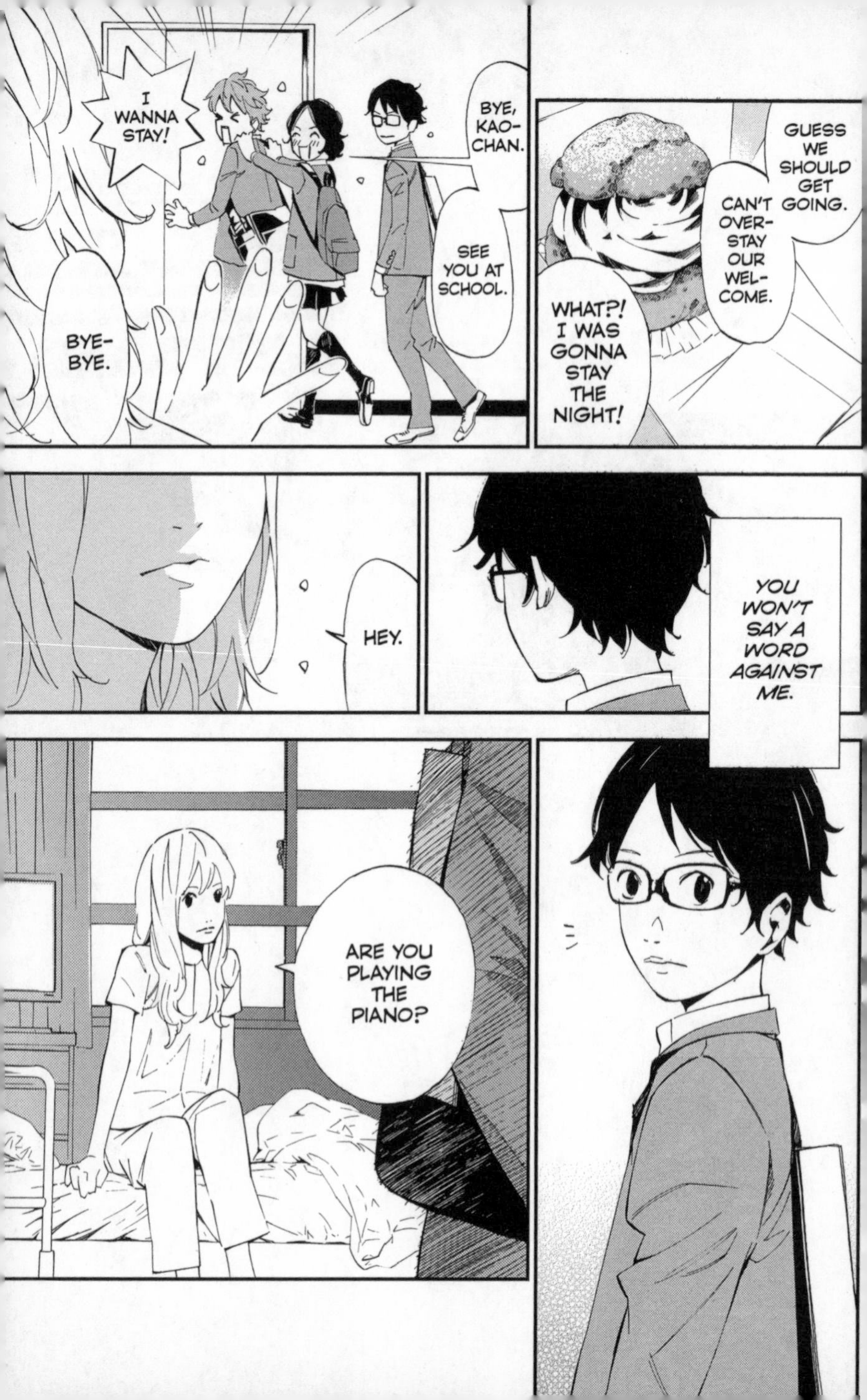
GUESS WE SHOULD GET GOING.
CAN'T OVERSTAY OUR WELCOME.
WHAT?! I WAS GONNA STAY THE NIGHT!
BYE, KAO-CHAN.
SEE YOU AT SCHOOL.
I WANNA STAY!
BYE-BYE.
YOU WON'T SAY A WORD AGAINST ME.
HEY.
ARE YOU PLAYING THE PIANO?

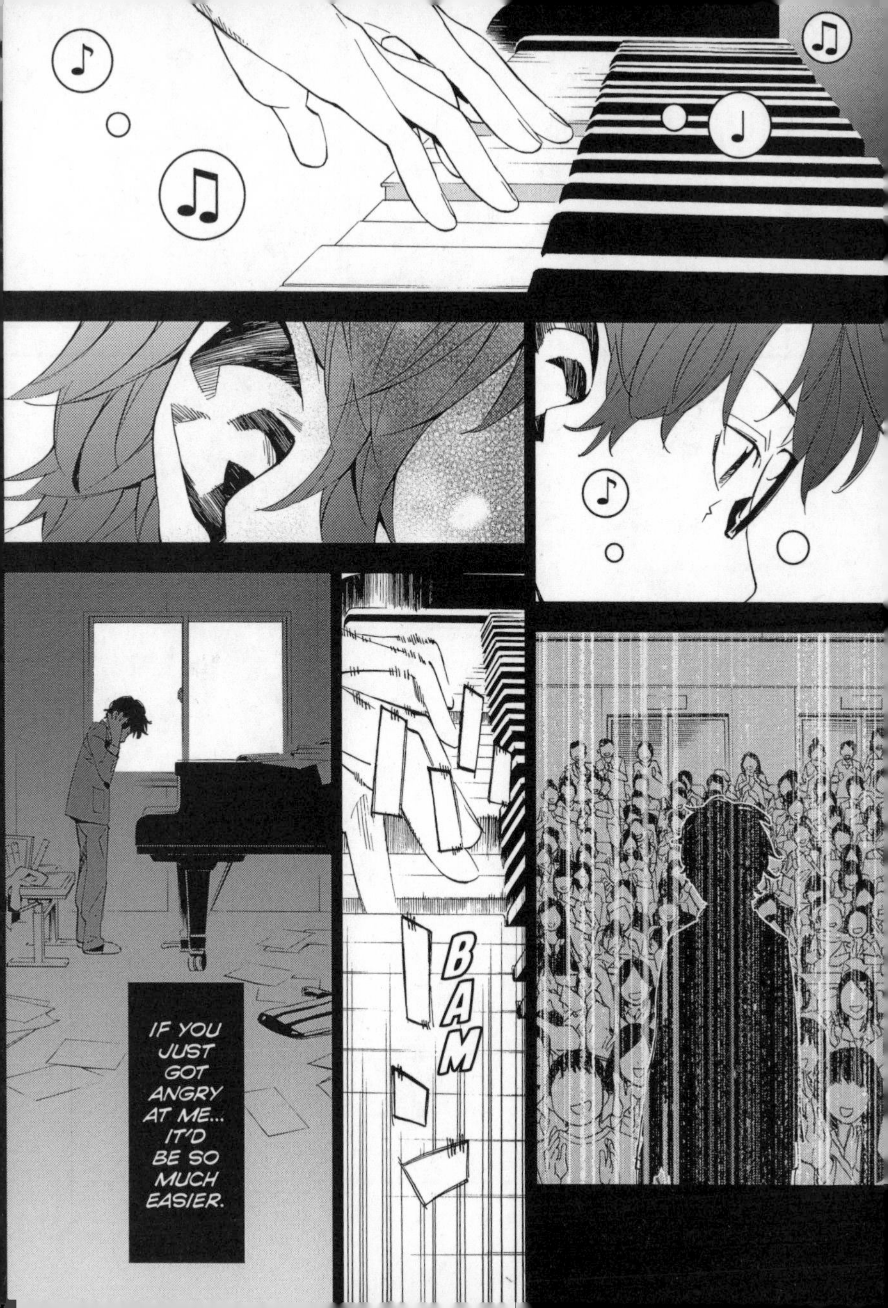
BAM
IF YOU JUST GOT ANGRY AT ME... IT'D BE SO MUCH EASIER.

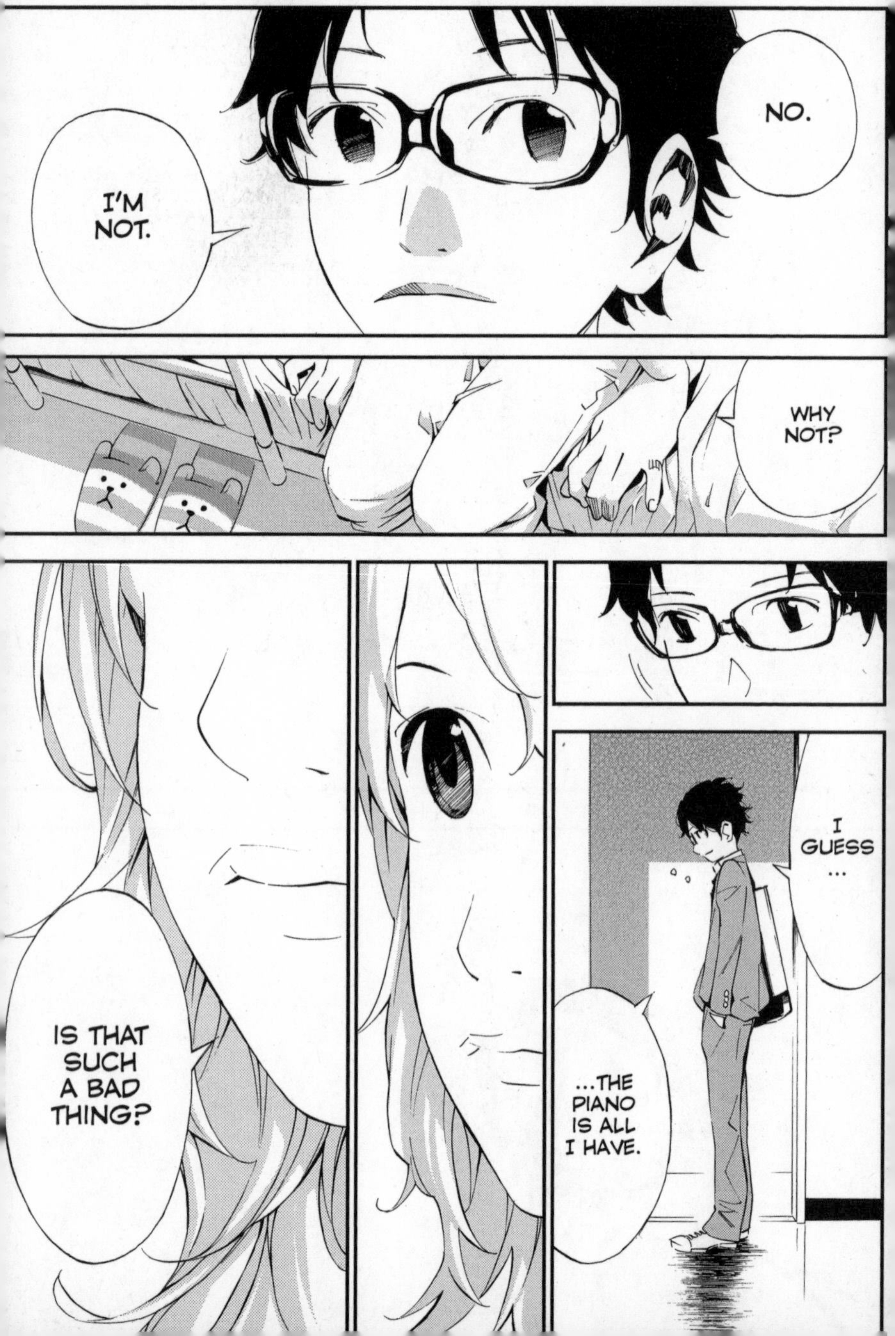
NO.
I'M NOT.
WHY NOT?
I GUESS ...
...THE PIANO IS ALL I HAVE.
IS THAT SUCH A BAD THING?

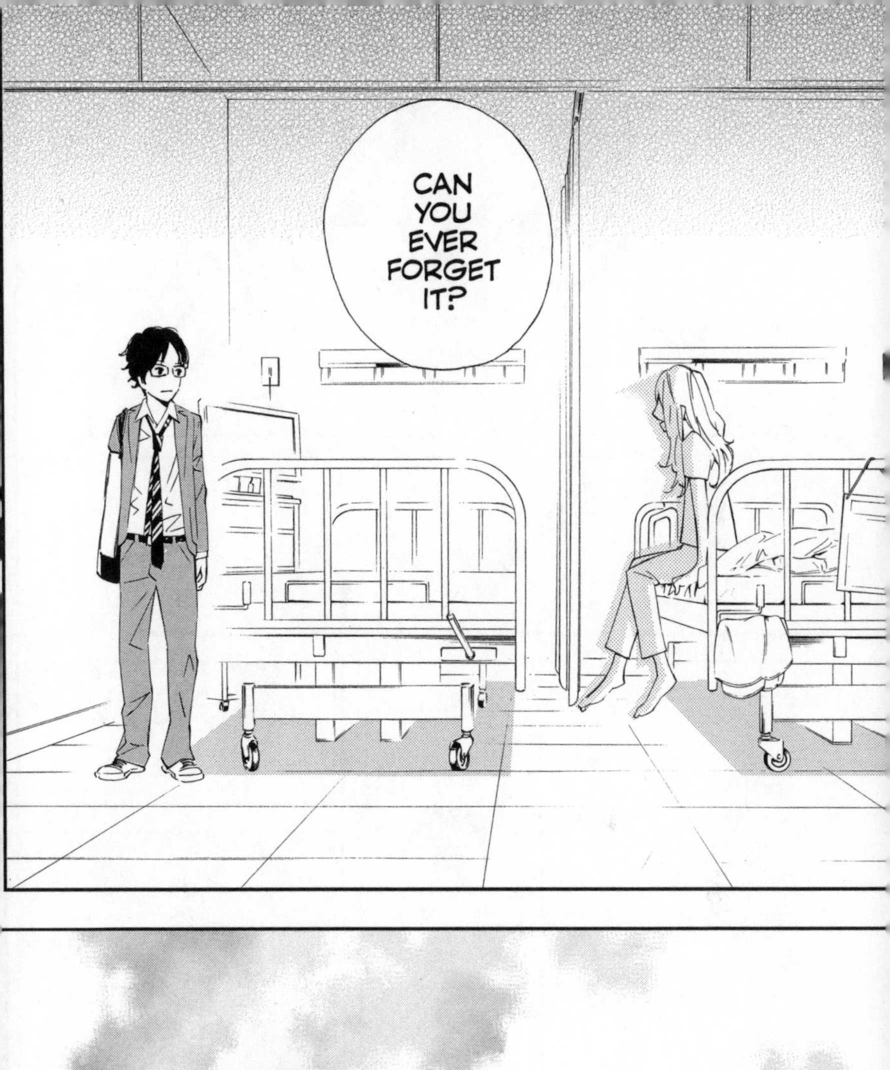
CAN YOU EVER FORGET IT?
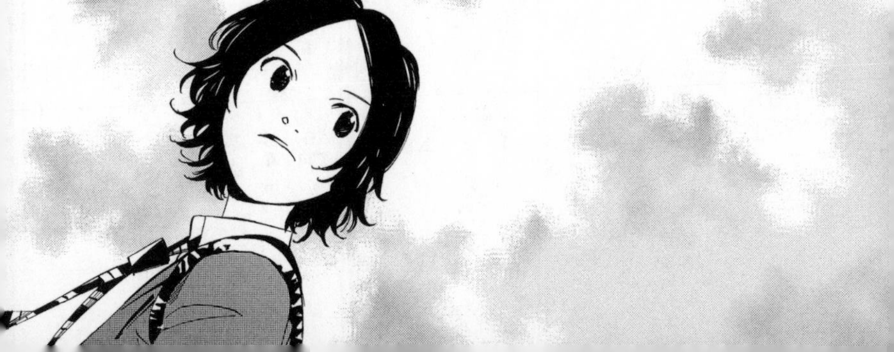

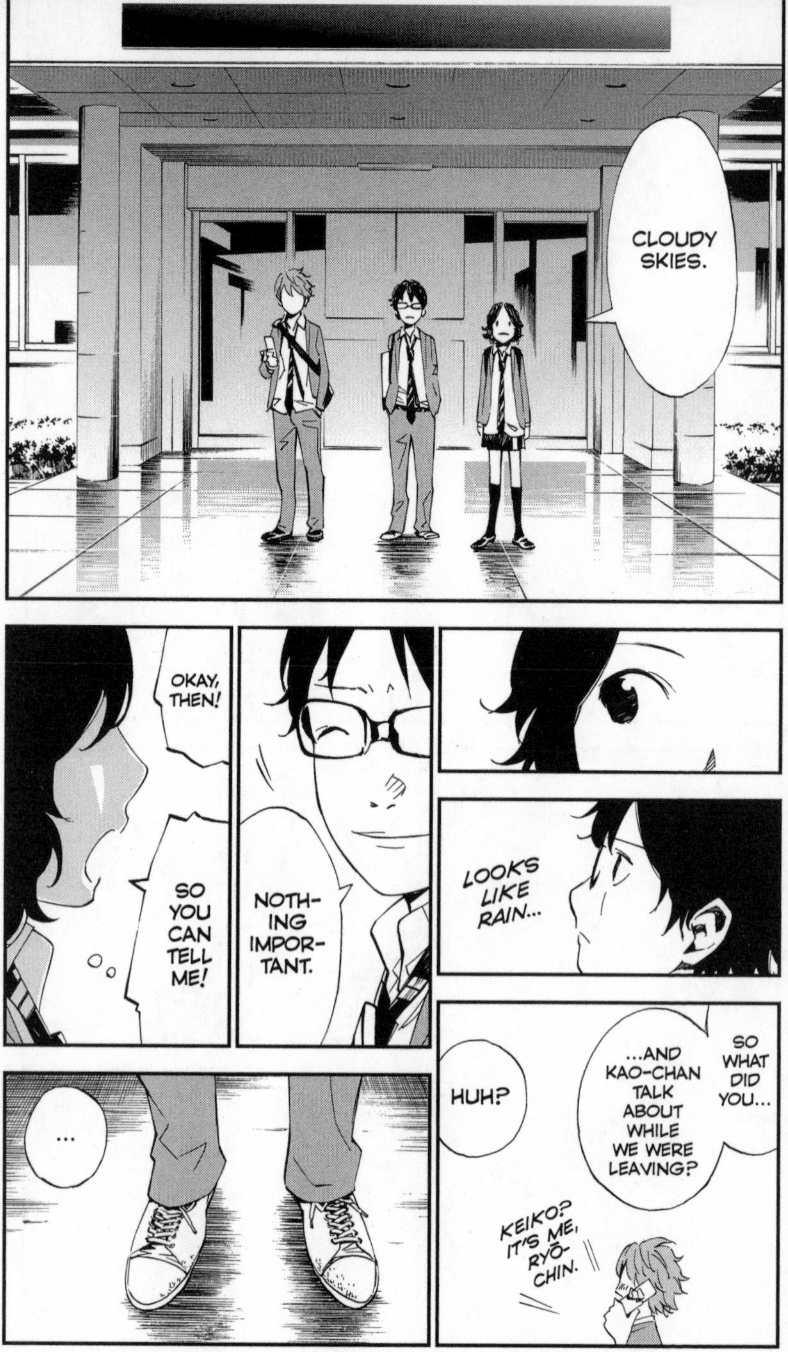
CLOUDY SKIES.
LOOKS LIKE RAIN...
NOTH-ING IMPOR-TANT.
OKAY, THEN!
SO YOU CAN TELL ME!
SO WHAT DID YOU...
...AND KAO-CHAN TALK ABOUT WHILE WE WERE LEAVING?
HUH?
KEIKO? IT'S ME, RYŌ-CHIN.
...

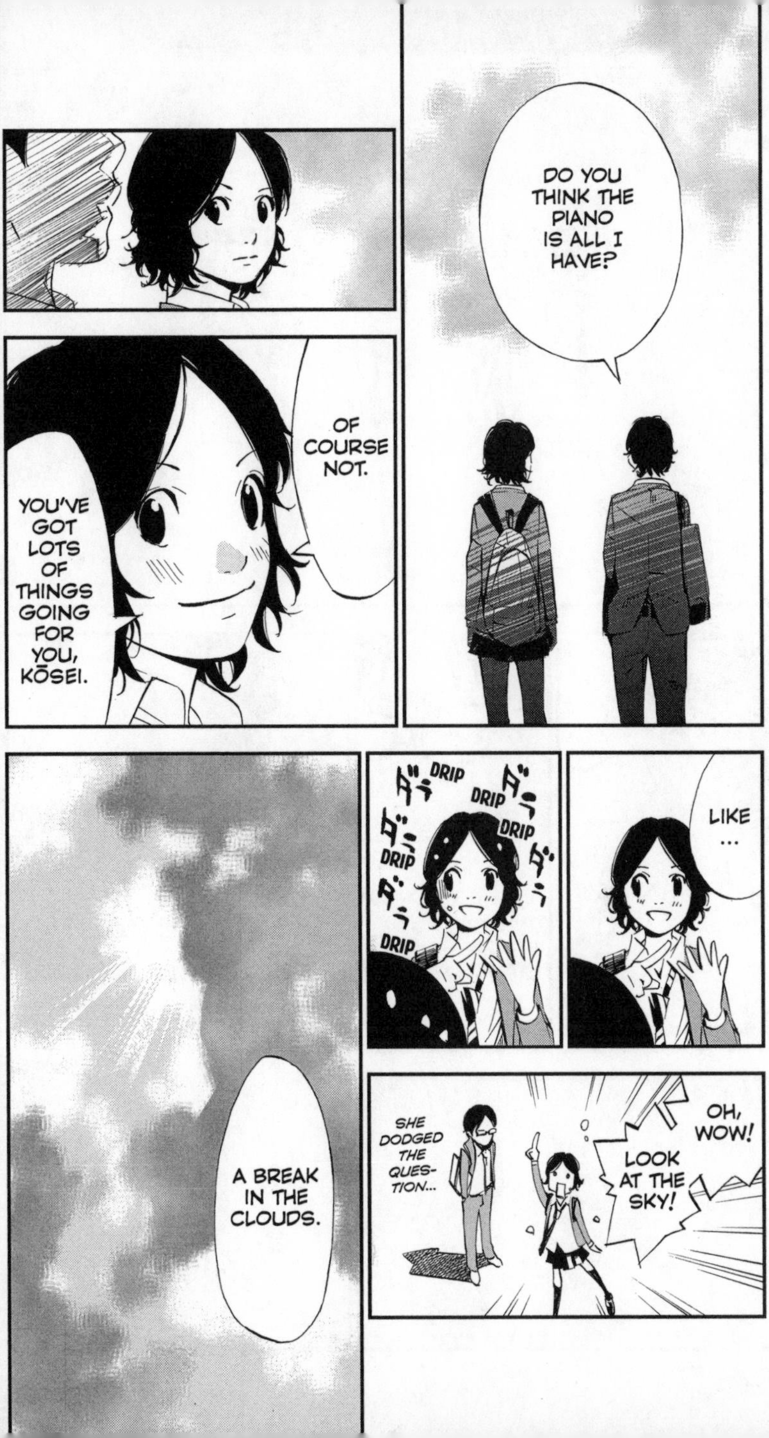
DO YOU THINK THE PIANO IS ALL I HAVE?
OF COURSE NOT.
YOU'VE GOT LOTS OF THINGS GOING FOR YOU, KŌSEI.
LIKE ...
DRIP
DRIP
DRIP
DRIP
DRIP
OH, WOW!
LOOK AT THE SKY!
SHE DODGED THE QUES-TION...
A BREAK IN THE CLOUDS.

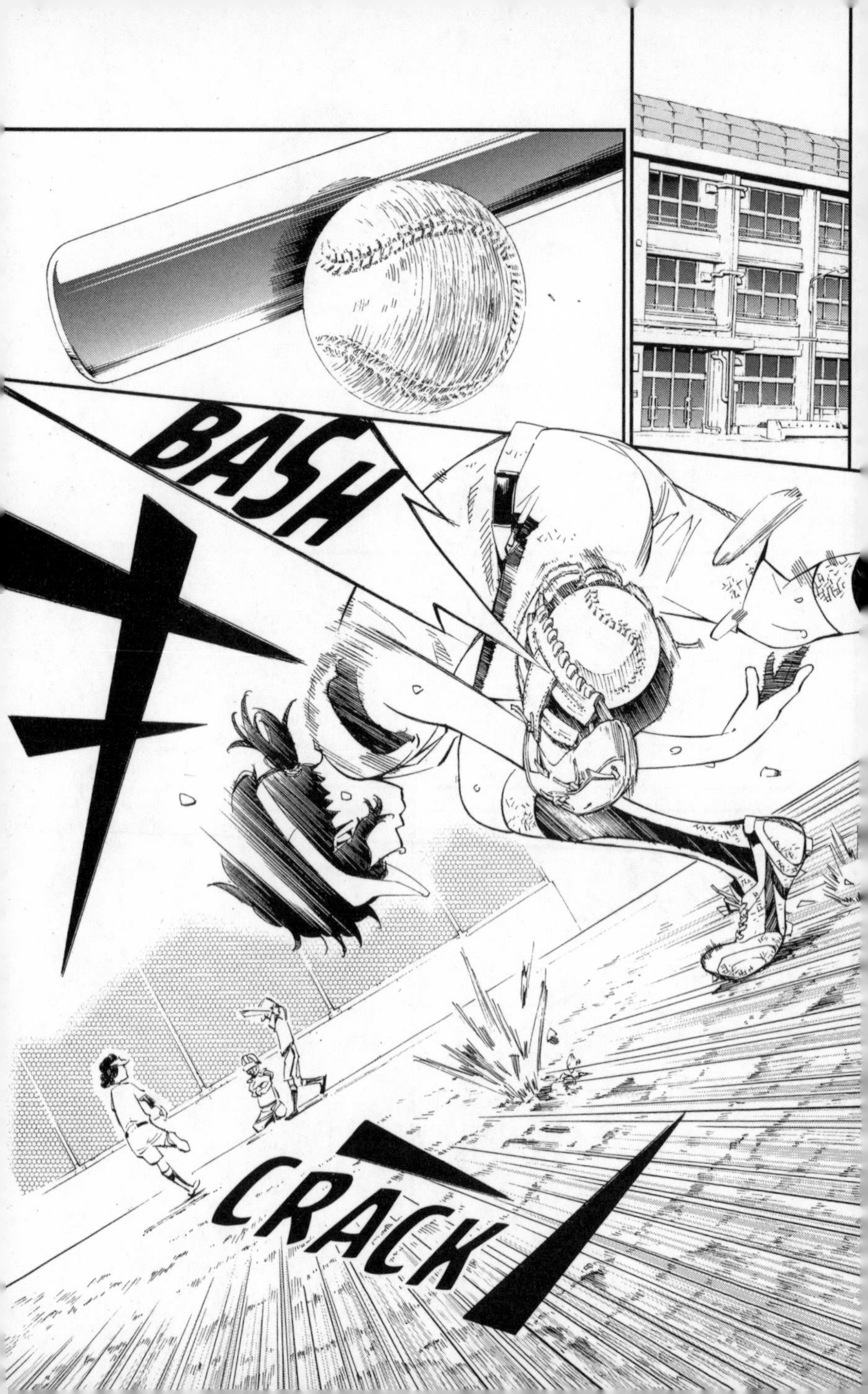
BASH
CRACK

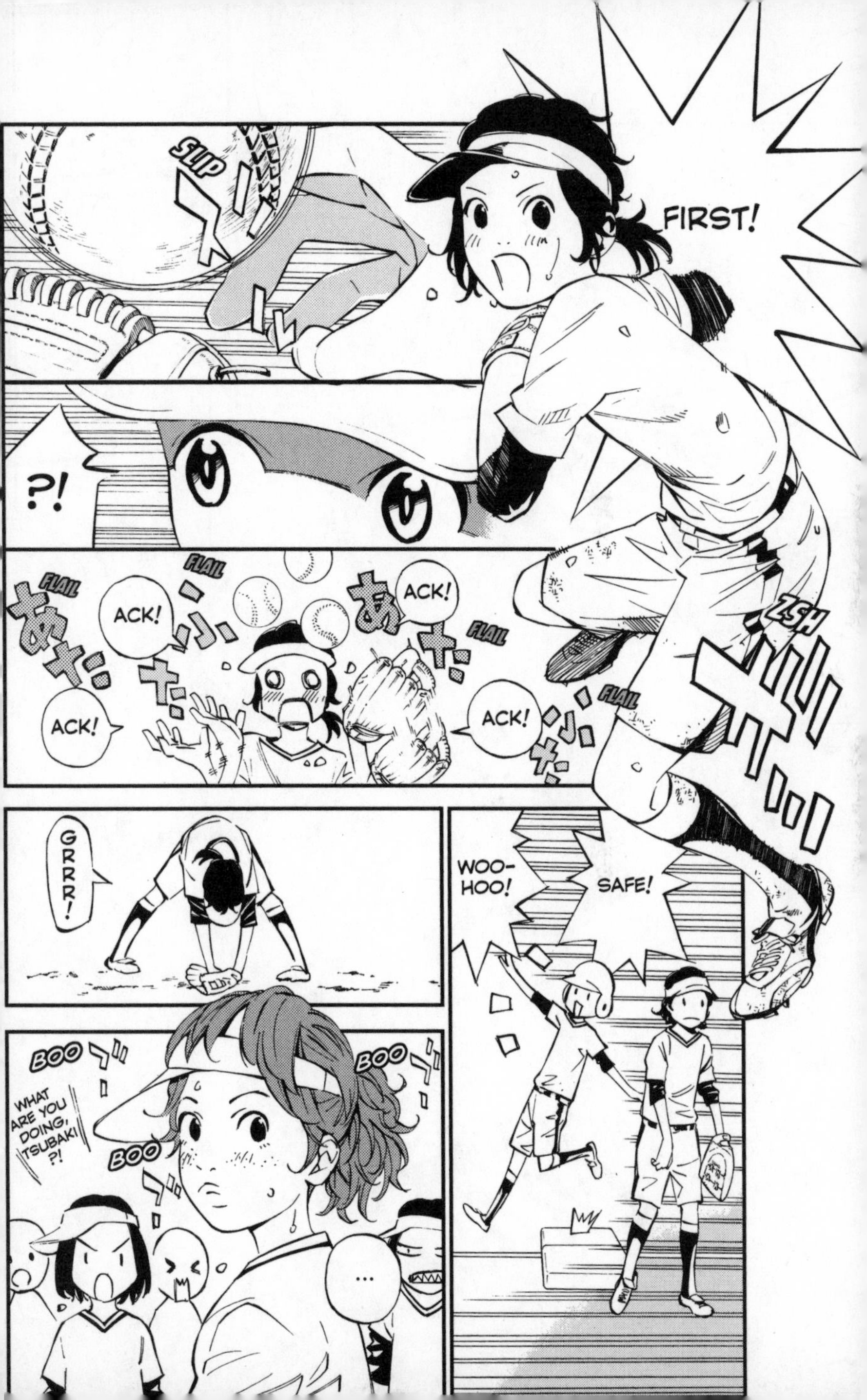
FIRST!
SLIP
?!
FLAIL
ACK!
FLAIL
ACK!
FLAIL
ACK!
ACK!
FLAIL
ZSH
SAFE!
WOO-HOO!
GRRR!
BOO
BOO
WHAT ARE YOU DOING, TSUBAKI?!
BOO
...

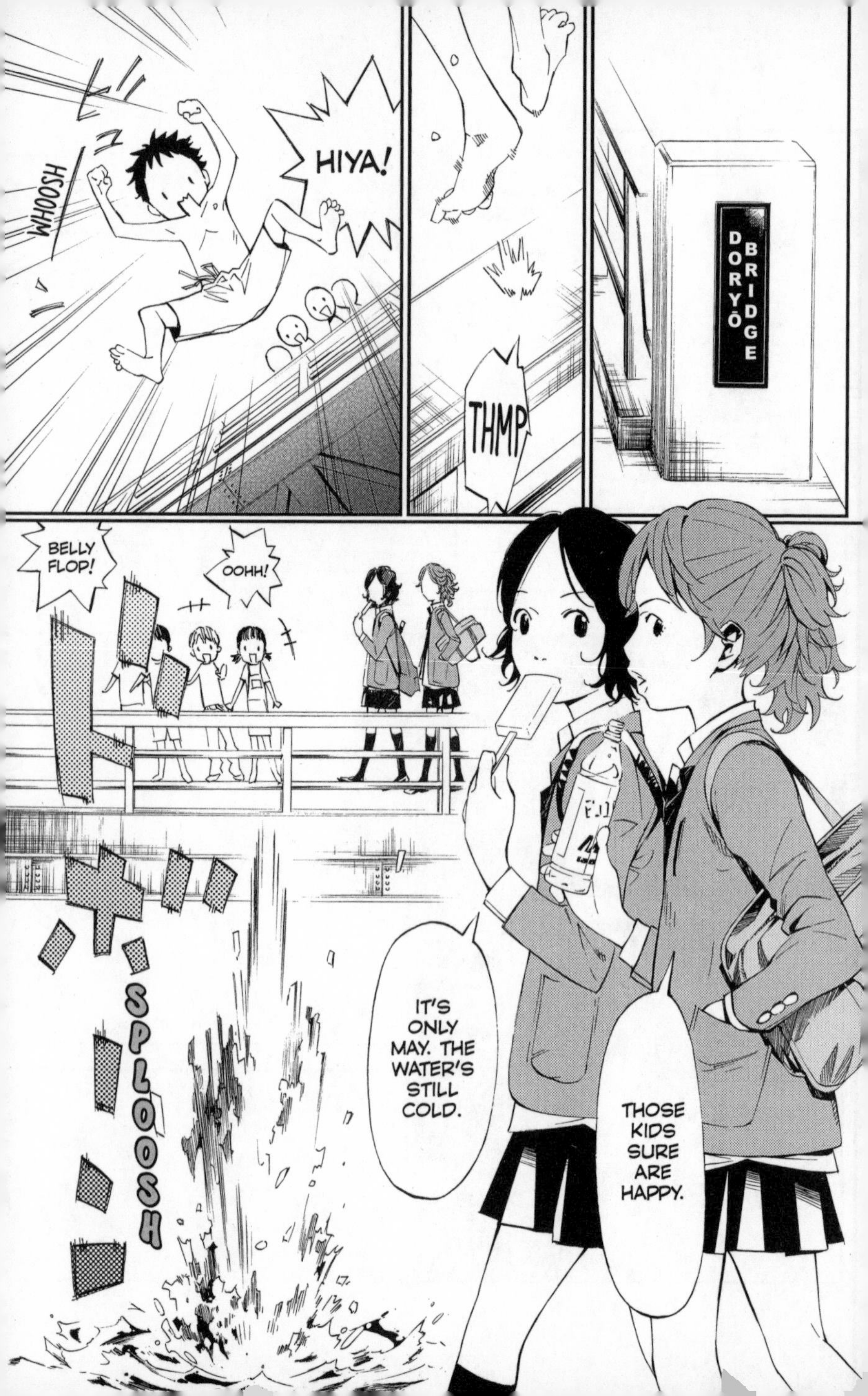
DORYŌ BRIDGE
THMP
HIYA!
WHOOSH
THOSE KIDS SURE ARE HAPPY.
IT'S ONLY MAY. THE WATER'S STILL COLD.
OOHH!
BELLY FLOP!
SPLOOSH

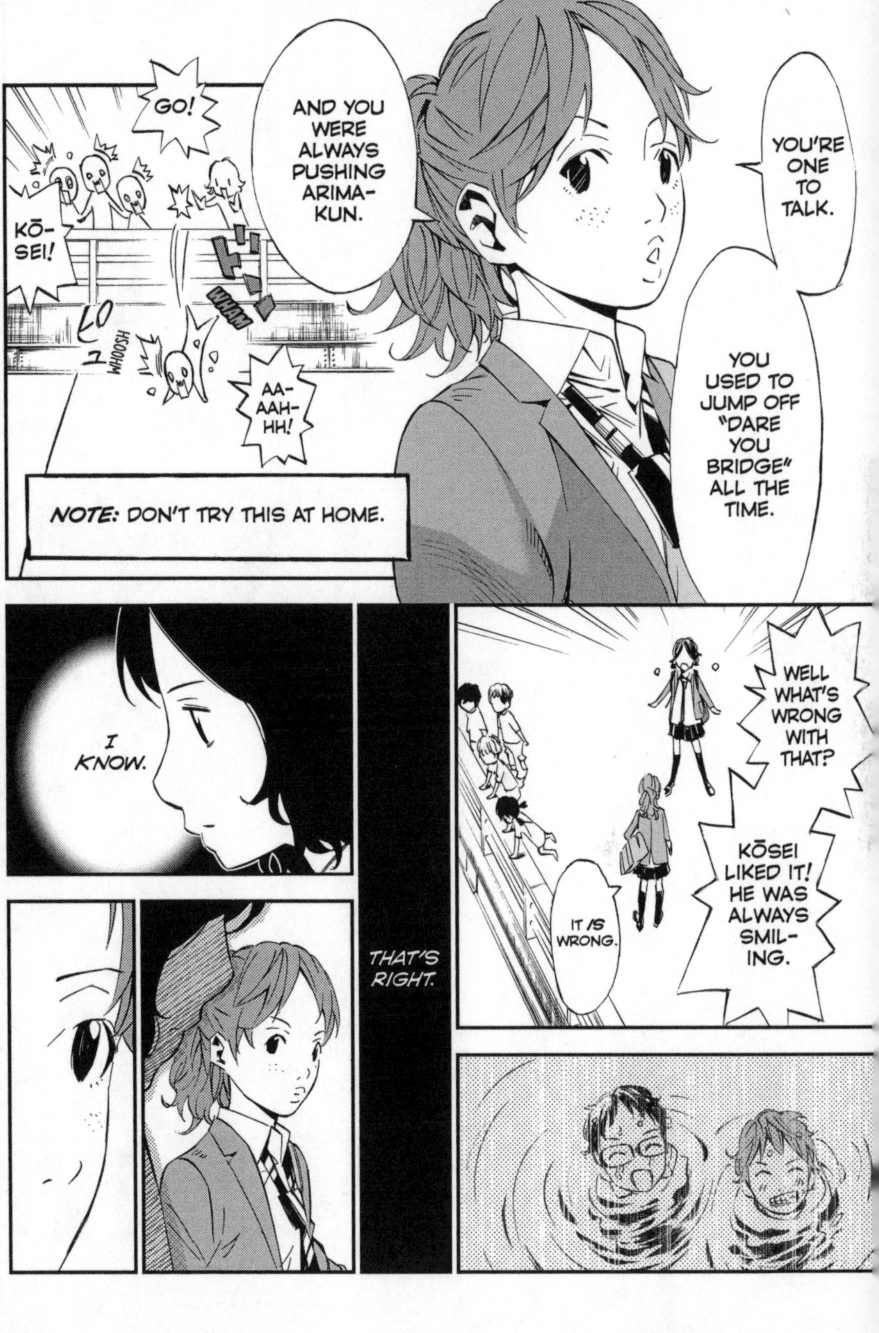
AND YOU WERE ALWAYS PUSHING ARIMA-KUN.
YOU'RE ONE TO TALK.
YOU USED TO JUMP OFF "DARE YOU BRIDGE" ALL THE TIME.
GO!
KŌSEI!
WHAM
WHOOSH
AA-AAH-HH!
NOTE: DON'T TRY THIS AT HOME.
WELL WHAT'S WRONG WITH THAT?
KŌSEI LIKED IT! HE WAS ALWAYS SMIL-ING.
IT IS WRONG.
THAT'S RIGHT.
I KNOW.

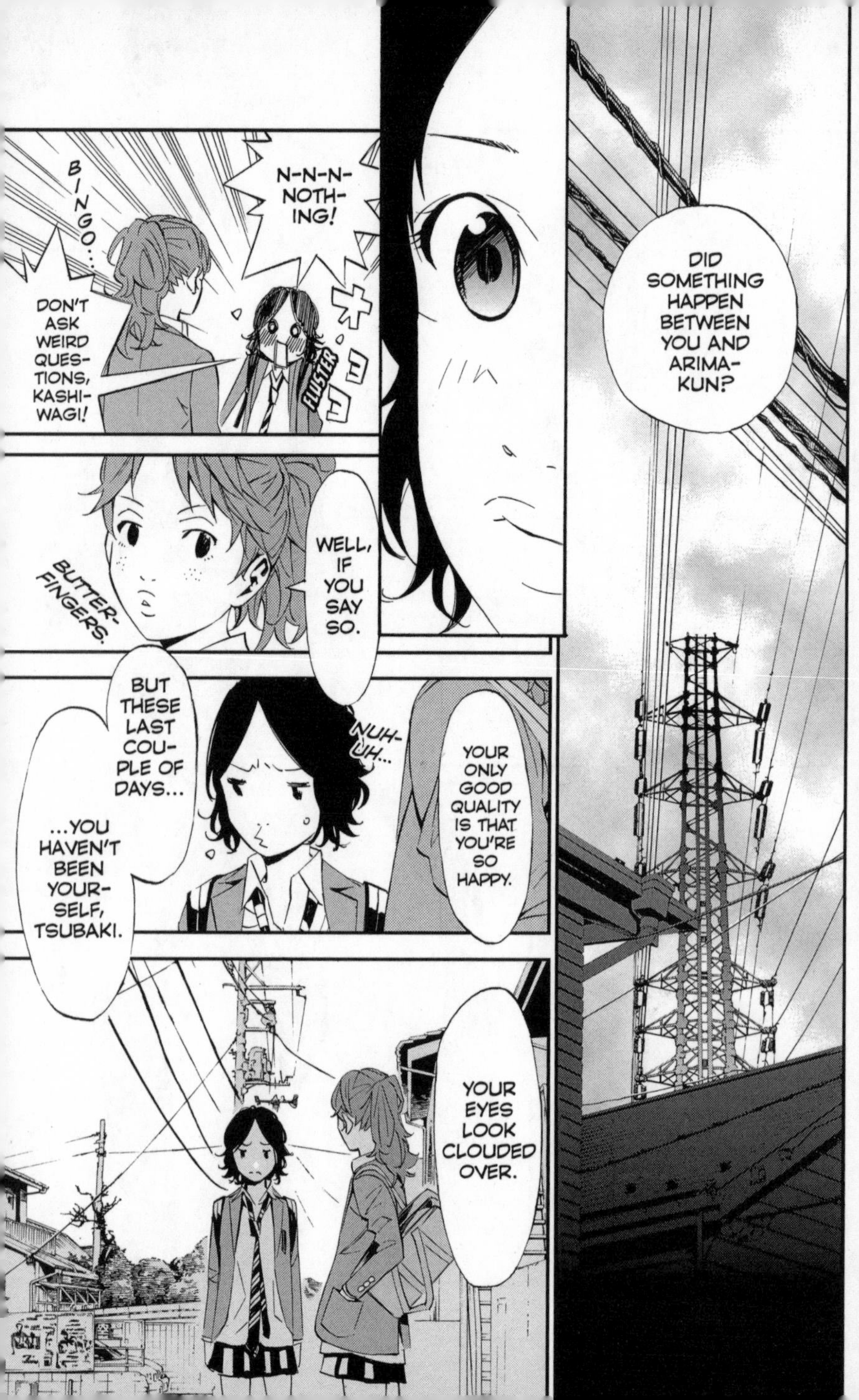
DID SOMETHING HAPPEN BETWEEN YOU AND ARIMA-KUN?
N-N-N-NOTHING!
FLUSTER
BINGO...
DON'T ASK WEIRD QUES-TIONS, KASHI-WAGI!
WELL, IF YOU SAY SO.
BUTTER-FINGERS.
YOUR ONLY GOOD QUALITY IS THAT YOU'RE SO HAPPY.
NUH-UH...
BUT THESE LAST COU-PLE OF DAYS...
...YOU HAVEN'T BEEN YOUR-SELF, TSUBAKI.
YOUR EYES LOOK CLOUDED OVER.

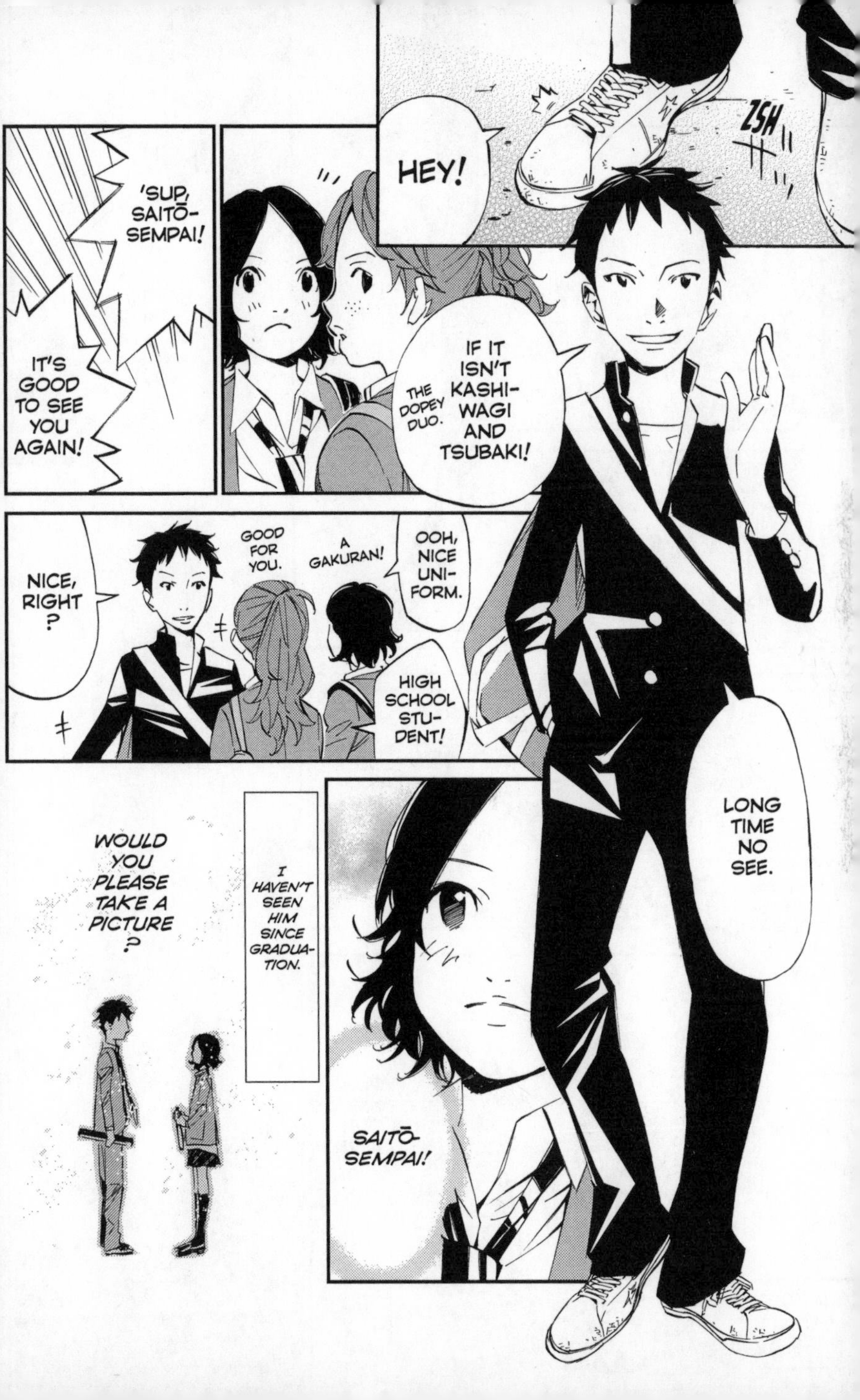
HEY!
ZSH
IF IT ISN'T KASHIWAGI AND TSUBAKI!
THE DOPEY DUO.
LONG TIME NO SEE.
'SUP, SAITŌ-SEMPAI!
IT'S GOOD TO SEE YOU AGAIN!
OOH, NICE UNIFORM.
A GAKURAN!
GOOD FOR YOU.
HIGH SCHOOL STUDENT!
NICE, RIGHT?
SAITŌ-SEMPAI!
I HAVEN'T SEEN HIM SINCE GRADUATION.
WOULD YOU PLEASE TAKE A PICTURE?

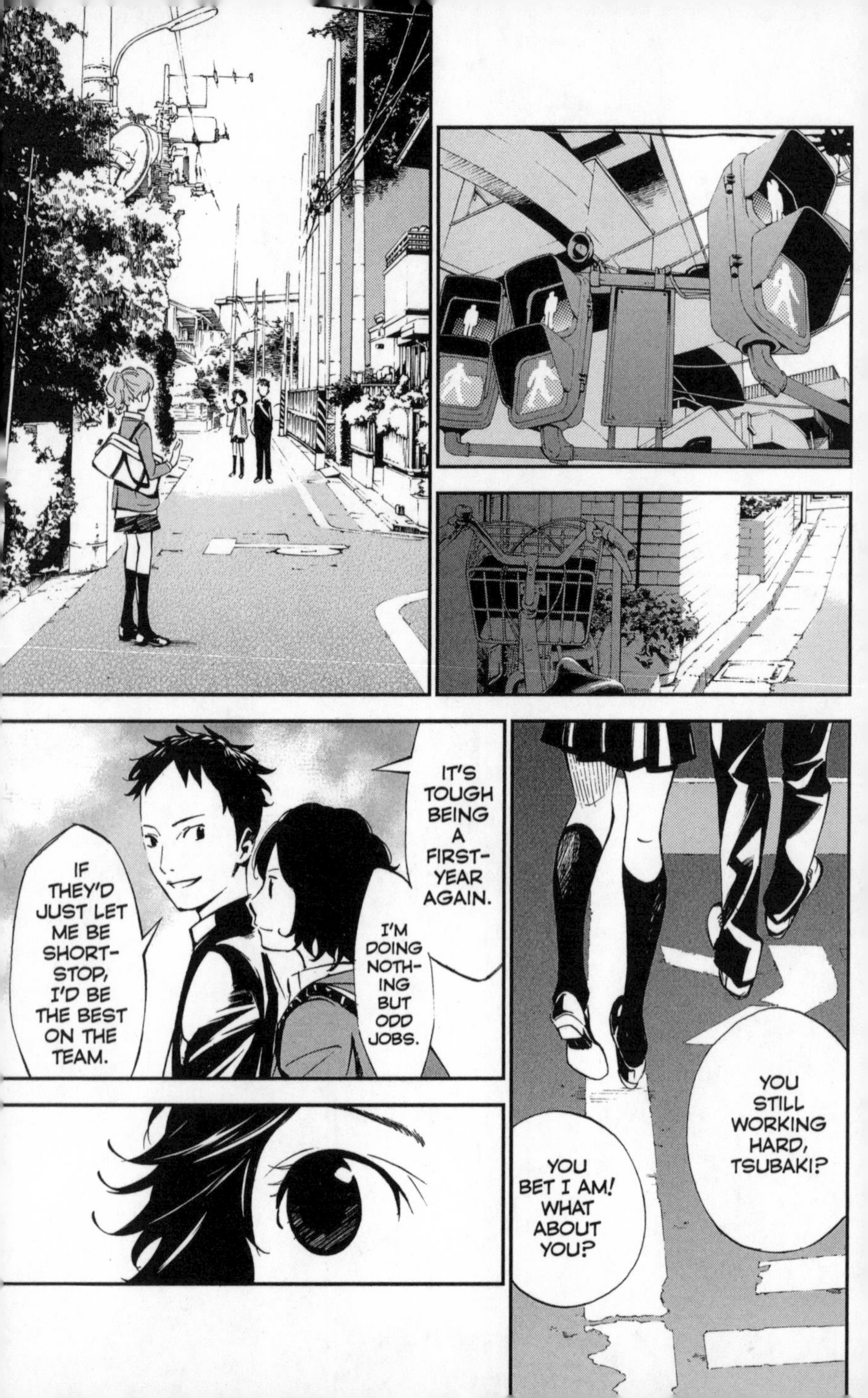
YOU STILL WORKING HARD, TSUBAKI?
YOU BET I AM! WHAT ABOUT YOU?
IT'S TOUGH BEING A FIRST-YEAR AGAIN.
I'M DOING NOTHING BUT ODD JOBS.
IF THEY'D JUST LET ME BE SHORTSTOP, I'D BE THE BEST ON THE TEAM.

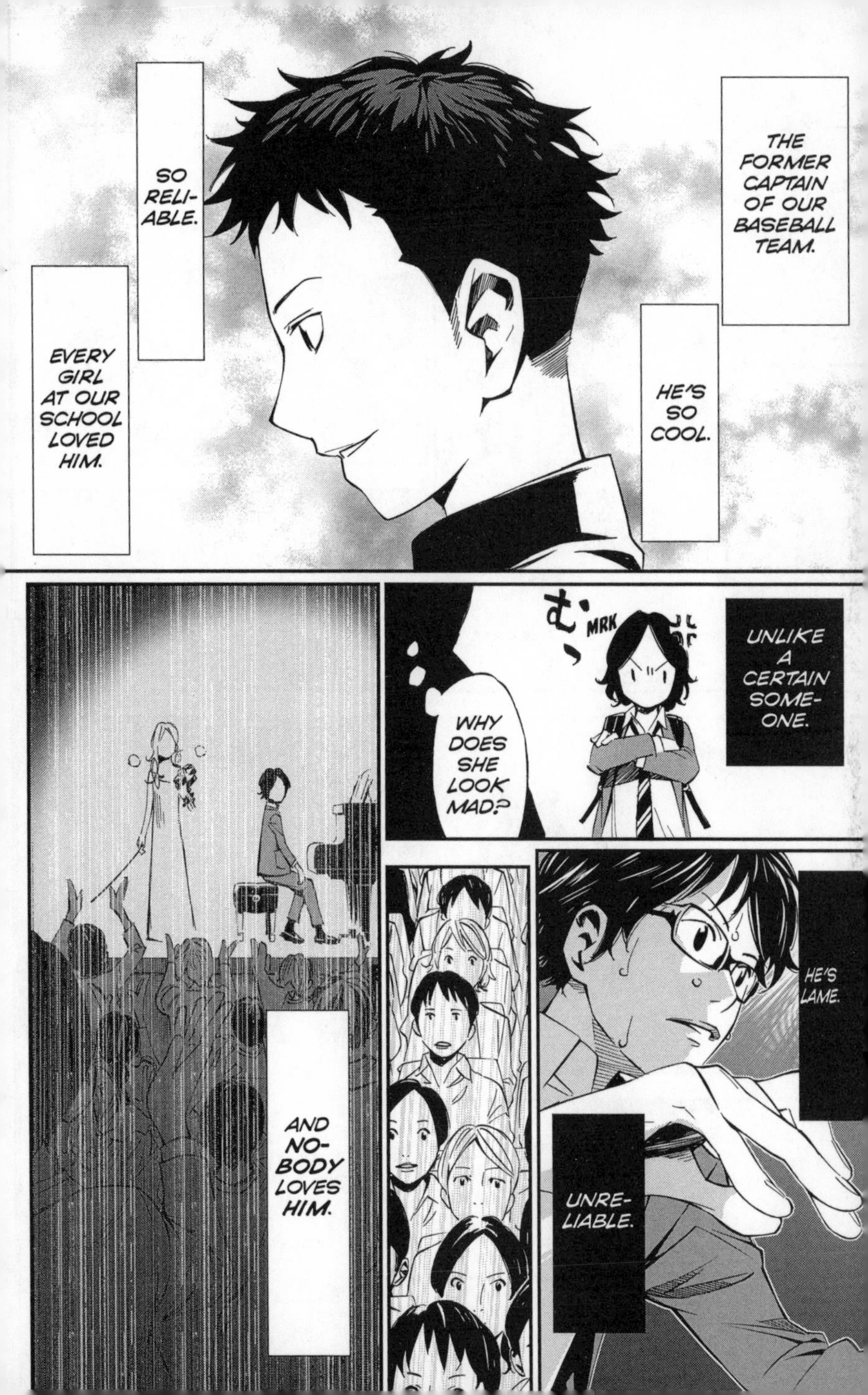
THE FORMER CAPTAIN OF OUR BASEBALL TEAM.
HE'S SO COOL.
SO RELI-ABLE.
EVERY GIRL AT OUR SCHOOL LOVED HIM.
UNLIKE A CERTAIN SOME-ONE.
MRK
WHY DOES SHE LOOK MAD?
HE'S LAME.
UNRE-LIABLE.
AND NO-BODY LOVES HIM.

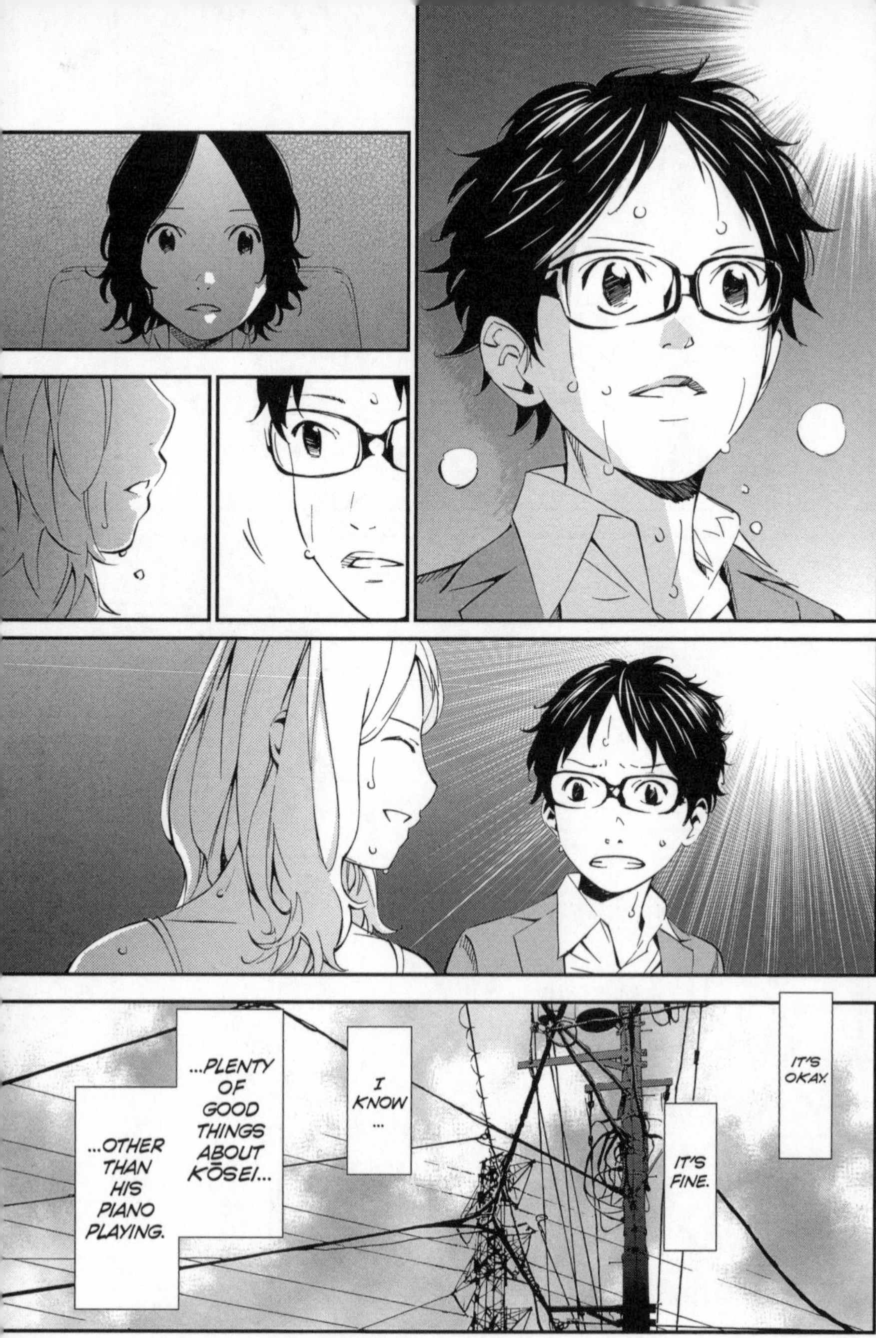
IT'S OKAY.
IT'S FINE.
I KNOW...
...PLENTY OF GOOD THINGS ABOUT KŌSEI...
...OTHER THAN HIS PIANO PLAYING.

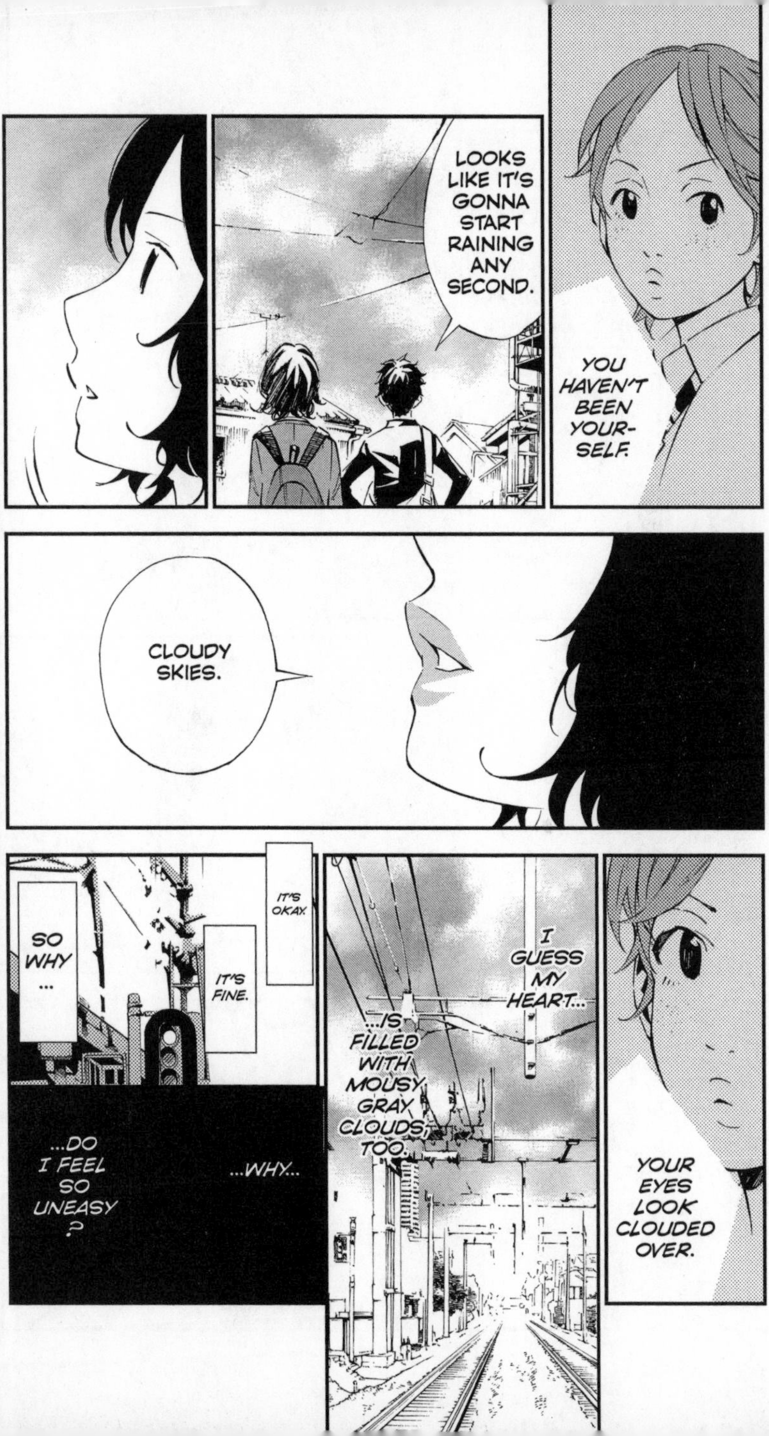
YOU HAVEN'T BEEN YOURSELF.
LOOKS LIKE IT'S GONNA START RAINING ANY SECOND.
CLOUDY SKIES.
YOUR EYES LOOK CLOUDED OVER.
I GUESS MY HEART...
...IS FILLED WITH MOUSY GRAY CLOUDS, TOO.
IT'S OKAY.
IT'S FINE.
SO WHY...
...WHY...
...DO I FEEL SO UNEASY?

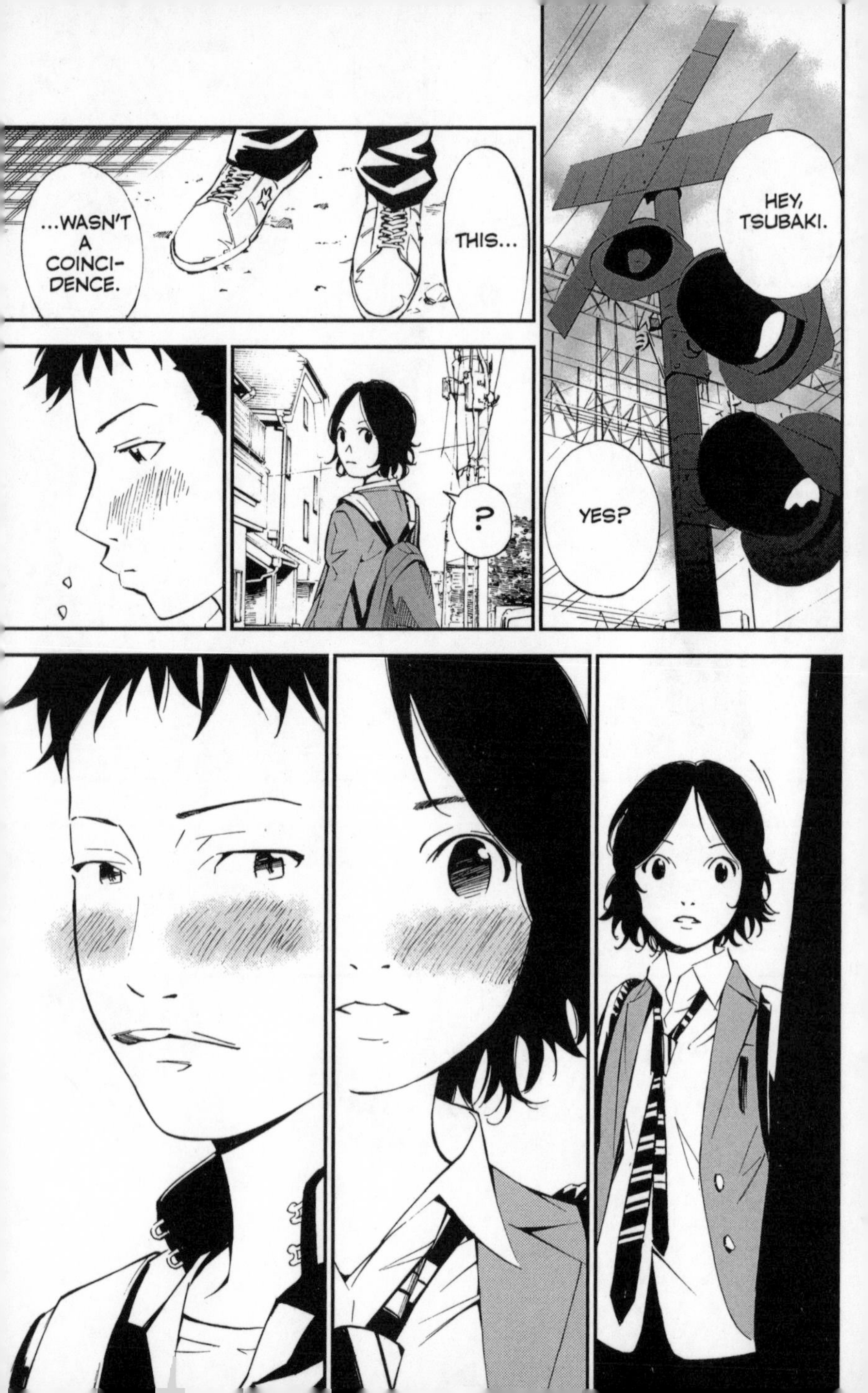
HEY, TSUBAKI.
YES?
THIS...
...WASN'T A COINCIDENCE.
?

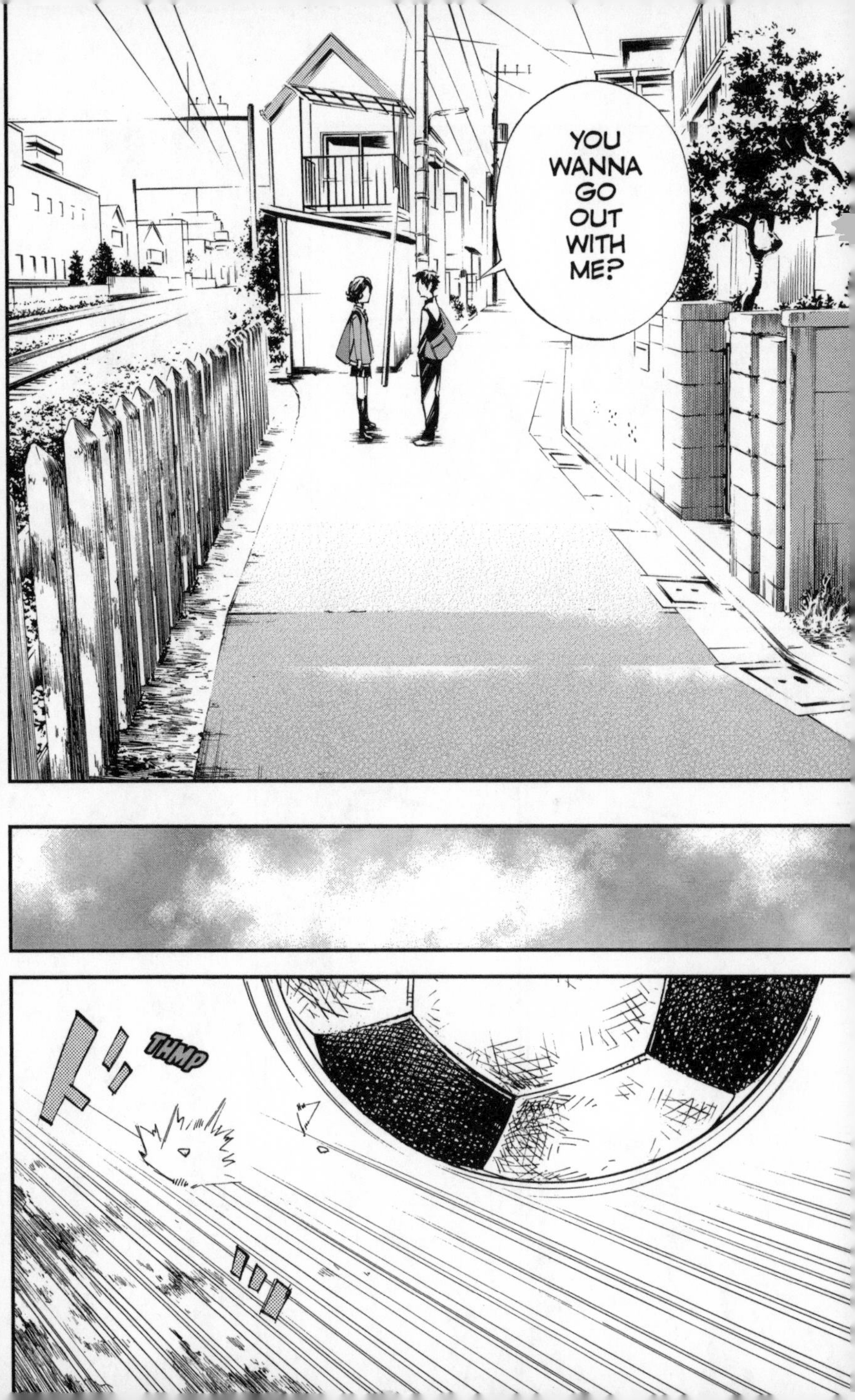
YOU WANNA GO OUT WITH ME?
THMP

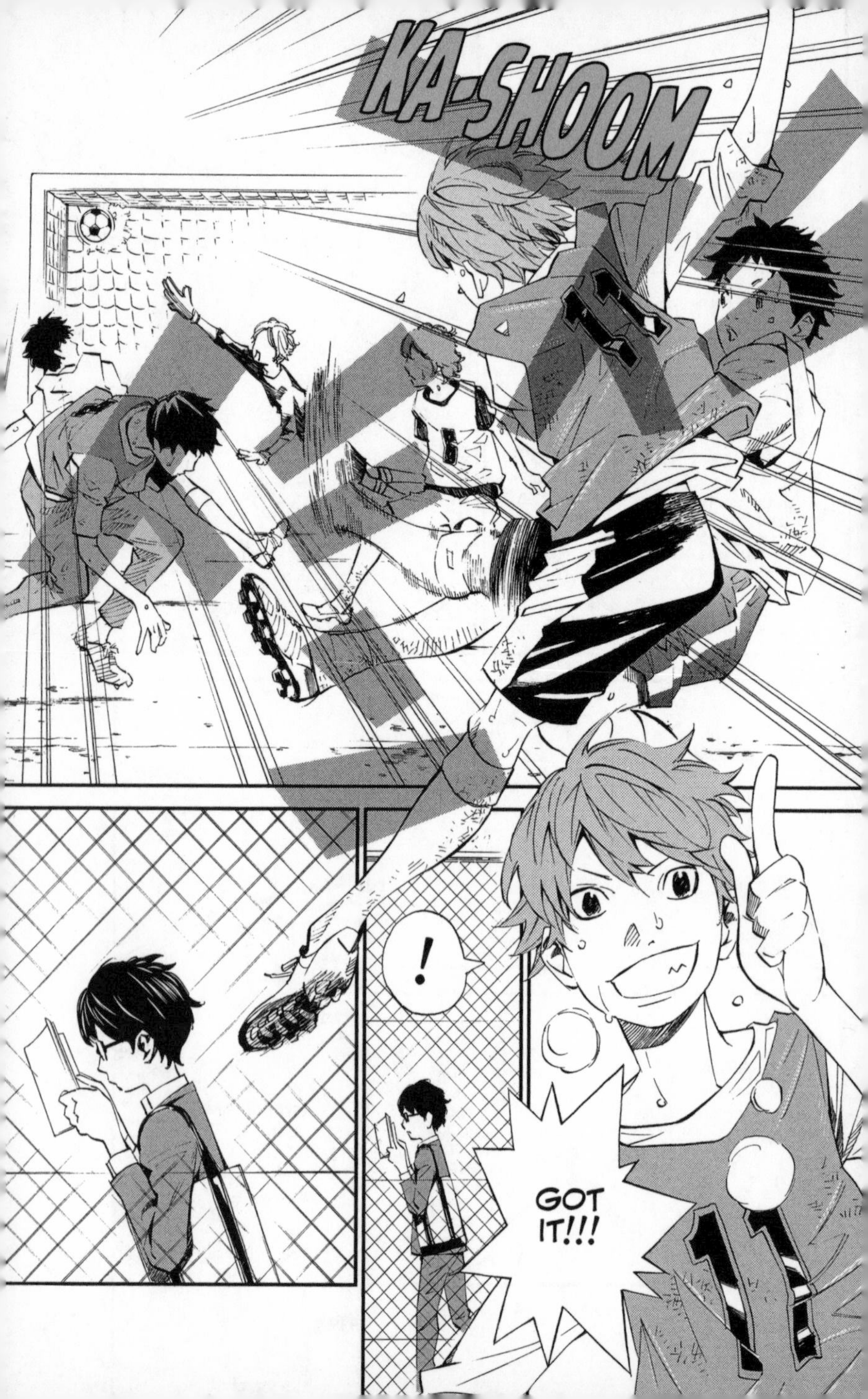
KA-SHOOM
GOT IT!!!
!

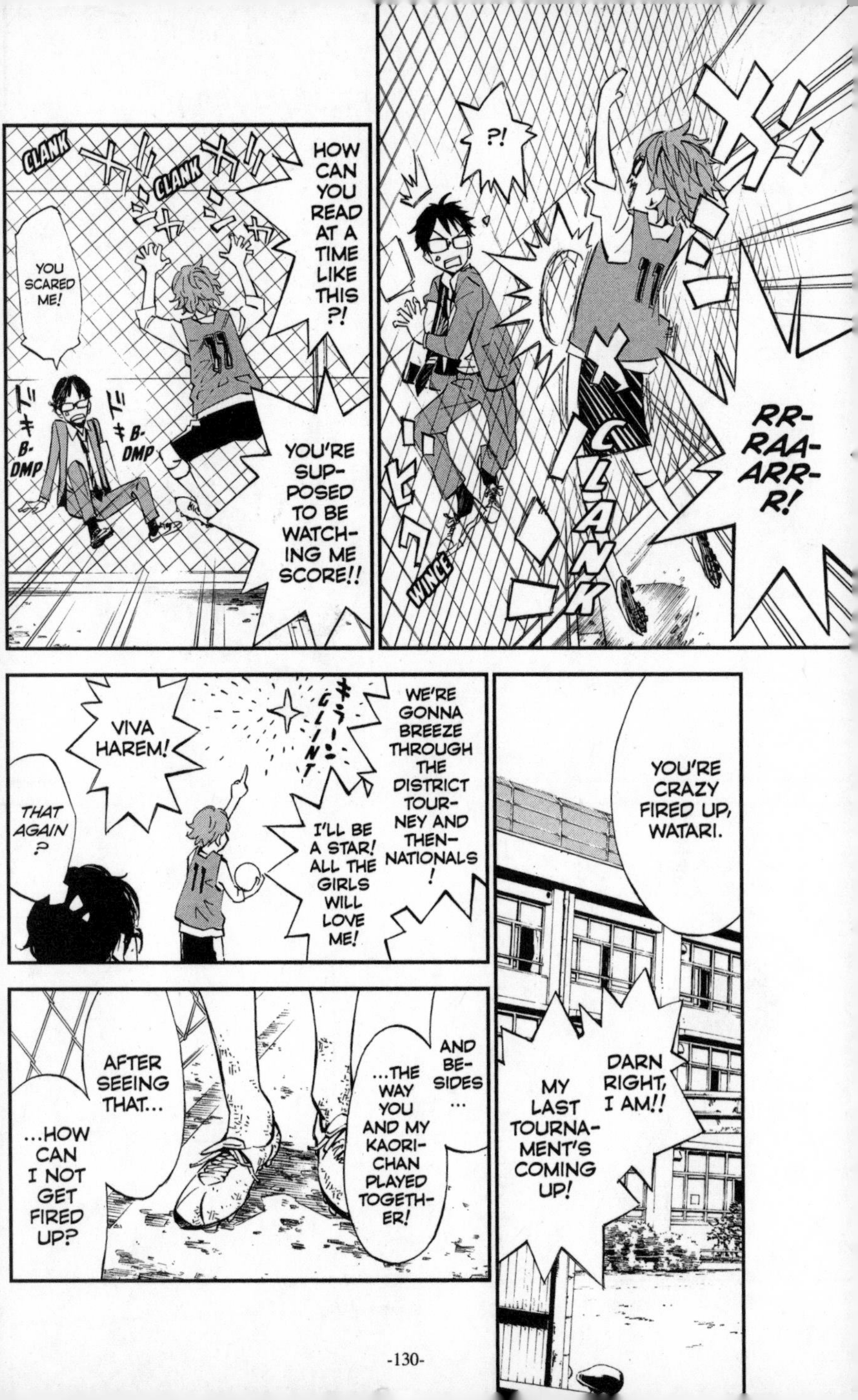
?!
RR-RAA-ARR-R!
CLANK
WINCE
HOW CAN YOU READ AT A TIME LIKE THIS?!
CLANK
CLANK
YOU SCARED ME!
B-DMP
B-DMP
YOU'RE SUPPOSED TO BE WATCHING ME SCORE!!
YOU'RE CRAZY FIRED UP, WATARI.
DARN RIGHT, I AM!!
MY LAST TOURNAMENT'S COMING UP!
WE'RE GONNA BREEZE THROUGH THE DISTRICT TOURNEY AND THEN—NATIONALS!
GLINT
I'LL BE A STAR! ALL THE GIRLS WILL LOVE ME!
VIVA HAREM!
THAT AGAIN?
AND BESIDES...
...THE WAY YOU AND MY KAORI-CHAN PLAYED TOGETHER!
AFTER SEEING THAT...
...HOW CAN I NOT GET FIRED UP?

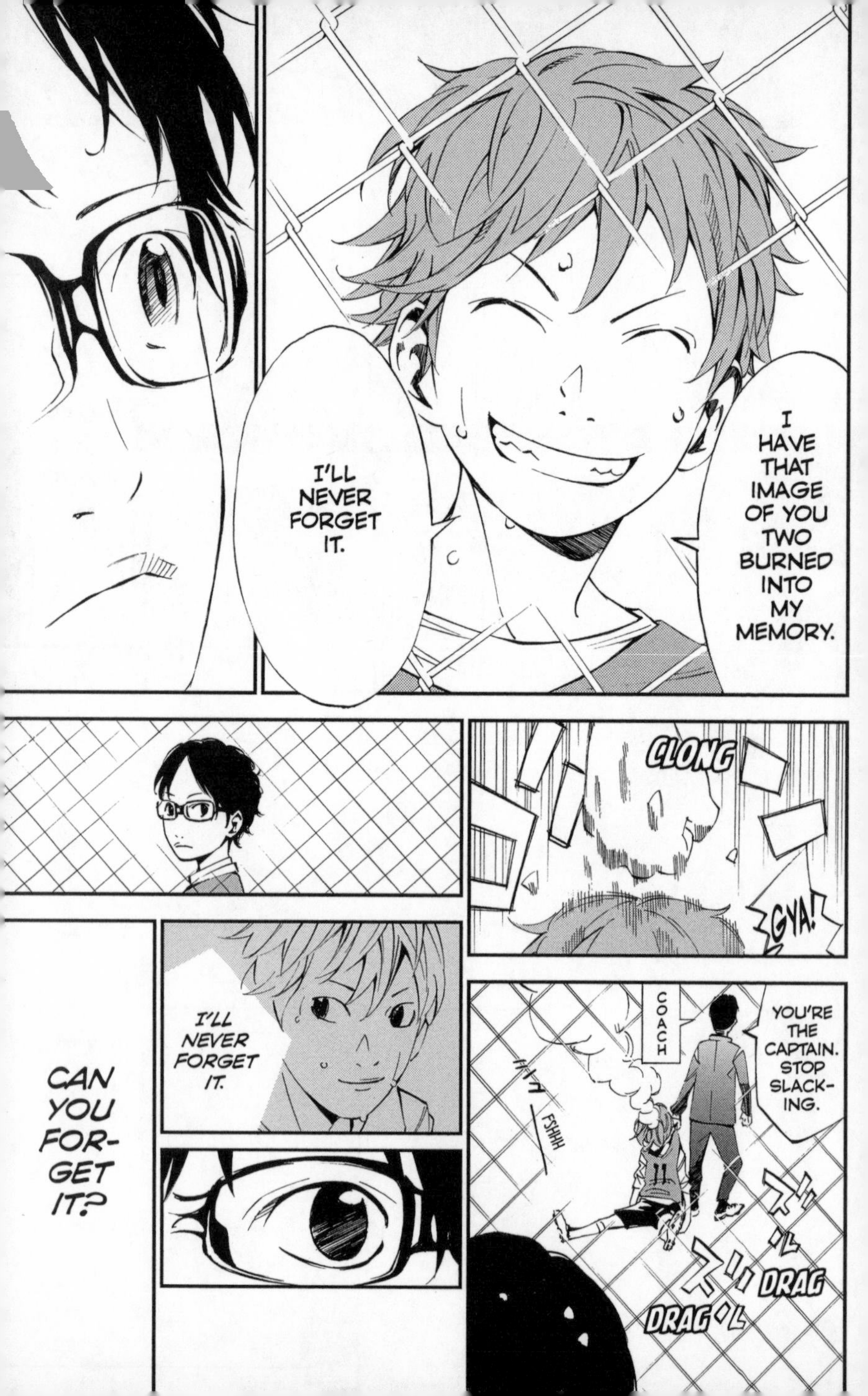
I HAVE THAT IMAGE OF YOU TWO BURNED INTO MY MEMORY.
I'LL NEVER FORGET IT.
CLONG
GYA!
COACH
YOU'RE THE CAPTAIN. STOP SLACK-ING.
FSHHH
DRAG
DRAG
I'LL NEVER FORGET IT.
CAN YOU FOR-GET IT?

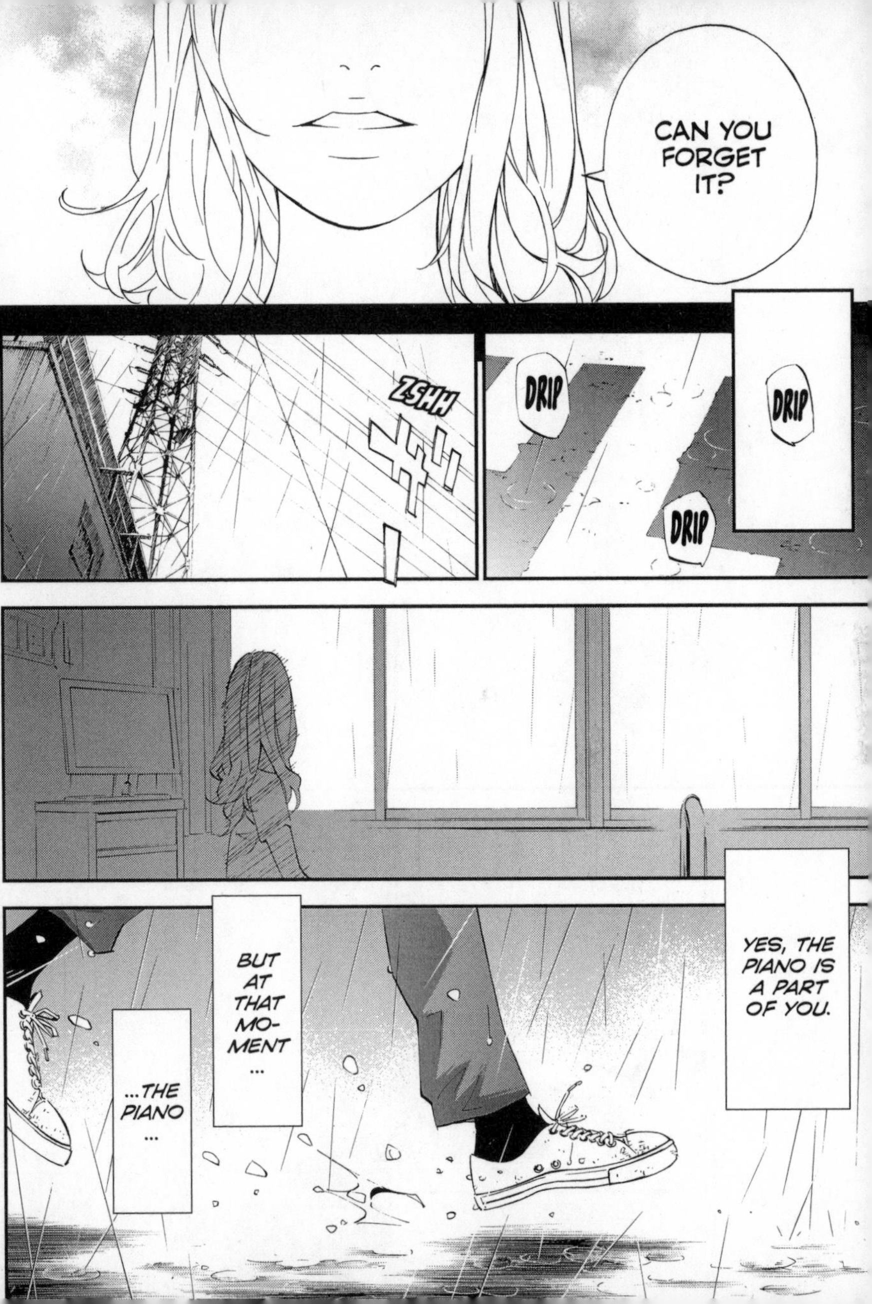
CAN YOU FORGET IT?
ZSHH
DRIP
DRIP
DRIP
YES, THE PIANO IS A PART OF YOU.
BUT AT THAT MO-MENT ...
...THE PIANO ...

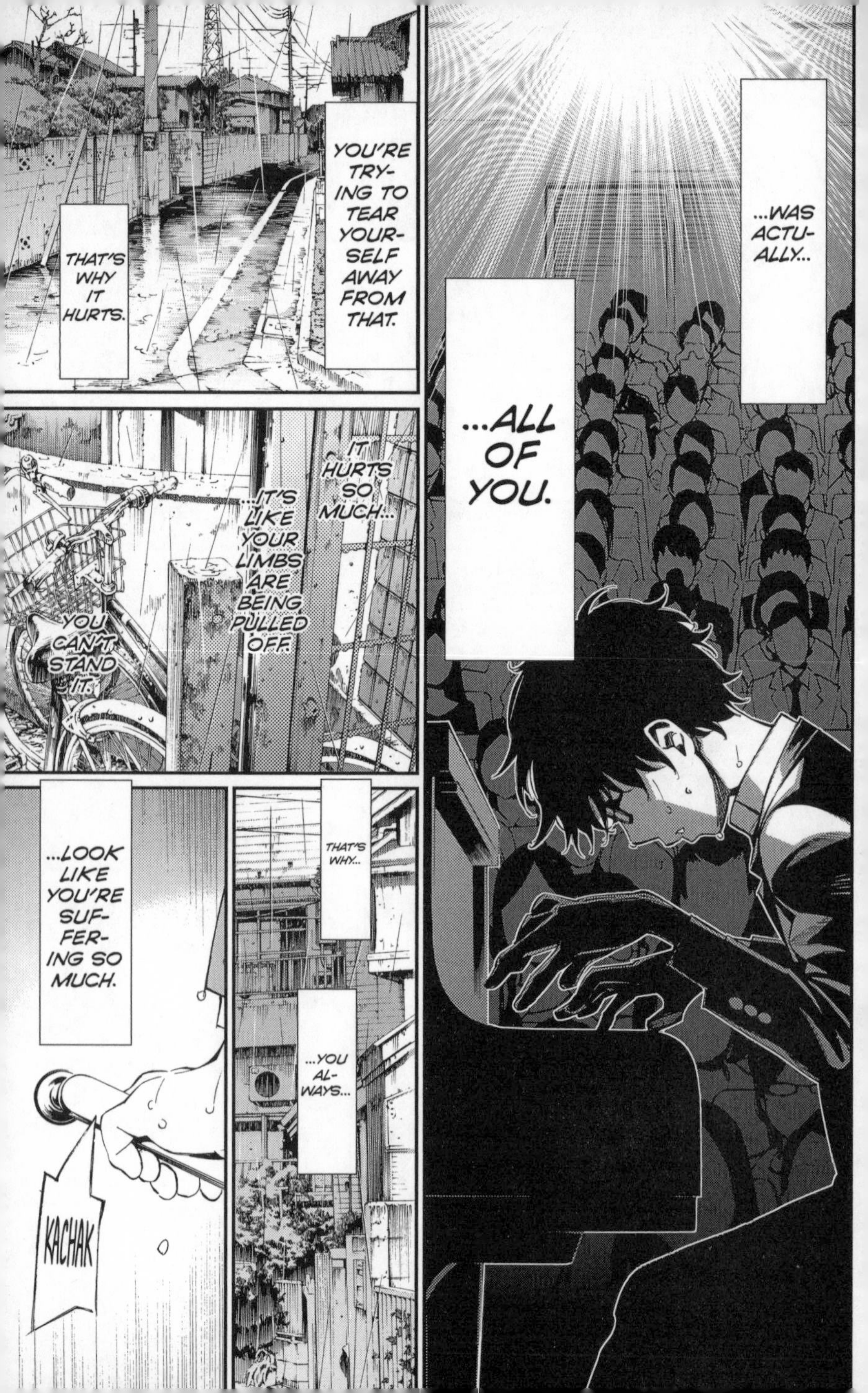
...WAS ACTUALLY...
...ALL OF YOU.
YOU'RE TRYING TO TEAR YOURSELF AWAY FROM THAT.
THAT'S WHY IT HURTS.
IT HURTS SO MUCH...
...IT'S LIKE YOUR LIMBS ARE BEING PULLED OFF.
YOU CAN'T STAND IT.
THAT'S WHY...
...YOU ALWAYS...
...LOOK LIKE YOU'RE SUFFERING SO MUCH.
KACHAK

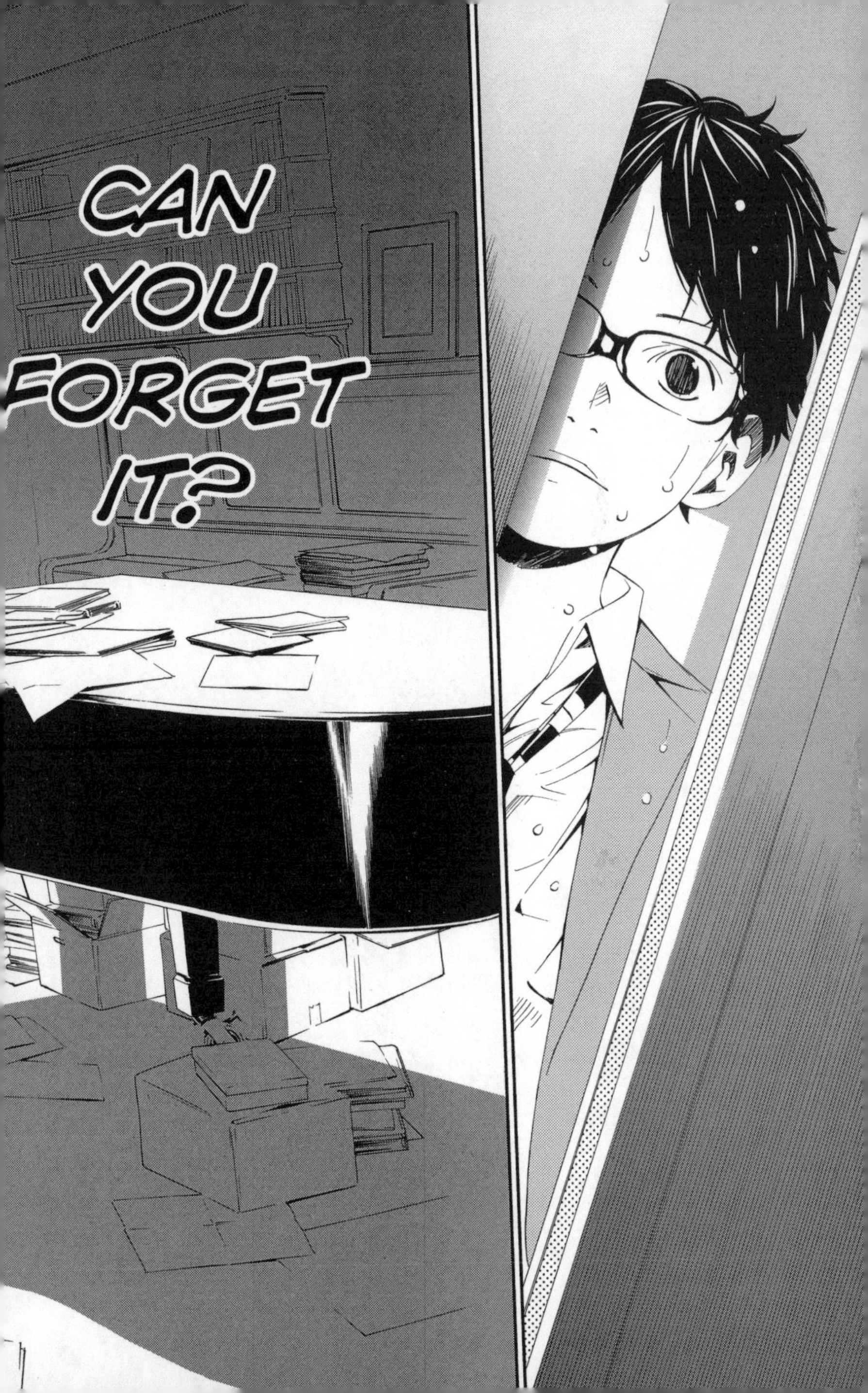
CAN YOU FORGET IT?

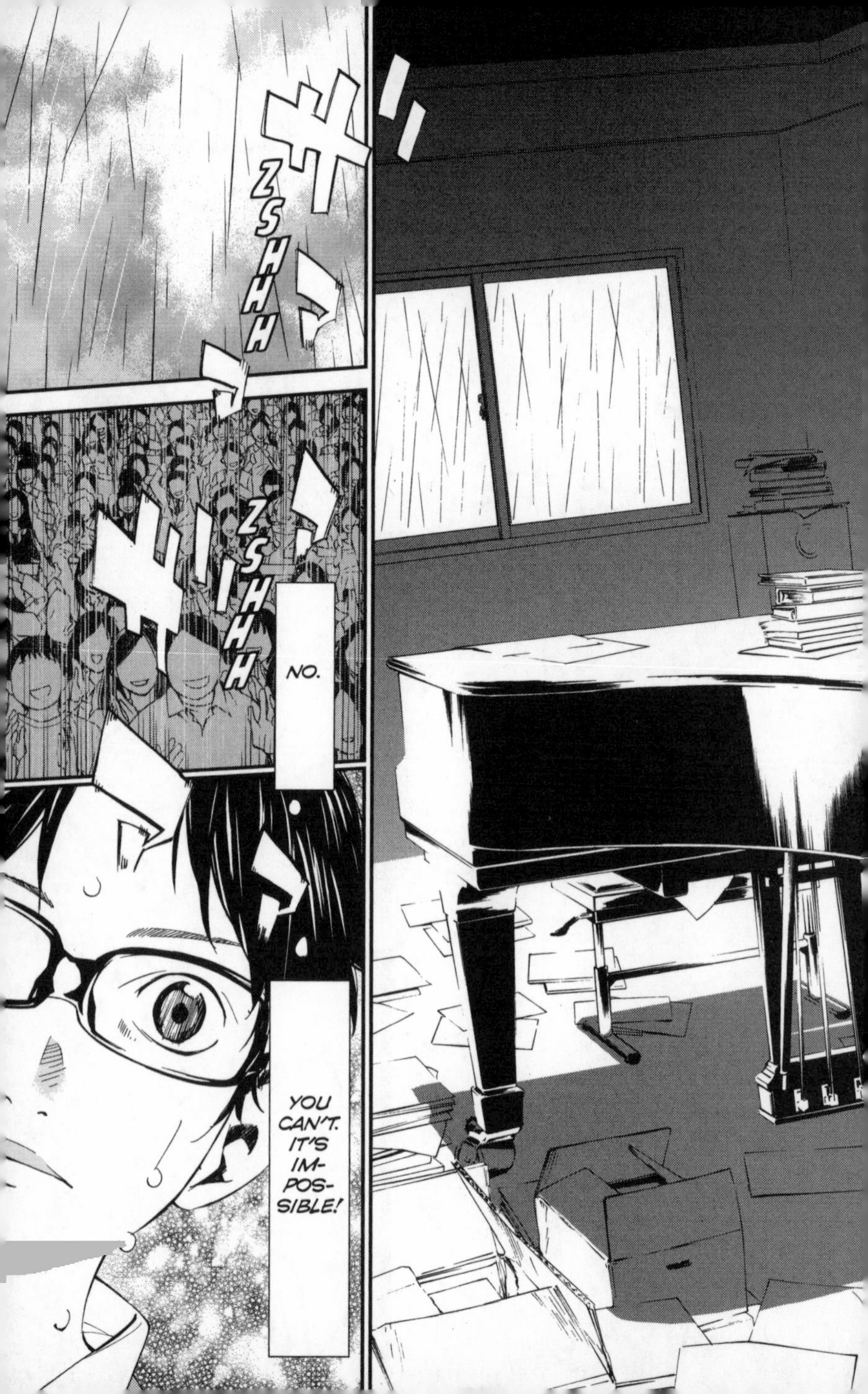
ZSHHHH
ZSHHHH
NO.
YOU CAN'T. IT'S IM-POS-SIBLE!

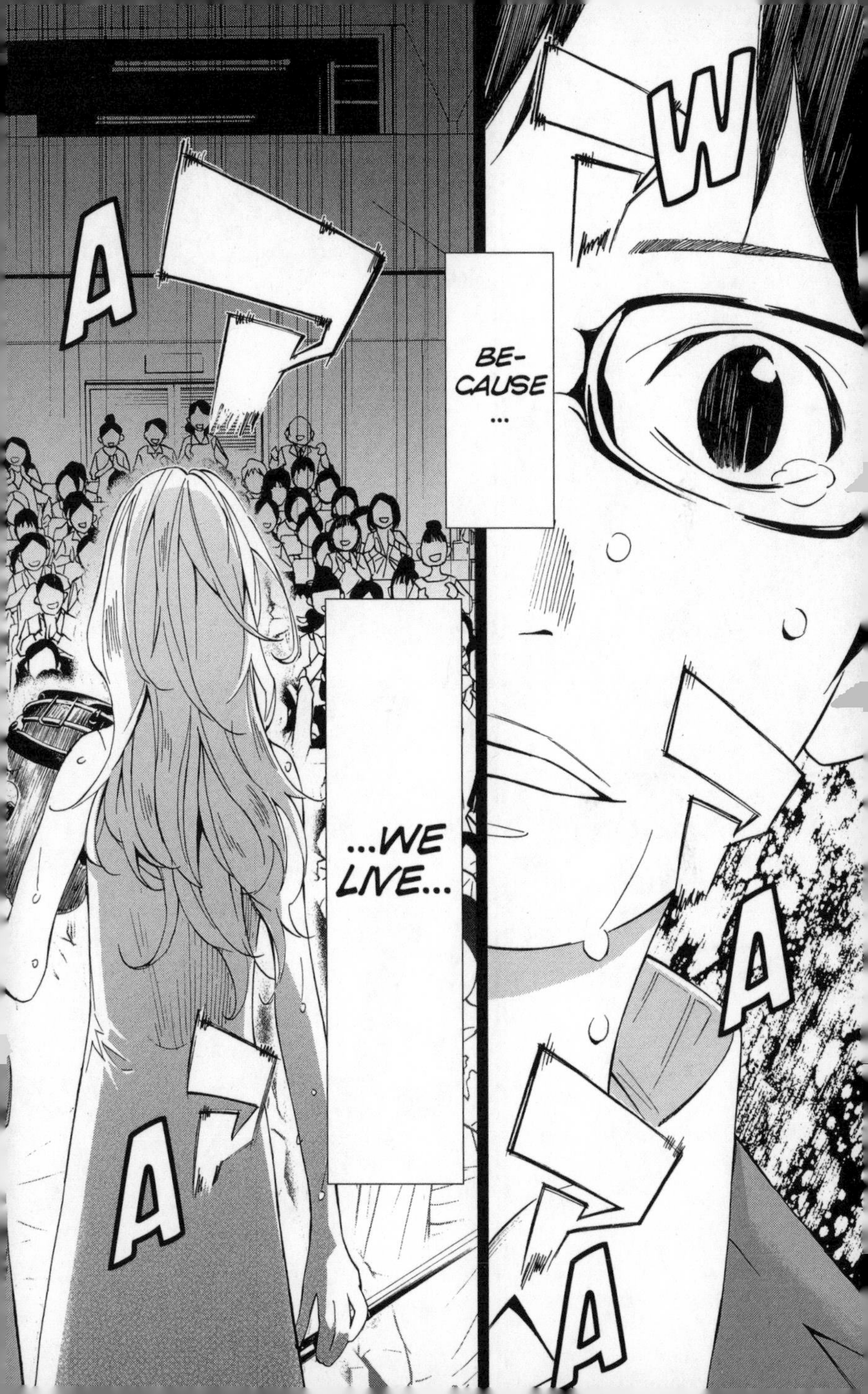
W
BE-CAUSE...
A
A
...WE LIVE...
A
A

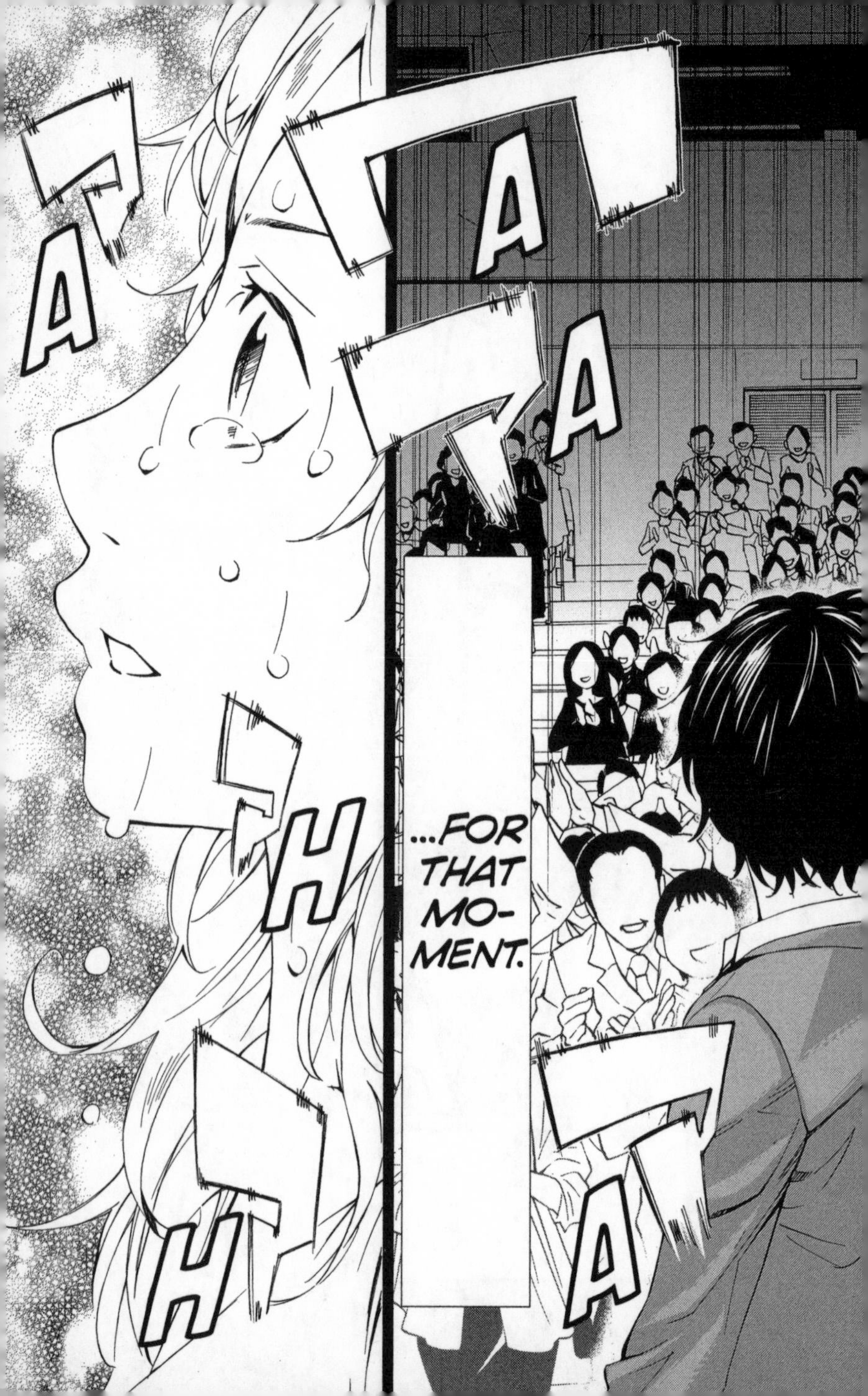
A
A
...FOR THAT MO-MENT.
A
A
H
H

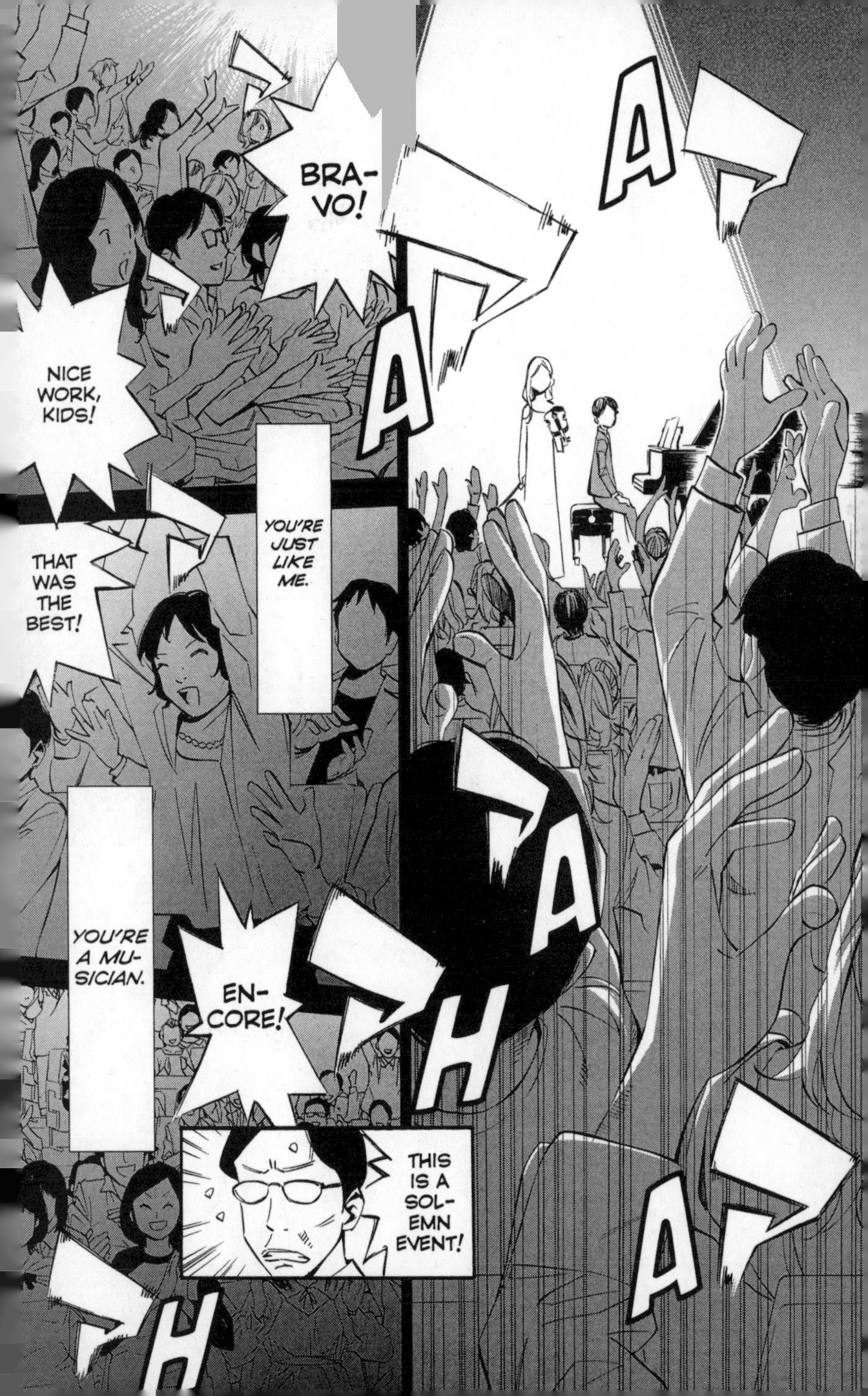

AA
BRA-VO!
NICE WORK, KIDS!
A
YOU'RE JUST LIKE ME.
THAT WAS THE BEST!
AAH
YOU'RE A MU-SICIAN.
EN-CORE!
THIS IS A SOL-EMN EVENT!
AA
H

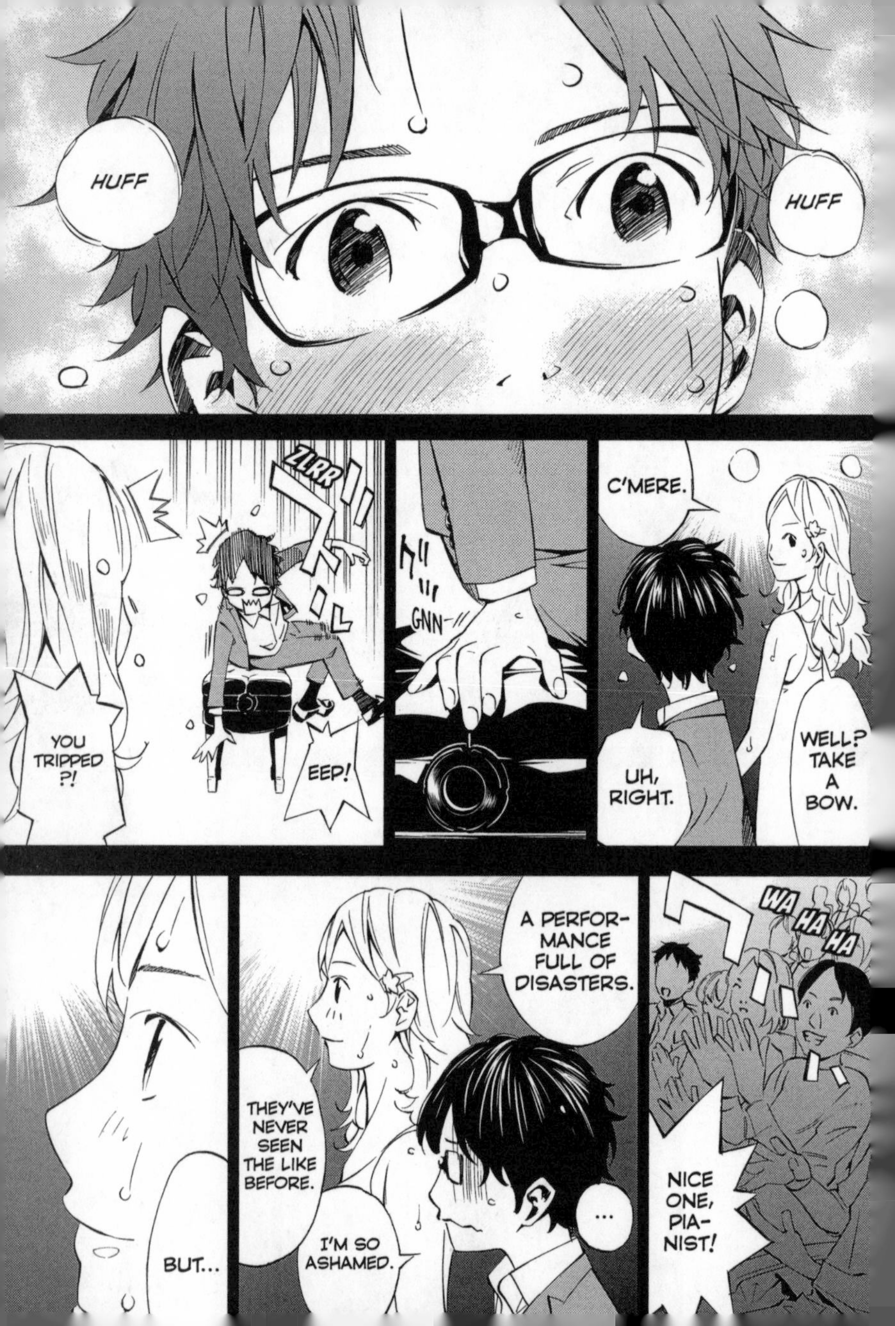
HUFF
HUFF
C'MERE.
WELL? TAKE A BOW.
UH, RIGHT.
GNN-
ZLRR
EEP!
YOU TRIPPED ?!
WA HA HA
NICE ONE, PIA-NIST!
A PERFOR-MANCE FULL OF DISASTERS.
THEY'VE NEVER SEEN THE LIKE BEFORE.
...
I'M SO ASHAMED.
BUT...

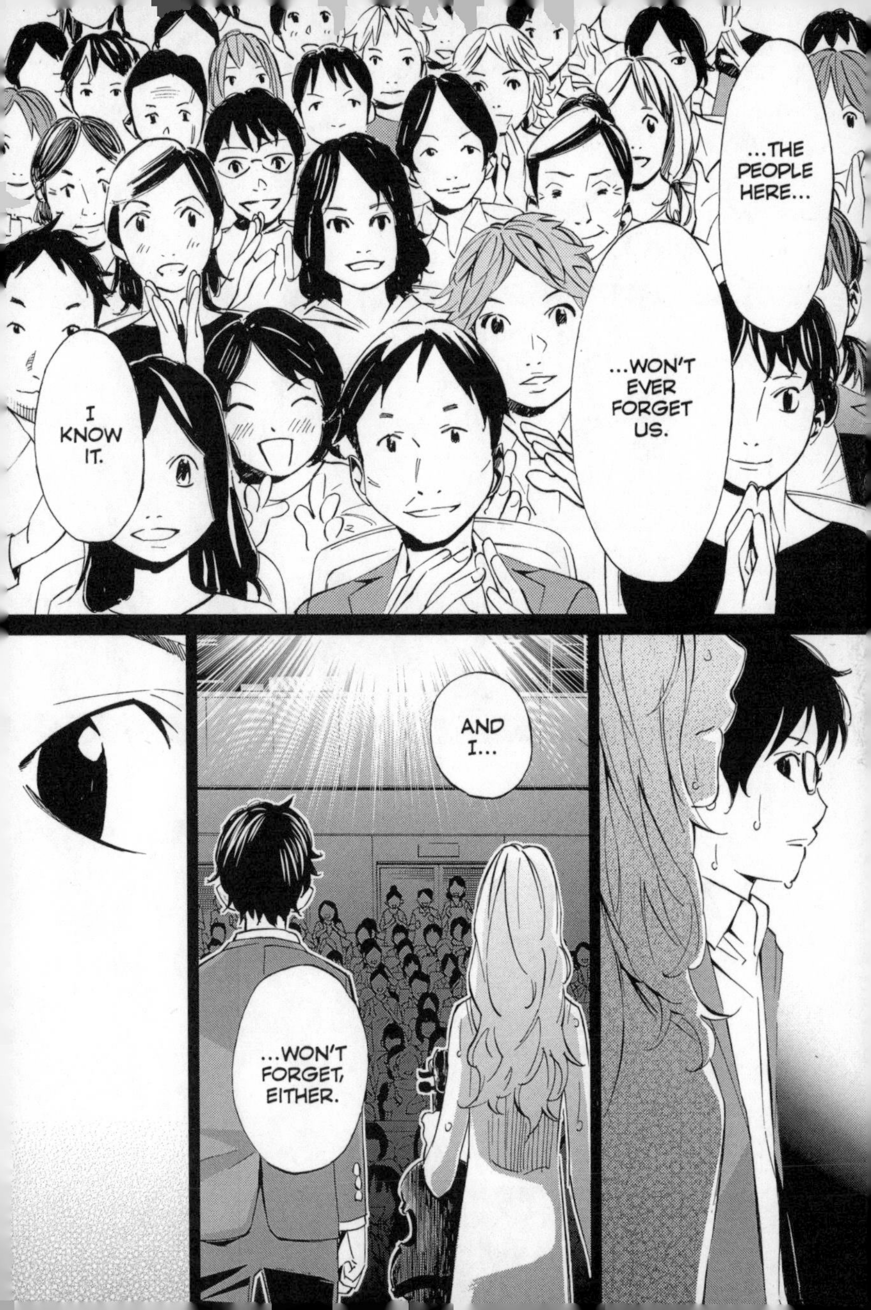
...THE PEOPLE HERE...
...WON'T EVER FORGET US.
I KNOW IT.
AND I...
...WON'T FORGET, EITHER.

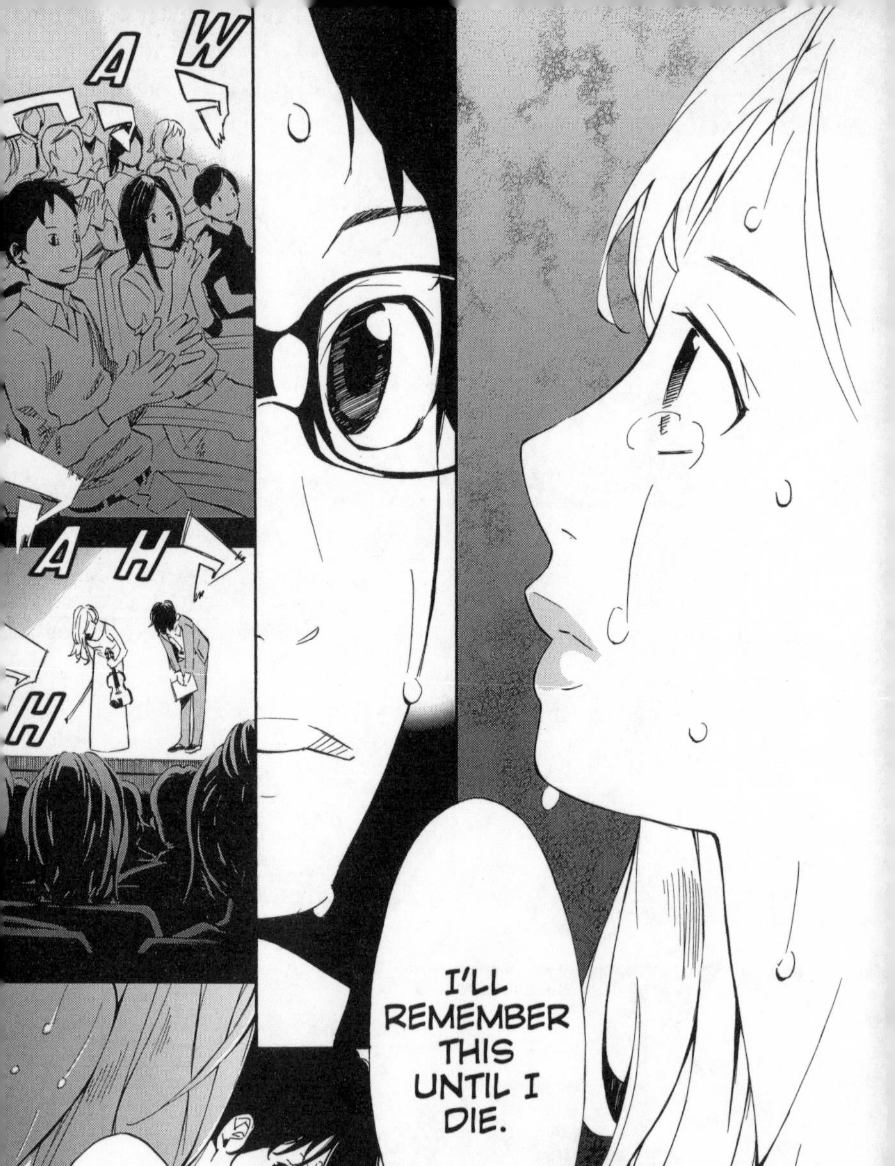
I'LL REMEMBER THIS UNTIL I DIE.
WA
AH
H
THANK YOU.

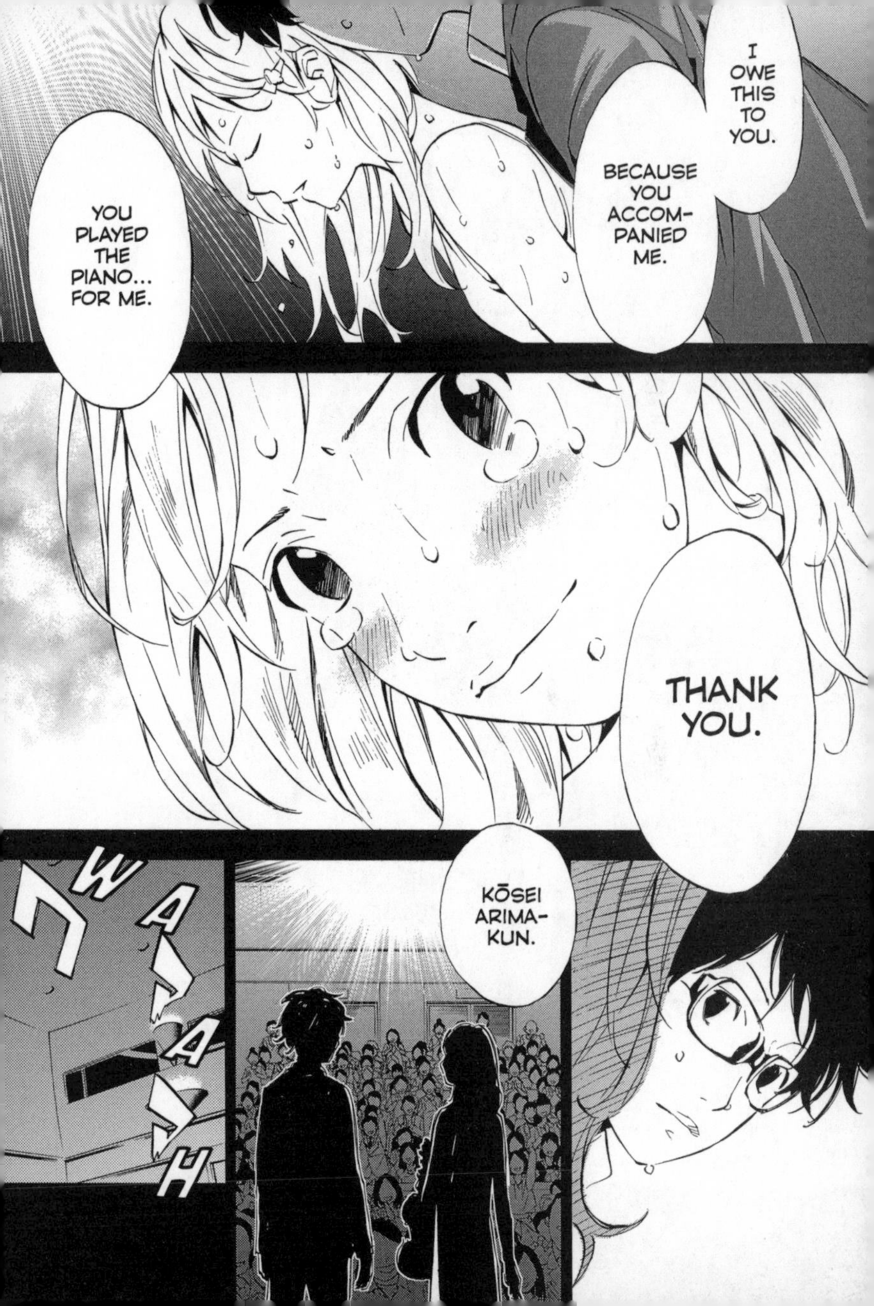
I OWE THIS TO YOU.
BECAUSE YOU ACCOMPANIED ME.
YOU PLAYED THE PIANO... FOR ME.
THANK YOU.
KŌSEI ARIMA-KUN.
WAAAH

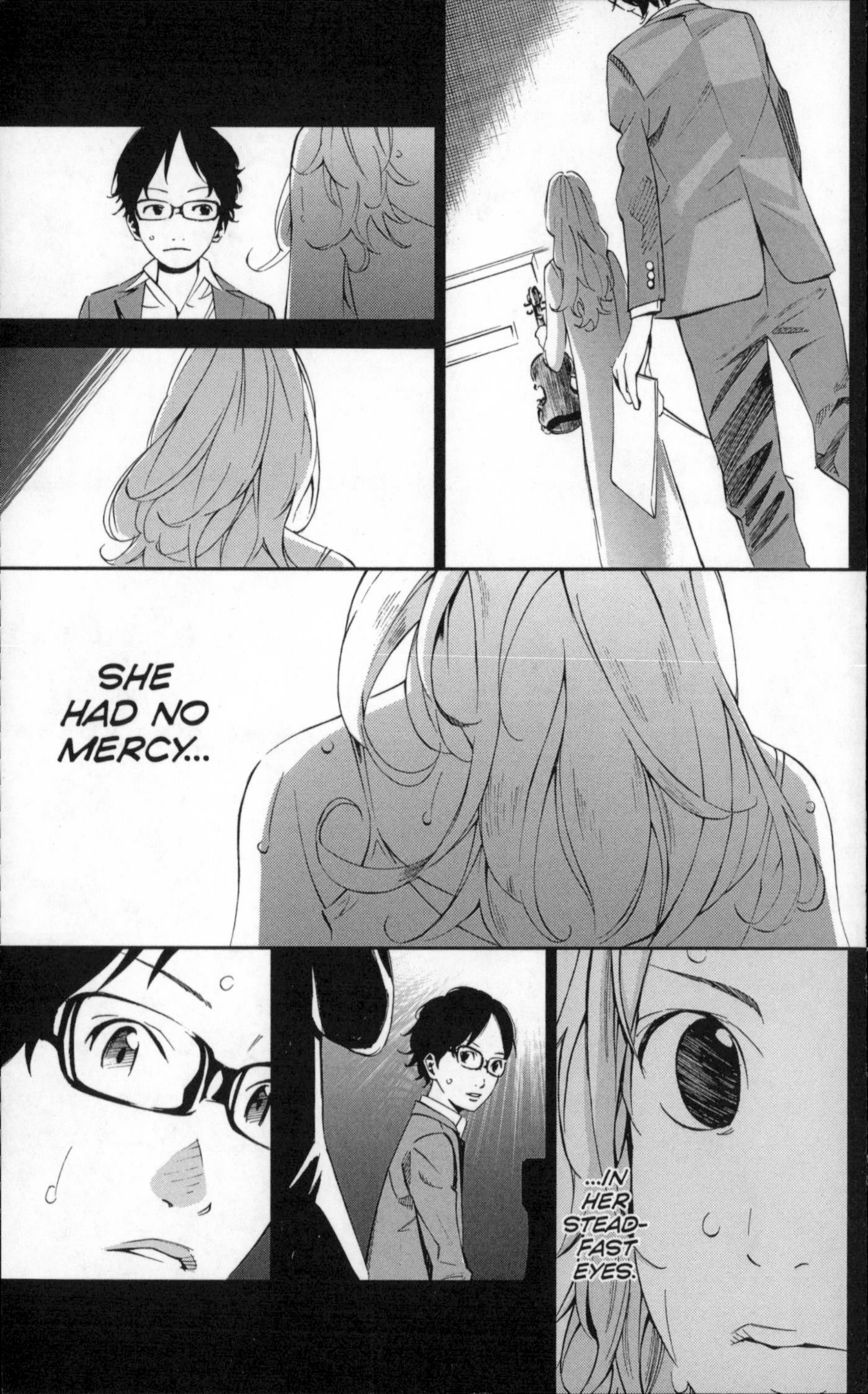
SHE HAD NO MERCY...
...IN HER STEAD-FAST EYES.

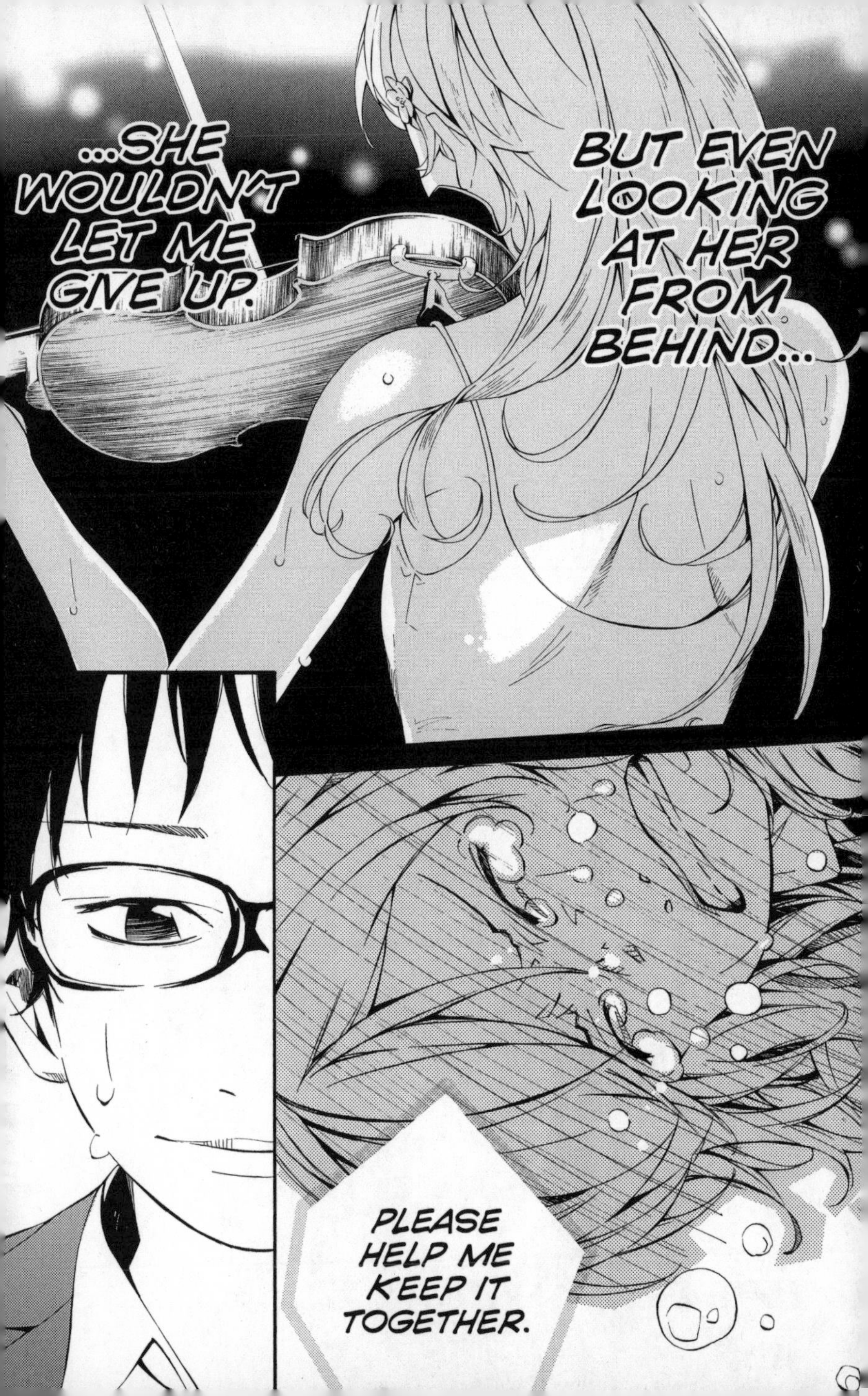
BUT EVEN LOOKING AT HER FROM BEHIND...
...SHE WOULDN'T LET ME GIVE UP.
PLEASE HELP ME KEEP IT TOGETHER.

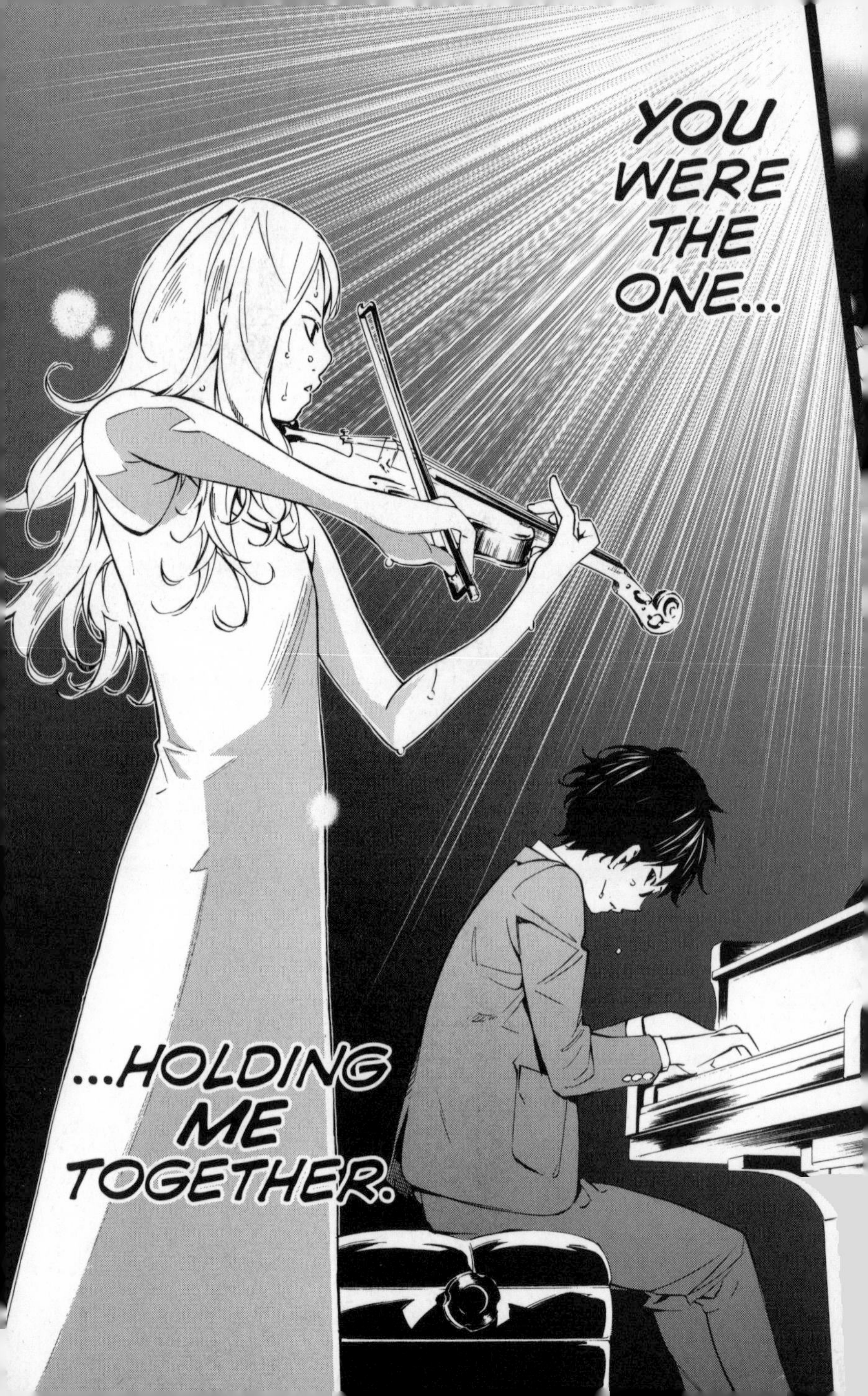
YOU WERE THE ONE...
...HOLDING ME TOGETHER.

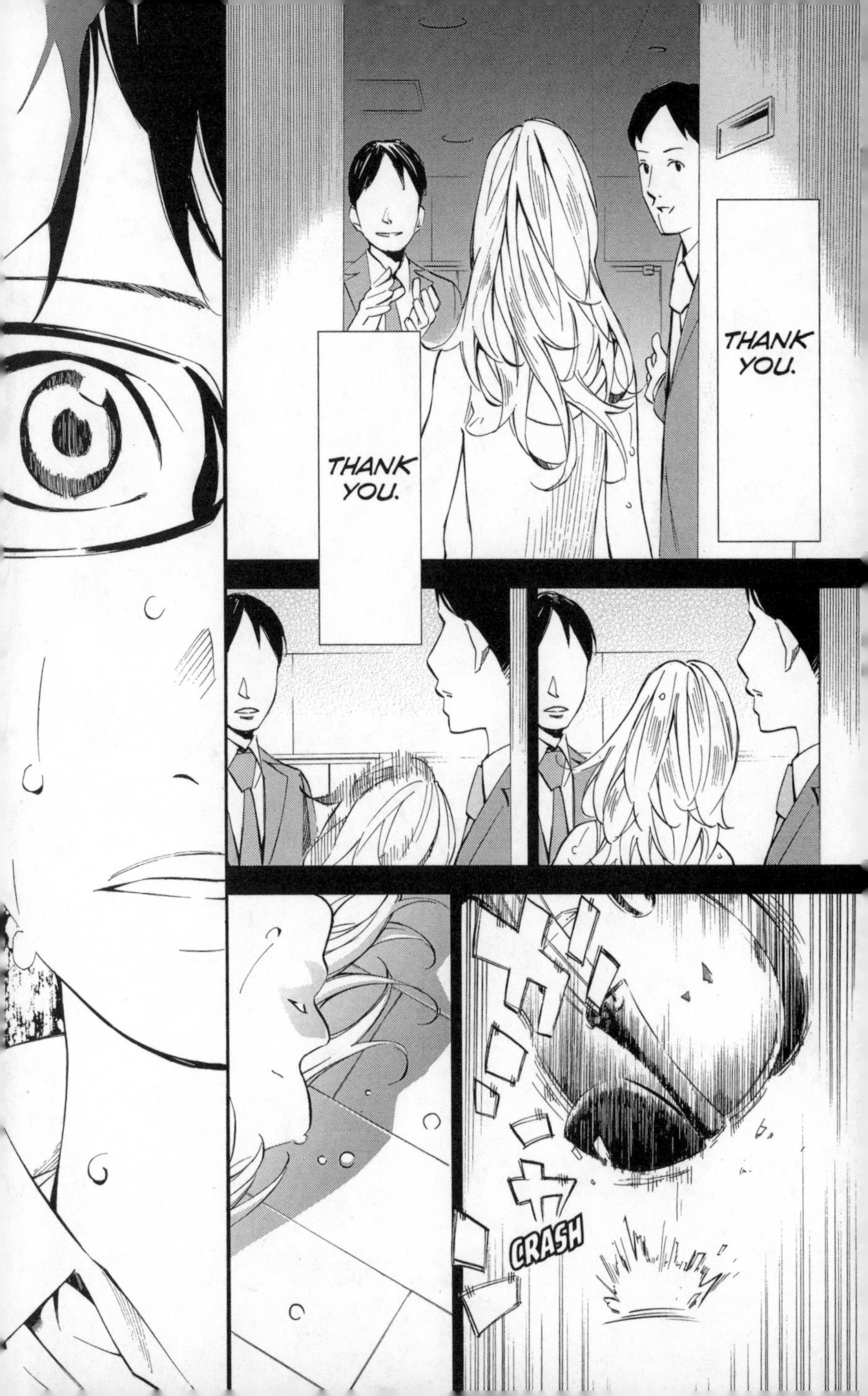
THANK YOU.
THANK YOU.
CRASH

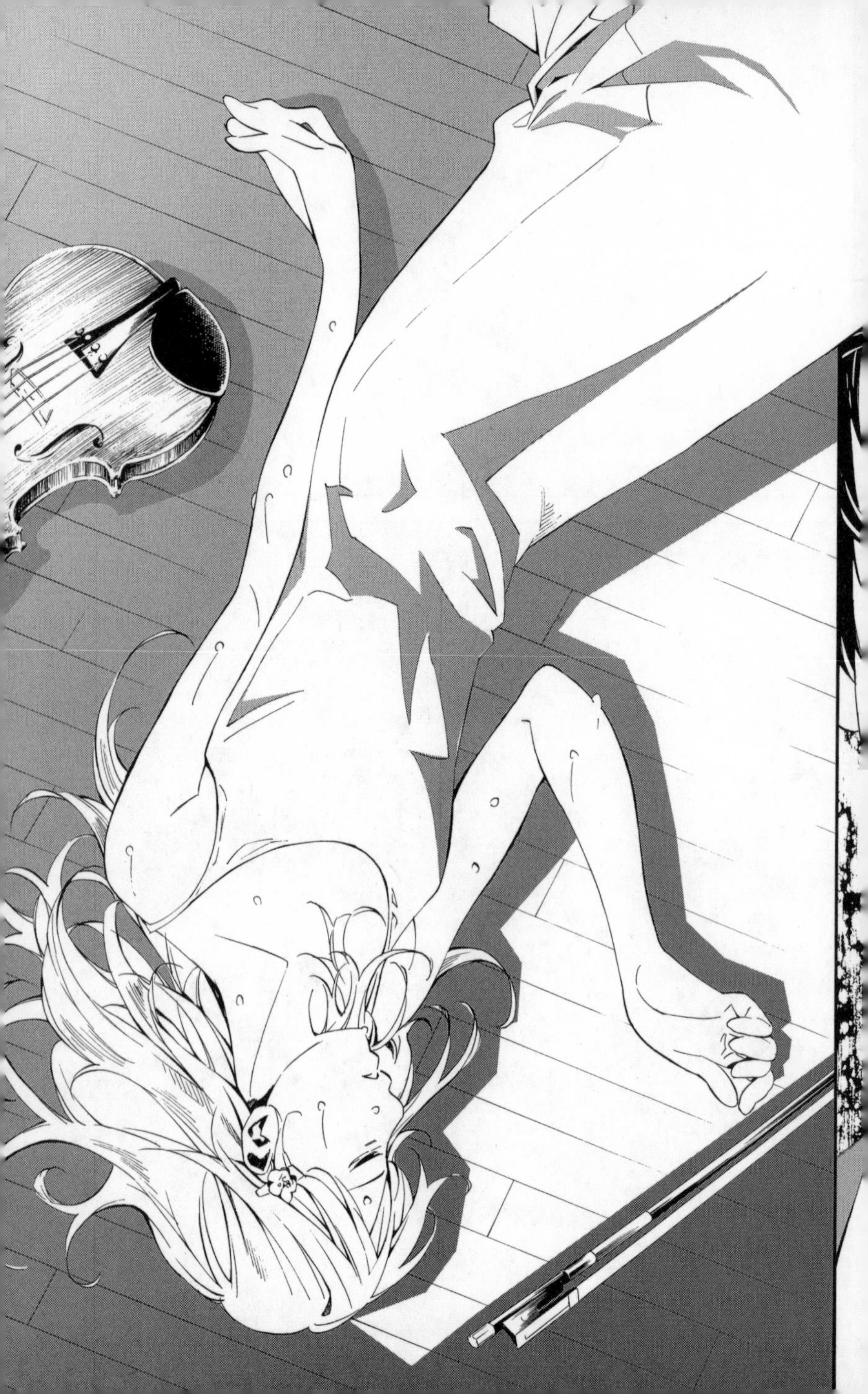

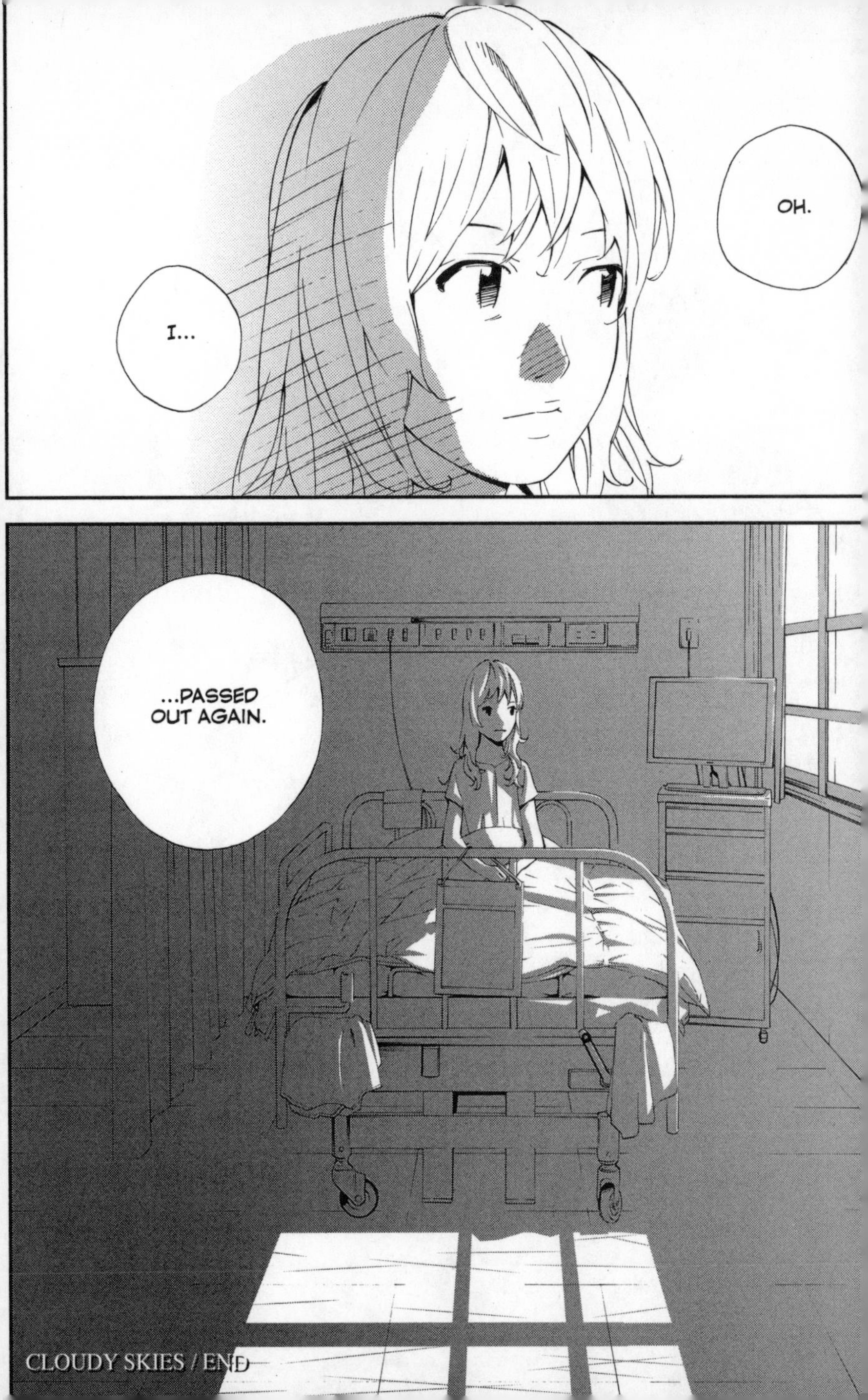
OH.
I...
...PASSED OUT AGAIN.
CLOUDY SKIES / END

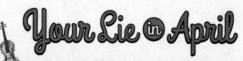

I met the girl under full-bloomed cherry blossoms, and my fate has begun to change.

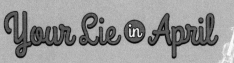

Your Lie in April

I met the girl under full-bloomed cherry blossoms, and my fate has begun to change.

Chapter 8: The Water's Surface

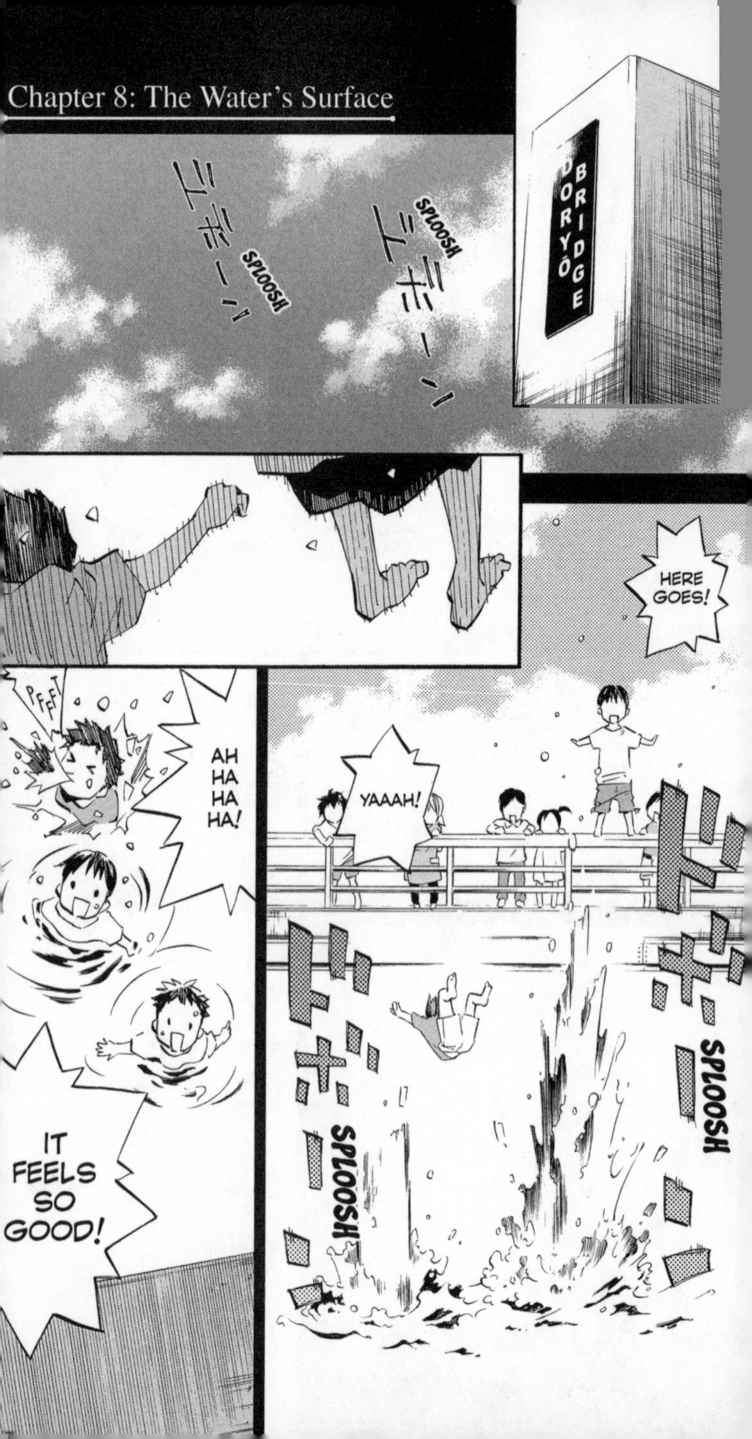
DORYŌ BRIDGE
SPLOOSH
SPLOOSH
HERE GOES!
YAAAH!
SPLOOSH
SPLOOSH
PFFT
AH HA HA HA!
IT FEELS SO GOOD!

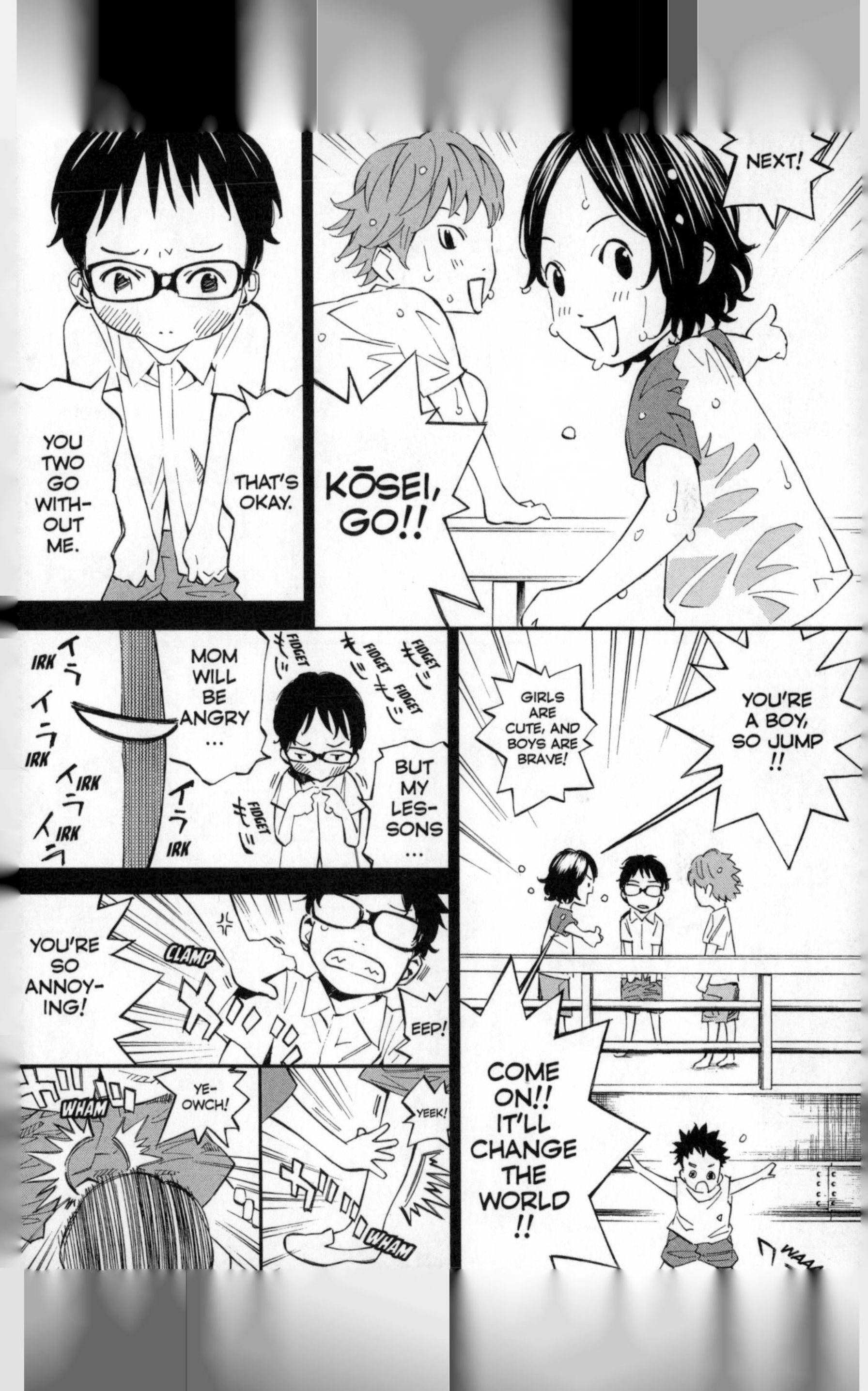
NEXT!
KŌSEI, GO!!
THAT'S OKAY.
YOU TWO GO WITH-OUT ME.
YOU'RE A BOY, SO JUMP!!
GIRLS ARE CUTE, AND BOYS ARE BRAVE!
COME ON!! IT'LL CHANGE THE WORLD!!
FIDGET FIDGET FIDGET FIDGET
MOM WILL BE ANGRY...
BUT MY LES-SONS...
IRK IRK IRK IRK IRK
YOU'RE SO ANNOY-ING!
CLAMP
EEP!
YEEK!
WHAM
YE-OWCH!
WHAM

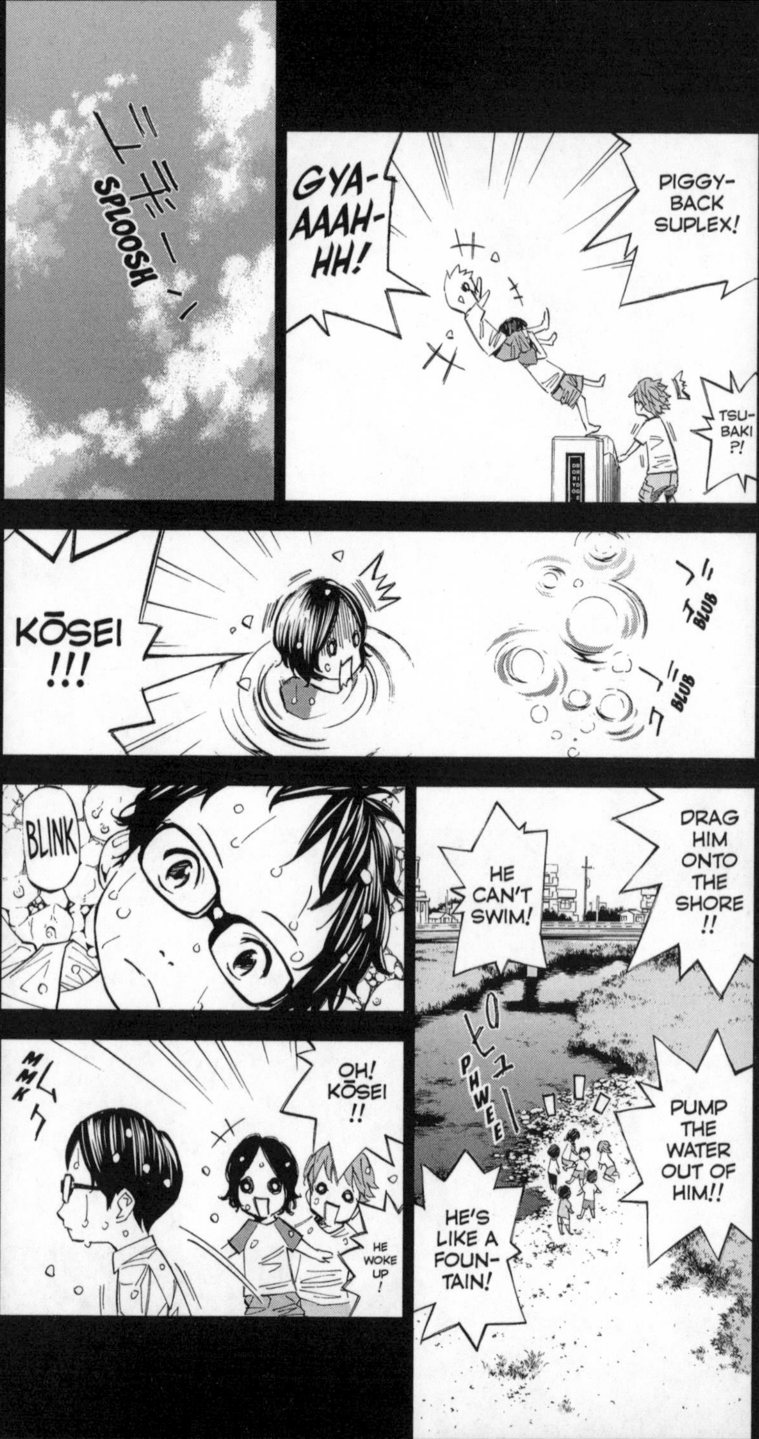
PIGGY-BACK SUPLEX!
GYA-AAAH-HH!
TSUBAKI?!
SPLOOSH
BLUB
BLUB
KŌSEI!!!
DRAG HIM ONTO THE SHORE!!
HE CAN'T SWIM!
PHWEE
PUMP THE WATER OUT OF HIM!!
HE'S LIKE A FOUNTAIN!
BLINK
OH! KŌSEI!!
HE WOKE UP!
MMK

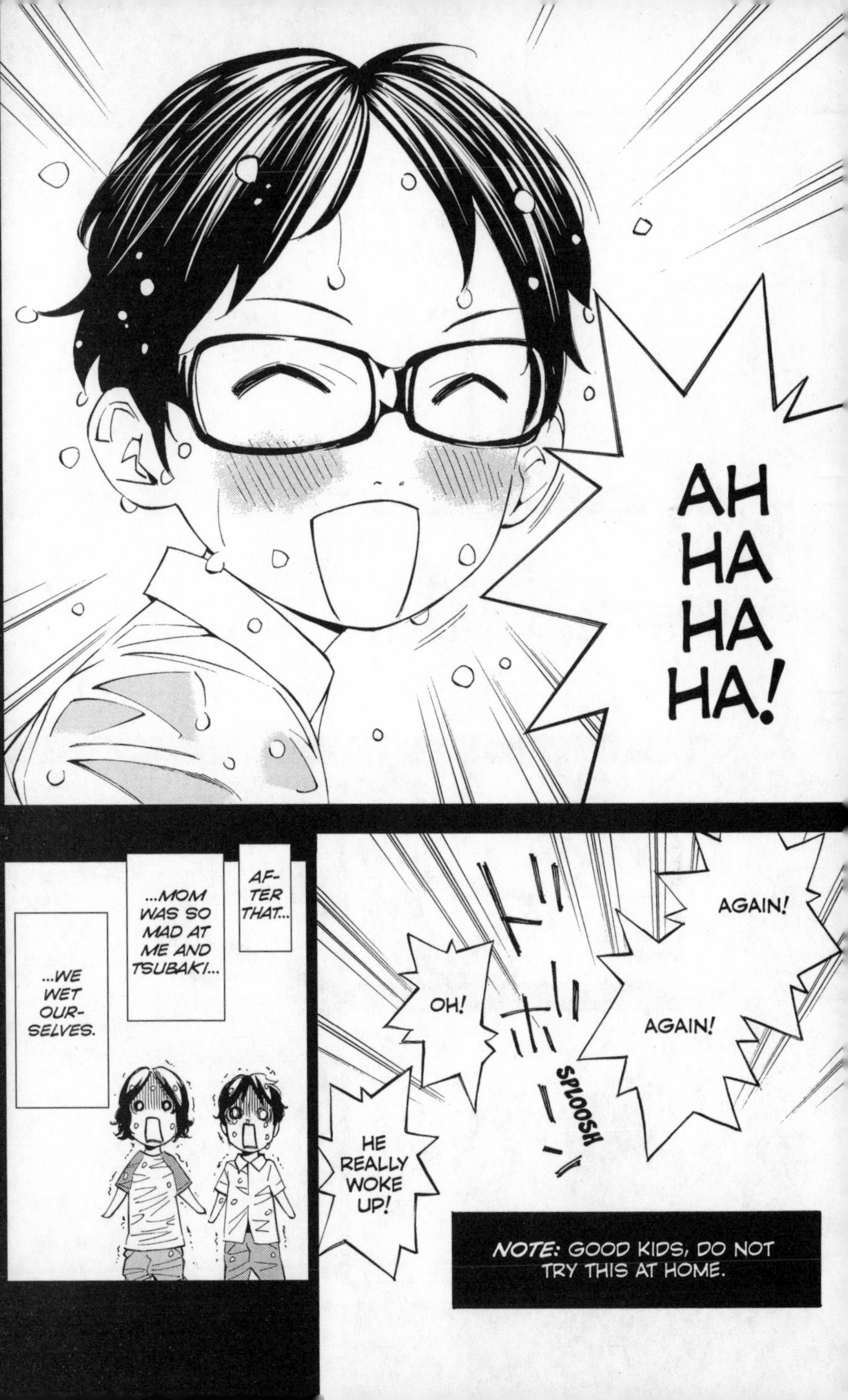
AH HA HA HA HA!
AGAIN!
AGAIN!
OH!
SPLOOSH
HE REALLY WOKE UP!
NOTE: GOOD KIDS, DO NOT TRY THIS AT HOME.
AFTER THAT...
...MOM WAS SO MAD AT ME AND TSUBAKI...
...WE WET OURSELVES.

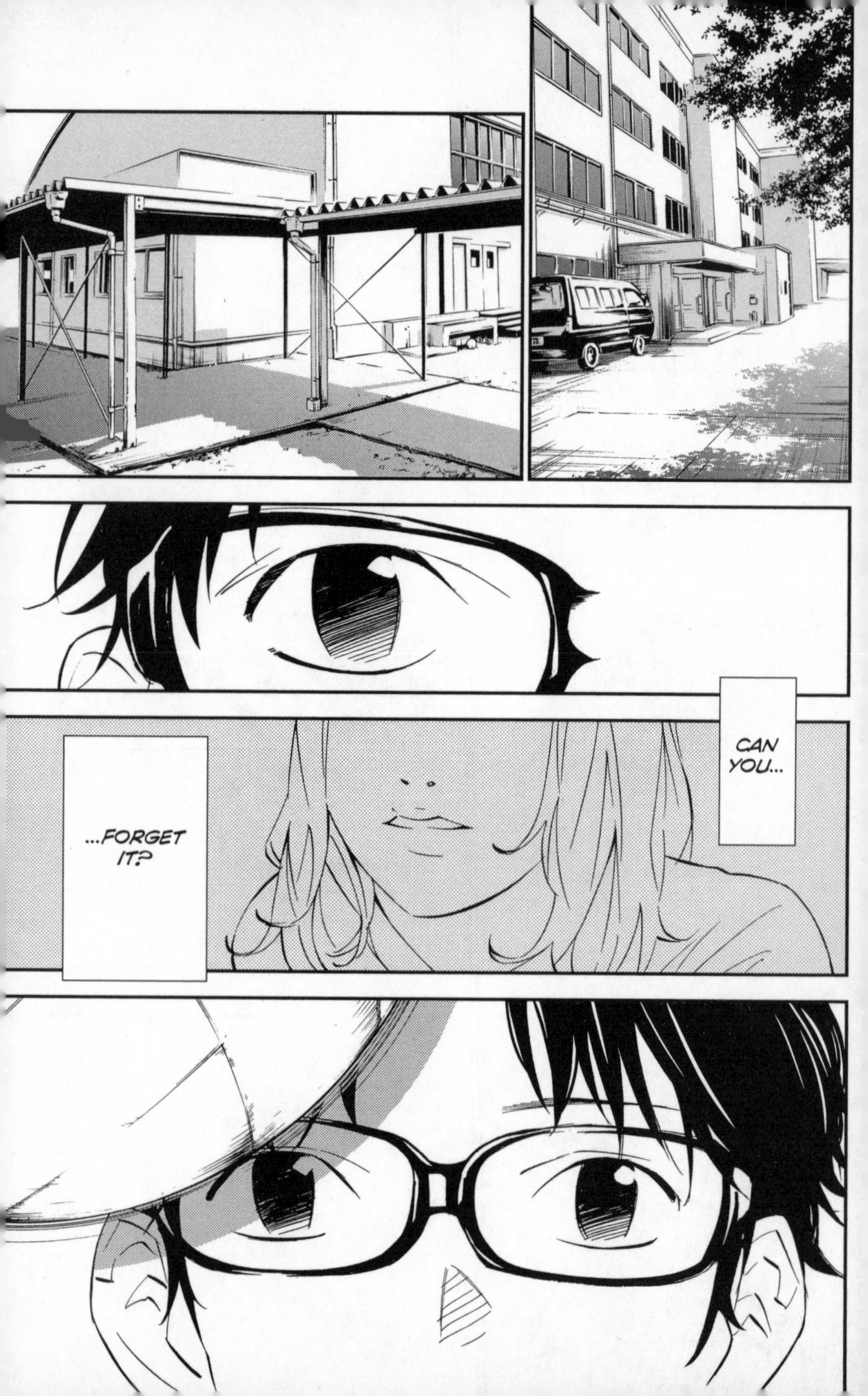
CAN YOU...
...FORGET IT?

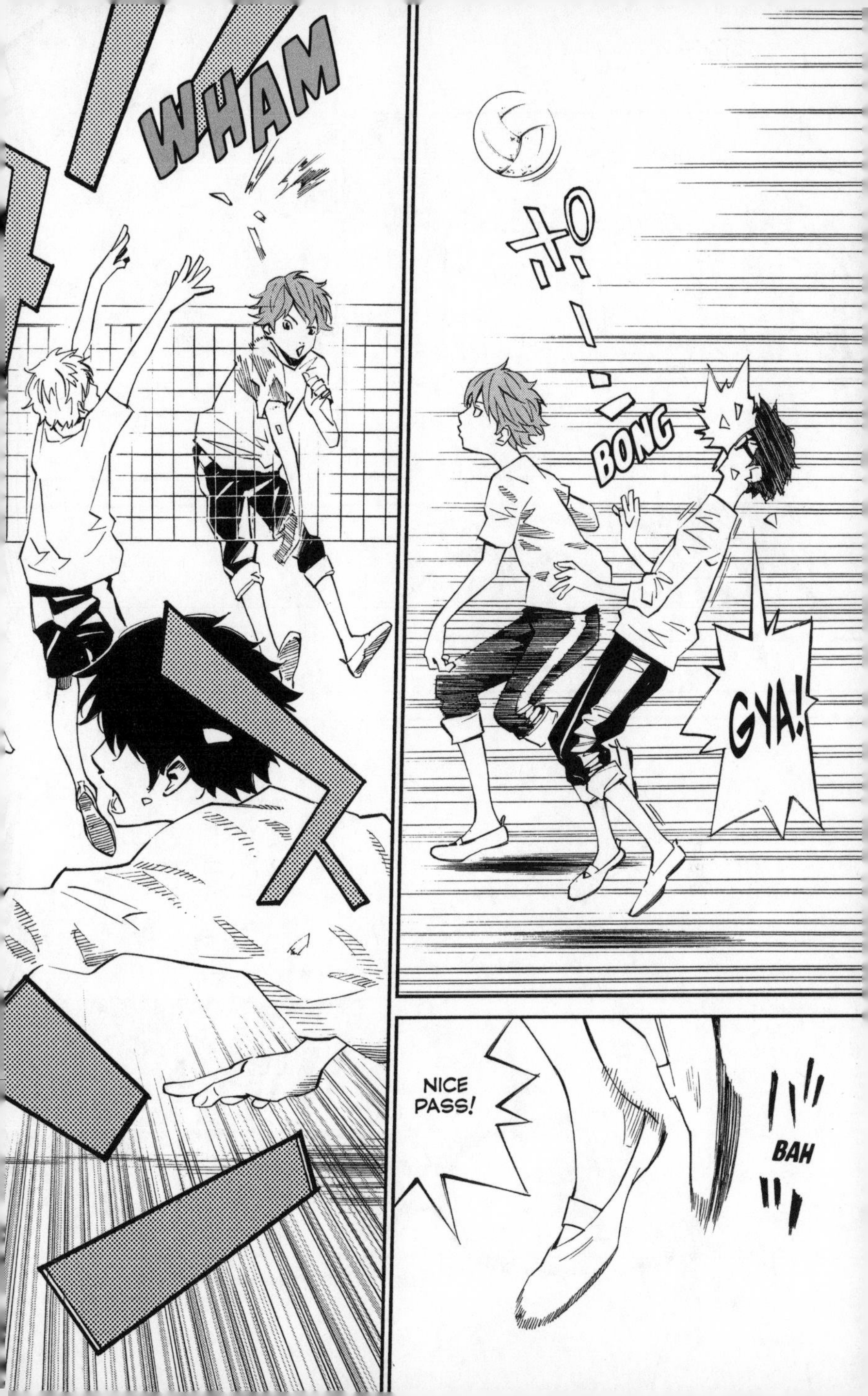
BONG
GYA!
NICE PASS!
BAH
WHAM

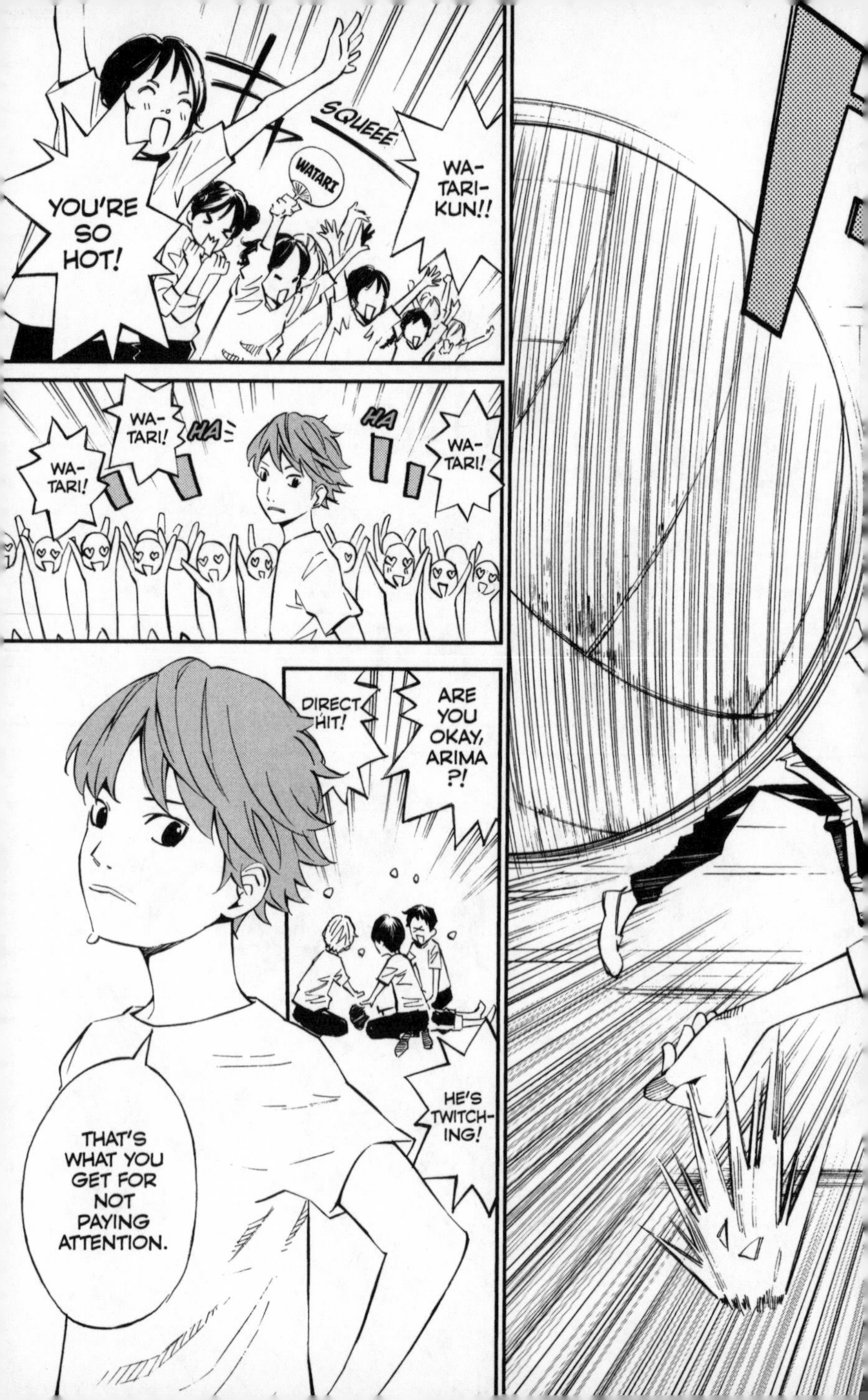
WA-TARI-KUN!!
SQUEEE
WATARI
YOU'RE SO HOT!
WA-TARI!
HA
HA
WA-TARI!
WA-TARI!
ARE YOU OKAY, ARIMA?!
DIRECT HIT!
HE'S TWITCH-ING!
THAT'S WHAT YOU GET FOR NOT PAYING ATTENTION.

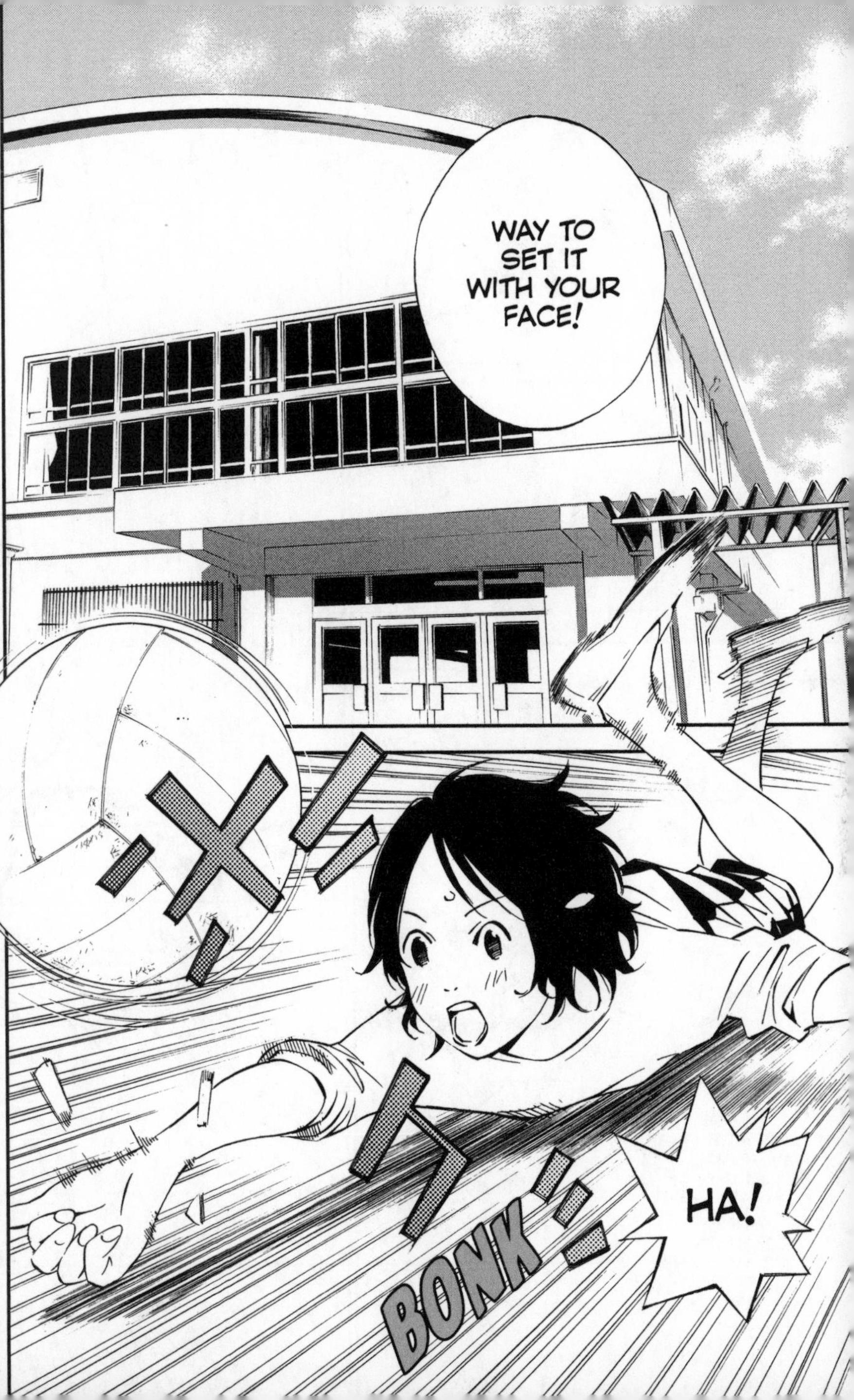
WAY TO SET IT WITH YOUR FACE!
BONK!!
HA!

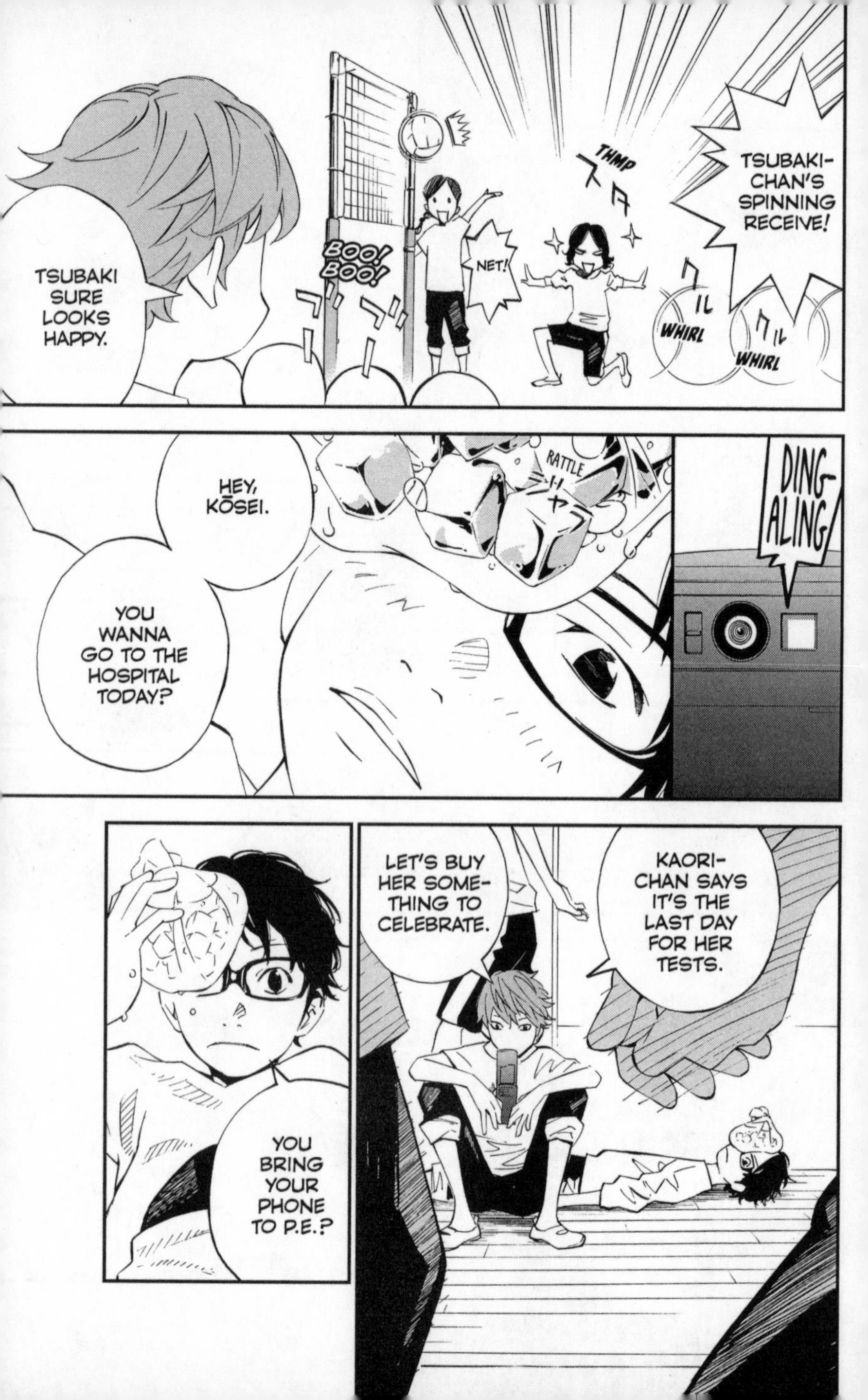
TSUBAKI-CHAN'S SPINNING RECEIVE!
WHIRL
WHIRL
THMP
NET!
BOO! BOO!
TSUBAKI SURE LOOKS HAPPY.
DING-ALING
RATTLE
HEY, KŌSEI.
YOU WANNA GO TO THE HOSPITAL TODAY?
KAORI-CHAN SAYS IT'S THE LAST DAY FOR HER TESTS.
LET'S BUY HER SOME-THING TO CELEBRATE.
YOU BRING YOUR PHONE TO P.E.?

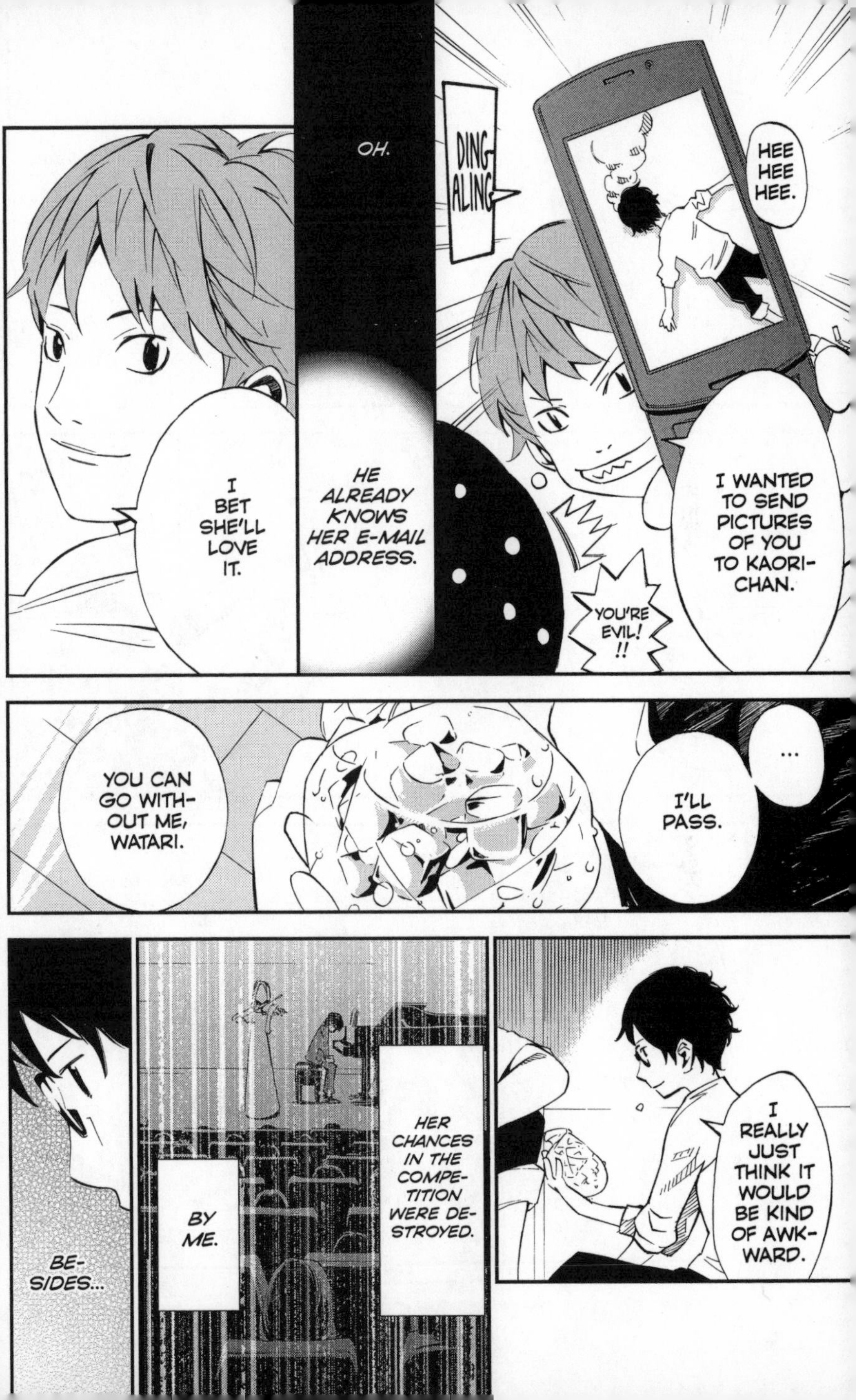
HEE HEE HEE.
DING-ALING
I WANTED TO SEND PICTURES OF YOU TO KAORI-CHAN.
YOU'RE EVIL! !!
OH.
HE ALREADY KNOWS HER E-MAIL ADDRESS.
I BET SHE'LL LOVE IT.
...
I'LL PASS.
YOU CAN GO WITHOUT ME, WATARI.
I REALLY JUST THINK IT WOULD BE KIND OF AWKWARD.
HER CHANCES IN THE COMPETITION WERE DESTROYED.
BY ME.
BESIDES...

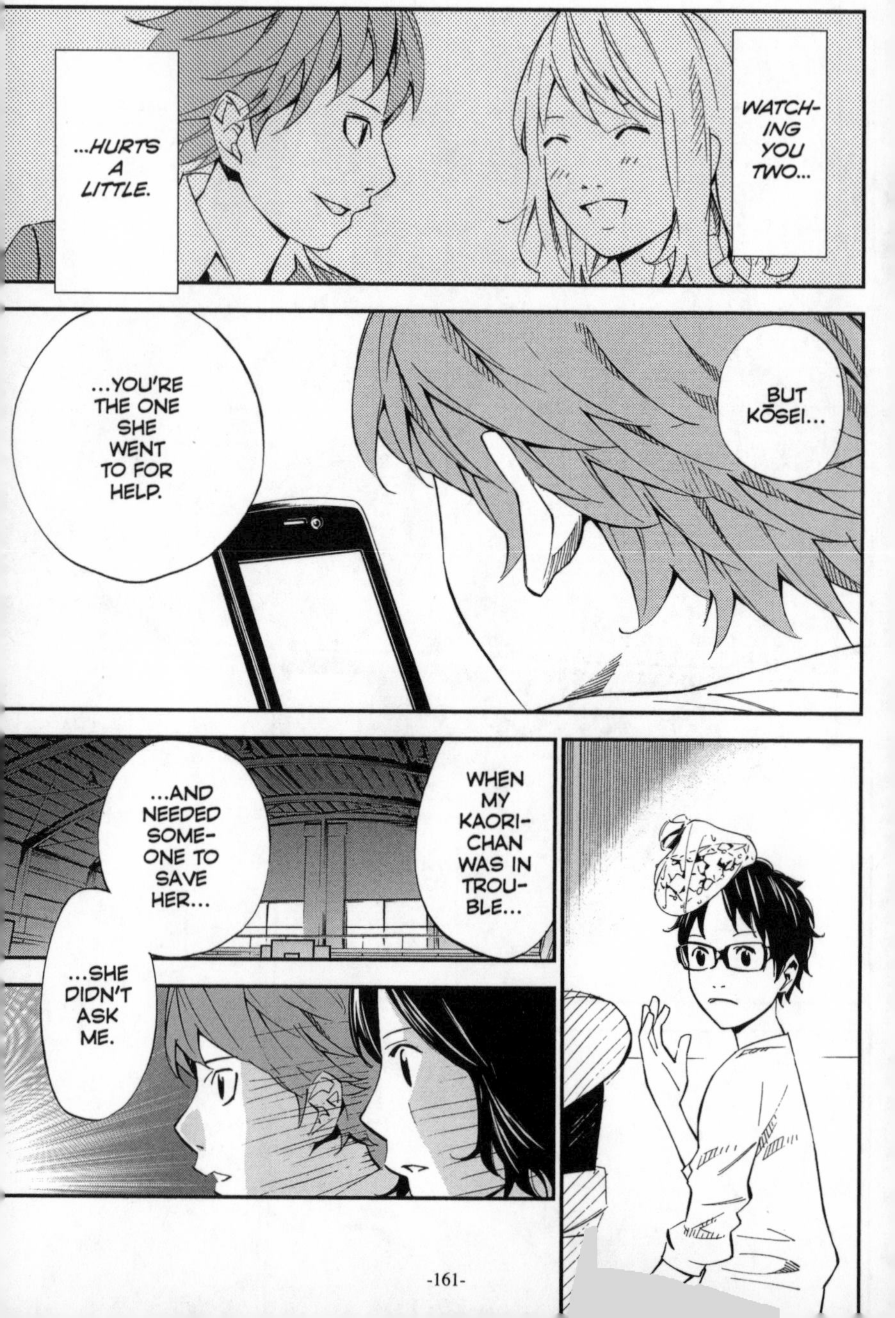
WATCH-ING YOU TWO...
...HURTS A LITTLE.
BUT KŌSEI...
...YOU'RE THE ONE SHE WENT TO FOR HELP.
WHEN MY KAORI-CHAN WAS IN TROU-BLE...
...AND NEEDED SOME-ONE TO SAVE HER...
...SHE DIDN'T ASK ME.

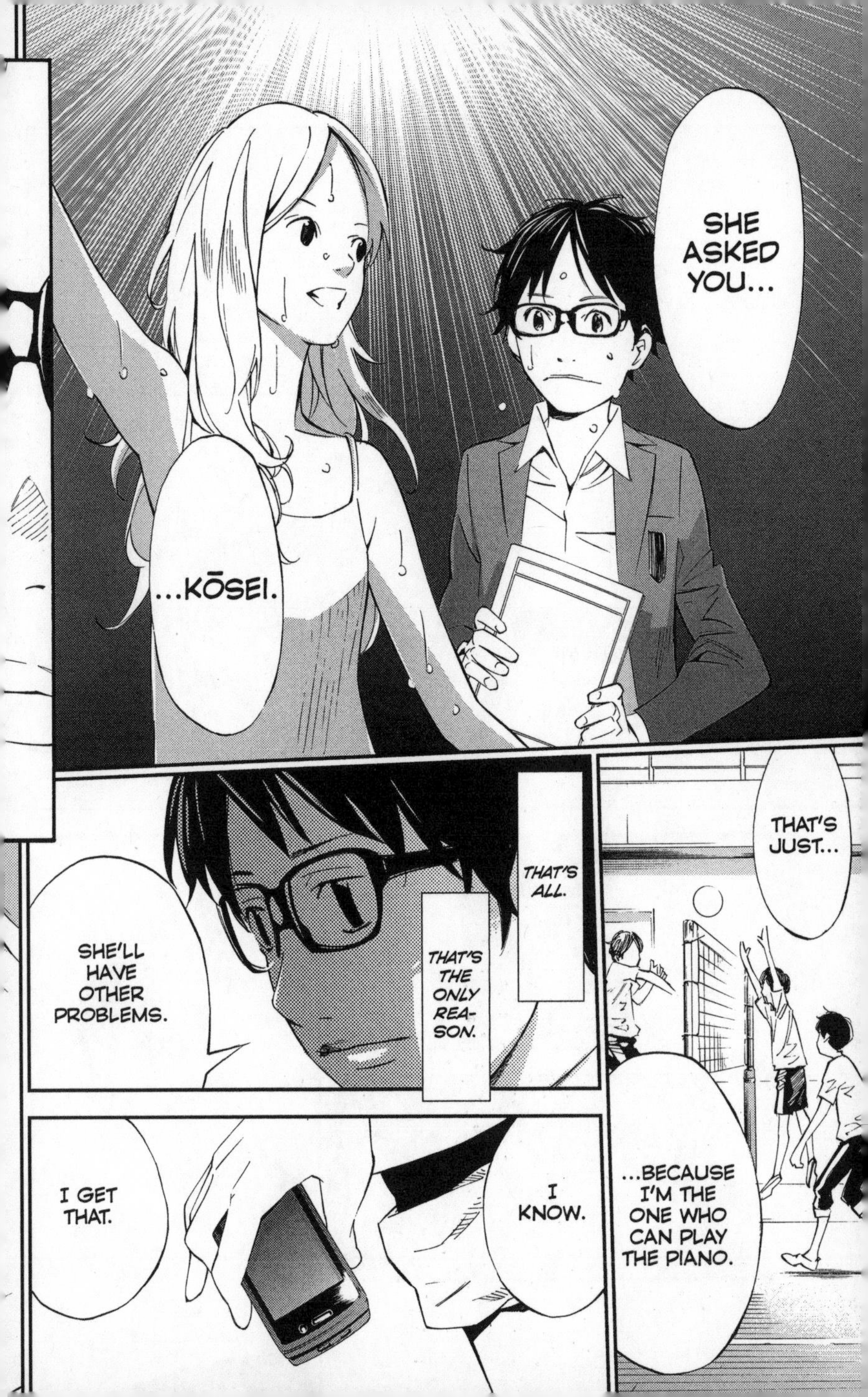
SHE ASKED YOU...
...KŌSEI.
THAT'S JUST...
...BECAUSE I'M THE ONE WHO CAN PLAY THE PIANO.
THAT'S ALL.
THAT'S THE ONLY REA-SON.
SHE'LL HAVE OTHER PROBLEMS.
I KNOW.
I GET THAT.

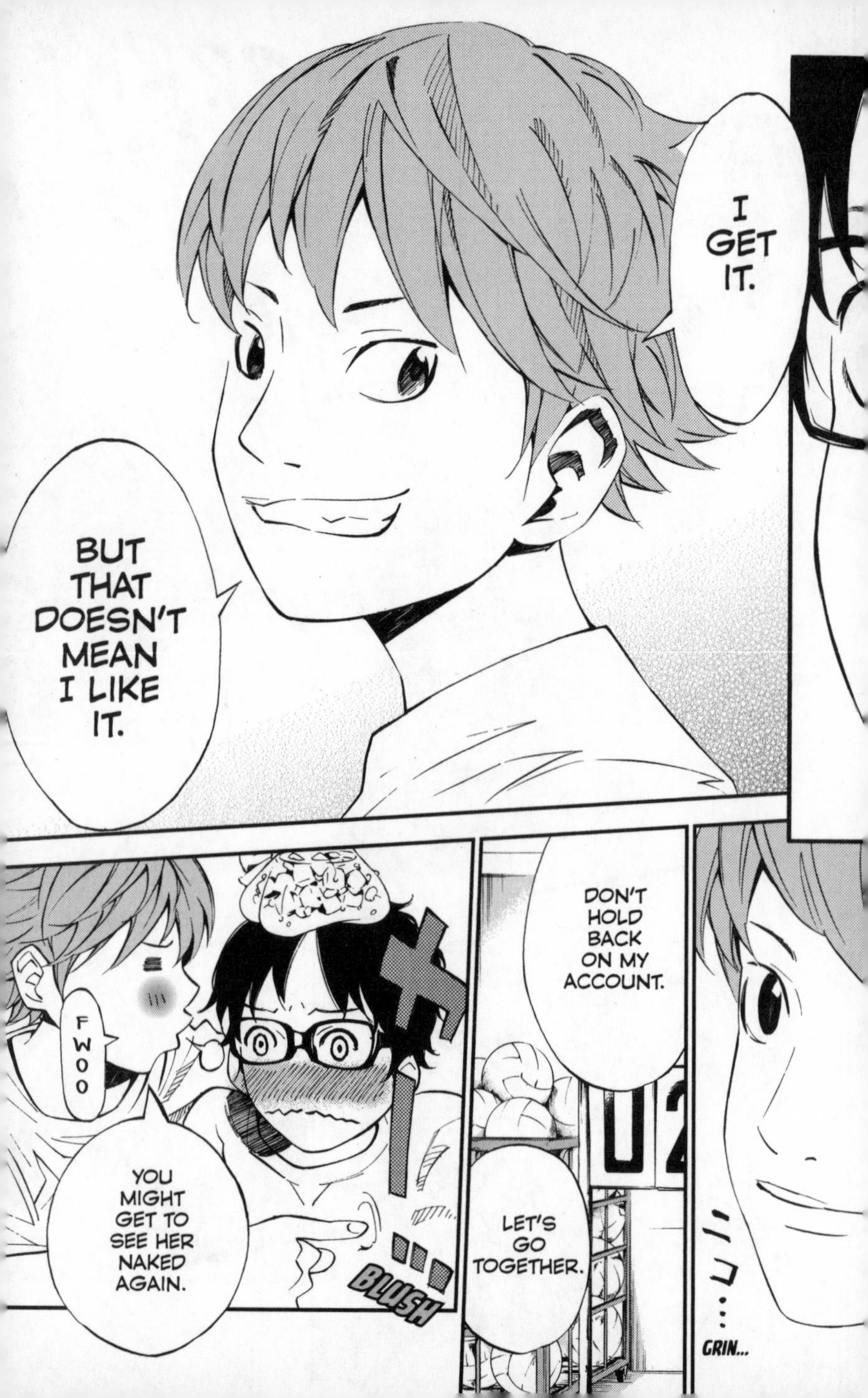
I GET IT.
BUT THAT DOESN'T MEAN I LIKE IT.
DON'T HOLD BACK ON MY ACCOUNT.
LET'S GO TOGETHER.
GRIN...
FWOO
YOU MIGHT GET TO SEE HER NAKED AGAIN.
BLUSH

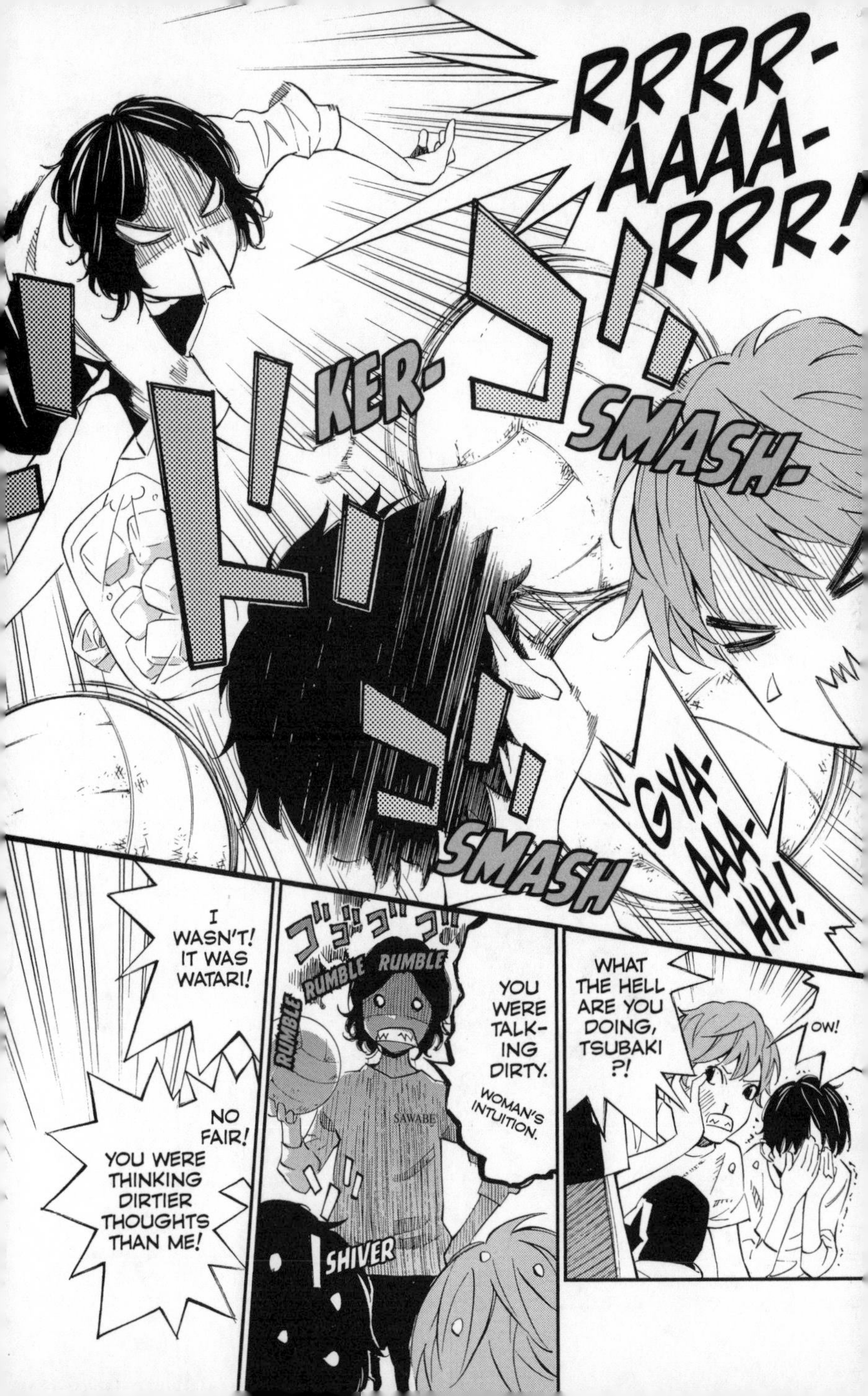
RRRR-AAAA-RRRR!
KER-
SMASH-
SMASH
GYA-AAA-HH!
WHAT THE HELL ARE YOU DOING, TSUBAKI ?!
OW!
YOU WERE TALKING DIRTY.
WOMAN'S INTUITION.
RUMBLE RUMBLE RUMBLE
SAWABE
SHIVER
I WASN'T! IT WAS WATARI!
NO FAIR!
YOU WERE THINKING DIRTIER THOUGHTS THAN ME!

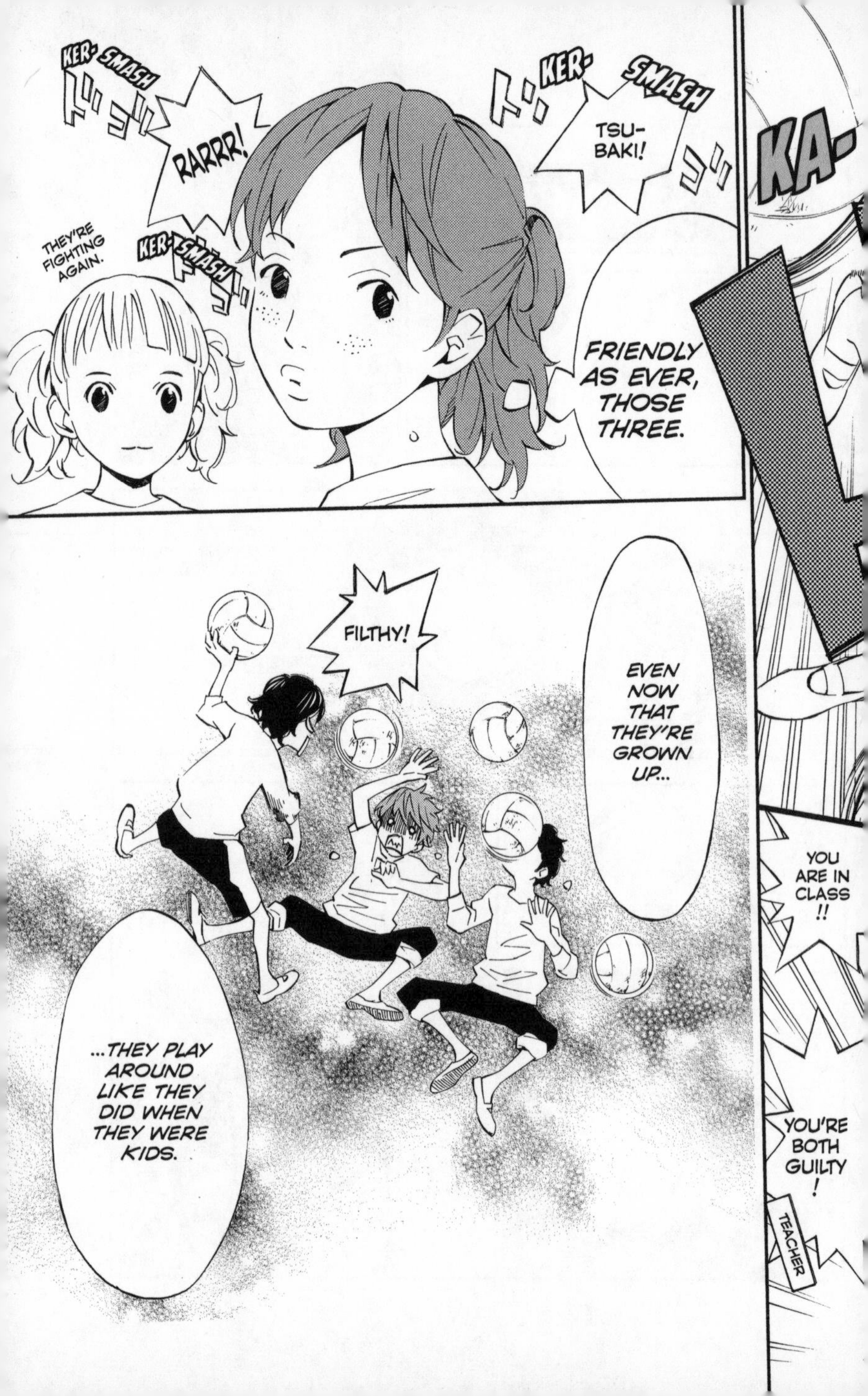
KA-
YOU ARE IN CLASS !!
YOU'RE BOTH GUILTY !
TEACHER
KER-SMASH
TSU-BAKI!
KER-SMASH
RARRR!
THEY'RE FIGHTING AGAIN.
KER-SMASH
FRIENDLY AS EVER, THOSE THREE.
EVEN NOW THAT THEY'RE GROWN UP...
FILTHY!
...THEY PLAY AROUND LIKE THEY DID WHEN THEY WERE KIDS.

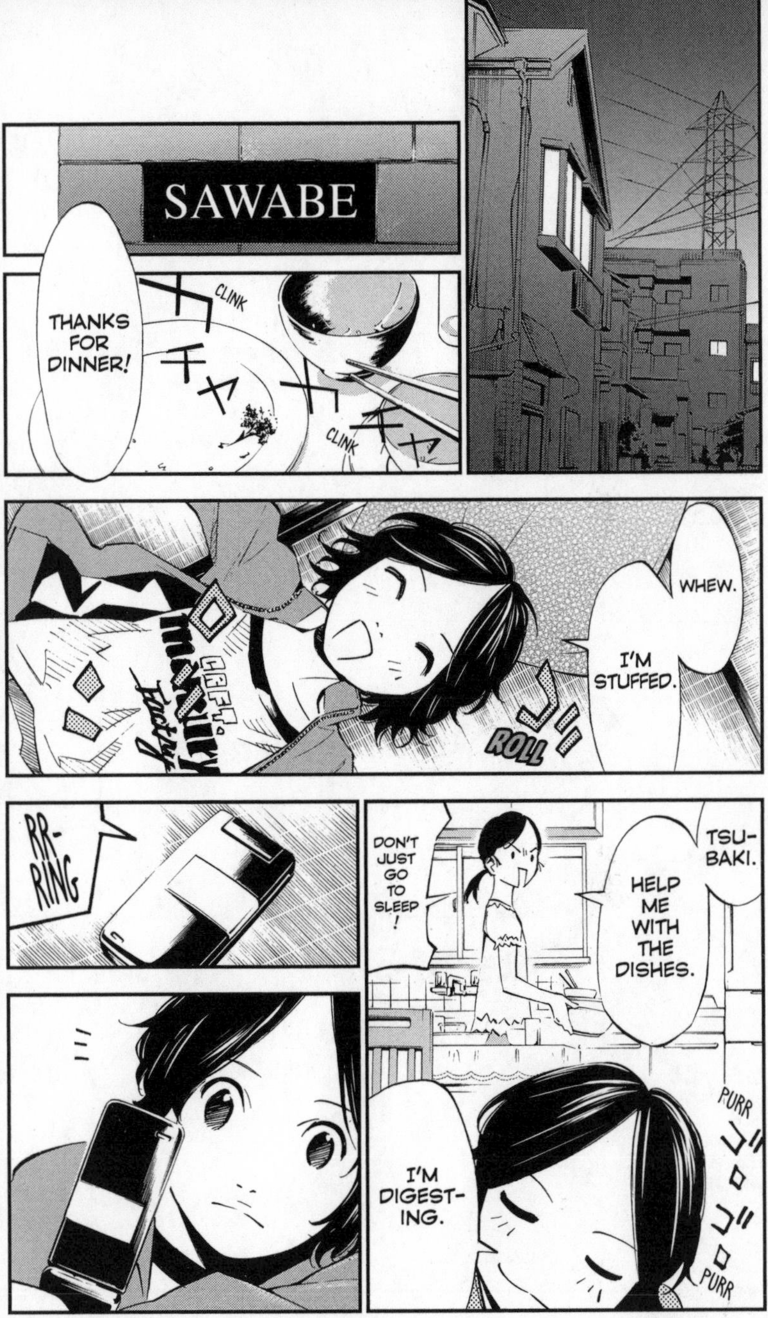
SAWABE
THANKS FOR DINNER!
CLINK
CLINK
WHEW.
I'M STUFFED.
ROLL
TSU-BAKI.
HELP ME WITH THE DISHES.
DON'T JUST GO TO SLEEP!
RR-RING
PURR
I'M DIGEST-ING.
PURR

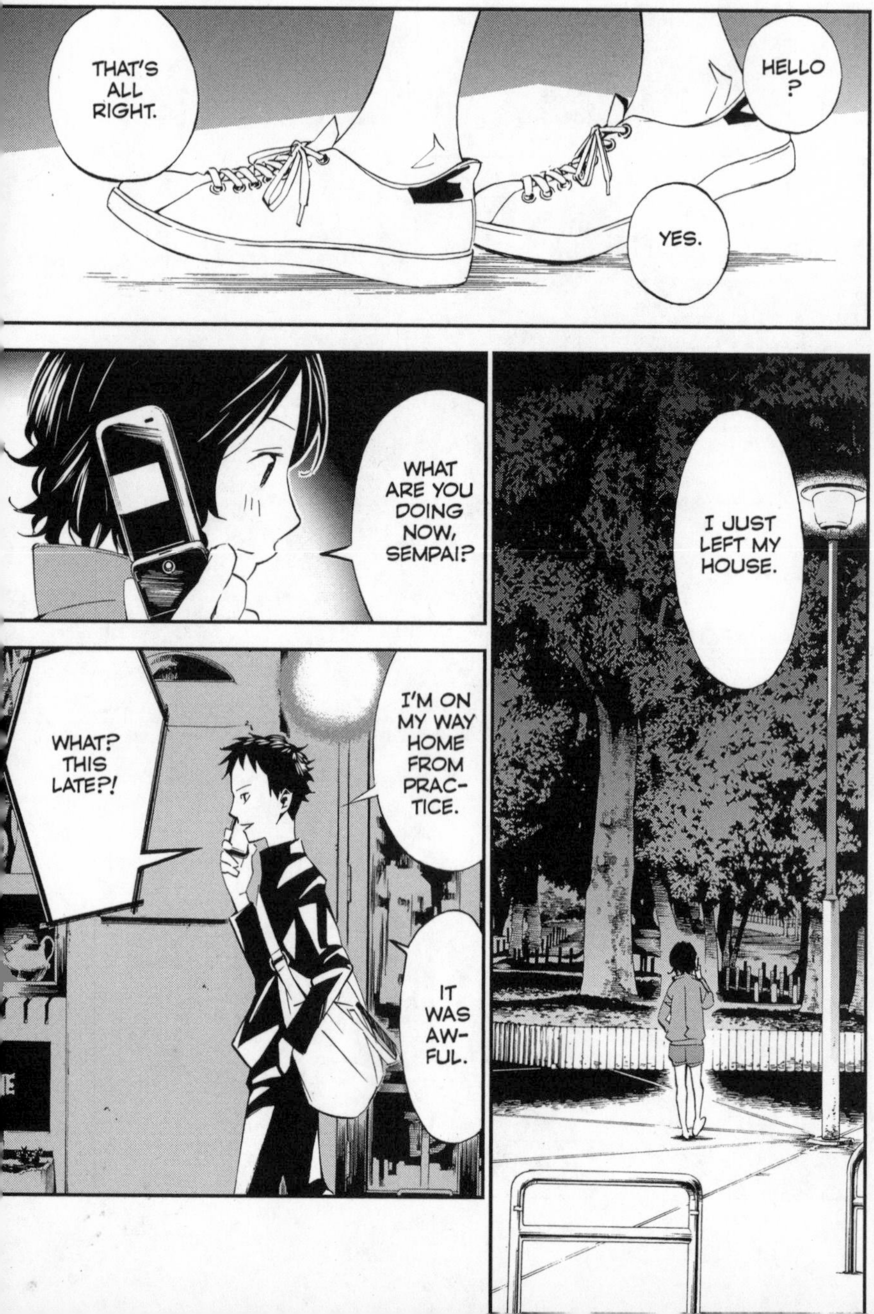
HELLO ?
YES.
THAT'S ALL RIGHT.
WHAT ARE YOU DOING NOW, SEMPAI?
I'M ON MY WAY HOME FROM PRAC- TICE.
IT WAS AW- FUL.
I JUST LEFT MY HOUSE.
WHAT? THIS LATE?!

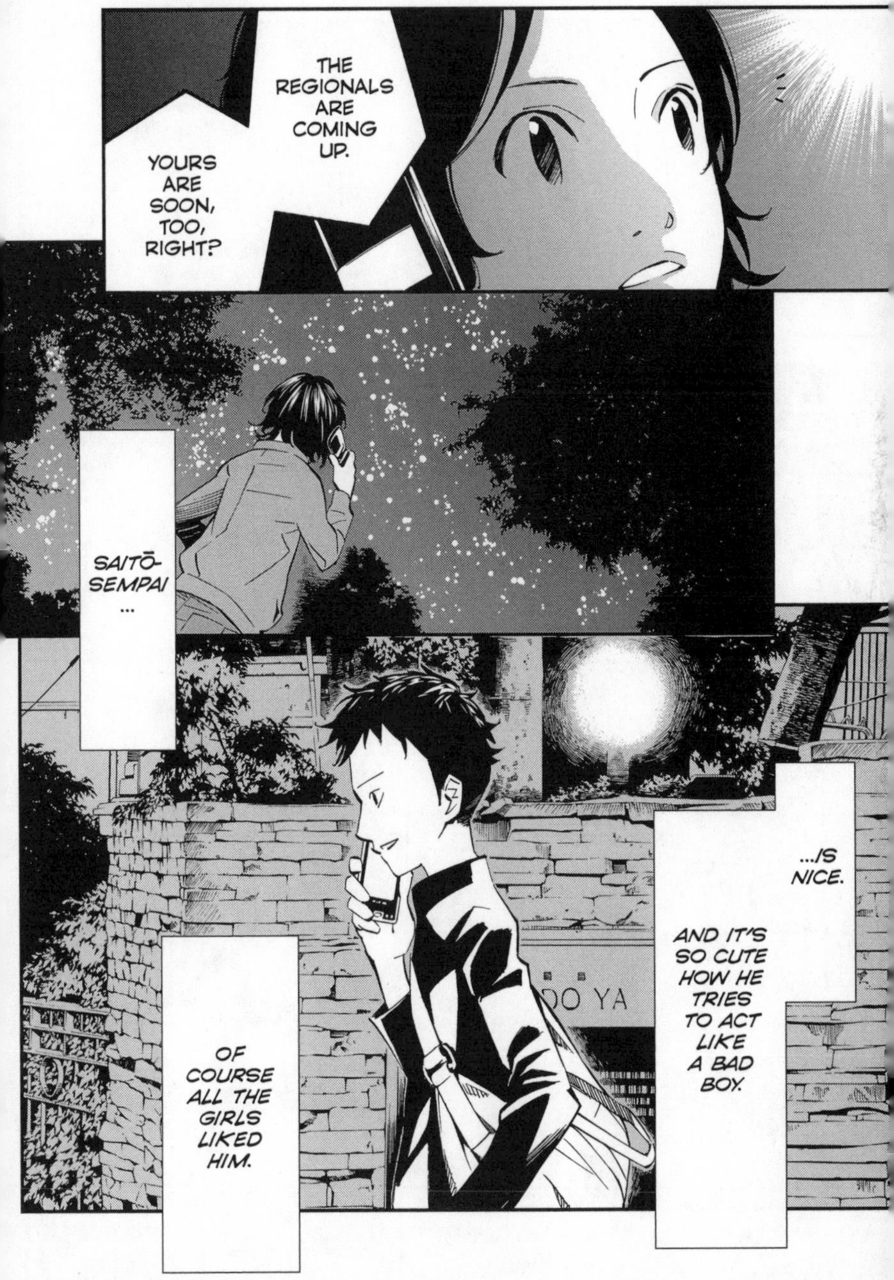
THE REGIONALS ARE COMING UP.
YOURS ARE SOON, TOO, RIGHT?
SAITŌ-SEMPAI ...
...IS NICE.
AND IT'S SO CUTE HOW HE TRIES TO ACT LIKE A BAD BOY.
OF COURSE ALL THE GIRLS LIKED HIM.

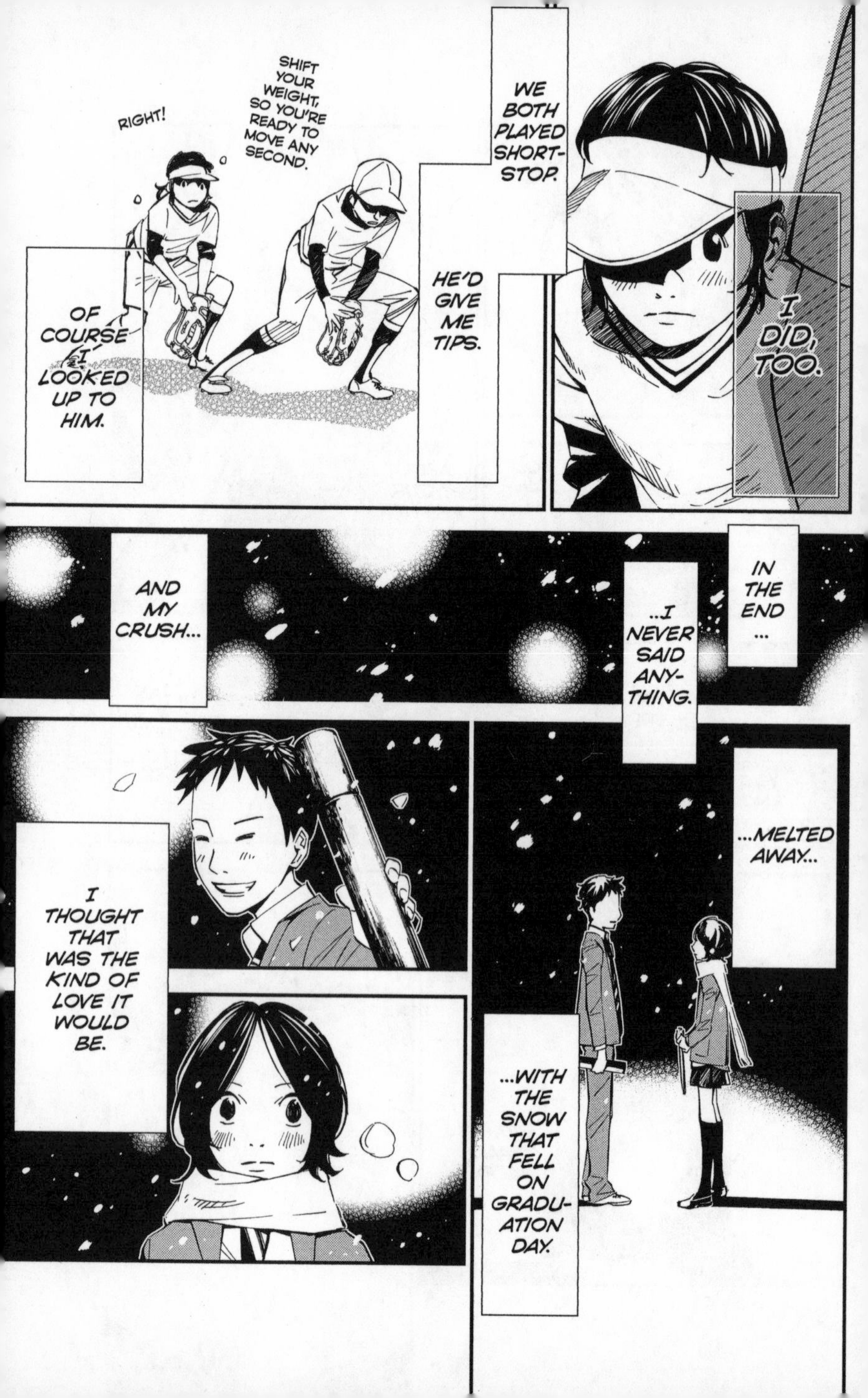
I DID, TOO.
WE BOTH PLAYED SHORT-STOP.
HE'D GIVE ME TIPS.
SHIFT YOUR WEIGHT, SO YOU'RE READY TO MOVE ANY SECOND.
RIGHT!
OF COURSE I LOOKED UP TO HIM.
IN THE END ...
...I NEVER SAID ANY-THING.
AND MY CRUSH...
...MELTED AWAY...
...WITH THE SNOW THAT FELL ON GRADU-ATION DAY.
I THOUGHT THAT WAS THE KIND OF LOVE IT WOULD BE.

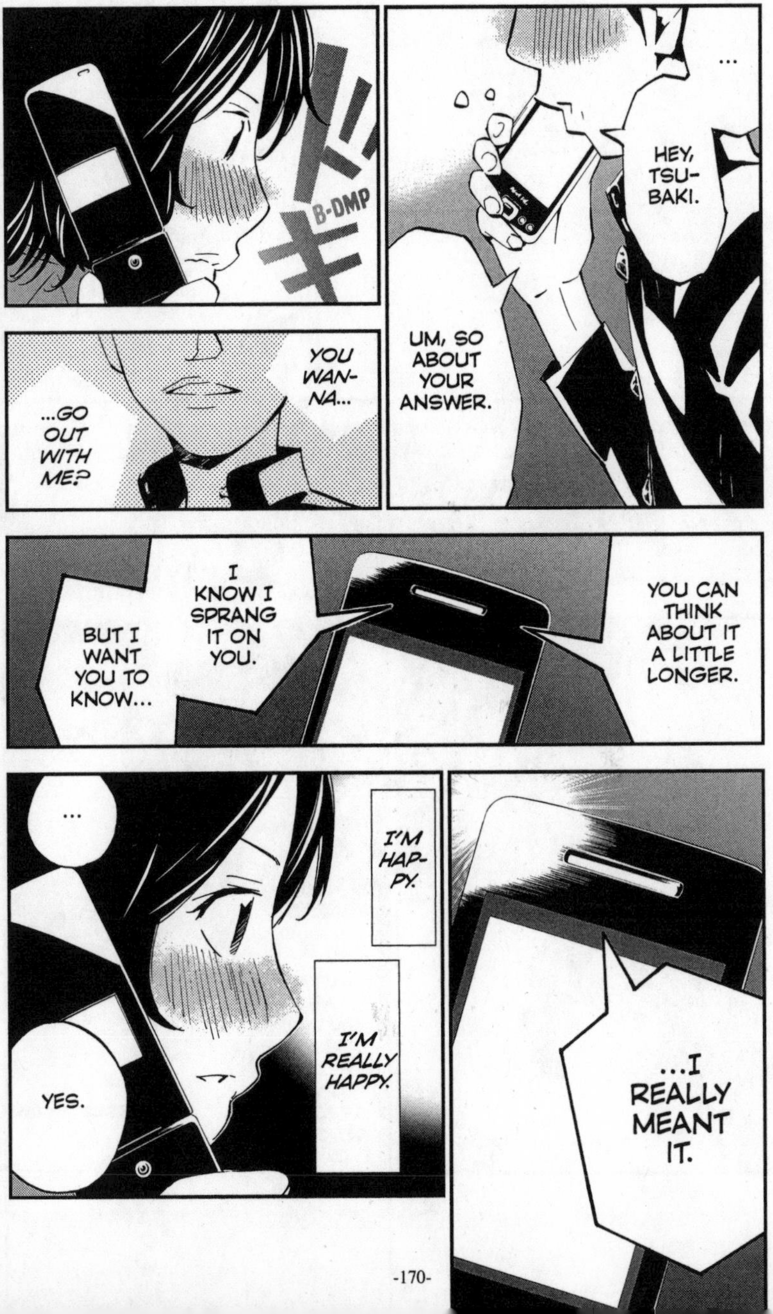
...
HEY, TSU-BAKI.
UM, SO ABOUT YOUR ANSWER.
B-DMP
YOU WAN-NA...
...GO OUT WITH ME?
YOU CAN THINK ABOUT IT A LITTLE LONGER.
I KNOW I SPRANG IT ON YOU.
BUT I WANT YOU TO KNOW...
...I REALLY MEANT IT.
I'M HAP-PY.
...
I'M REALLY HAPPY.
YES.

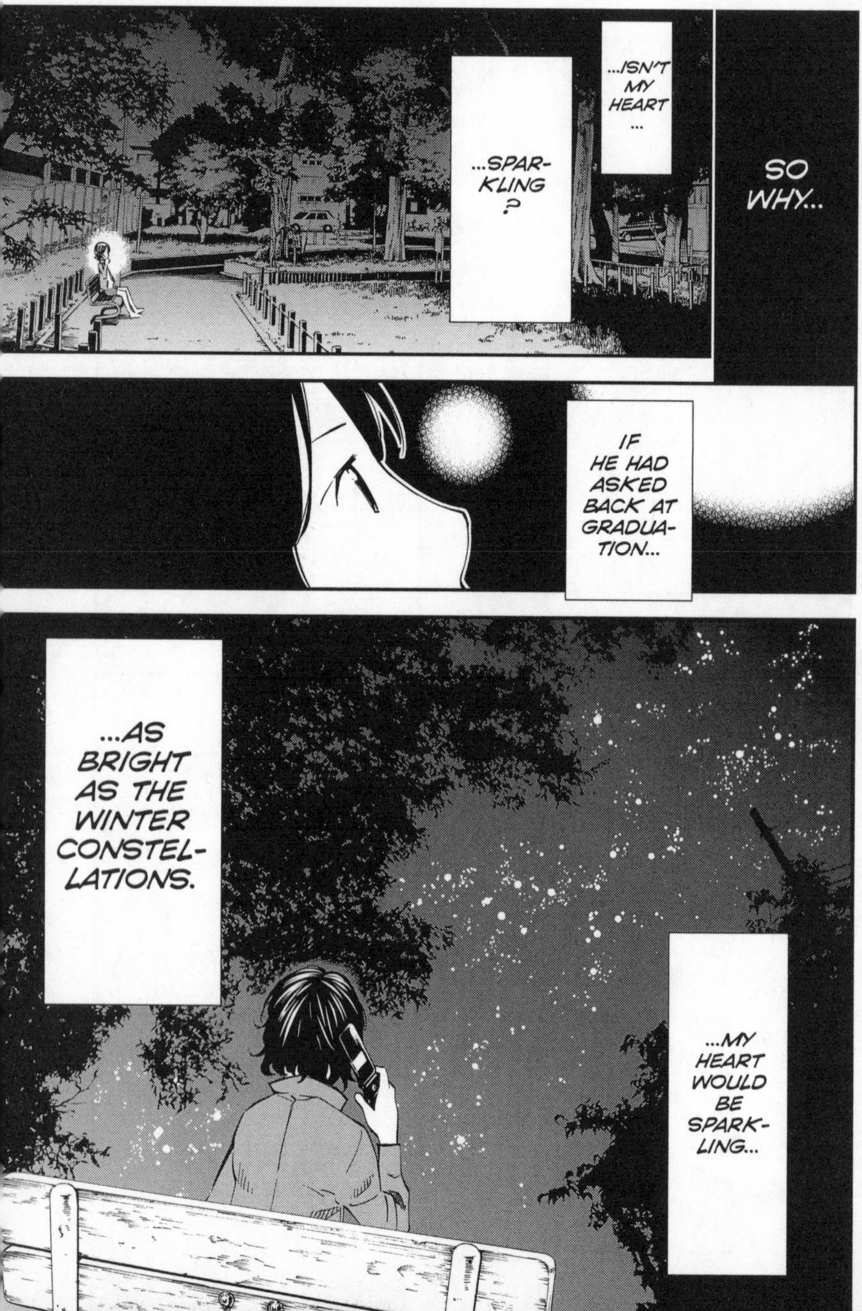
SO WHY...
...ISN'T MY HEART...
...SPAR-KLING?
IF HE HAD ASKED BACK AT GRADUA-TION...
...MY HEART WOULD BE SPARK-LING...
...AS BRIGHT AS THE WINTER CONSTEL-LATIONS.

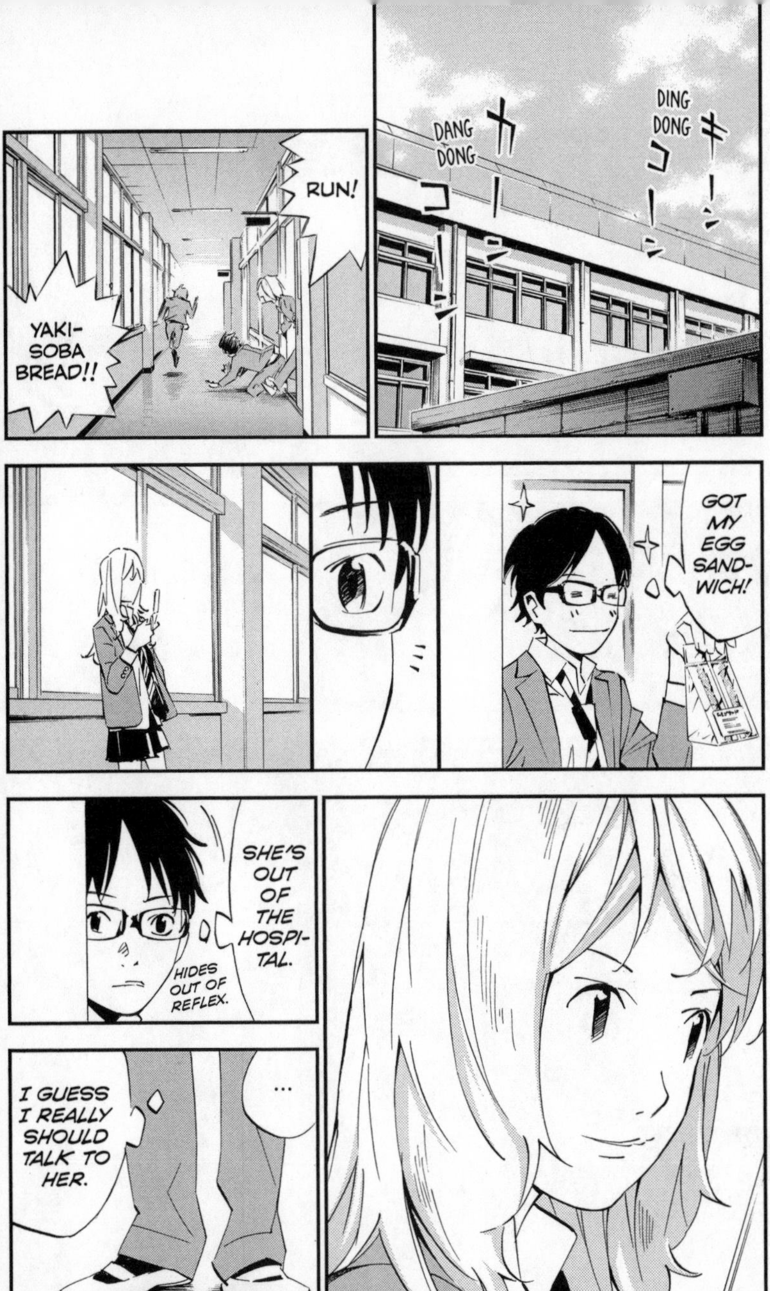
DING DONG
キーンコーン
DANG DONG
カーンコーン
RUN!
YAKI-SOBA BREAD!!
GOT MY EGG SANDWICH!
SHE'S OUT OF THE HOSPITAL.
HIDES OUT OF REFLEX.
...
I GUESS I REALLY SHOULD TALK TO HER.

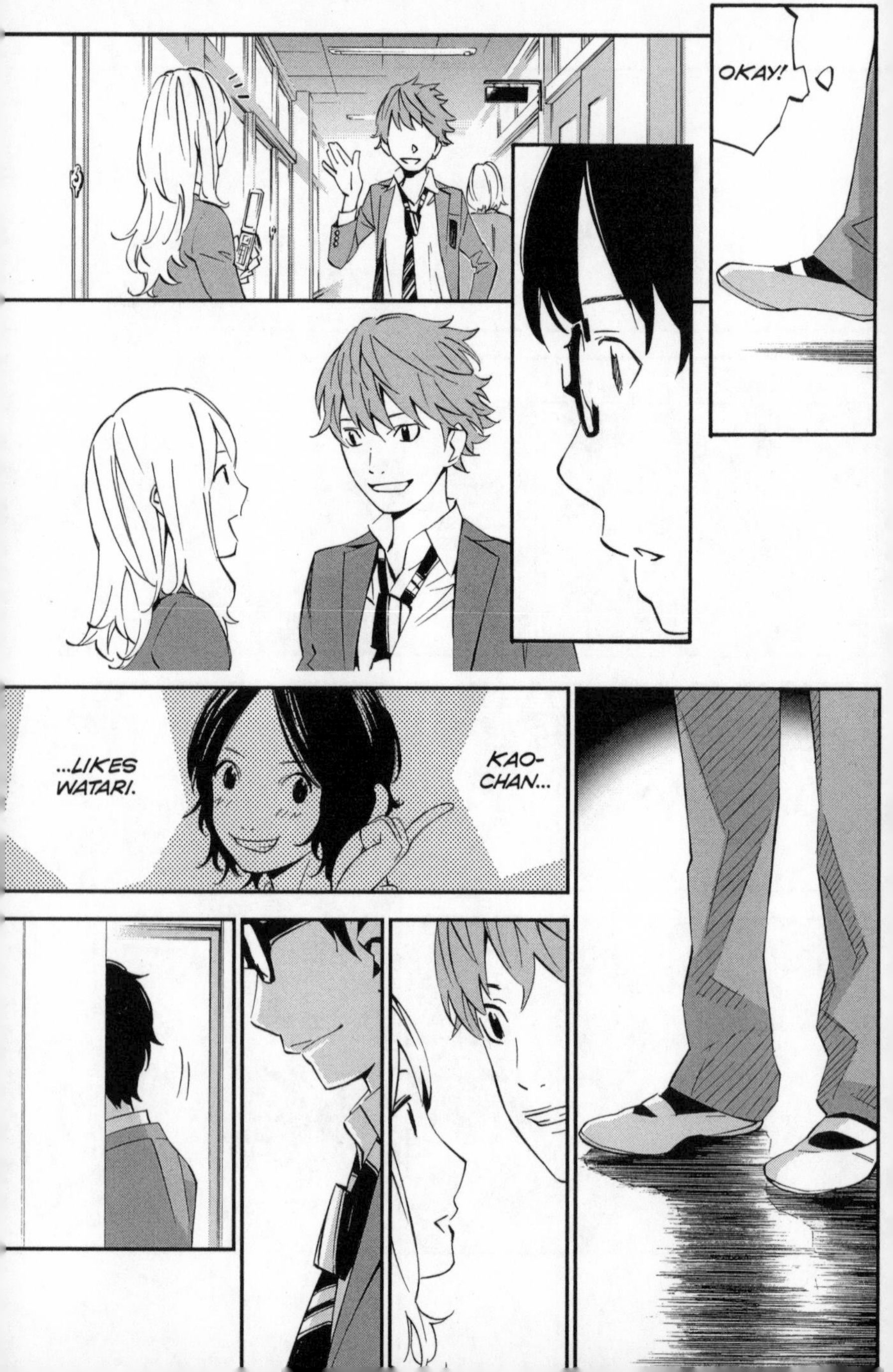
OKAY!
KAO-CHAN...
...LIKES WATARI.

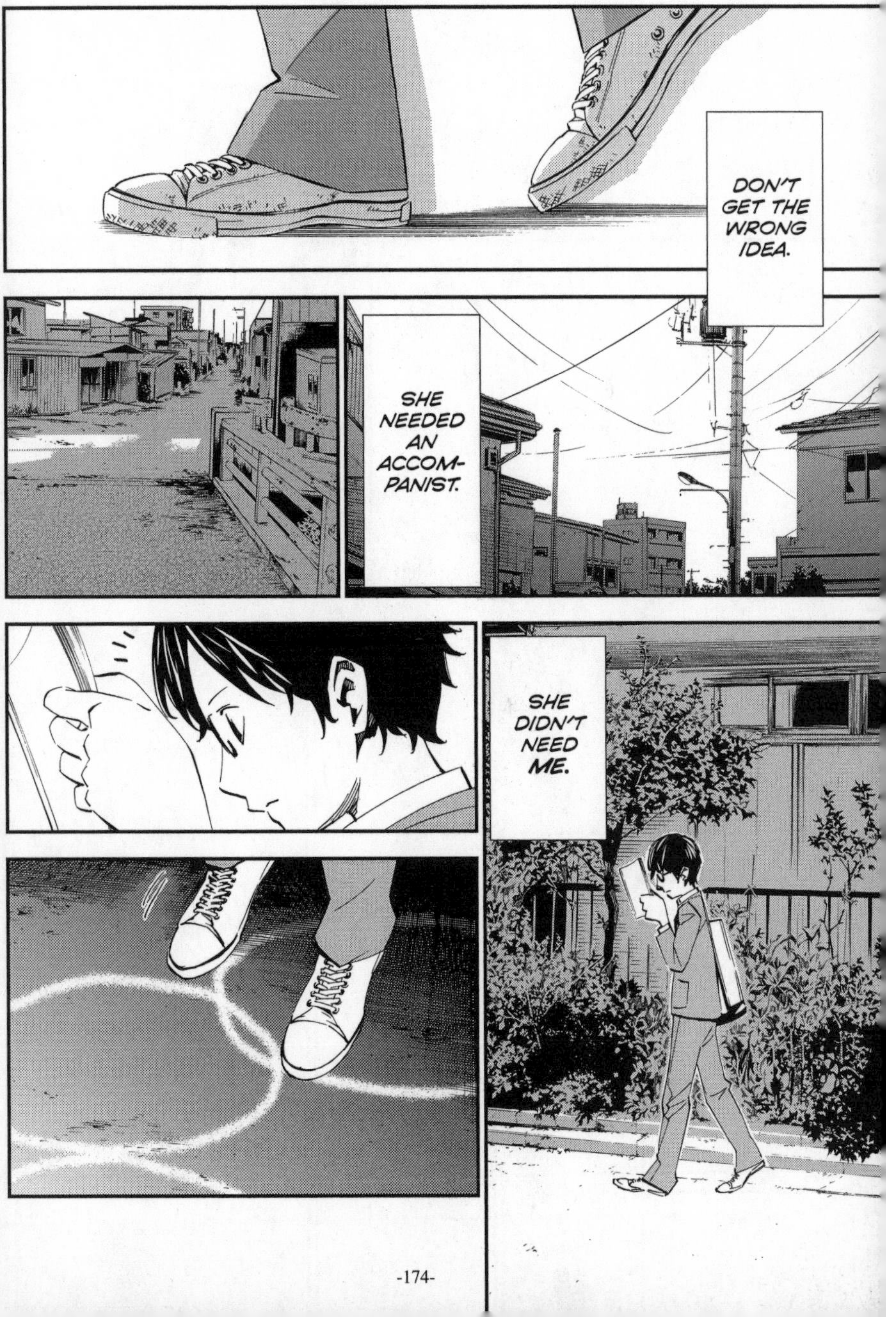
DON'T GET THE WRONG IDEA.
SHE NEEDED AN ACCOM-PANIST.
SHE DIDN'T NEED ME.

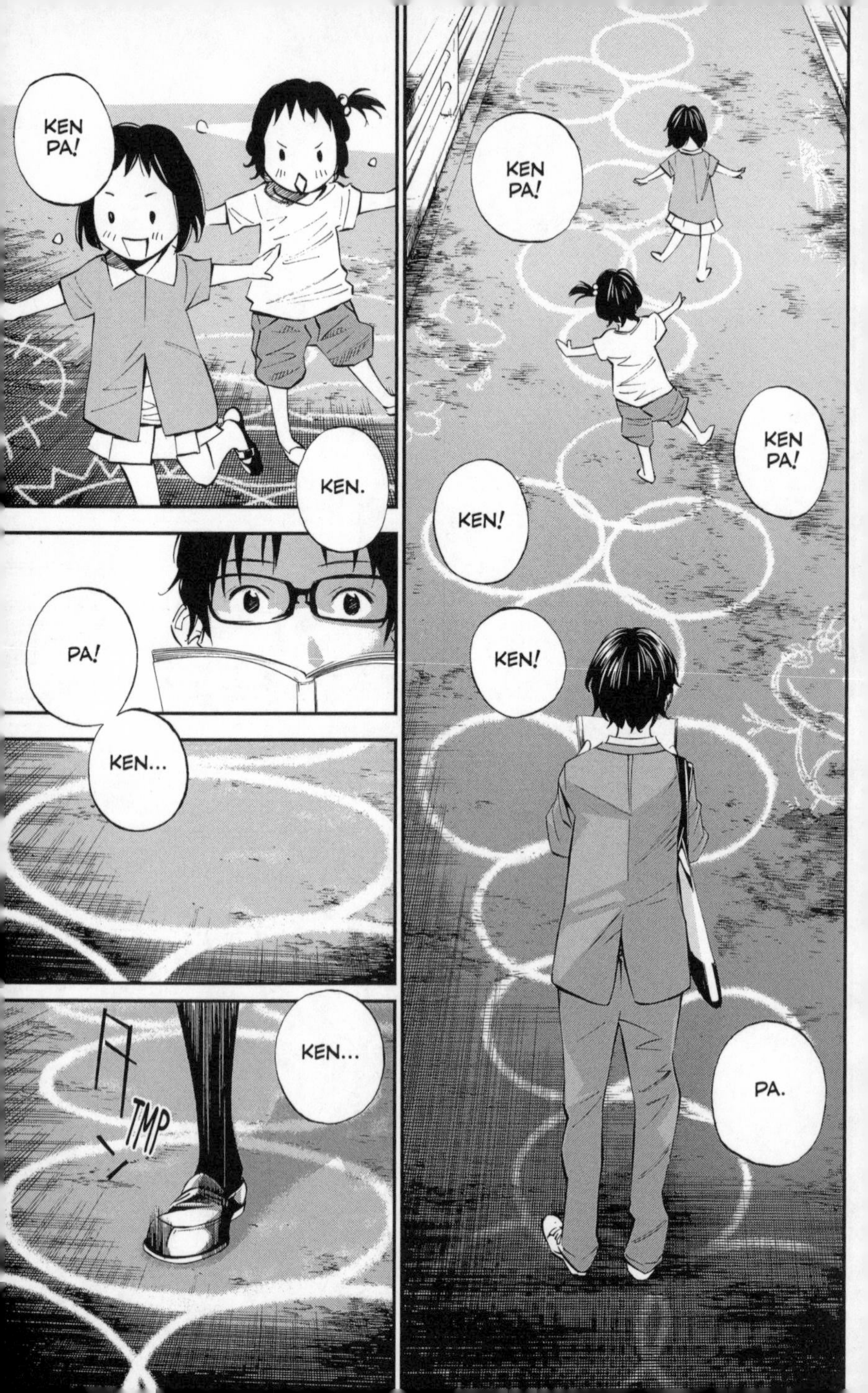
KEN PA!
KEN PA!
KEN!
KEN!
PA.
KEN PA!
KEN.
PA!
KEN...
KEN...
TMP

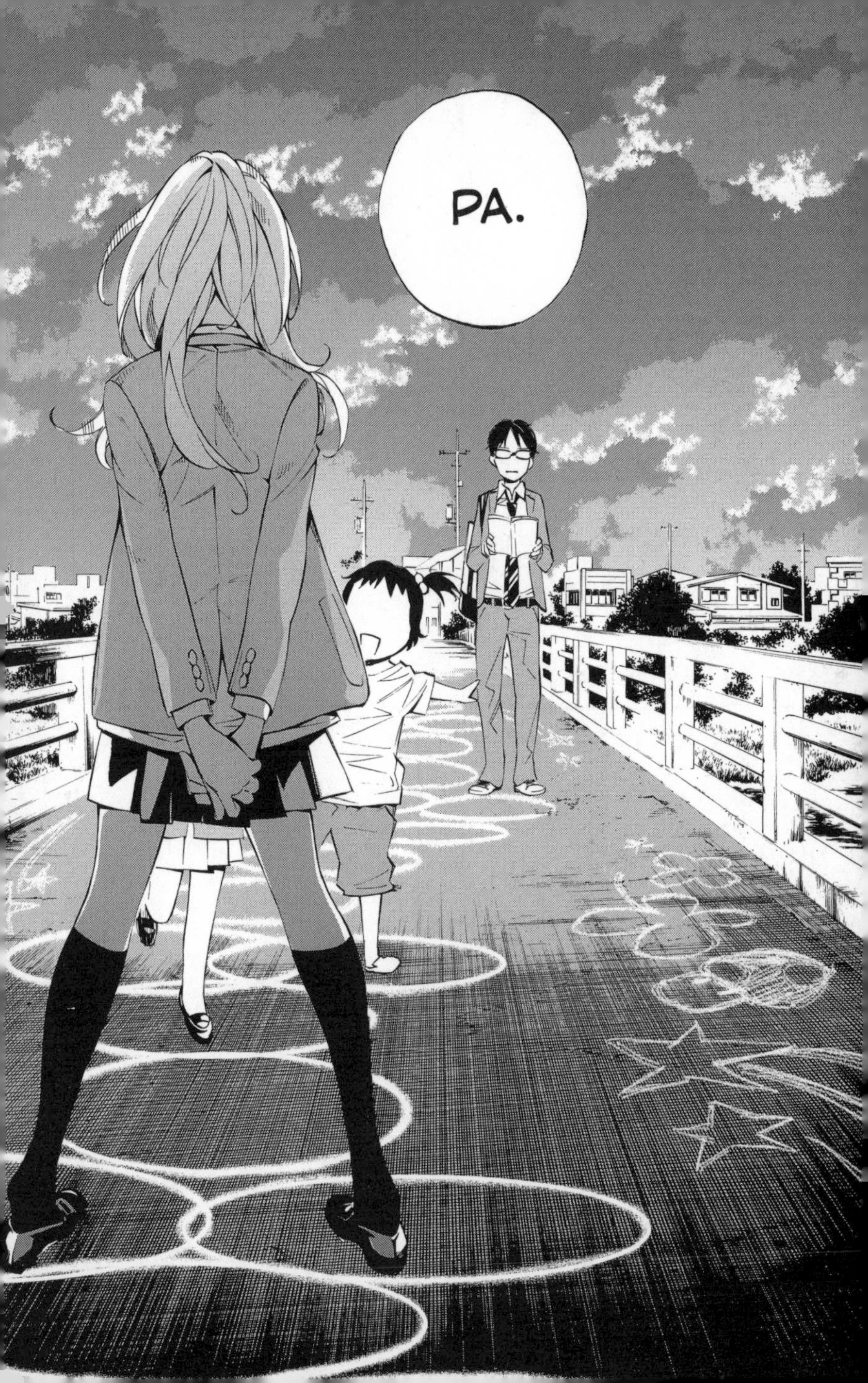
PA.

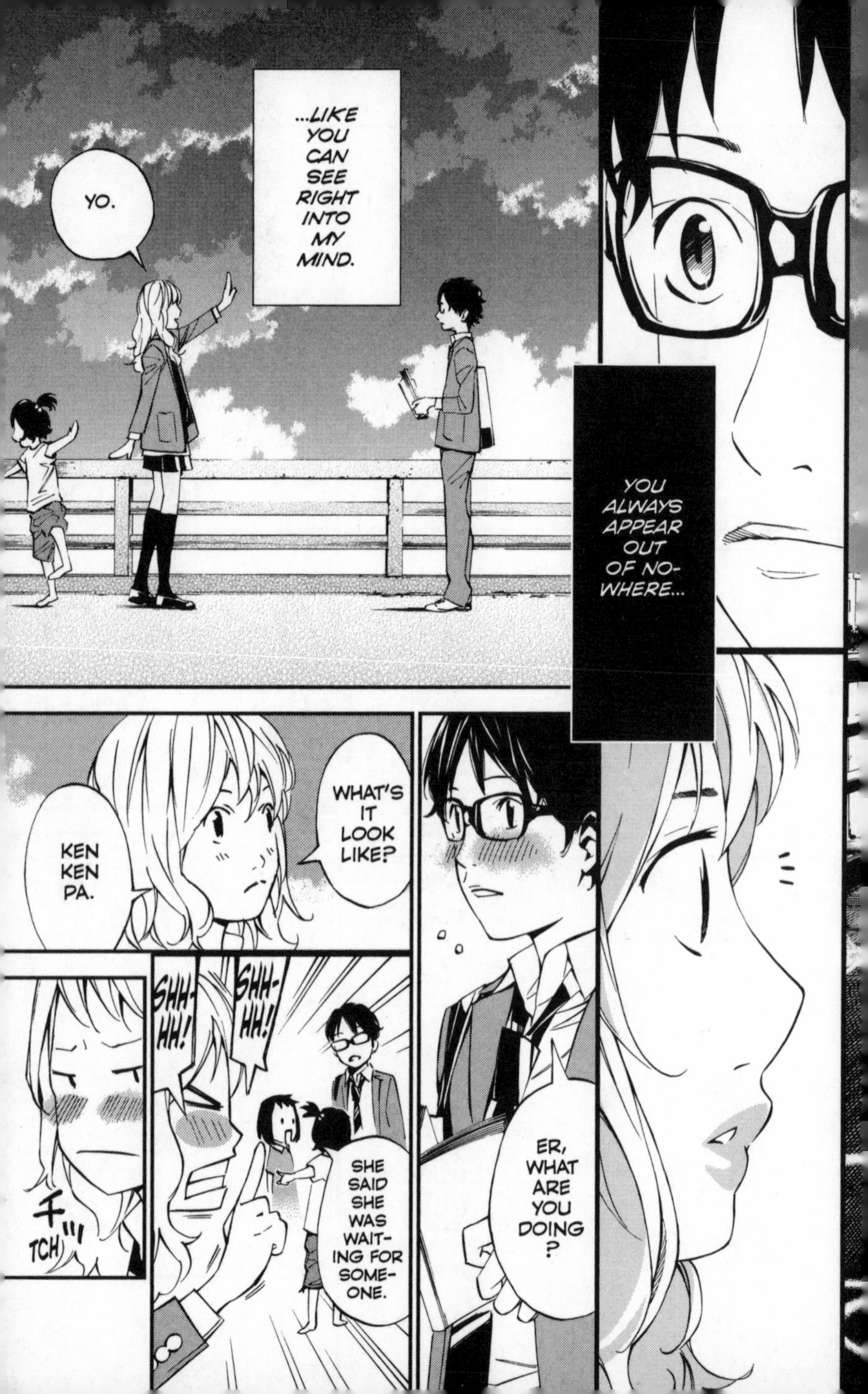
YOU ALWAYS APPEAR OUT OF NO-WHERE...
...LIKE YOU CAN SEE RIGHT INTO MY MIND.
YO.
ER, WHAT ARE YOU DOING?
WHAT'S IT LOOK LIKE?
KEN KEN PA.
SHE SAID SHE WAS WAIT-ING FOR SOME-ONE.
SHH-HH!
SHH-HH!
チッ
TCH

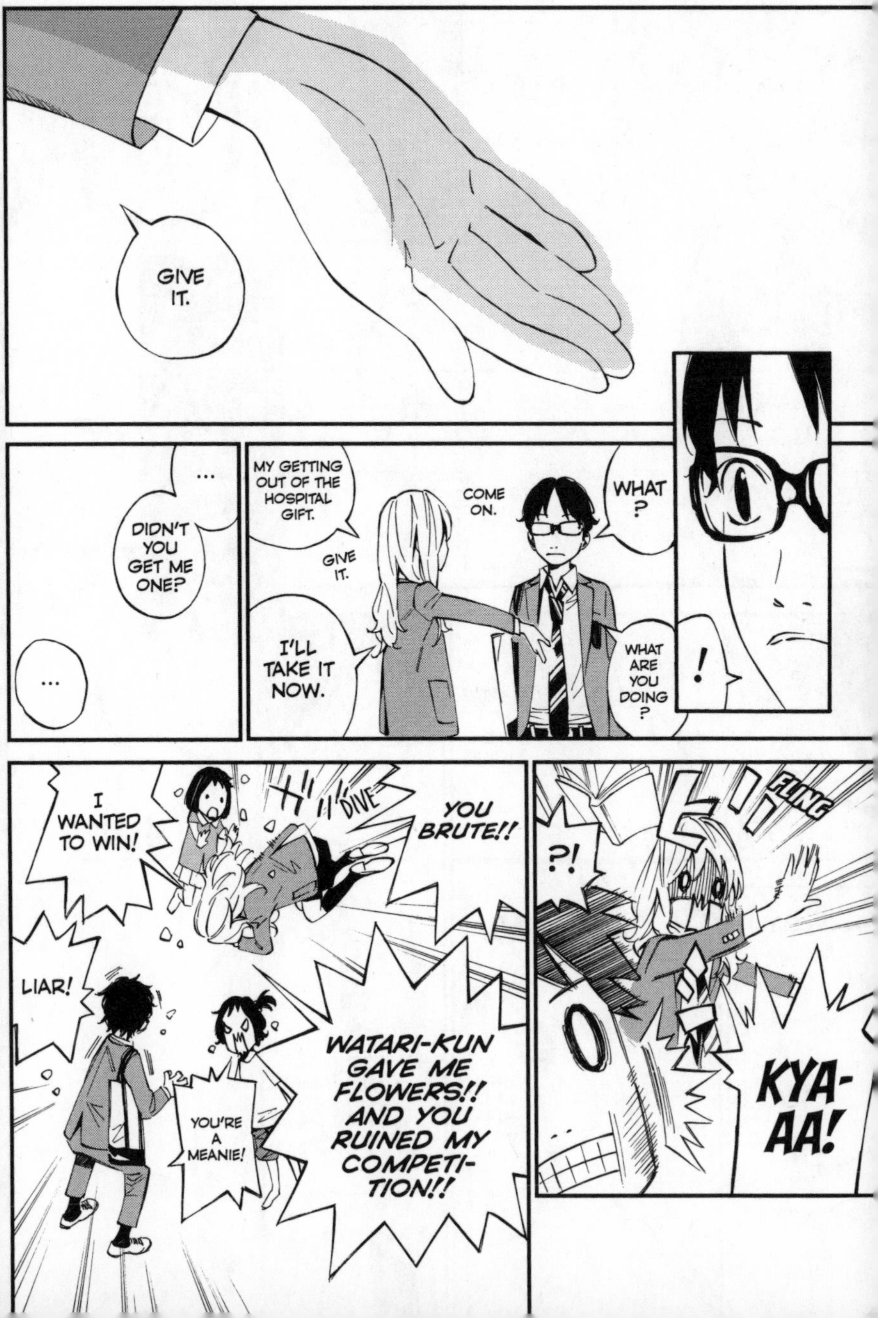
GIVE IT.
!
WHAT ?
COME ON.
MY GETTING OUT OF THE HOSPITAL GIFT.
GIVE IT.
WHAT ARE YOU DOING ?
I'LL TAKE IT NOW.
...
DIDN'T YOU GET ME ONE?
...
FLING
?!
KYA-AA!
YOU BRUTE!!
DIVE
I WANTED TO WIN!
WATARI-KUN GAVE ME FLOWERS!! AND YOU RUINED MY COMPETI-TION!!
LIAR!
YOU'RE A MEANIE!

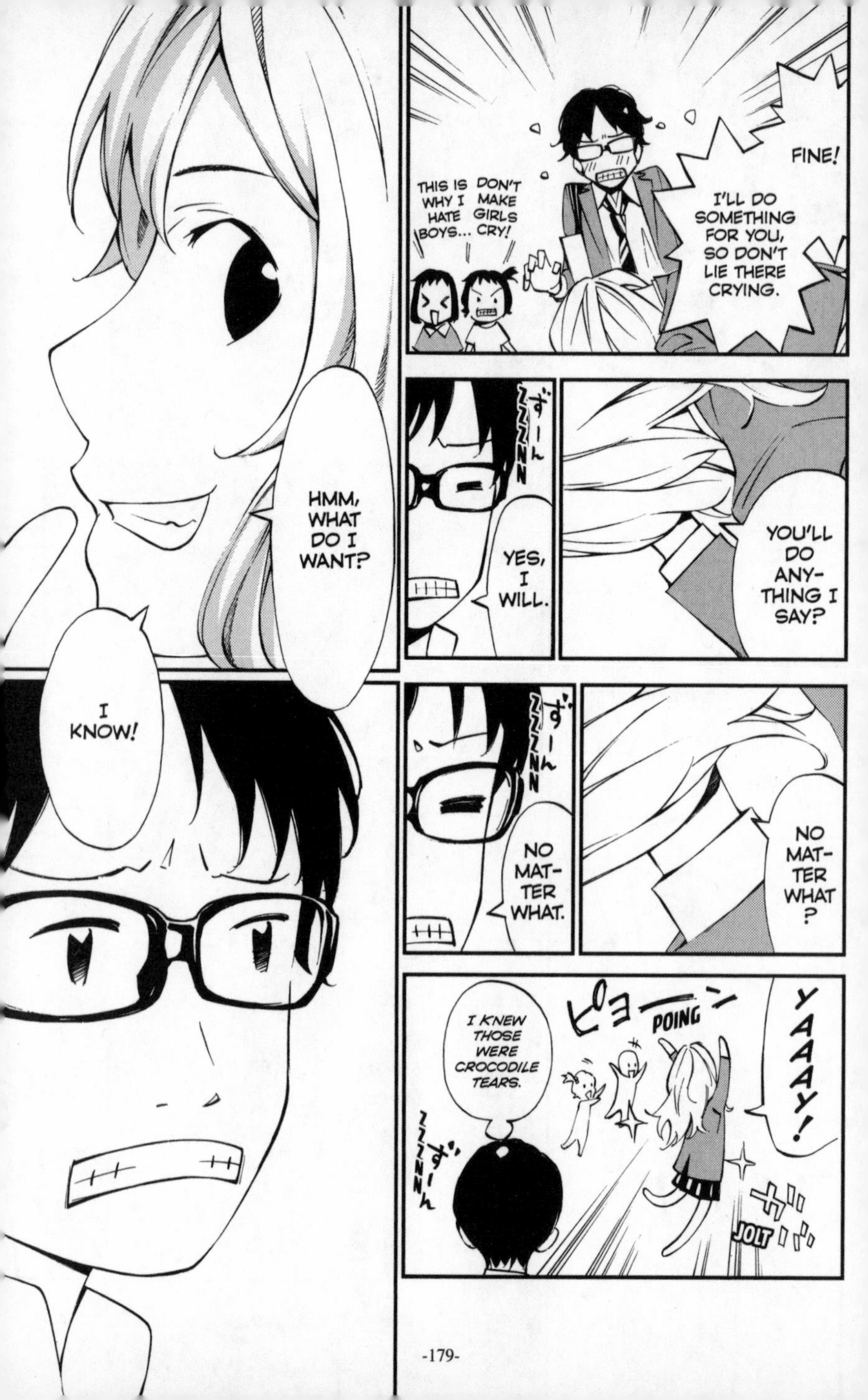
FINE!
I'LL DO SOMETHING FOR YOU, SO DON'T LIE THERE CRYING.
DON'T MAKE GIRLS CRY!
THIS IS WHY I HATE BOYS...
YOU'LL DO ANYTHING I SAY?
ずーん ZZZNN
YES, I WILL.
NO MATTER WHAT?
ずーん ZZZNN
NO MATTER WHAT.
YAAAAY!
ピョーン POING
I KNEW THOSE WERE CROCODILE TEARS.
ずーん ZZZNN
JOLT
HMM, WHAT DO I WANT?
I KNOW!

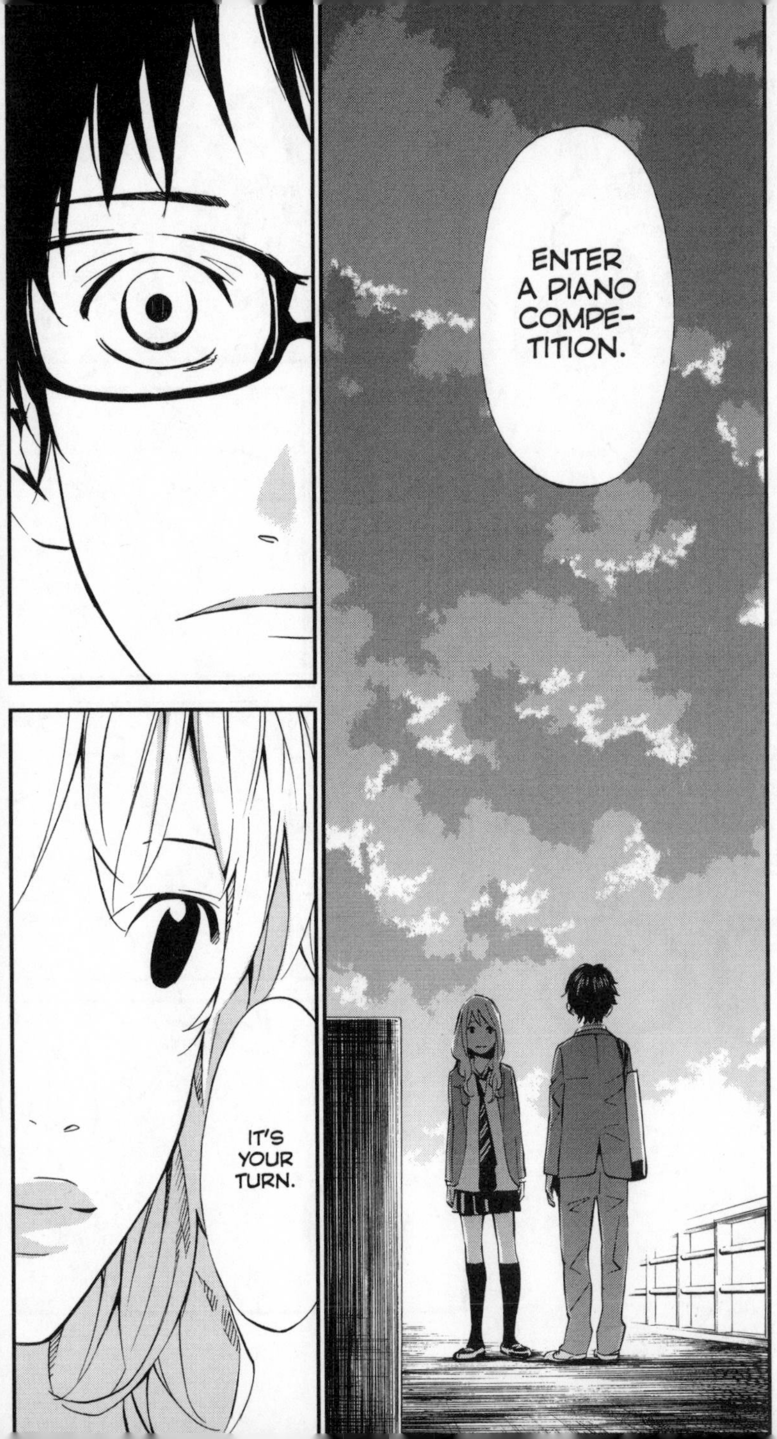
ENTER A PIANO COMPETITION.
IT'S YOUR TURN.

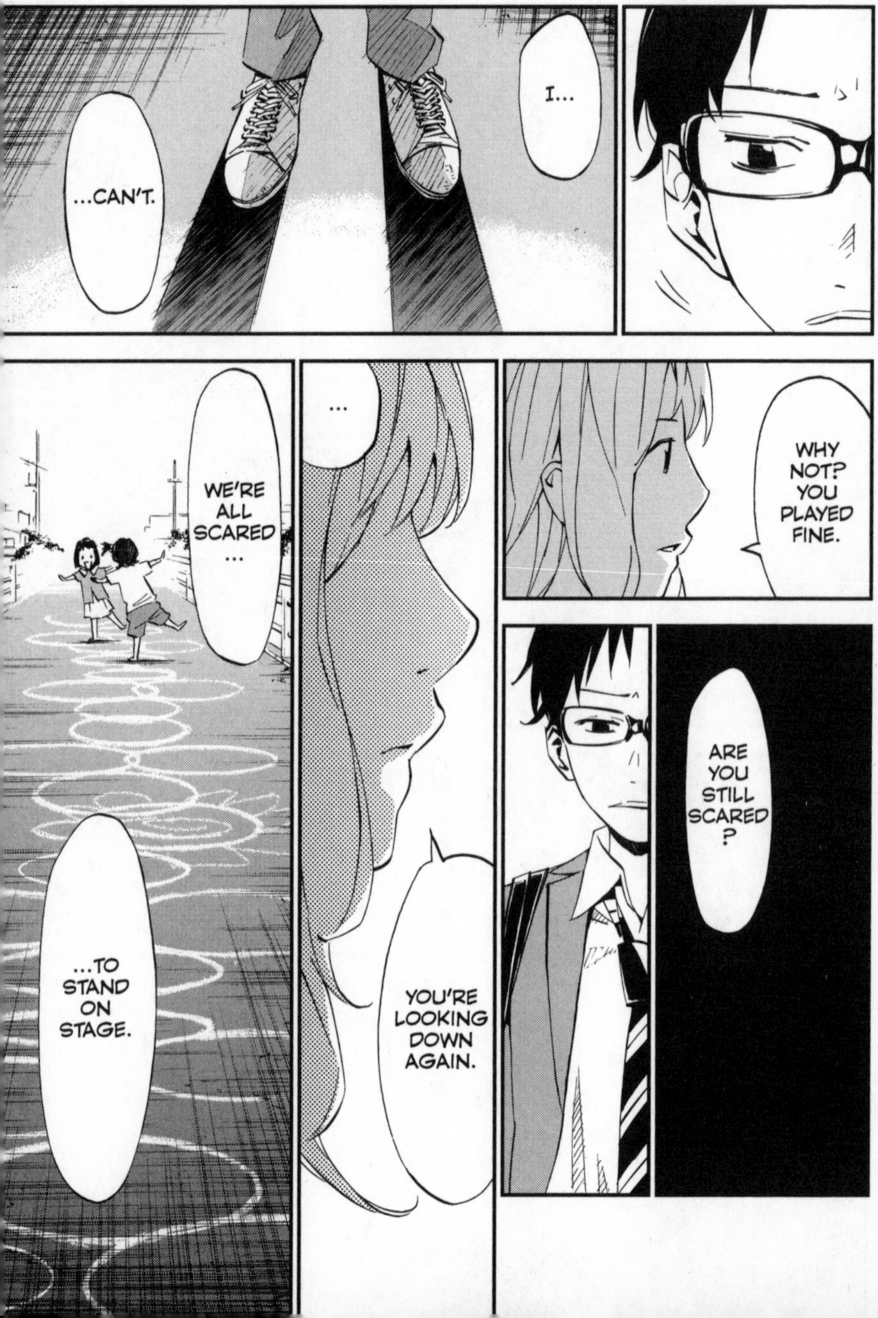
I...
...CAN'T.
WHY NOT? YOU PLAYED FINE.
ARE YOU STILL SCARED?
...
YOU'RE LOOKING DOWN AGAIN.
WE'RE ALL SCARED...
...TO STAND ON STAGE.

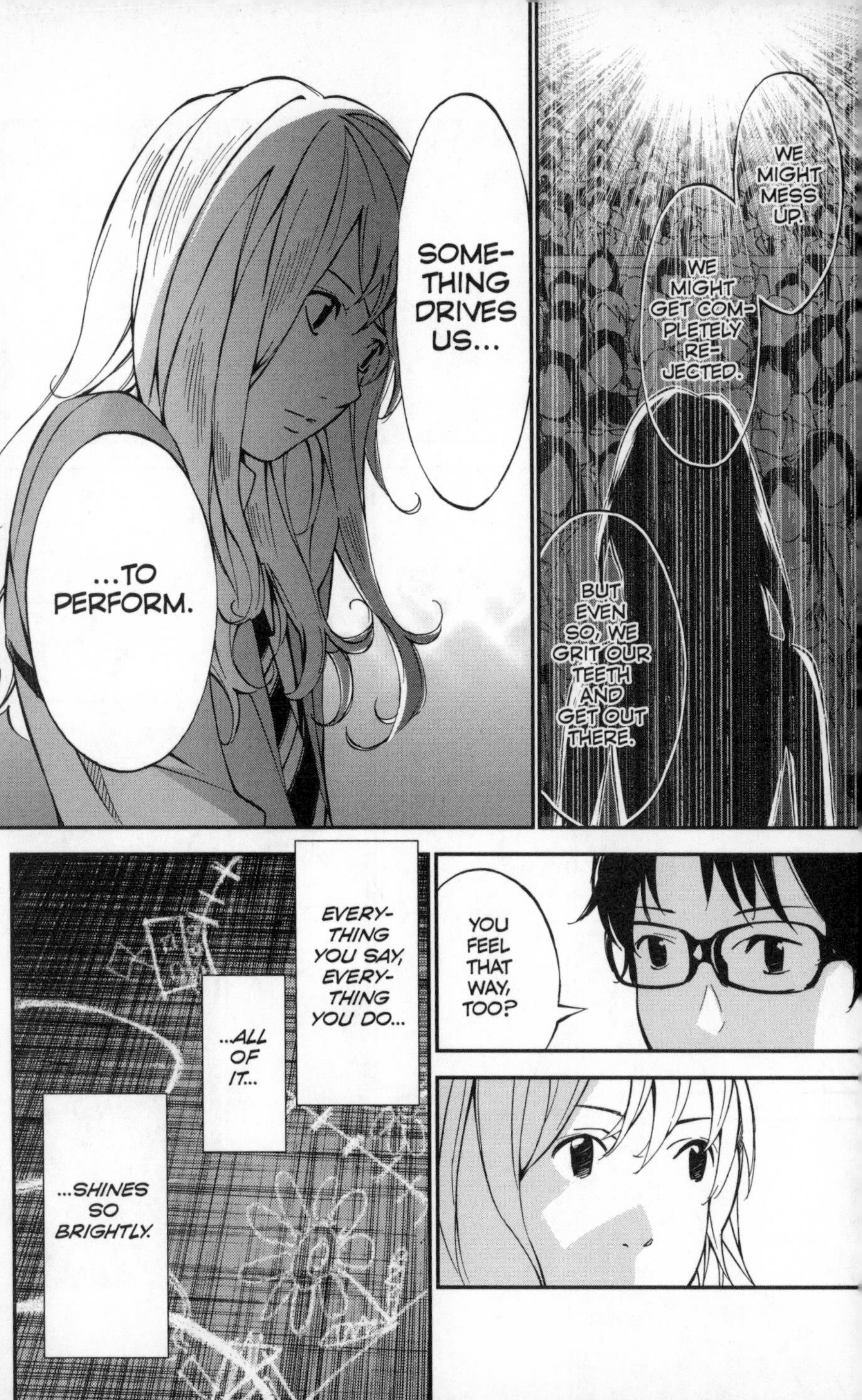
WE MIGHT MESS UP.
WE MIGHT GET COM-PLETELY RE-JECTED.
BUT EVEN SO, WE GRIT OUR TEETH AND GET OUT THERE.
SOME-THING DRIVES US...
...TO PERFORM.
YOU FEEL THAT WAY, TOO?
EVERY-THING YOU SAY, EVERY-THING YOU DO...
...ALL OF IT...
...SHINES SO BRIGHTLY.

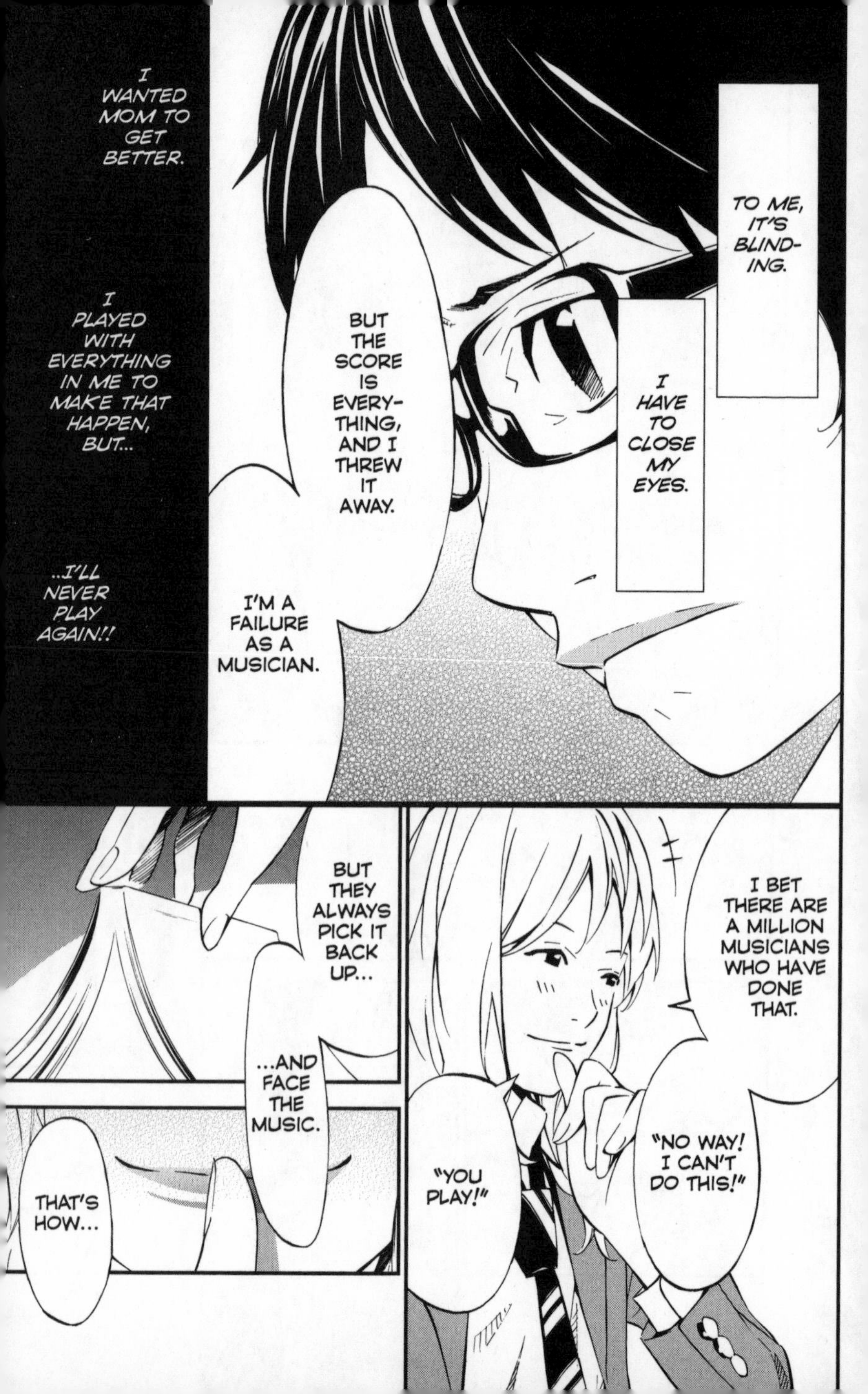
TO ME, IT'S BLINDING.
I HAVE TO CLOSE MY EYES.
BUT THE SCORE IS EVERYTHING, AND I THREW IT AWAY.
I'M A FAILURE AS A MUSICIAN.
I WANTED MOM TO GET BETTER.
I PLAYED WITH EVERYTHING IN ME TO MAKE THAT HAPPEN, BUT...
...I'LL NEVER PLAY AGAIN!!
I BET THERE ARE A MILLION MUSICIANS WHO HAVE DONE THAT.
"NO WAY! I CAN'T DO THIS!"
"YOU PLAY!"
BUT THEY ALWAYS PICK IT BACK UP...
...AND FACE THE MUSIC.
THAT'S HOW...

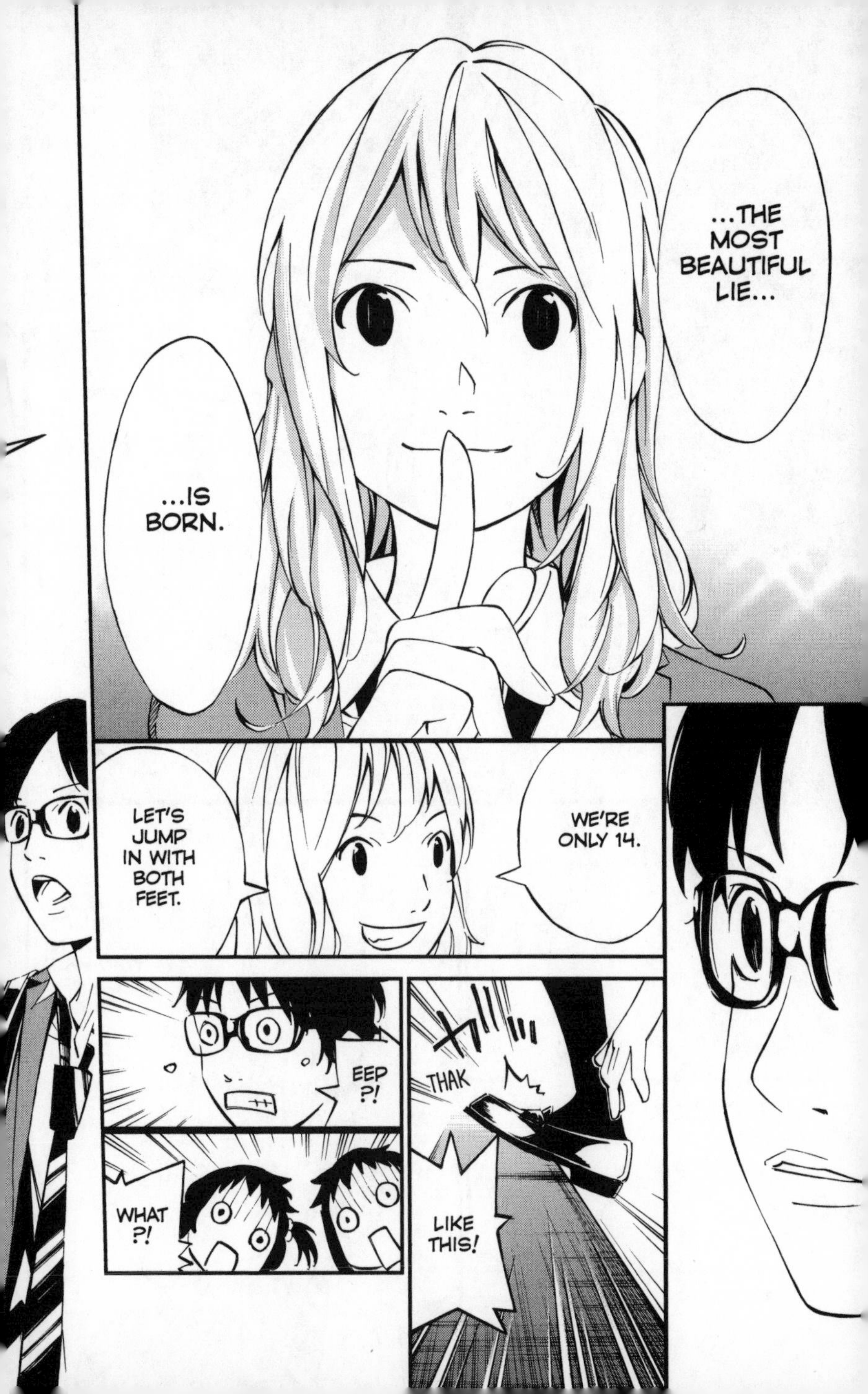
...THE MOST BEAUTIFUL LIE...
...IS BORN.
WE'RE ONLY 14.
LET'S JUMP IN WITH BOTH FEET.
THAK
LIKE THIS!
EEP ?!
WHAT ?!

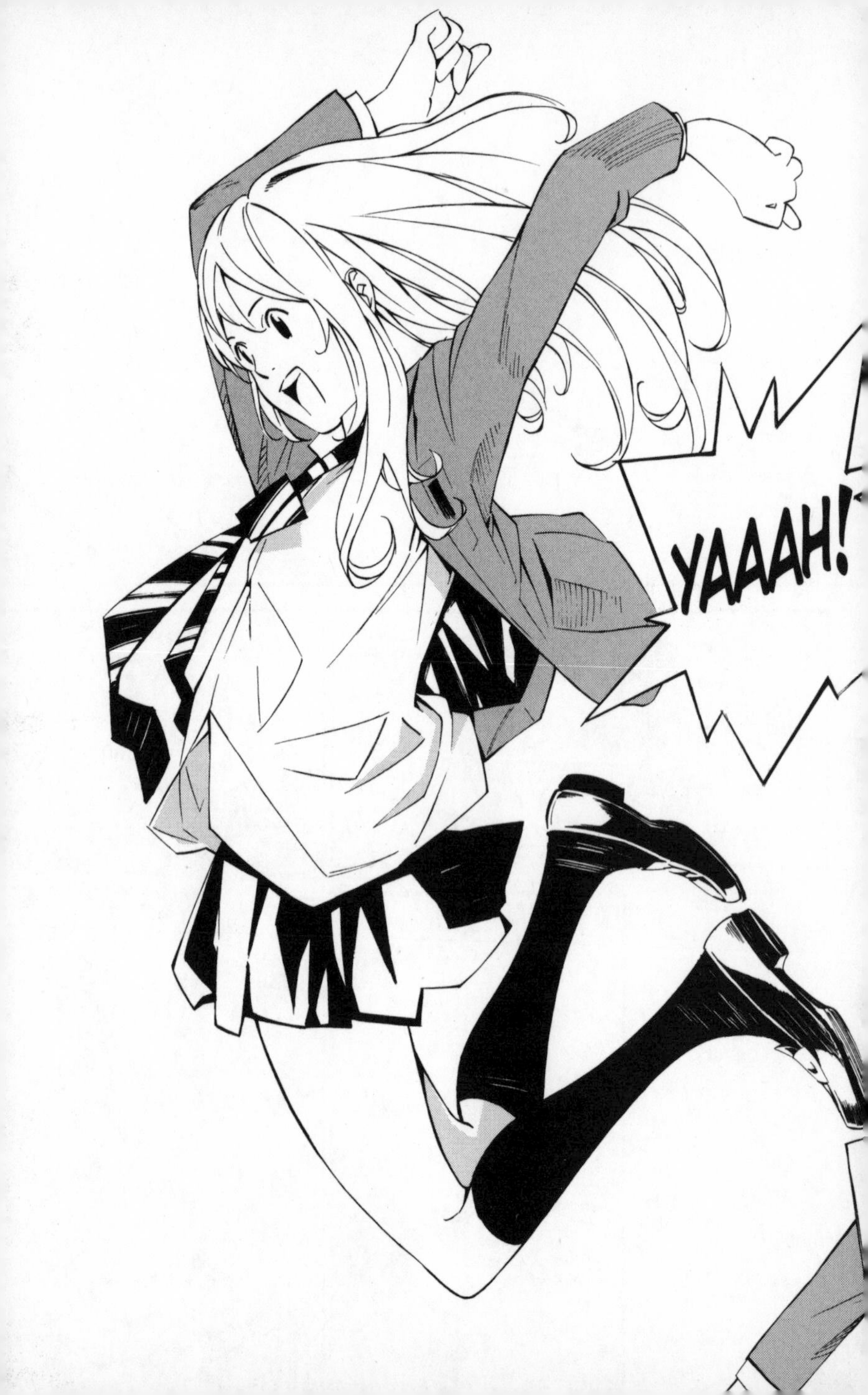
YAAAH!

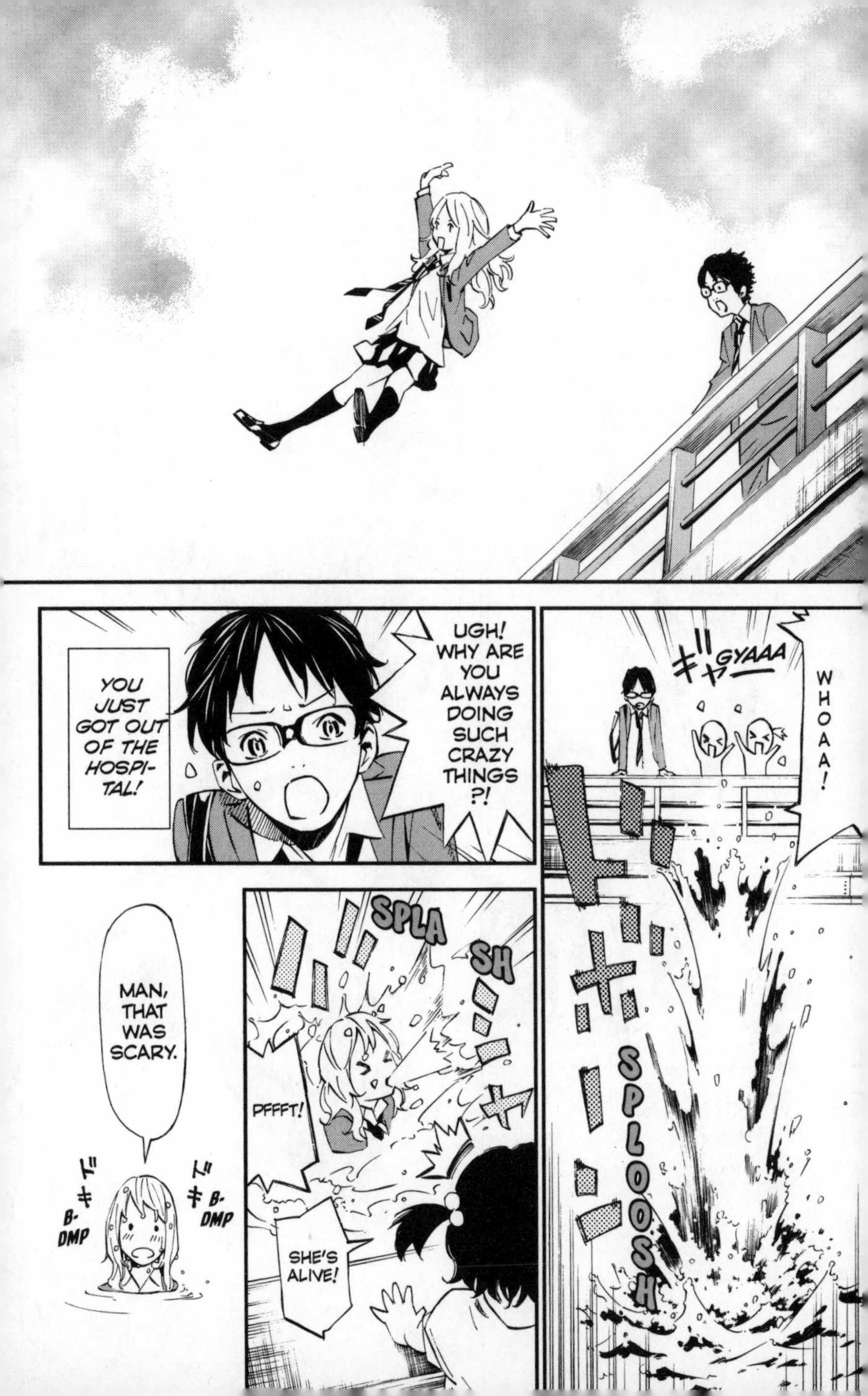
WHOAA!
GYAAA
SPLOOSH
UGH! WHY ARE YOU ALWAYS DOING SUCH CRAZY THINGS?!
YOU JUST GOT OUT OF THE HOSPITAL!
SPLASH
PFFFT!
SHE'S ALIVE!
MAN, THAT WAS SCARY.
B-DMP
B-DMP

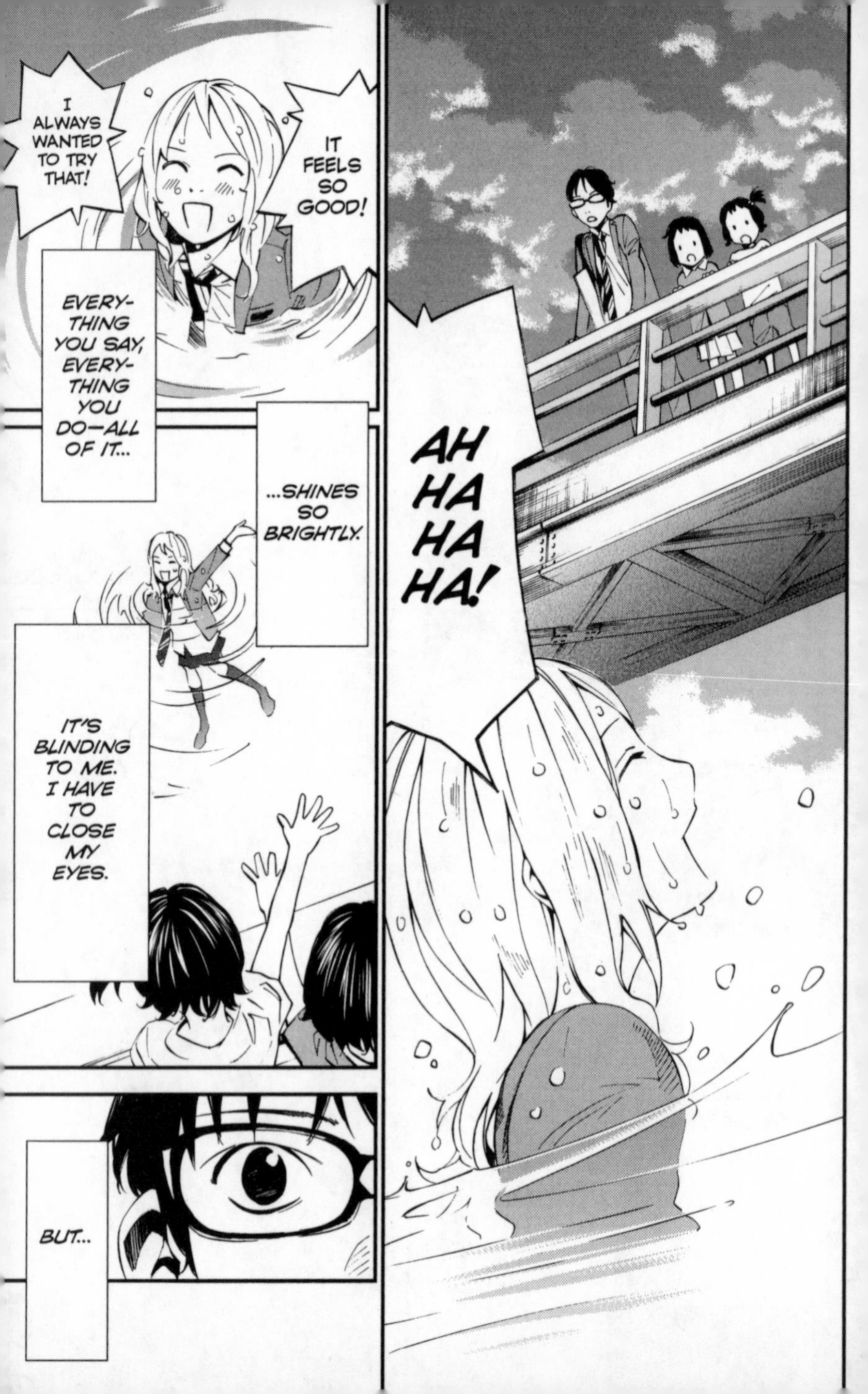
AH HA HA HA!
IT FEELS SO GOOD!
I ALWAYS WANTED TO TRY THAT!
EVERYTHING YOU SAY, EVERYTHING YOU DO—ALL OF IT...
...SHINES SO BRIGHTLY.
IT'S BLINDING TO ME. I HAVE TO CLOSE MY EYES.
BUT...

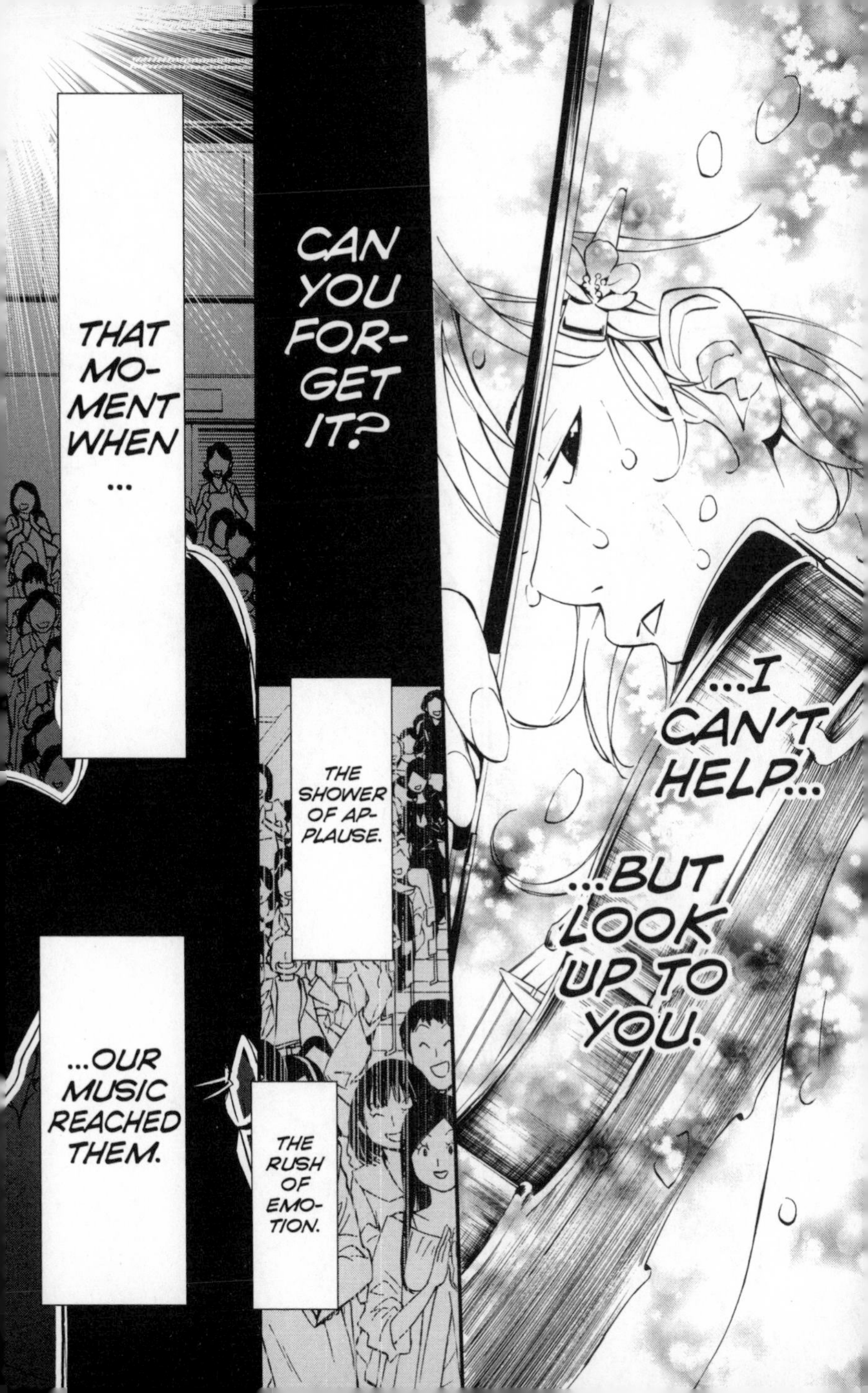
...I CAN'T HELP...
...BUT LOOK UP TO YOU.
CAN YOU FOR-GET IT?
THE SHOWER OF AP-PLAUSE.
THE RUSH OF EMO-TION.
THAT MO-MENT WHEN ...
...OUR MUSIC REACHED THEM.

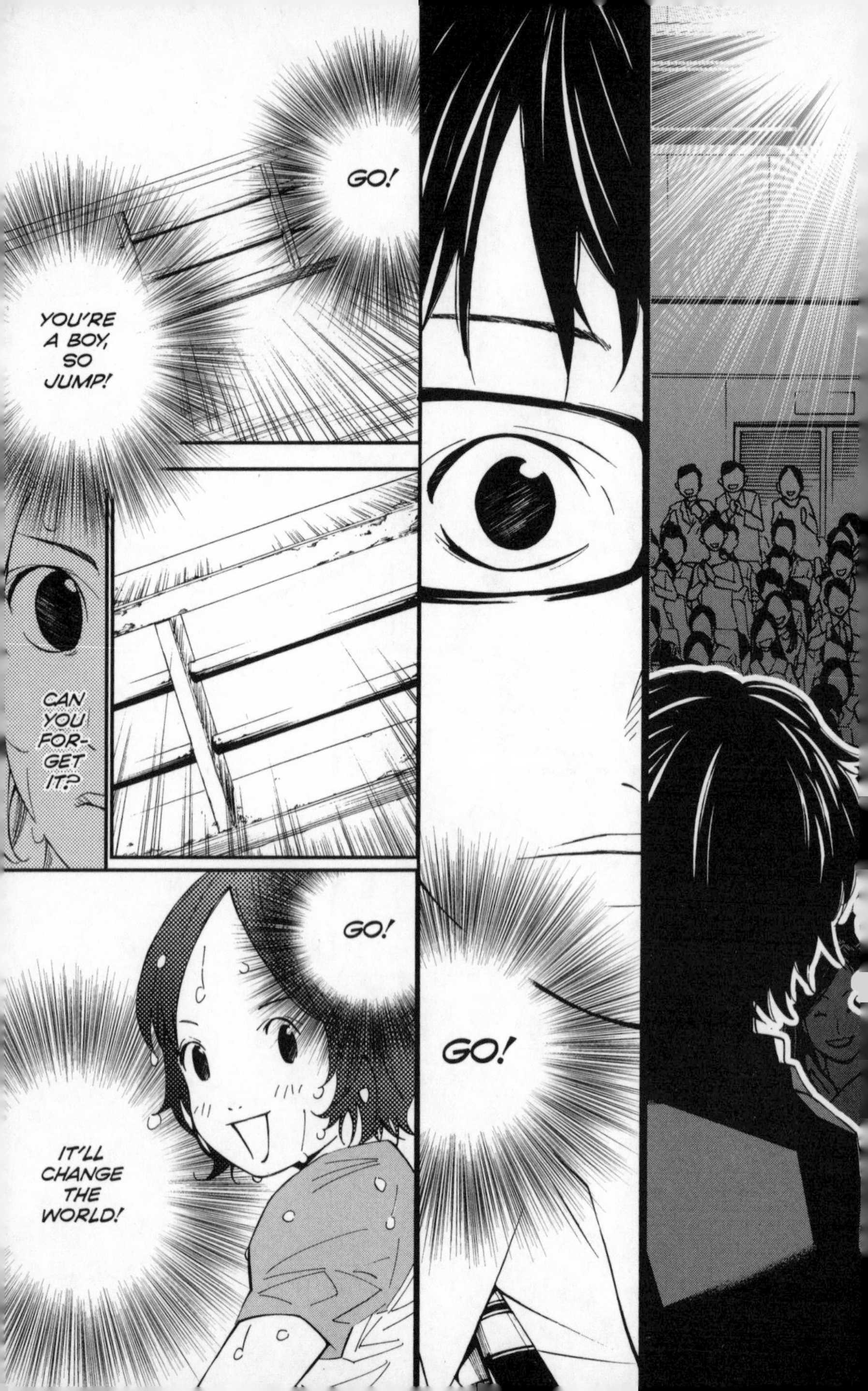
GO!
GO!
YOU'RE A BOY, SO JUMP!
CAN YOU FOR-GET IT?
GO!
IT'LL CHANGE THE WORLD!

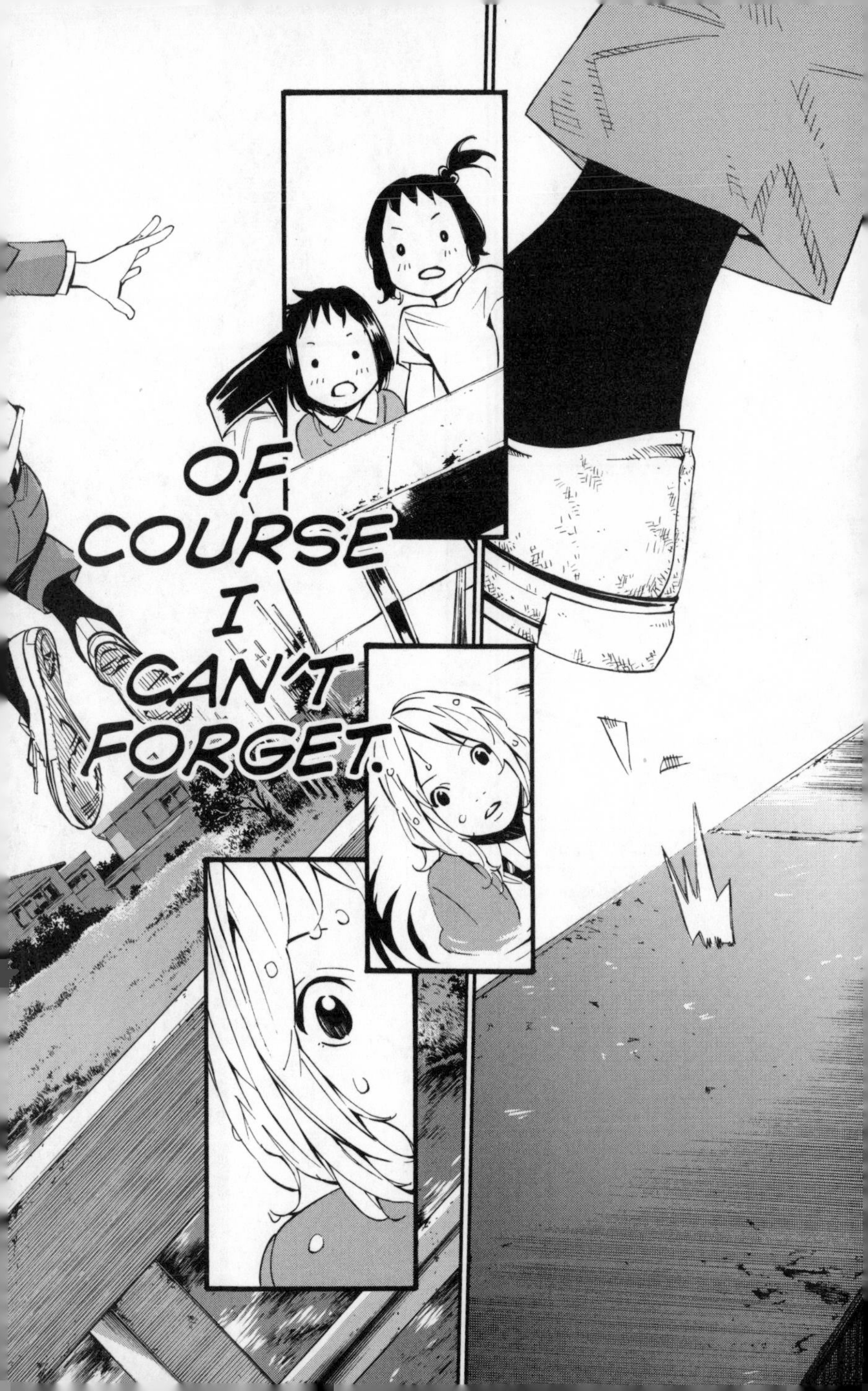
OF COURSE I CAN'T FORGET.

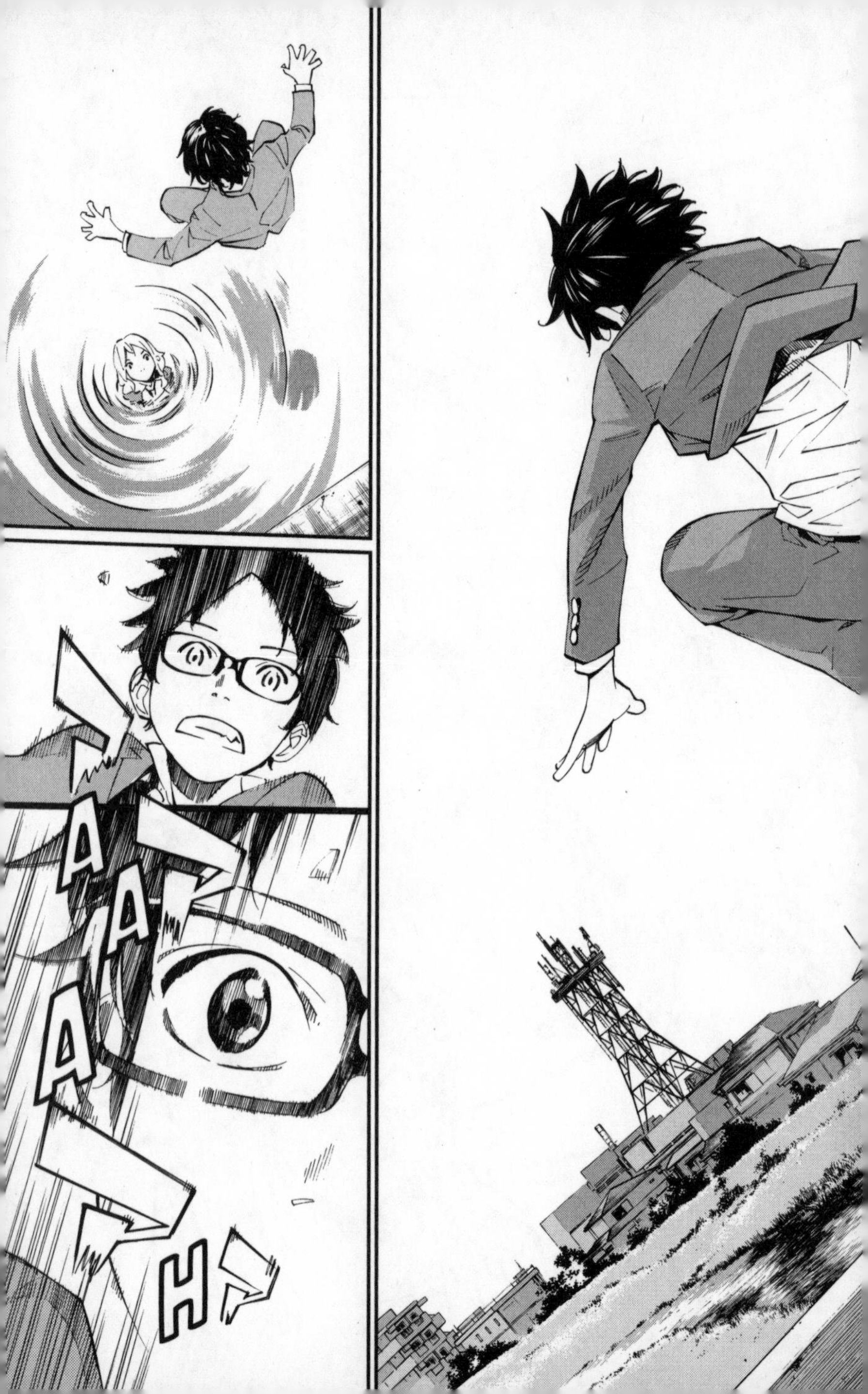
AAAH

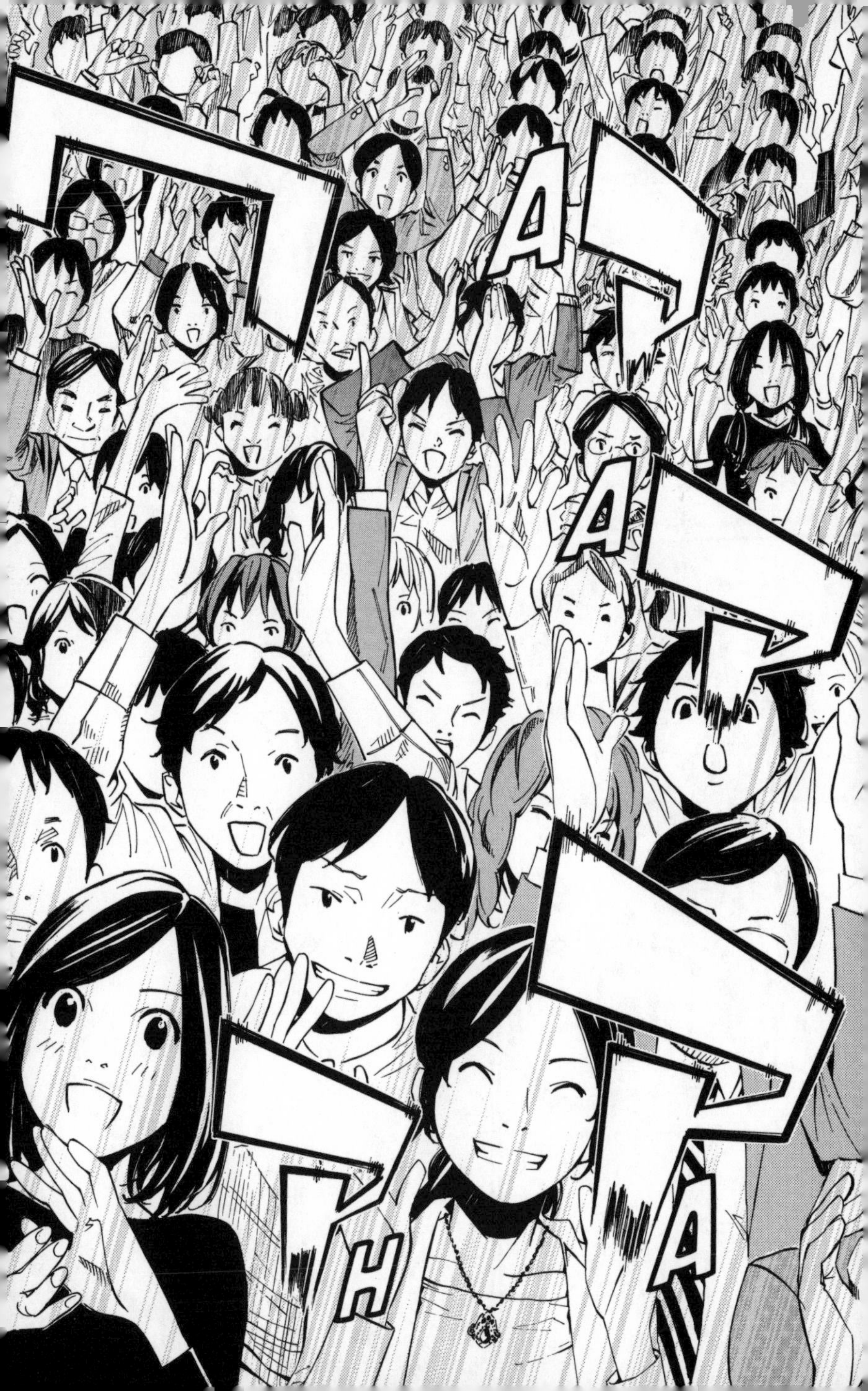
A
A
H
A

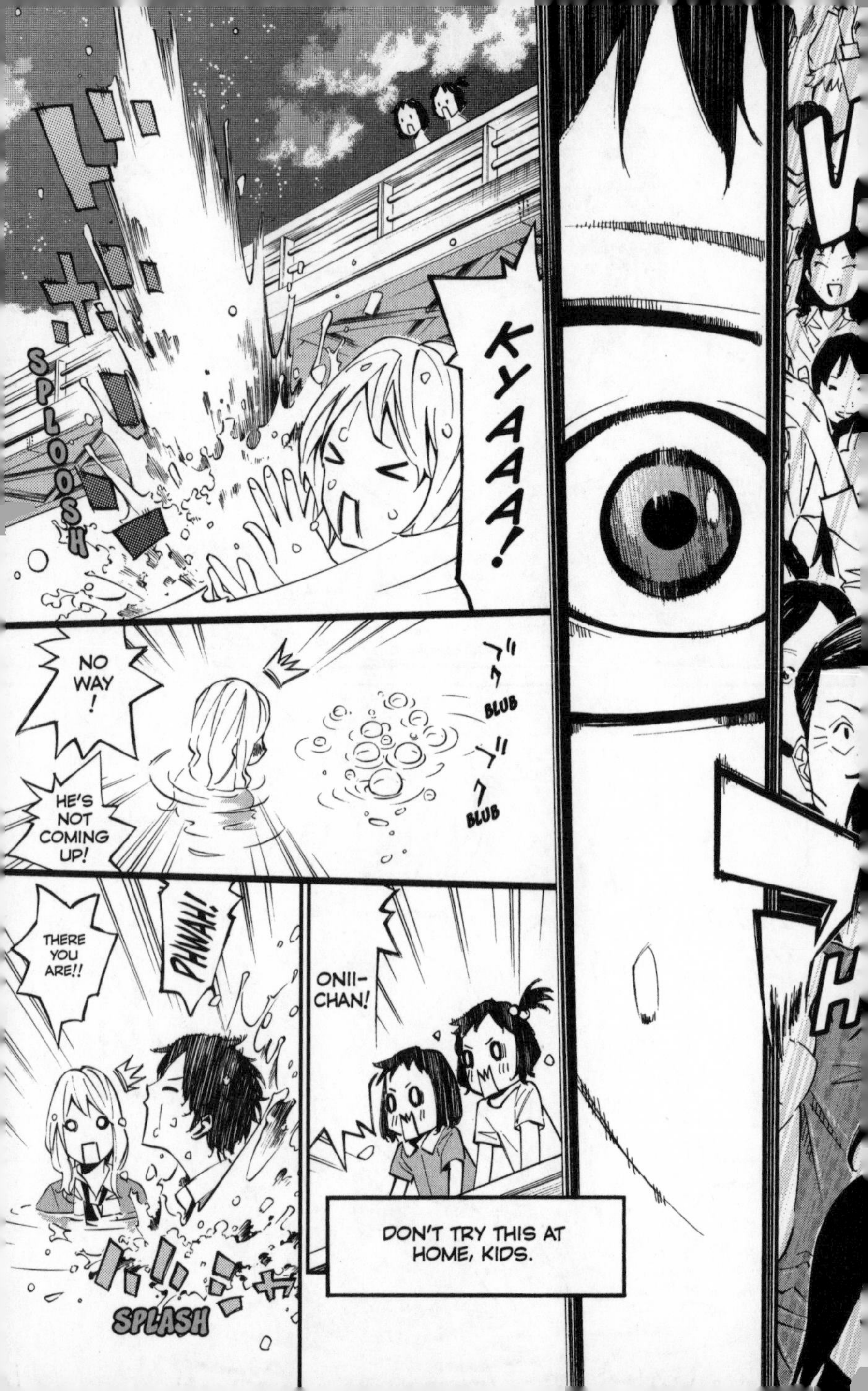
KYAAAA!
SPLOOSH
BLUB
BLUB
NO WAY!
HE'S NOT COMING UP!
ONII-CHAN!
DON'T TRY THIS AT HOME, KIDS.
PHWAH!
THERE YOU ARE!!
SPLASH

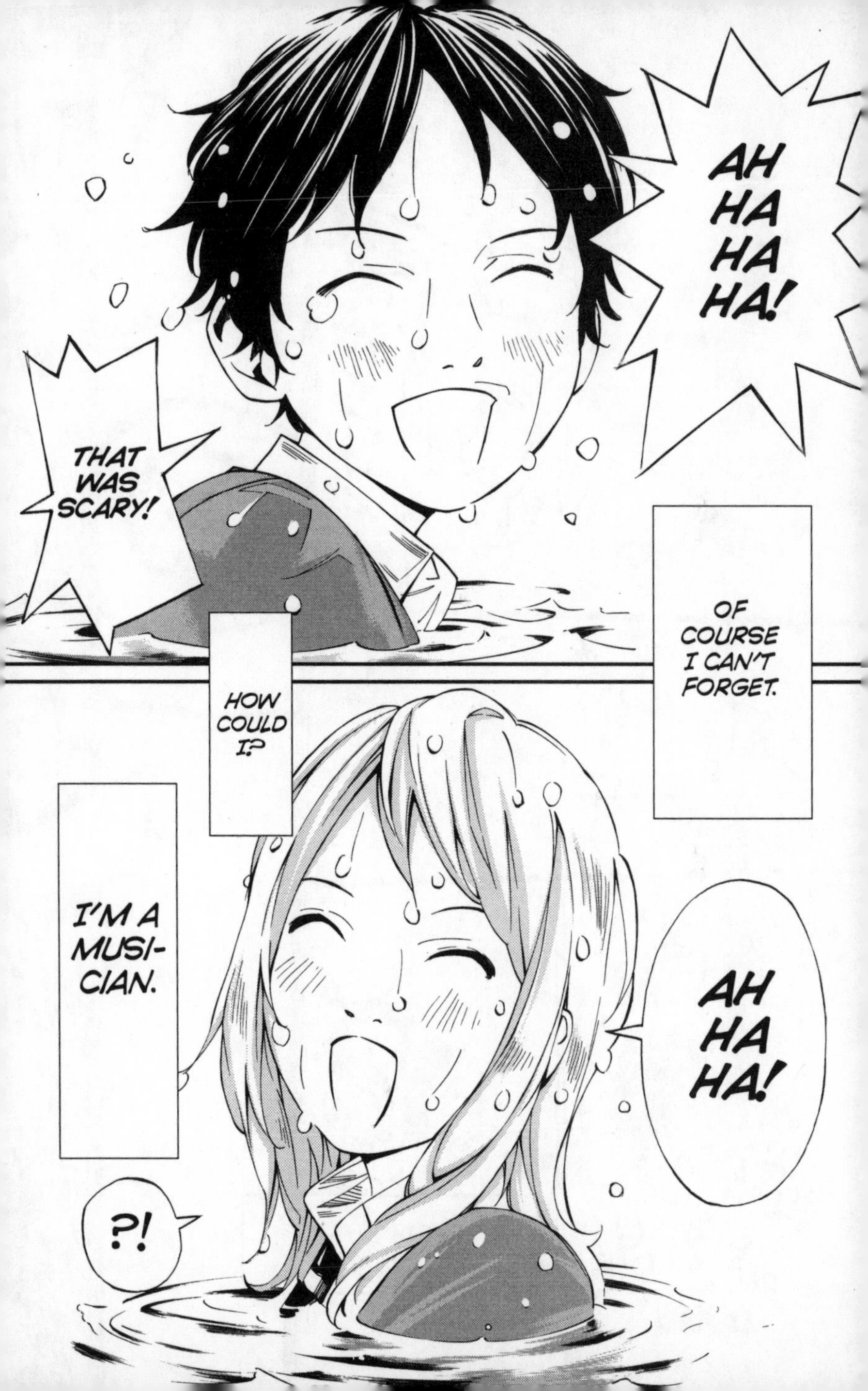
AH HA HA HA!
THAT WAS SCARY!
OF COURSE I CAN'T FORGET.
HOW COULD I?
AH HA HA!
I'M A MUSI-CIAN.
?!

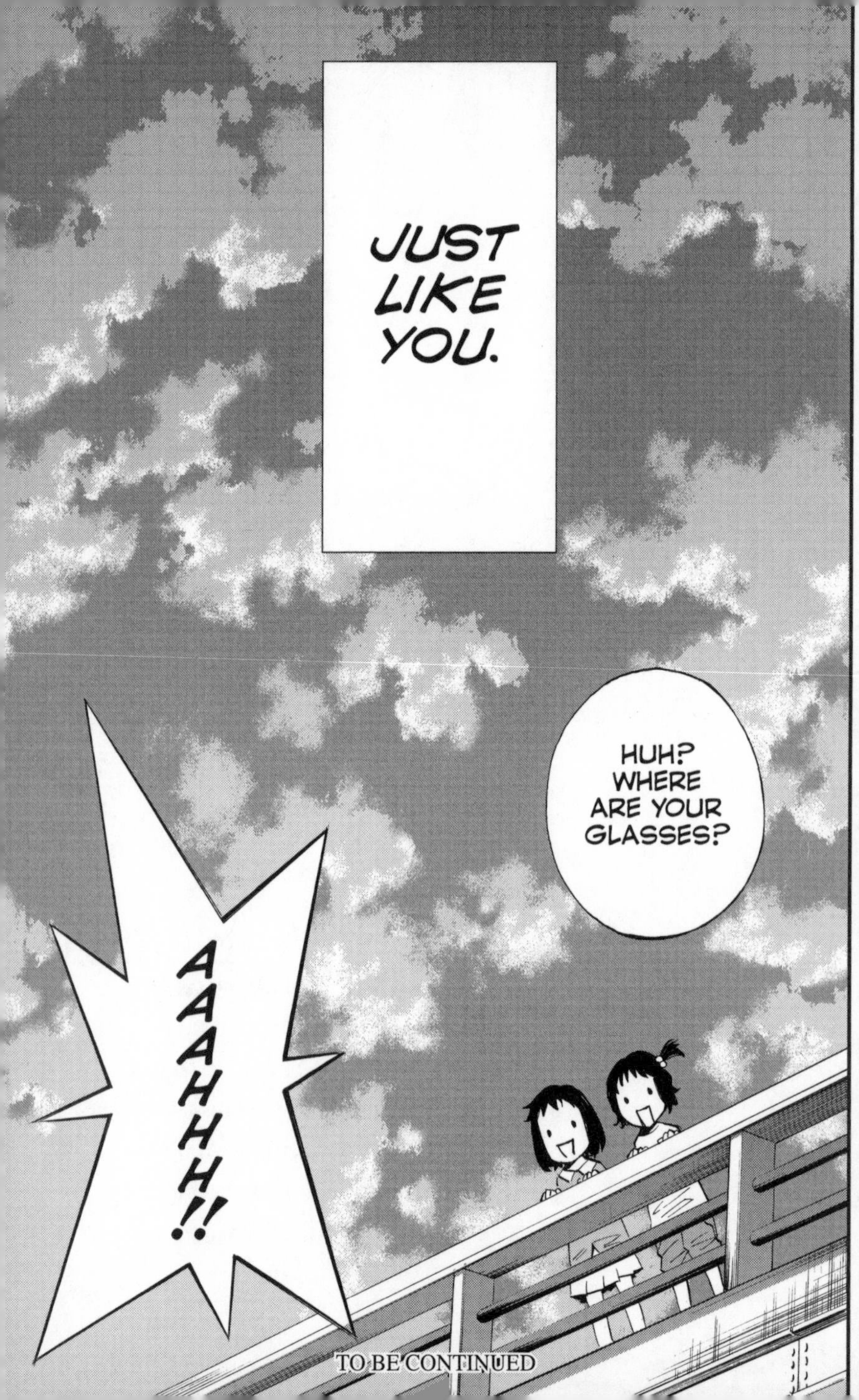
JUST LIKE YOU.
HUH? WHERE ARE YOUR GLASSES?
AAAHHH!!
TO BE CONTINUED

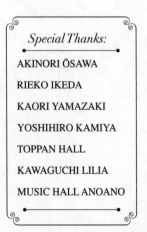

Special Thanks:

AKINORI ŌSAWA

RIEKO IKEDA

KAORI YAMAZAKI

YOSHIHIRO KAMIYA

TOPPAN HALL

KAWAGUCHI LILIA

MUSIC HALL ANOANO

Translation Notes

"Go on a journey," page 23

Mozart once said, "I assure you, without travel, at least for people from the arts and sciences, one is a miserable creature!" He also said, "A man of ordinary talent will always be ordinary, whether he travels or not; but a man of superior talent will go to pieces if he remains forever in the same place." Either way, the idea is that if Kaori and Kōsei are talented musicians, they must go on a journey or they will be miserable forever. And so, according to Kaori, Mozart is urging them from beyond the grave to stand on the stage as part of their journey.

Dare You Bridge, page 120

The name of the bridge is Doryō Bridge, which sounds very much like Dokyō Bridge. Dokyō means "bravery" or "grit." It is usually translated to "guts," and refers to a person's ability to remain undaunted in the face of whatever challenge confronts them, such as jumping off a high bridge into a river. The translators chose to render the bridge's nickname as "Dare You Bridge," in the hopes that it would count as wordplay.

Gakuran, page 122

Here, Tsubaki is noticing the new school uniform Saitō is sporting now that he's moved on to high school. It's called a *gakuran*, and is noted for its button-down jacket with a standing collar, a style that was originally imported from Europe. The *gaku* refers to school or learning, while the *ran* refers to Western culture or Western clothes, so together the name means "Western-style school clothes." The school year starts in April, and it's not quite May in the story, so it makes sense that she wouldn't have seen him wearing his new uniform until now.

Ken Ken Pa, page 175

As the reader may have guessed from the pictures, Ken Ken Pa is a game very much like Hopscotch. It's so much like Hopscotch, in fact, that the rules are almost exactly the same: first, draw circles on the ground as shown, then throw a rock into one of the circles. Hop across the circles, and when you get to the end, turn around and come back, picking up your rock on the way. One difference is the chanting of "ken" and "pa." "Ken" is for when you land with one foot, and "pa" is for when you land with both (each in a different circle, of course).

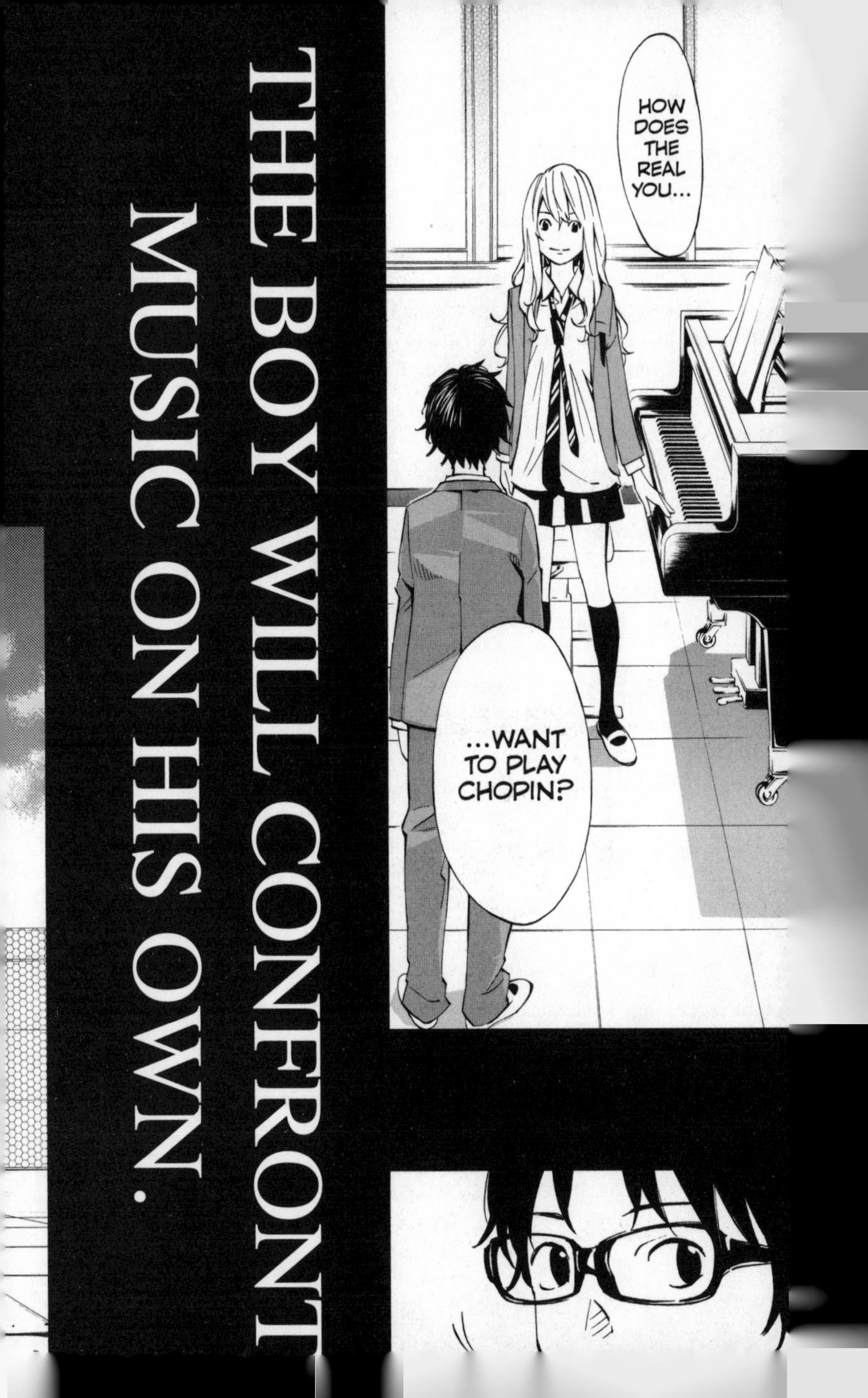
HOW DOES THE REAL YOU...
...WANT TO PLAY CHOPIN?
THE BOY WILL CONFRONT MUSIC ON HIS OWN.

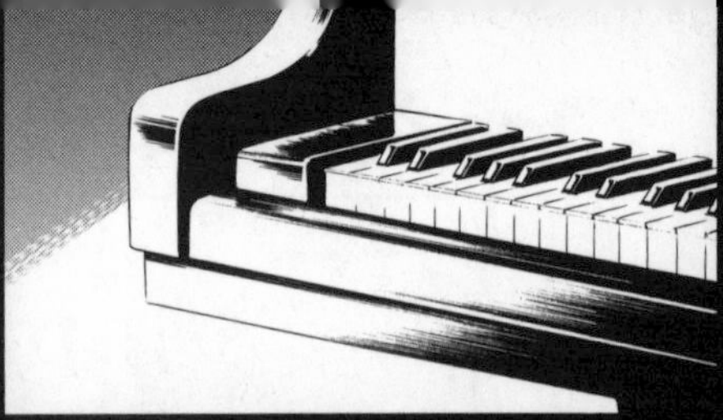

"ENTER A PIANO COMPETITION!" STRUCK BY KAORI'S DESPERATE FEELINGS, KŌSEI MAKES UP HIS MIND TO GO ON STAGE. YEARS WITHOUT PRACTICE, AN INABILITY TO HEAR THE NOTES, AND YET THE BOY FACES THE MUSIC IN EARNEST. WHAT SORT OF ANSWER WILL HE FIND...?

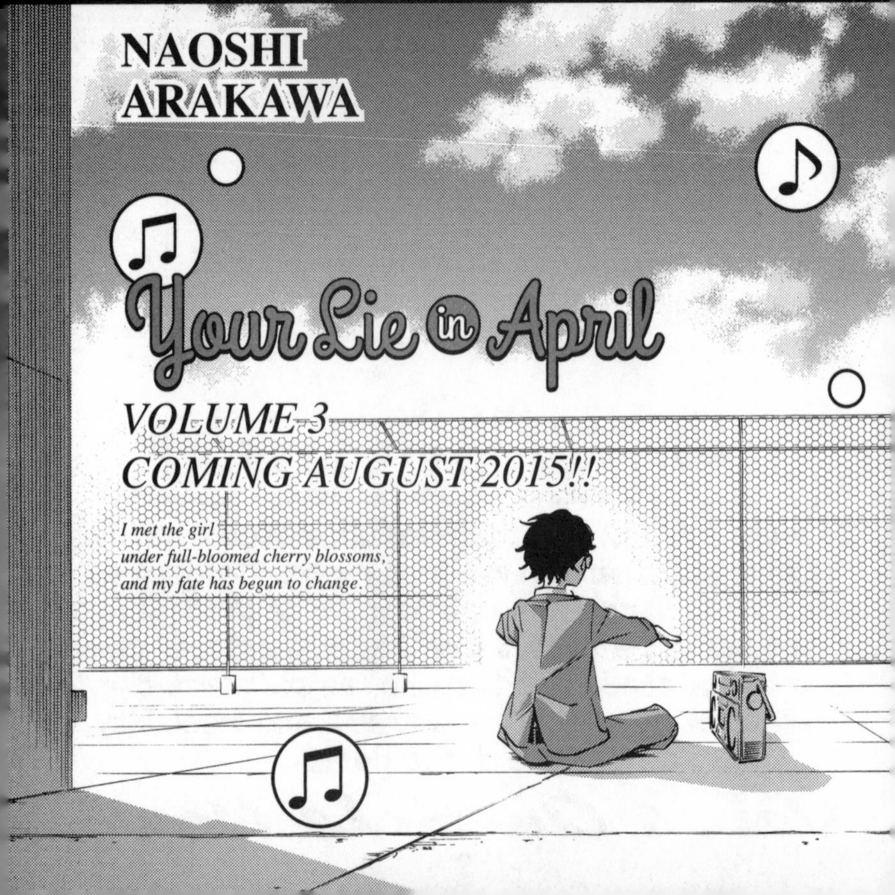
NAOSHI
ARAKAWA
Your Lie in April
VOLUME 3
COMING AUGUST 2015!!
I met the girl
under full-bloomed cherry blossoms,
and my fate has begun to change.

Destined to Dance!

1
Let's Dance a Waltz
NATSUMI ANDO

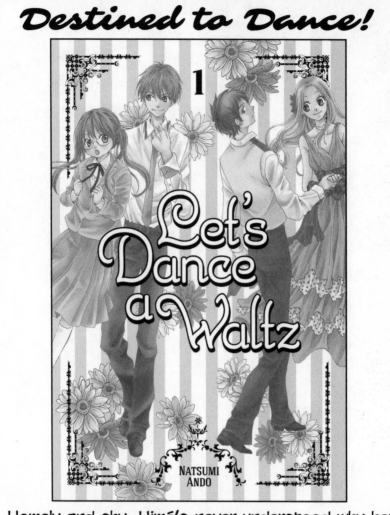

Homely and shy, Himé's never understood why her mother gave her a name that means "Princess." Meanwhile, Tango is a ballroom dance prodigy who keeps his gift a secret from his classmates. When fate brings these two together as partners, they'll help each other overcome shame and insecurity, on the dance floor!

Vol. 1 On Sale Now!

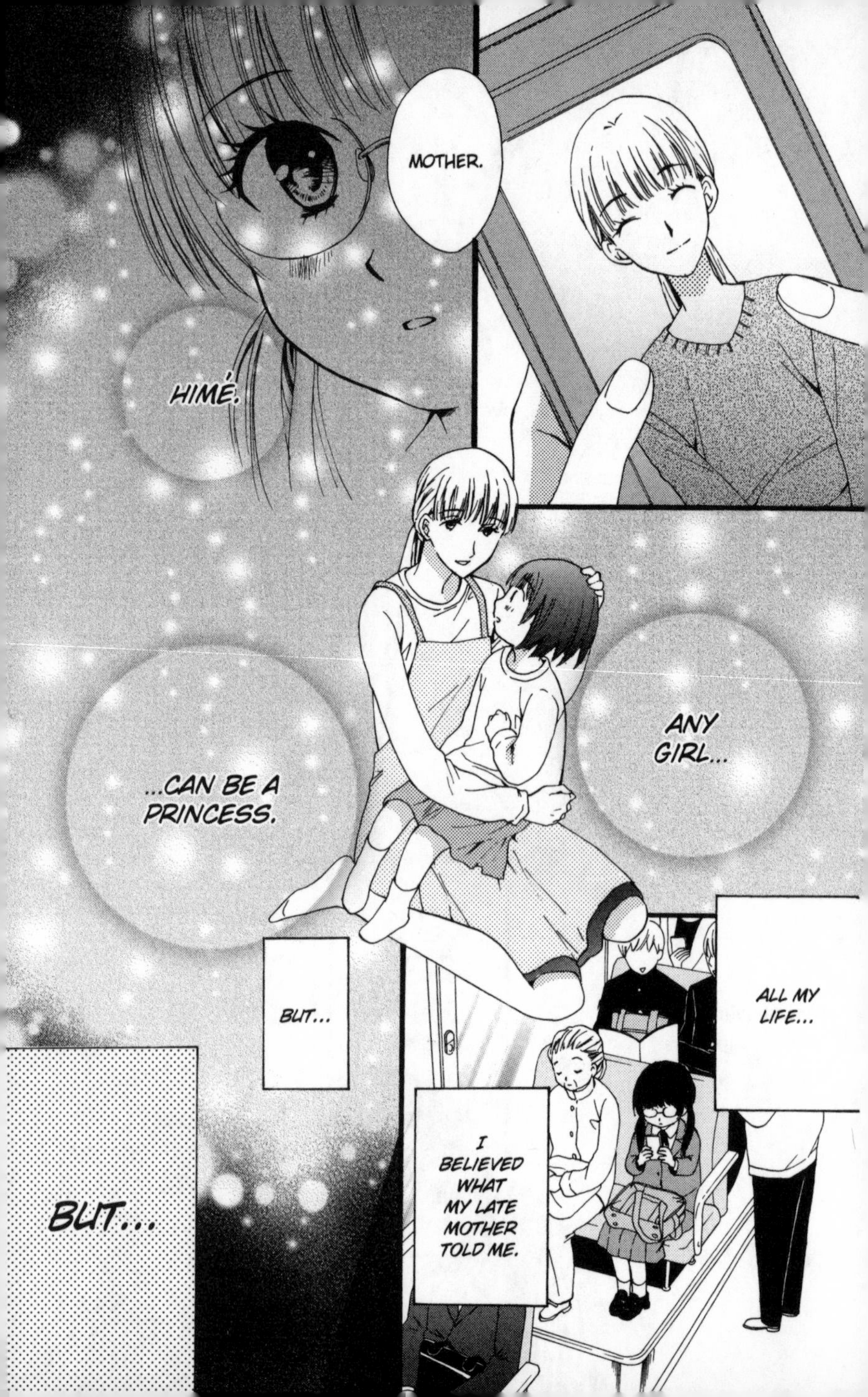

MOTHER.
HIMÉ.
ANY GIRL...
...CAN BE A PRINCESS.
ALL MY LIFE...
I BELIEVED WHAT MY LATE MOTHER TOLD ME.
BUT...
BUT...

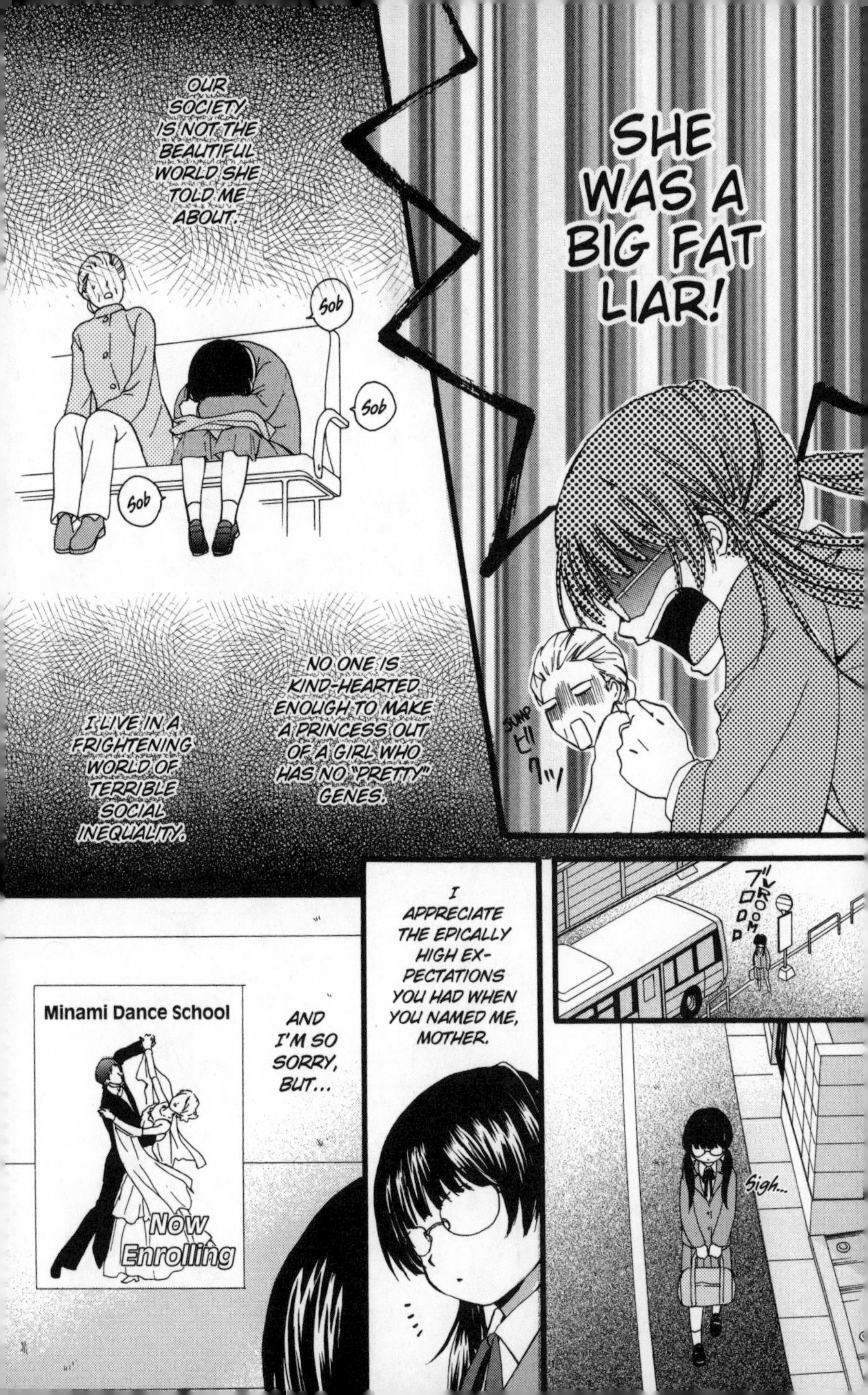
SHE WAS A BIG FAT LIAR!
OUR SOCIETY IS NOT THE BEAUTIFUL WORLD SHE TOLD ME ABOUT.
Sob
Sob
Sob
NO ONE IS KIND-HEARTED ENOUGH TO MAKE A PRINCESS OUT OF A GIRL WHO HAS NO "PRETTY" GENES.
I LIVE IN A FRIGHTENING WORLD OF TERRIBLE SOCIAL INEQUALITY.
VROOM
Sigh...
I APPRECIATE THE EPICALLY HIGH EX-PECTATIONS YOU HAD WHEN YOU NAMED ME, MOTHER.
AND I'M SO SORRY, BUT...
Minami Dance School
Now Enrolling

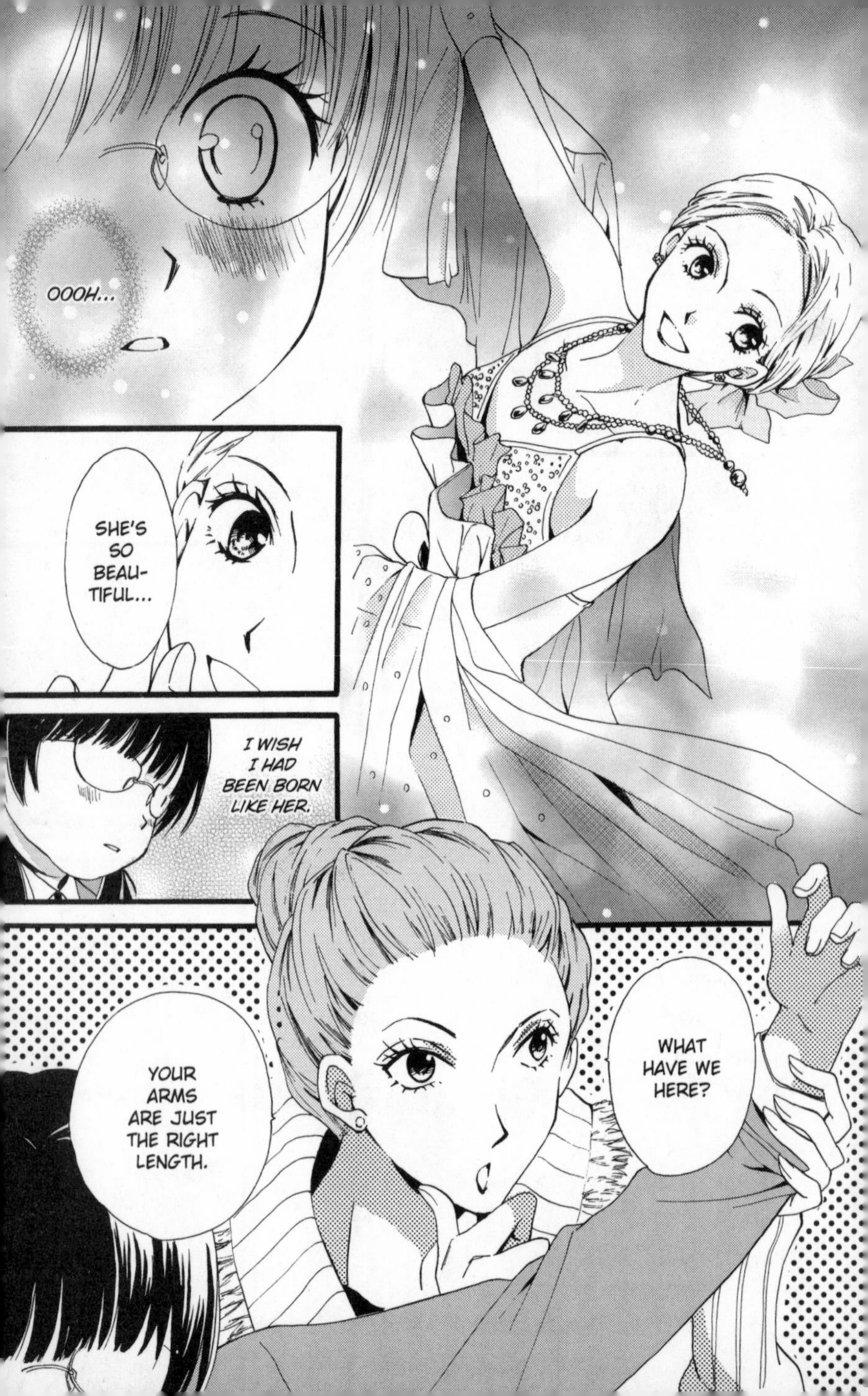
OOOH...
SHE'S SO BEAUTIFUL...
I WISH I HAD BEEN BORN LIKE HER.
WHAT HAVE WE HERE?
YOUR ARMS ARE JUST THE RIGHT LENGTH.

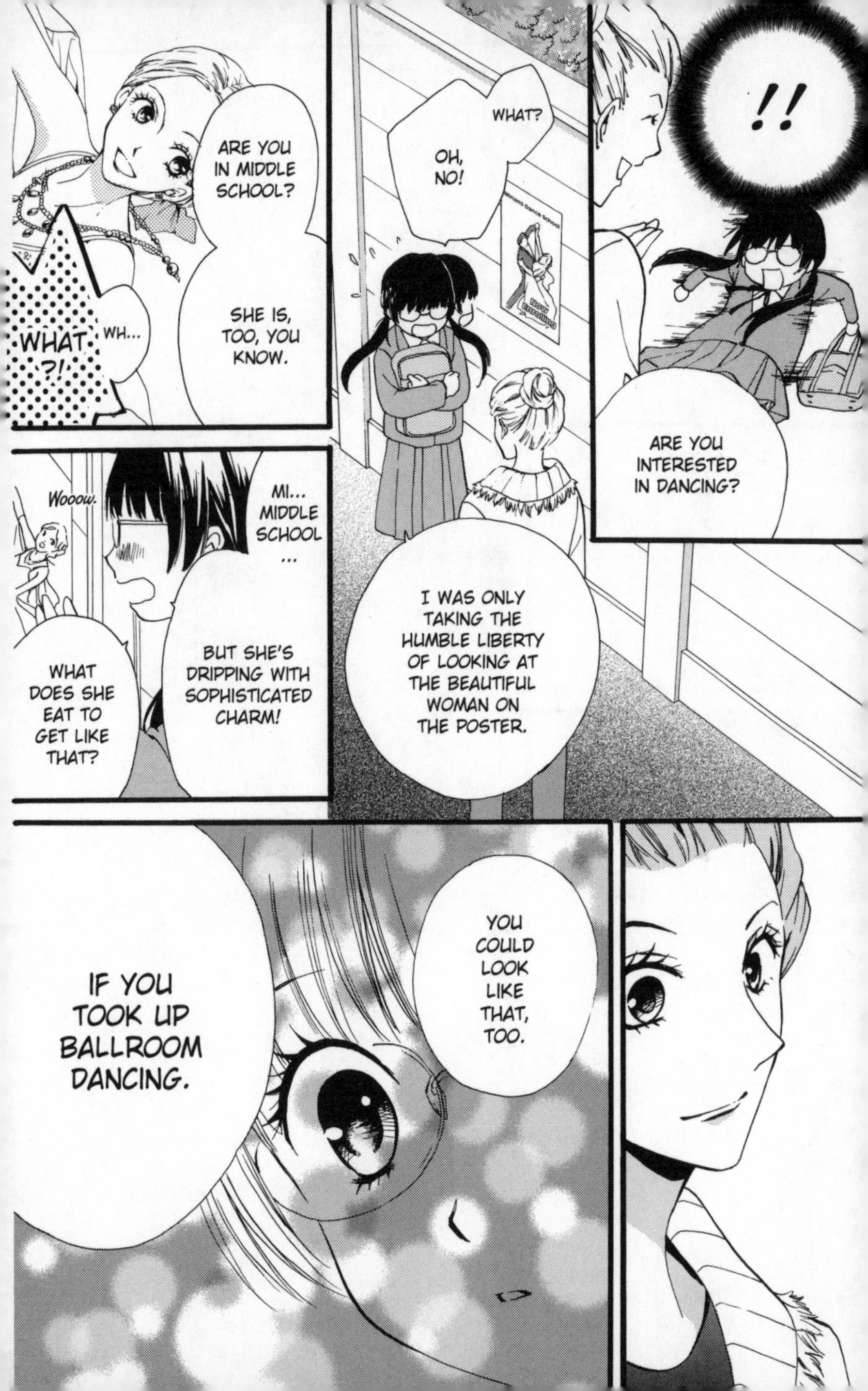
!!
ARE YOU INTERESTED IN DANCING?
WHAT?
OH, NO!
I WAS ONLY TAKING THE HUMBLE LIBERTY OF LOOKING AT THE BEAUTIFUL WOMAN ON THE POSTER.
ARE YOU IN MIDDLE SCHOOL?
SHE IS, TOO, YOU KNOW.
WH...
WHAT?!
MI... MIDDLE SCHOOL...
Wooow.
BUT SHE'S DRIPPING WITH SOPHISTICATED CHARM!
WHAT DOES SHE EAT TO GET LIKE THAT?
YOU COULD LOOK LIKE THAT, TOO.
IF YOU TOOK UP BALLROOM DANCING.

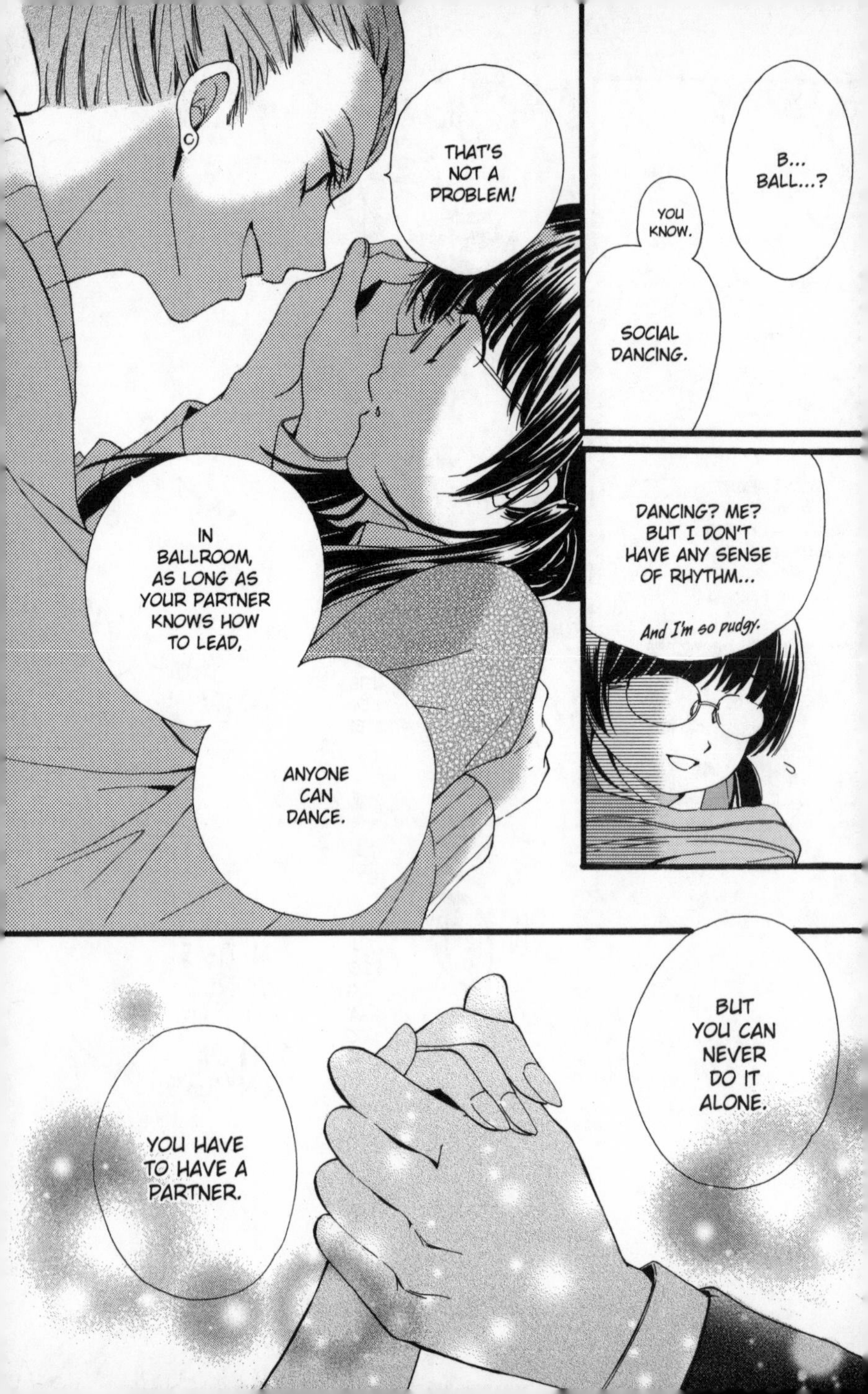
B... BALL...?
YOU KNOW.
SOCIAL DANCING.
DANCING? ME? BUT I DON'T HAVE ANY SENSE OF RHYTHM...
And I'm so pudgy.
THAT'S NOT A PROBLEM!
IN BALLROOM, AS LONG AS YOUR PARTNER KNOWS HOW TO LEAD,
ANYONE CAN DANCE.
BUT YOU CAN NEVER DO IT ALONE.
YOU HAVE TO HAVE A PARTNER.

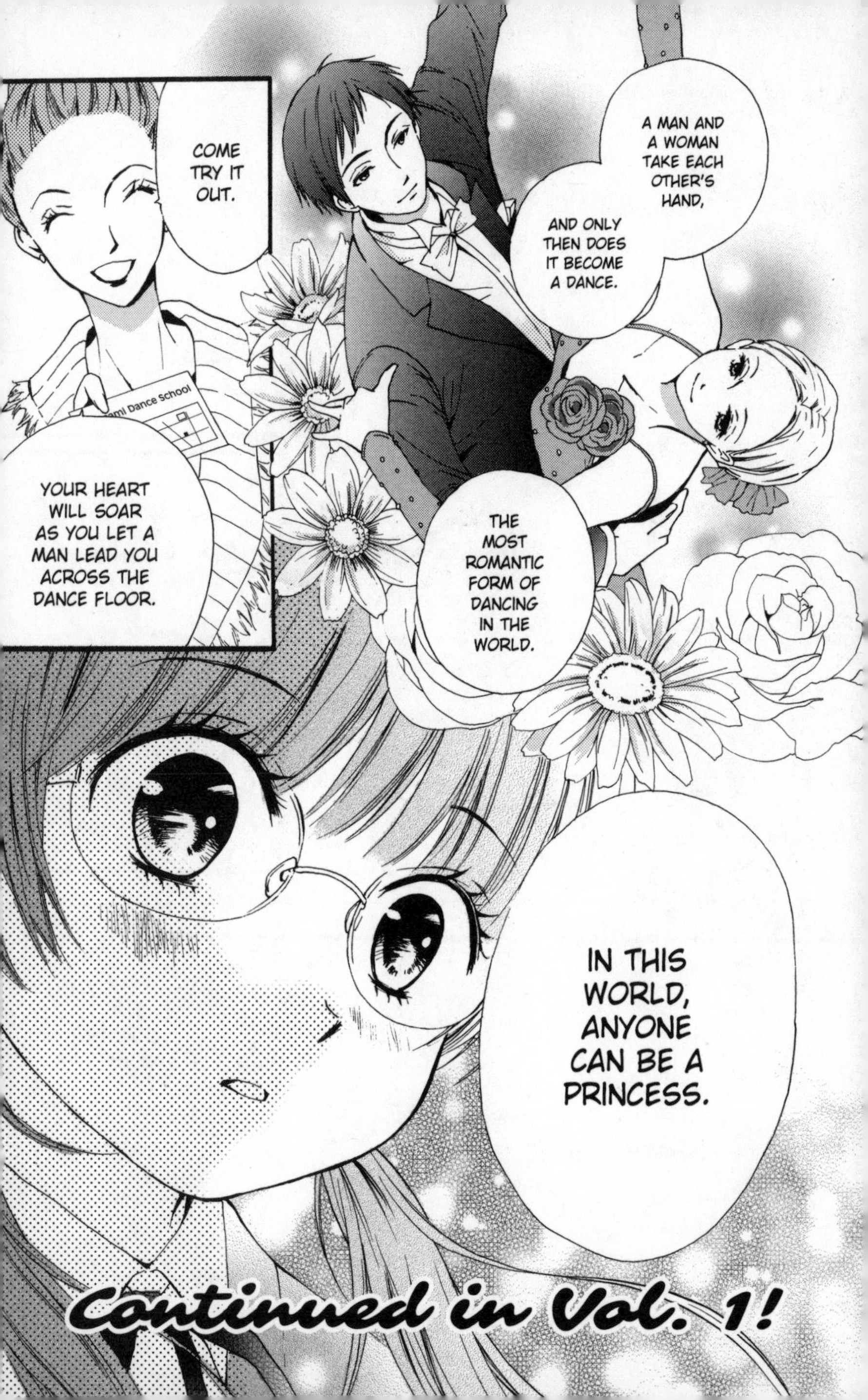
A MAN AND A WOMAN TAKE EACH OTHER'S HAND,
AND ONLY THEN DOES IT BECOME A DANCE.
THE MOST ROMANTIC FORM OF DANCING IN THE WORLD.
COME TRY IT OUT.
YOUR HEART WILL SOAR AS YOU LET A MAN LEAD YOU ACROSS THE DANCE FLOOR.
IN THIS WORLD, ANYONE CAN BE A PRINCESS.
Continued in Vol. 1!

STORY & CHARACTERS

When his mother died in the autumn of his 12th year, piano prodigy Kōsei Arima lost his ability to play. Without a purpose, his days lost all color and continued on in a drab monotone. But in the spring when he was 14, the boy met a girl. The cheerfully violent, ill-tempered, and exceptionally talented violinist Kaori Miyazono has started to change Kōsei's gray world.

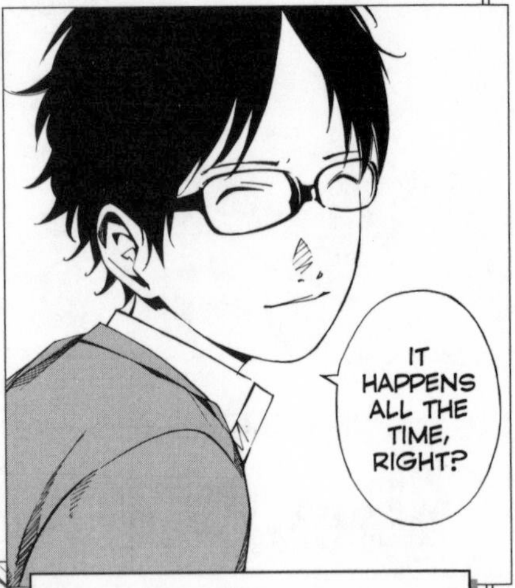
IT HAPPENS ALL THE TIME, RIGHT?

Kōsei Arima

An ex-piano prodigy who lost his ability to play when his mother died the autumn he was 11. His meeting with Kaori leads him to once again dedicate himself to the world of music.

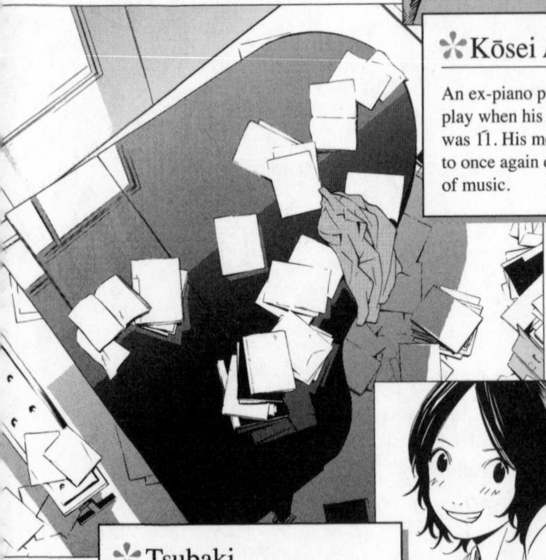

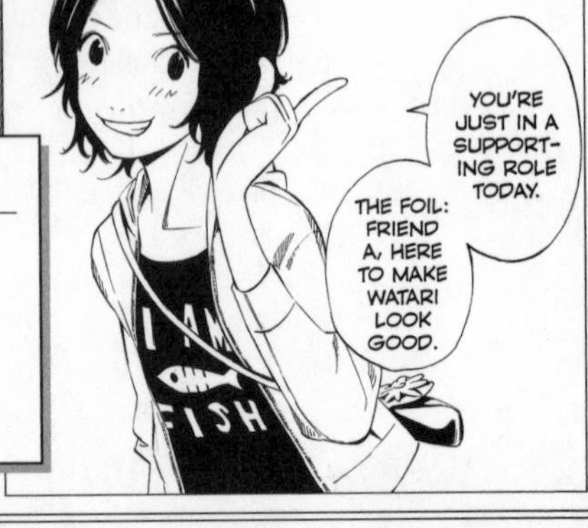
YOU'RE JUST IN A SUPPORTING ROLE TODAY.
THE FOIL: FRIEND A, HERE TO MAKE WATARI LOOK GOOD.
I AM FISH

Tsubaki

The school softball team's power hitter. A longtime friend and next-door neighbor of Kōsei, She believes that time has frozen for him, and she helps Kaori in an attempt to start it moving again.

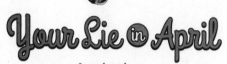

*I met the girl
under full-bloomed cherry blossoms,
and my fate has begun to change.*

2

Naoshi Arakawa